HOW TO BUY AND SELL USED GUNS

HOW TO BUY AND SELL USED GUNS

JOHN E. TRAISTER

Stoeger Publishing Company

Published by Stoeger Publishing Company
55 Ruta Court
South Hackensack, New Jersey 07606

International Standard Book Number (ISBN): 0-88317-114-7
Library of Congress Catalog Card Number: 82-61425
Manufactured in the United States of America

Distributed in the U.S. by Stoeger Industries, 55 Ruta Court, South Hackensack, New Jersey 07606, (201) 440-2700; in Canada, by Stoeger Canada Ltd., 169 Idema Road, Markham, Ontario, L3R 1A9, (416) 475-6682.

Acknowledgments

No book of this type can be written entirely by one person; it requires the help of many individuals. To name each and every person who made a contribution to my gun trading knowledge would take more space than this book allows. However, I must mention a few special people so I won't feel too guilty about taking credit for authorship of this book.

First of all comes my Dad who took me afield at a very early age and got me started on the right foot. His two brothers—my uncles, Bill and Charles—did more than their share to make sure I could hit a few of the quail that my old dog Rusty and I would flush during my days off from school during the hunting season. Then, of course, comes Mom who never could see how anyone could spend hard-earned money (probably hers) on such foolish things as guns, ammo, outdoor magazines and the like, but somehow put up with me anyway.

In recent years, Ben Toxvard of Shenandoah Guns in Berryville, Virginia, has been more than a friend in helping me with my own business (even though I'm really his competitor) and getting me out of many "holes." Johnny Clark of Clark Brothers in Warrenton, Va., has also given me great assistance in appraising certain rare firearms.

Thanks to the many manufacturers, suppliers, other writers, and the like who cooperated 100 percent to meet any and all my needs in completing this book.

I'm indeed indebted to Ruby Updike who helped with the research and typing, and also to Charlene Cruson, who expertly edited my manuscript for Stoeger Publishing Company.

Last, but certainly not least, is my family who made life a little easier than usual during my final weeks of work on this book to make the publisher's deadline.

—J.E.T.

ABOUT THE AUTHOR

As a young boy, John Traister eagerly watched his father and uncles as they pursued hunting and other activities involving firearms. So it is not surprising that by the time he was 13 years old, he was allowed to trade and collect guns, an avid hobby that developed into a full-time occupation. In 1978, he started his own gun trading business in Virginia (he presently lives in Bentonville), and has bought and sold guns nationwide ever since. He is also a firearm consultant for Stoeger Industries.

When not repairing or dealing in guns, Traister can be found writing about them. He has authored more than 50 titles to date, including *Basic Gunsmithing, Professional Care and Finishing of Guns* and *Learn Gunsmithing: The Trouble-Shooting Method.* In addition, he has sold over 300 articles to such magazines as The American Rifleman, Fur-Fish-Game, The Shooting Industry and Handloader's Digest.

Preface

Gun trading is an old American tradition. Its practice provided many people with the only means of owning a firearm. Gunsmiths usually bought and sold used guns to boost their profits, while others found gun trading an excellent means of building up a gun collection. The practice continues today.

Every gun enthusiast—whether hunter, shooter, collector or dealer—will, at sometime in his life, engage in the practice of buying and selling used guns. The main objective of this practice is to pick up a real "buy" and not get stuck. To accomplish this objective, you first have to know just what the gun is, its model rarity and condition. If parts are missing, do you know if they are readily available—and for how much? Are the parts in a particular gun all original, or has the gun been assembled from several junked guns? Is the finish original, or has the arm been refinished? If the gun is a very rare model, are you sure it is authentic—or is it a fake? These are just a few of the factors you'll need to know about and consider when buying and selling used guns.

In HOW TO BUY AND SELL USED GUNS the reader will learn how to identify and inspect practically every gun made—both modern and antique; what to look for when trading and collecting shotguns, centerfire and rimfire rifles, handguns and the growing branch of black powder arms; how to make sound investments; firearm safety as well as the most effective security measures for your collection. You are given hints on how to protect your gun collection from deterioration. Making sure your used gun is safe is a "must" for every shooter, so you'll find out how to test your guns for safety, too.

Gun dealers should be especially pleased with the contents of this book, as the data within can mean the difference, literally, between making a profit and filing for bankruptcy. And, since every gun enthusiast will at some time engage in trading used guns (most are already doing so), everyone even peripherally associated with firearms will want a copy of this book for study and reference.

When using this book, please remember that the values shown represent approximate retail prices for used guns in excellent condition, without accessories, and may vary from region to region.

Also, for easy reference, the manufacturers and suppliers mentioned throughout the text are listed, with addresses, in the back of the book in the Appendix section.

HOW TO BUY AND SELL USED GUNS is designed to help all buyers and sellers of used guns—potential ones and present ones—approach the practice more intelligently and profitably, enabling them to enjoy the practice as well as the end product more fully.

—JOHN E. TRAISTER

Table of Contents

1.
Getting Started In Gun Trading

Firearms enthusiasts engage in gun trading for many reasons. Some may want to save money on the price of a new gun and buy a used one instead. A collector may have duplicates in his collection and wish to trade them for other guns not yet obtained. A hunter may like a certain model shotgun that is now obsolete and, therefore, a used gun in that model is all that's available. Gun dealers, of course, are in the business of buying and selling used guns to make a profit, and many dealers are finding this a good way to compete with the discount houses that merchandise predominantly new guns.

Where to Start

The first requirement for trading in used guns is to know how to evaluate them. There are several books on the market that will give you the basic prices, but just remember that these published prices are only starting points—don't take each and every listing as gospel. Here are a few key references; other references are listed in Appendix IV:

Gun Trader's Guide
Stoeger Publishing Co.
55 Ruta Court
South Hackensack, New Jersey 07606

Modern Gun Values
DBI Books, Inc.
One Northfield Plaza
Northfield, Illinois 60093

The Firearms Price Guide
Crown Publishers, Inc.
1 Park Avenue
New York, New York 10016

Williams Blue Book of Gun Dealing
Williams Gun Sight Company
7389 Lapeer Road
Davison, Michigan 48423

Flayderman's Guide to Antique American Firearms
DBI Books, Inc.
One Northfield Plaza
Northfield, Illinois 60093

Another pricing guide for antique firearms should be out shortly after this book is published, and you may want to reserve a copy from Stoeger Publishing Company, 55 Ruta Court, South Hackensack, N.J. 07606.

When using any of the pricing guides listed above, make certain you understand how to use each one. The

GUN TRADER'S GUIDE, for example, lists prices for guns in "excellent" condition, while another lists prices for firearms in "very good" condition. The NRA Condition Guidelines are those most used in describing the condition of firearms and will be fully explained later in this chapter.

One word of caution. Anyone who purchases a used gun runs the risk of buying a stolen gun, and you're the one who is likely to get stuck. If the potential seller seems nervous or in a hurry, or will let the gun go for an unrealistically low price, beware. It might be that the seller has been out of work and needs cash, and his gun is the only thing of value he has to sell. On the other hand, the gun could be stolen and result in an endless amount of trouble for you to go through—not to mention your having to give up the gun to the authorities.

If you're a dealer and someone drops in and wants to sell a gun outright, stress the fact that the gun's serial number, along with the seller's name, will be recorded in your firearms records and these will be available to local law enforcement agencies. This action alone will usually discourage a person from knowingly selling a stolen firearm.

Letting a person know that your firearms records are available to local law enforcement agencies is usually enough to deter him from knowingly selling you a stolen gun.

Gun Control Act of 1968

The Gun Control Act of 1968 restricts the selling and buying of firearms. Under this law, if you're not a dealer or gunsmith, you are permitted to sell personal firearms in most states to another individual in your state without a Federal Firearms License (FFL), but you must check the state and local firearms regulations with your municipal law enforcement people; new ordinances are continually cropping up. Without an FFL you may also, depending on state laws, sell to residents of contiguous, or adjoining, states.

If you want to mail-order firearms or buy guns and ammunition for resale to others particularly via interstate or foreign commerce, you'll need an FFL. To qualify for a Federal Firearms License, you:

1. Must be 21 years of age or over.

2. Must not: (1) be under indictment for or have been convicted of a crime punishable by imprisonment for a term exceeding one year (not including business offenses or misdemeanors not involving a firearm or explosive that are punishable by a term of imprisonment for two years or less); (2) be a fugitive from justice; (3) be an unlawful user or addicted to marijuana or any depressant, stimulant or narcotic drug; or (4) have been adjudicated as a mental defective or been committed to a mental institution.

3. Must not be an alien, unlawfully or illegally, in the United States.

4. Must not, being a United States citizen, have renounced citizenship.

5. Must not have willfully failed to disclose any material information or made any false statements as to any material fact in connection with an application for an FFL.

6. Must have premises from which business is conducted or from which you intend to conduct a dealer's business within a reasonable period of time.

Once you obtain an FFL, you will be entitled to buy and sell either commercially or privately firearms and ammunition on an interstate basis. You may buy and sell guns through the mail or UPS from other holders of an FFL, and anyone in the United States (unless prohibited by state laws) may ship a firearm to you by UPS for your purchase. So you can see, it's a nice piece of paper to have.

1. Name

TRAISTER ARMS COMPANY

2. License Number 8 54 069 06 C3 17698

3. Expiration Date 3-1-83

5. Type of License 06

01 Dealer in firearms other than destructive devices or ammunition for other than destructive devices.

02 Pawnbroker dealing in firearms other than destructive devices or ammunition for firearms other than destructive devices.

03 Collector of curios and relics.

06 Manufacturer of ammunition for firearms other than destructive devices.

07 Manufacturer of firearms other than destructive devices.

08. Importer of firearms other than destructive devices or ammunition for firearms other than destructive devices.

09 Dealer in destructive devices or ammunition for destructive devices.

10 Manufacturer of destructive devices or ammunition for destructive devices.

11 Importer of destructive devices or ammunition for destructive devices.

4. Issued by Regional Regulatory Administrator, ATF at (Address) #2 Penn Center Plaza
Philadelphia, Pa. 19102

6. Signature of Regional Regulatory Administrator

ATF Form 8 (5310.11) (5-80) PART II

Copy of License (18 U.S.C. Chapter 44)

I certify that this is a true copy of a license issued to me to engage in the business specified in item 5.

(Signature of Licensee)

PURCHASING COPY

The licensee named herein may use this form, a reproduction thereof, or a reproduction of his license, to assist a transferor of firearms to verify the identity and the licensed status of the licensee as provided in 27 CFR Part 178.

John E. Traister
t/a Traister Arms Company
Route 1 Box 300
Bentonville, Virginia 22610

DEPARTMENT OF THE TREASURY — BUREAU OF ALCOHOL, TOBACCO AND FIREARMS

A Federal Firearms License is required to purchase and sell guns (other than antiques or relics) through the mails or via interstate or foreign commerce.

You may operate out of your home, a garage, an outbuilding or a regular place of business, but you must be open to the public during the hours you specify on your application. Remember, however, that some local zoning laws may prohibit you from operating any business out of your home or may prohibit the storage of ammunition. Be sure to look into your local requirements for a business license to operate from your home before making application for an FFL if you intend to be open to the public.

To apply for your license, write to the Department of the Treasury, Bureau of Alcohol, Tobacco, and Firearms, to the same address you use when filing your federal income tax. Request an "Application for License Under U.S.C. Chapter 44, Firearms." You will receive an application shortly afterward and it should be self-explanatory. They will also send you a manual telling how to log guns in and out as you receive them.

Perhaps, for various reasons, you choose not to obtain an FFL. There are still ways you can receive firearms from out-of-state dealers; merely have a local dealer (with an FFL) order the gun for you. He will then have you fill out the proper forms and sell you the gun locally. The usual fee for such a transaction varies, but 10 percent of the sale is common. Here's how it works.

Suppose you see a used gun advertised in *Shotgun News* that you want to purchase, but the seller is located in another state a thousand miles away. Show your local dealer the ad and ask him if he'll order the gun for you. He will usually require full payment in advance plus his commission, or at least a sizable deposit. He then sends his check, enclosing a copy of his FFL with his original signature on it, to the seller. When the gun arrives, the dealer will notify you, have you fill out Form 4473 and, if everything checks out, you can take the gun home. This is probably the best route to take if you anticipate buying only a few guns each year.

Federally Licensed Firearms Collectors

A collector of curios and relics may obtain a collector's license under the Gun Control Act of 1968. The privileges conferred by this license extend only to transactions in curios and relics. A person *need not* be federally licensed to collect curios and relics. He must be licensed, however, in order to receive curios and relics lawfully in interstate or foreign commerce.

The curios and relics listed in Appendix I of this book have been determined by the Bureau of Alcohol, Tobacco and Firearms (ATF) to have special value as

DEPARTMENT OF THE TREASURY - BUREAU OF ALCOHOL, TOBACCO, AND FIREARMS

FIREARMS TRANSACTION RECORD

PART II — CONTIGUOUS-STATE OR NON-OVER-THE-COUNTER

TRANSFEROR'S TRANSACTION NO.

NOTE: PREPARE IN DUPLICATE. ALL ENTRIES OTHER THAN SIGNATURES MUST BE TYPED OR CLEARLY PRINTED IN INK. ALL SIGNATURES ON THIS FORM MUST BE IN INK.

SECTION A - MUST BE COMPLETED PERSONALLY BY TRANSFEREE OR BUYER (See notices and instructions on reverse)

1. TRANSFEREE'S *(Buyer's)* NAME *(Last, First, Middle) (Mr., Mrs., Miss.)*
2. HEIGHT
3. WEIGHT
4. RACE
5. RESIDENCE ADDRESS *(No., Street, City, State, Zip Code)*
6. DATE OF BIRTH
7. PLACE OF BIRTH
8. CERTIFICATION OF TRANSFEREE *(Buyer)* — An untruthful answer may subject you to criminal prosecution. Each question must be answered with a "yes" or a "no" inserted in the box at the right of the question:

a. Are you under indictment or information in any court for a crime punishable by imprisonment for a term exceeding one year?

b. Have you been convicted in any court of a crime punishable by imprisonment for a term exceeding one year? (Note: The actual sentence given by the judge does not matter—a yes answer is necessary if the judge could have given a sentence of more than one year. Also, a "yes" answer is required even if a conviction has been discharged, set aside, or dismissed pursuant to an expugment or rehabilitation statute.)

c. Are you a fugitive from justice?

d. Are you an unlawful user of, or addicted to marihuana or a depressant, stimulant or narcotic drug?

e. Have you ever been adjudicated mentally defective or have you ever been committed to a mental institution?

f. Have you been discharged from the Armed Forces under dishonorable conditions?

g. Are you an alien illegally in the United States?

h. Are you a person who having been a citizen of the United States, has renounced his citizenship?

Subject to penalties provided by law, I swear that, in the case of any firearm other than a shotgun or a rifle, I am 21 years or more of age, or that, in the case of a shotgun or a rifle, I am 18 years or more of age; that I am not prohibited by the provisions of Chapter 44 of Title 18, United States Code, from receiving a firearm in interstate or foreign commerce, and that my receipt of this firearm will not be in violation of any statute of the State and published ordinance applicable to the locality in which I reside. Further, the true title, name, and address of the principal law enforcement officer of the locality to which the firearm will be delivered are:

TITLE

NAME

ADDRESS

I also hereby certify that the answers to the above are true and correct. I understand that a person who answers any of the above questions in the affirmative is prohibited by Federal law from purchasing and/or possessing a firearm. I also understand that the making of any false oral or written statement or the exhibiting of any false or misrepresented identification with respect to this transaction is a crime punishable as a felony.

TRANSFEREE'S *(Buyer's)* SIGNATURE

DATE

SECTION B - MUST BE COMPLETED BY TRANSFEROR OR SELLER (See notices and instructions on reverse)

On the basis of (1) the statements in Section A; (2) my notification of the chief law enforcement officer designated above; and (3) the information in the current list of Published Ordinances, it is my belief that it is not unlawful for me to sell, deliver, transport, or otherwise dispose of the firearm described below to the person identified in Section A.

9. TYPE *(Pistol, Rifle, etc.)*
10. MODEL
11. CALIBER OR GUAGE
12. SERIAL NO.
13. MANUFACTURER *(and importer, if any)*
14. TRADE/CORPORATE NAME AND ADDRESS OF TRANSFEROR *(Seller) (Hand stamp may be used)*
15. FEDERAL FIREARMS LICENSE NO.
16. TRANSFEROR'S *(Seller's)* SIGNATURE
17. TRANSFEROR'S TITLE
18. TRANSACTION DATE

ATF F 4473 (5300.9) PART II (10-76) EDITION OF 2-75 MAY BE USED

If you don't have a Federal Firearms License, you can usually purchase guns that are for sale in another state through a licensed dealer. He will send for them and, when they arrive, will have you fill out Form 4473 to complete the transaction.

collectors' items as of 1981. To be recognized as curios or relics, firearms must satisfy at least one of the following requirements:

1. The weapon (not including replicas) must have been manufactured at least 50 years ago;

2. The weapon must be certified by the curator of a municipal, state or federal museum exhibiting firearms to be of museum interest;

3. A substantial part of the weapon's monetary value must be derived from the fact that it is novel, rare or bizarre, or was associated with some historical figure, period or event.

Collectors who wish to obtain a curio or relic determination from the ATF on a specific firearm not appearing in Appendix I may submit a letter to the Chief of the Firearms Technology Branch, Bureau of Alcohol, Tobacco and Firearms, Washington, DC 20226. The letter should include a complete physical description of the firearm, reasons why the collector believes that the weapon in question merits classification as a relic or curio, as well as any supporting data concerning the history of the firearm.

Antique Firearms

Antique firearms are exempt from the Gun Control Act of 1968. In other words, unless state laws dictate otherwise, anyone may order antique firearms through the mail or buy them in any state without an FFL. The ATF defines an antique firearm as:

> Any firearm not designed or redesigned for using rimfire or conventional centerfire ignition with fixed ammunition and manufactured in or before 1898 (including any matchlock, flintlock, percussion cap, or similar type of ignition system or replica thereof, whether actually manufactured before or after the year 1898), and also any firearm using fixed ammunition manufactured in or before 1898, for which ammunition is no longer manufactured in the United States and is not readily available in the ordinary channels of commercial trade.

From the above definition, it would seem that a Winchester Model 94, chambered for the .30-30 cartridge and manufactured in, say, 1895, would come under modern weapons, whereas a Winchester Model 94, manufactured in 1895 and chambered for the .32-40, would fall under the antique category. However, at a recent meeting with ATF inspectors in Richmond, Virginia, they told me that all firearms manufactured in 1898 or before—regardless of the caliber or cartridge—are classified as antiques and are exempt from the Gun Control Act of 1968. They can be bought, sold and shipped the same as a cap pistol. Again, check with your local authorities just to be sure.

NRA Standards of Condition for Modern Firearms

In every instance, condition is a prime factor in determining the value of a used gun. The following NRA Standards of Condition for Modern Firearms are used almost universally in grading such items offered for sale:

New: Guns not previously sold at retail, in the same condition as current factory production.

New, discontinued: Same as **New**, except discontinued model.

Perfect: In new condition in every respect.

Excellent: New condition; used but little, no

A NO-GO headspace gauge is a handy gadget that can save your life.

noticeable marring of wood or metal, bluing perfect (except at muzzle or sharp edges).

Very Good: In perfect working condition; no appreciable wear on working surfaces, no corrosion or pitting, only minor surface dents or scratches on wood.

Good: In safe working condition, minor wear on working surfaces; no broken parts, no corrosion or pitting that will interfere with proper functioning.

Fair: In safe working condition, but well worn, perhaps requiring replacement of minor parts or adjustments which should be indicated in advertisement; no rust, but may have corrosion pits which do not render the article unsafe or inoperable.

Poor: A firearm that is badly worn, rusty and battered is considered to be in "poor" condition. Many in this condition require major adjustments or repairs to put them in safe operating condition.

Things to Consider When Making a Purchase

If you're looking for a good used gun buy, bear in mind that *dealers must make a profit to stay in business.* There was a time when a retail dealer could count on making from 20 to 25 percent on new gun sales, but in these times when discount stores are cutting prices like mad, it's difficult to sell a new gun for even 10 percent above cost! This is why many gun dealers count on used guns to keep themselves in business. Few used gun dealers will take less than 20 percent profit on any gun —even those high-quality shotguns that sell for thousands of dollars. Most try to make 40 percent profit, but usually end up with 25 to 30 percent. So if you're trying to sell a used gun to a dealer, be aware that you're not going to get full retail price. If the dealer thinks that he can get around, say, $200 for a gun, he will usually offer no more than $120 for it. There are exceptions, however.

For example, let's assume you have a Winchester

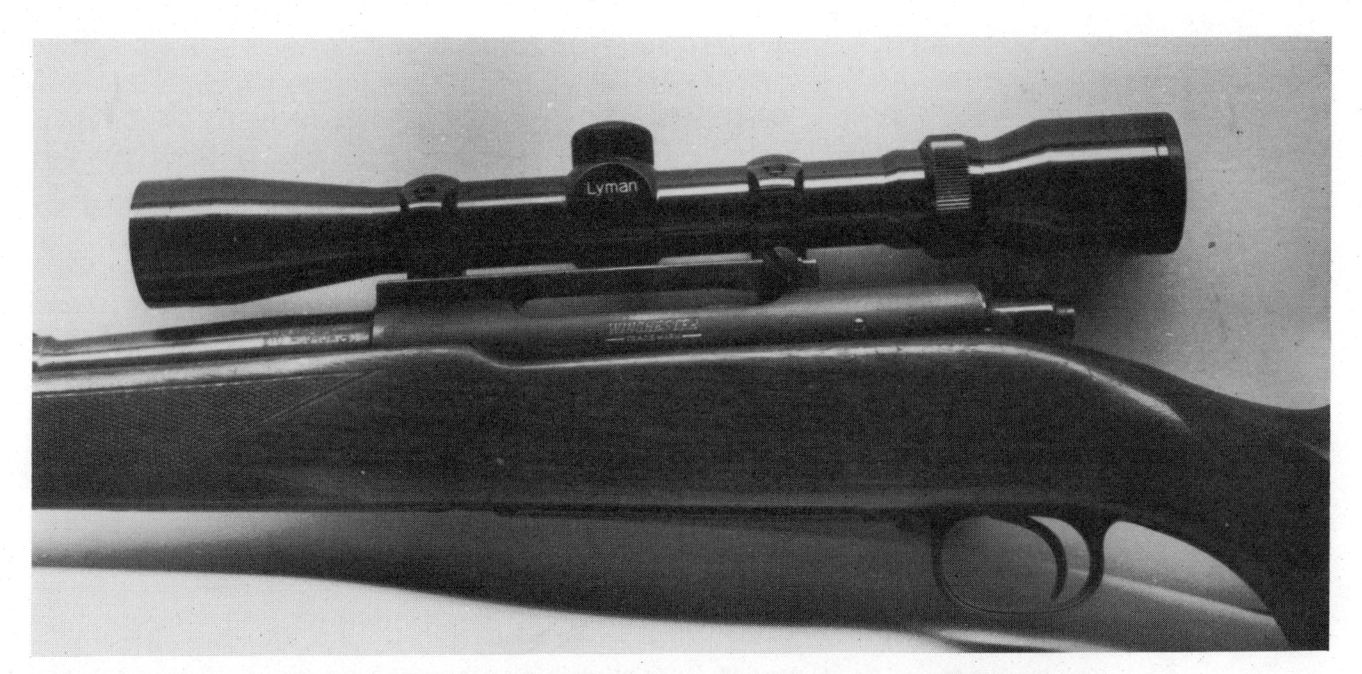

This pre-WWII Winchester Model 70 was rechambered from .270 Winchester to .270 Weatherby Magnum. Although the rifle has lost its collector value, it is still worth something as a useful hunting rifle.

Model 61, a .22 rimfire pump in excellent condition that you want to sell. The current retail value of this gun is about $350. Normally, a dealer should offer around $210 to $250 for it. However, perhaps a customer has told a dealer to look out for a Winchester 61 in excellent condition, for which he will immediately pay $350. The dealer may then offer you $300 for your gun, knowing that he will make $50 from his customer in only a few hours after calling him.

The time of year plays an important role in obtaining the best gun buys, although collector guns seem to have no particular "good time" to buy. They are always in demand, with new ones being added to the list constantly. Hunting guns are a different story. As a rule, you will normally obtain the best deals from January through July of each year. When August and September roll around, you can bet that dealers are going to have their hunting arms marked at top dollar, and will usually get it, to supply the demand for the forthcoming hunting season.

Consider the condition a firearm should be in to suit your needs best. Let's say you want a safe single-shot, single-barrel shotgun to keep around your summer cabin as a utility gun. You walk into a used gun shop and find an Iver Johnson Champion shotgun; it's almost like new and you think this is just what you need. This particular model is now obsolete and in the condition mentioned will bring around $100 to $125 from a collector. For your purpose, one in good condition is really all you need, and you can probably find one for around $50.

By the same token, you may be in the market for a Winchester Model 12 pump shotgun for duck hunting. A standard grade Winchester Model 12 in excellent condition will run you around $500 to $650, and although it may look nice to you, one in good condition will serve the purpose just as well, and you could save $200 to $350.

Difficult-to-obtain replacement parts. Obsolete guns that are not in the collectible class don't resell very well, and usually bring the lowest prices. Some of these include rifles and shotguns manufactured by U.S. and foreign firms for mail-order houses; you know, J.C. Higgins and the like. Considerable time and expense are often involved when a replacement part for one of these obsolete weapons is needed. The only solution is often a hand-made part which can cost a pretty penny—depending on the time it takes to make it.

For example, one common problem with some of the obsolete pump shotguns supplied by the large chains is the breaking of the operating handle bar. Apparently, a low-grade steel was used in these bars, because I've had dozens come in for repair over the past couple of years. Replacement parts are no longer available, so existing parts must be repaired or new parts constructed by hand. Some owners have taken the bar to the local welding shop and had the parts brazed together. The high heat required to braze the parts to-

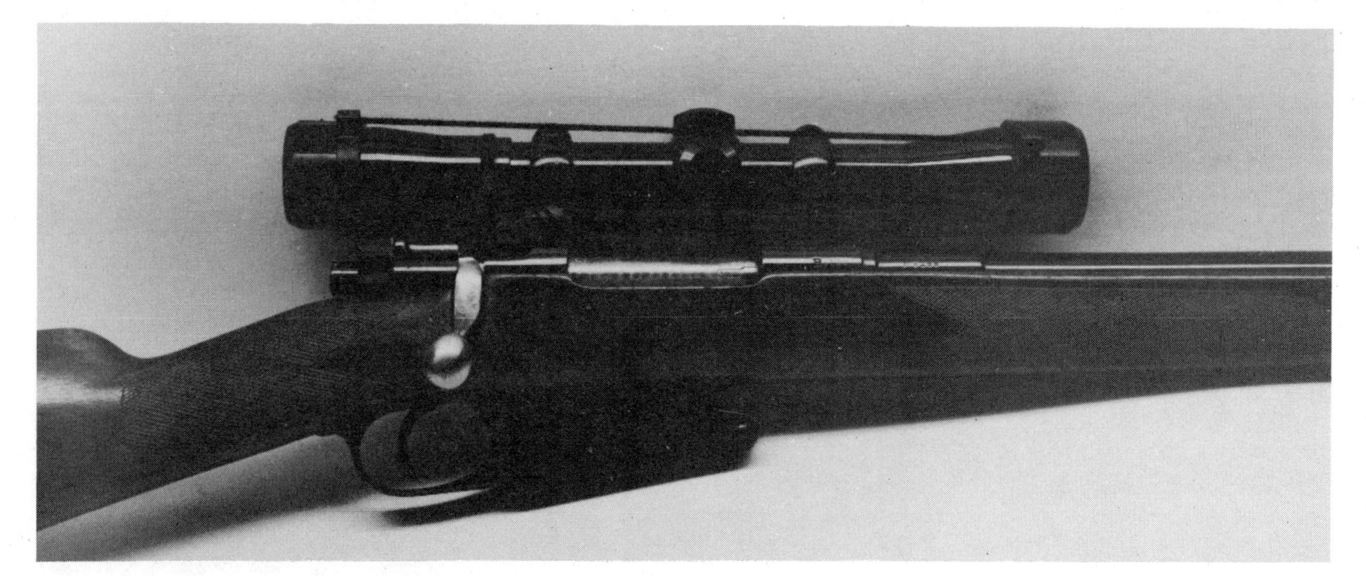

This Model 1891 Argentine Mauser is safe for use with its original chambering, but it can be extremely dangerous when converted to a different cartridge with higher pressure.

Many older obsolete centerfire cartridges can be found on the shelves of hardware and sporting goods stores that have been in business for some time.

gether often softened and weakened the metal even more, so they would usually break again in a very short time.

To repair these bars requires that the weak metal be cut away and a new piece be silver-soldered (not to exceed 1100°F in temperature) and then shaped to operate properly. The job costs about $35 or more, and the gun is not worth a hundred dollars!

Some Spanish and Italian double-barreled shotguns of recent manufacture are in this same category. The manufacturer is either out of business or has started making other models, or the importer has dropped the line. Under these circumstances, replacement parts are nearly impossible to obtain. Profits made on guns that later prove irreparable are seldom worth the ill will that follows. All guns can usually be repaired by a capable gunsmith, of course, but at current labor prices, it is usually not worth the expense. These are the type of guns to avoid.

Is headspace correct? Oftentimes a used gun is sold because it doesn't function right. The extractor may be damaged, the locking lugs are worn and the fired cases show head separation or extruding primers. If any or all of these conditions exist, the gun probably has excessive headspace and needs to be corrected.

If you don't have a headspace gauge for a particular firearm, shims can be used with reasonably good results as explained in Chapter 11. If an expensive gun does have headspace problems, it requires that the barrel be set back or else a rebarreling job is necessary—both jobs often costing more than the gun is worth.

Trigger pull may or may not be a problem. If it's too heavy, it can usually be lightened without too much difficulty. If too light, it could mean a simple trigger adjustment, in the case of an adjustable trigger. However, a light trigger pull can also mean excessive wear on the trigger and sear, or both. Is the gun worth the price if a new trigger and sear have to be replaced?

While on the subject of trigger pull, *always check to see if the empty gun "fires" when the bolt closes or when the buttstock is lightly tapped on the floor.* Place the safety "on" and squeeze the trigger firmly; does it hold? With the safety "on" and then "off," see if the gun can be made to fire by twisting the bolt and/or exerting pressure against the hammer or the cocking piece.

Should the gun fire (causing the firing pin to fall) under any of the above circumstances, do not attempt to buy or sell until the problem can be determined and the cost of repair estimated.

Rechambering a modern rifle from one high-intensity cartridge to another is perfectly acceptable, providing the work is done right. However, any collector value is lost (with rare exceptions) when such a conversion is made. *Converted weapons should be examined extra carefully* before buying, giving consideration to the workmanship of the conversion and several other factors, such as age of the gun, type of conversion, etc.

A Winchester Model 92 rifle in good condition is considered safe when correctly converted to handle .357 Magnum cartridges and hundreds of these conversions have been made. However, this same conversion made to a Winchester Model 73 could be hazardous.

When you encounter a converted rifle, look closely at the workmanship. I once was about to buy a Winchester High Wall rifle that had been converted to a .22 K Hornet. A Winchester Model 70 barrel, originally chambered for the 22 Hornet, was used. Instead of turning the face of the barrel off and then rechambering, the person who converted this rifle merely screwed in the '70 barrel and rechambered it, leaving several threads showing ahead of the action or receiver. Although this gun was probably safe, the appearance of this conversion was enough to discourage me and I didn't purchase it because of the sloppy workmanship.

Also beware of conversions of older rifles—those manufactured before, say, 1930 or thereabouts. Some of these guns were often made of comparatively soft steel, and while safe for the smokeless cartridges which they were originally chambered for, they were not stressed for modern loads. Unless the serial number indicates that the converted gun is of fairly recent manufacture and/or in excellent condition, it's usually best to pass it by.

When buying a modern gun for shooting, always check the bore to make sure it is in good shape. If not, you'd better let this go also unless you can live with a rebarreled job and can buy the gun accordingly. Rust in rifle bores leaves pits which can't be removed, and although the gun may still deliver adequate accuracy, guns in this condition are always more difficult to sell than those with good bores. Rust is often an indication that the entire gun has been neglected.

A loose rifle action or a break-open shotgun action with excessive play can have many causes: firing high pressure Magnum loads, wear, abuse or improper gunsmithing. When such a condition exists, the cost usually prohibits having the problem repaired, except in high-quality firearms.

To check for excessive play, open the action on the shotgun, holding the forearm tightly in your left hand and the grip tightly in your right hand. Twist in opposite directions; any "play" should be readily detected.

Bolt actions are first checked with the bolt open, then closed; by twisting and jiggling the cocking piece and bolt, excessive wear should be readily detected. Some will even "fire" when the cocking piece is twisted. Such guns are obviously in need of repair, and this should be taken into consideration when trading.

There are *several models* floating around, although in good condition, that *are not of much value because ammunition is all but nonexistent.* This category includes, for example, the 7.65 Argentine Mauser. Sure, Norma manufactures ammo in this caliber, but the current price is over one dollar per round. However, some shooters can use this scarceness of ammo to their advantage. Let's assume that a person wants a centerfire rifle to use once a year during deer season; he doesn't care to use it any other time. Any bolt-action centerfire rifle in good condition will cost in excess of $200 if chambered for a modern, readily available cartridge. In this case, it may pay to buy a rifle chambered for an obsolete cartridge and pay the premium price for the hard-to-find ammo, since a box of 20 cartridges will probably last for years.

Brass for most obsolete centerfire cartridges can be formed from existing cartridges and then reloaded. In fact, in recent years, some small firms have again manufactured obsolete brass. If there's a way to save money by buying a particular rifle chambered for an obsolete cartridge, this could possibly be the route to take. However, as a rule of thumb, obsolete guns with little or no collector value should be left alone or else bought at a price so low that you can use them for wall hangers.

In general, you should only purchase used guns that are in good condition and that will sell fast should you ever decide to get rid of them. If work is required to make a particular gun safe, more accurate, operable or presentable, make sure that the cost of this extra labor and parts is taken into consideration. Remember, it's best to pass up a marginal "bargain," or one that you're not sure of, than to buy and lose money because the gun won't perform the way you want or it won't sell at the price you thought.

2.

How To Make a Preliminary Inspection

When shopping for a used gun, most potential buyers do not have all the time they may need to evaluate the arm completely. Trading usually takes place across the counter of a busy gun shop, with other customers waiting in line for service. Perhaps you'll see a gun at one of the gun shows, where again your time and facilities for inspecting the gun will be limited.

Most reputable gun dealers will allow a short inspection period of, say, three days after the firearm is purchased. In other words, the buyer may return the firearm for a full refund any time within three days after purchasing it. However, gun dealers, pawnbrokers and others who buy guns from individuals do not enjoy this privilege. Once a dealer buys a gun from an individual, chances of him recovering money on a defective or stolen firearm are practically nil. Therefore, the dealer must be extremely cautious when purchasing used guns from individuals.

Another problem—especially on the high-priced items—is being sold fakes. The opportunity and temptation for easy money is too much for a few unscrupulous people.

Various organizations over the years have drawn guidelines for gun dealing applicable to both dealers and collectors. Probably the most widely known is the "Code of Ethics for Gun Collectors and Dealers," compiled by the National Rifle Association. A copy of this code follows and lists practices considered to be unethical.

1. The manufacture or sale of a spurious copy of a valuable firearm. This shall include the production of full-scale replicas of historic models and accessories, regardless of easily effaced modern markings, and it also shall include the rebuilding of any authentic weapon into a rarer and more valuable model. It shall not include the manufacture or sale of firearms or accessories which cannot be easily confused with the rare models of famous makers. Such items are: plastic or pottery products, miniatures, firearms of original design or other examples of individual skill, plainly stamped with the maker's name and date, made up as examples of utility and craftsmanship and not representative of the designs or models of any old-time arms makers.

2. The alteration of any marking or serial number, or the assembling and artificially aging of unrelated parts for the purpose of creating a more valuable or unique firearm, with or without immediate intent to defraud. This shall not include the legitimate restoration or completion of missing parts with those of original type, provided that such completions or restorations are indicated to a prospective buyer.

3. The refinishing (bluing, browning or plat-

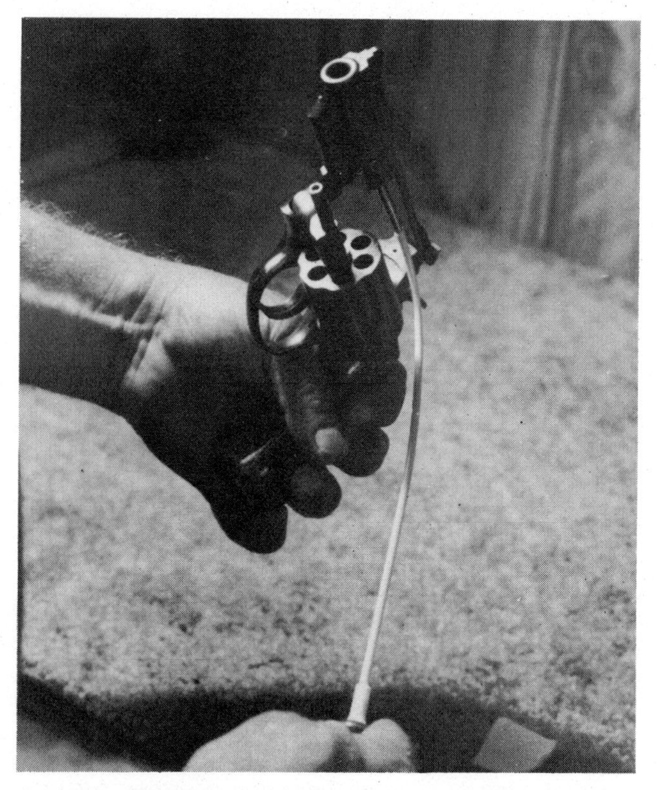

An inspection light is invaluable for examining the inside area of a firearm.

A bore gauge is a helpful, inexpensive item that can be carried in your pocket to determine the gauge, caliber and choke of different weapons.

ing) or engraving of any collector's weapons, unless the weapons may be clearly marked under the stocks or elsewhere to indicate the date and nature of the work, and provided the seller unequivocally shall describe such nonoriginal treatment to a buyer.

4. The direct or indirect efforts of a seller to attach a spurious historical association to a firearm in an effort to inflate its fair value; efforts to "plant" a firearm under circumstances which are designed to inflate the fair value.

5. The employment of unfair or shady practices in buying, selling or trading at the expense of young and inexperienced collectors or anyone else; the devious use of false appraisals, collusion and other sharp practices for personal gain.

6. The use of inaccurate, misleading or falsified representations in direct sales or in selling by sales list, catalog, periodical advertisement and other media; the failure to make prompt refunds, adjustments or other proper restitution on all just claims which may arise from arms sales, direct or by mail.

In general, most reputable gun dealers follow the above code of ethics, to some degree, if not to the fullest. Seldom will you find a marking under the stock of a firearm indicating date and nature of work performed when an antique arm is refinished or repaired with new parts. Even if the restorer marks such arms, it is a relatively easy matter for someone to remove them at a later date. Such restoration work is often played down during the trading process, and after a few transactions (the gun changing hands several times), even a "played-down" version may be omitted altogether. Therefore, the best way to determine if a firearm has been refinished or restored is to learn to detect characteristics of refinished arms. These are many and it will take much experience to be an expert at it, but after reading this chapter you should at least have the basic knowledge to get you started on the right foot.

Making the Preliminary Inspection

A bore light or inspection light should be available when examining a firearm, since the bore of any shotgun, rifle or handgun can tell the potential buyer a lot. Another handy item is an inexpensive bore gauge to help determine the choke and caliber of various weapons.

Before getting into the often complicated task of determining fakes or if a rare firearm has been refinished or otherwise restored to look better in the eyes of the buyer, let's look at used guns from the standpoint of functioning alone. Proper operation of a firearm will be the concern of most used gun buyers, as most will be "working" guns—those used for hunting, plinking or target shooting.

Let's assume you are looking for a good functional pump shotgun, one that will be used solely for hunting. Your main objective is to find a reasonably priced arm that is safe, operates properly and patterns reasonably well. On your first visit to a local gun dealer, you see a J.C. Higgins pump shotgun that looks brand new and is priced at $95. You don't have to be concerned whether the gun has been refinished or not . . . who cares? In this situation, an expertly finished arm will bring more (is worth more) than one in poor original condition, so don't waste your time looking for tell-tale signs of refinishing.

Rather, *be more concerned with the operation of the action.* Does it slide easily, or does it feel rough and sluggish? Use a bore light and inspect the bore. Is it pitted? If so, how badly? Inspect the muzzle very carefully to see if you can detect whether the barrel has been shortened. If it has, chances are you will have a cylinder bore (no choke) and you will then have a less-than-adequate hunting pattern.

Another way to tell if a shotgun barrel has been shortened is to *look for the choke marking on the side of the barrel.* If it says "full" and the manufacturer's specifications indicate that full-choked models were available only in 28- or 30-inch lengths, be cautious if the barrel length is, say, 26 inches. Of course, the barrel could have been 30 inches originally and cut off to 26 inches to "cure" a damaged muzzle. In this case, your bore gauge should be able to provide the answer. The following bore and choke diameters recommended by the Sporting Arms & Ammunition Manufacturers Institute (SAAMI) are the common standards for most U.S. manufacturers—although the dimensions will vary slightly.

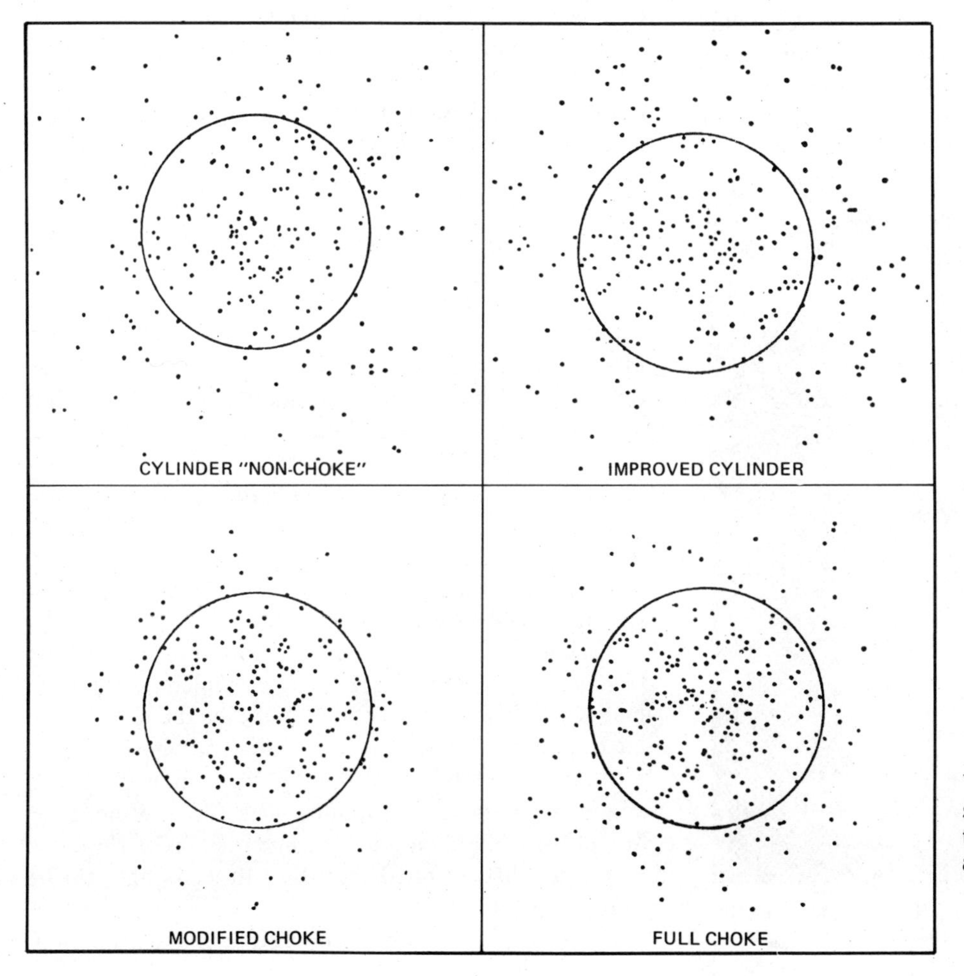

Various choke patterns showing pellet concentration inside a 20-inch circle at 40 yards.

Gauge	Bore	Full Choke Diam.	Modified Choke Diam.	Improved Cylinder Diam.
10	.775	.735	.765	.775
12	.729	.694	.710	.729
16	.667	.639	.652	.660
20	.617	.592	.603	.610
28	.550	.528	.538	.545
.410	.410	.393	.402	.406

You will find shotguns of different makes having slightly different dimensions, but if a 12-gauge shotgun, for example, is supposed to have a full-choked barrel and your bore gauge shows approximately .729, this indicates that the barrel has either been shortened or reamed out, since the measurement is bore size, with no choke.

Of course, *the true test is how the gun shoots.* As a rule of thumb, a full-choked barrel will place 70 percent of its pellets (shot) inside a 20-inch circle at 40 yards; a modified choke, 55 to 60 percent; and an improved cylinder, 45 to 50 percent. If a shotgun barrel has been shortened, this does not mean the gun is worthless. On the contrary, a competent gunsmith can rechoke the barrel or install a multi-choke device, such as the Poly-Choke or Cutts Compensator. However, such work will cost you and if it is determined that the barrel has been shortened, this leaves room for negotiating a lower price on the shotgun. It is also interesting to note that the plastic shot cup used in modern shotshells keeps the shot together longer—resulting in reduced pattern spread. With this in mind, a cylinder bore shotgun may be just what is needed for a close-range upland shotgun for use on quail and rabbit. It's at least worth a try, especially since you should be able to buy such a shotgun at less than market rate.

Plastic shot cups keep the shot together longer and, in most cases, reduce the pattern spread.

The next item to look for is the *gun's operating condition.* Oftentimes, a firearm will malfunction and the owner will sometimes take the gun down to see if he can find the problem. Many of these do-it-yourselfers should not attempt anything more mechanically difficult than tying a pair of shoes, because during the disassembly, parts are marred or broken, or eventually reassembled incorrectly. If you run into an inexpensive firearm that was put through this abuse, chances are the expense of repairing the arm will be more than it is worth. Look for marred screw heads. This is a sure sign that an amateur has taken the gun apart at some point. If these are present, make sure you examine the gun especially carefully before purchasing it.

If the bore looks good, the choke dimensions seem in order and the action functions properly, you probably have a good buy. However, if possible, always try to get the option to return the goods within a reasonable time should you later find out that the gun malfunctions. Most reputable dealers usually allow a certain inspection time and will refund the customer's money in full if a discrepancy is found. Dealers, on the other hand, usually do not enjoy this privilege. Once they get out the cash, or take one gun in trade for another, they are usually stuck with it. This is one reason why many dealers handling new firearms will not accept trade-ins. Those who do must be extremely careful so they will stay in business successfully.

When buying a used hunting arm, it is usually best to stay away from the off-brands for which parts are no longer available. Replacement parts for the most popular brands are nearly always available, whereas those for the less popular ones are very scarce indeed. For example, it is easier to obtain parts for a Winchester Model 1873 rifle than it is for some mail-order shotguns that were discontinued less than 10 years ago. So be cautious in this area.

The most important item when buying a used hunting rifle—besides proper operation of the action and safety—is the rifling and bore. If the rifling is shot out or badly pitted, the rifle will be inaccurate and an inaccurate rifle is about as useless as birth control pills are to a 93-year-old woman. Again, a bore light is invaluable when examining a used rifle. A quick glance at the bore will reveal its condition and tell you immediately if it's pitted, leaded or whatever. Also check the muzzle for any damage, as this will affect accuracy, too. A badly leaded barrel can be corrected by methods described in Chapter 13. It may require lapping by a gunsmith, but accuracy can usually be restored if the rifling is not completely shot out. However, you should not be expected to pay full price for such a weapon, which again leaves room for negotiation. A damaged muzzle may also be cut back and recrowned, but we are talking about $35 worth of work by the average gunsmith. This amount should be deducted from the asking price if the seller has not already done so.

Most reputable dealers of used hunting firearms will test each gun prior to selling it to a customer. During the past couple of years, I've had double-barreled shotguns that fired both barrels when one trigger was pulled, guns that fired upon closing the action, a .22 rimfire semiautomatic that fired automatically—all potentially dangerous situations. Each and every firearm that comes into my shop for repair or resale (other than factory new ones) is inspected and tested and is fired in hand (not from a mechanical rest) before any one is released to a customer. If I'm uneasy about firing a particular weapon, I certainly don't want to sell it to a customer with the possibility of injuring him. Then, if the customer is not completely satisfied, he has one week to return the gun—in the same condition in which it was originally purchased—for a full refund. Any reputable dealer will follow the same procedure.

Of course, you always have to be cautious with a used firearm. It could have some defect that has been overlooked, which in turn could cause serious injury to the shooter or nearby people. For example, a Hunter Special Grade shotgun was recently purchased by a neighbor of mine and, after looking it over, he decided that it was safe to fire. Taking it to a field beside his country home, he loaded two 20-gauge shells into the chambers, pointed it in a safe direction upward and closed the action. The right barrel went off immediately upon closing the action and the shot charge peppered the soffit of his house with No. 6 shot. The problem was easily corrected by a local gunsmith, but had he been a little less cautious, a serious accident could have resulted.

Has the Gun Been Refinished?

Refinishing a "working" gun is both legitimate and recommended, but such work on an antique or collectible firearm is generally frowned upon. For guidelines about restoring arms, see Chapter 14.

When a person has a collectible arm refinished in

Damaged screw heads are a sure indication that an amateur has disassembled the gun at one time or another.

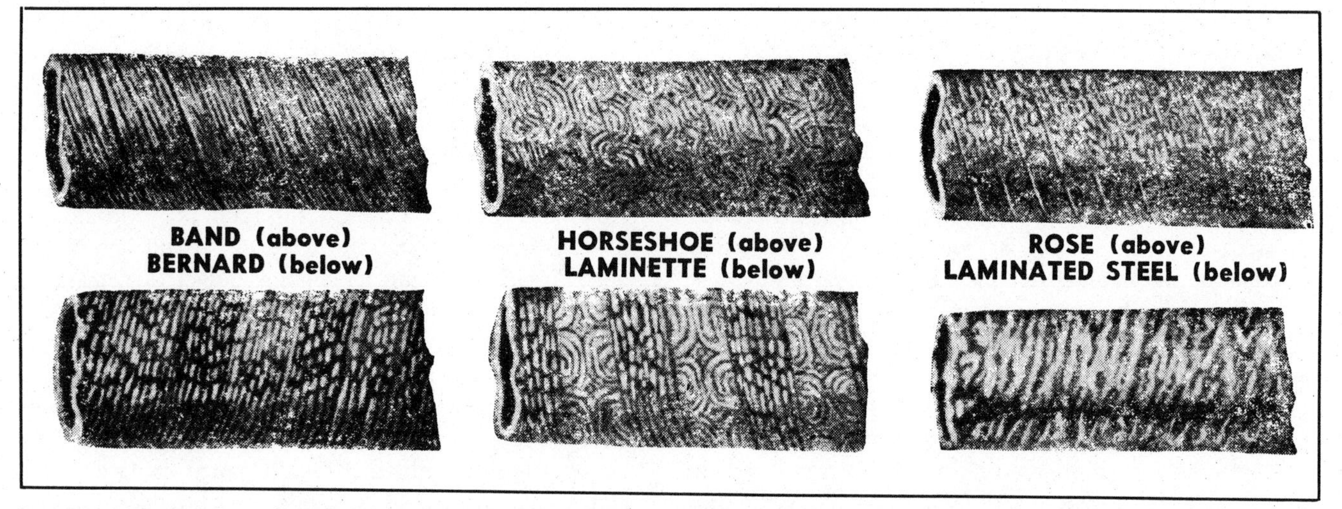

Damascus barrels consist of a combination of forged iron and steel, which is braided in different forms into a band. This band is then wound around a mandrel and welded.

an attempt to fool a collector or to inflate the value of the weapon, there is no other word but downright "crooked" for it. However, there may be times when an antique weapon has been refinished sometime in the past, but the present owner is not aware of it and sells it as an original finish. The latter instance frequently happens until it is detected by an expert, usually causing the last owner to lose considerable money since he would then have to sell it as a refinished model.

Detecting a refinished firearm is not always easy. In fact, some have been so expertly done, that it's next to impossible, but here are some hints that will enable you to detect most of them:

1. Carefully inspect the gun in a good strong light—preferably daylight—using a magnifying glass.

2. Look for scratch marks, light rust pitting and similar tell-tale signs *underneath* the finish. If such marks are shiny or above the finish, they occurred after the finish was applied. However, if underneath, chances are the gun has been refinished.

3. Look closely at all edges, such as those on octagonal barrels, receivers and other areas. Rounded edges that were originally sharp are a sure sign the gun has been polished and refinished. If possible, remove screws and examine screw holes. A person who intends to fool someone will usually not take the time to perform a perfect polishing job on the metal prior to bluing, and oftentimes one or more of the screw holes will be funneled or otherwise deformed.

4. Carefully examine all markings and lettering. When the polishing is done, markings are often lightened or even partially worn away. Some fakers are aware of this and, for this reason, purposely do little polishing around markings and lettering—usually leaving some small pits close to the lettering. Look for these.

5. Learn to detect the type of bluing on gun metal. The satin blue-black sheen characteristic of the slow rust bluing method used on many of the better firearms of the past is easily detected from the glossy deep-black finish used on most modern firearms (and most refinished old guns). A little practice is all that is required.

6. Look for better-than-original finishes. This may seem a little strange, but it's true. The lower grade utility guns of the past usually did not sport as high a grade of finish as did the more expensive models. Careful scrutiny of the original finish will reveal some polishing marks left by the factory. When these models are refinished, the refinisher will sometimes surpass the factory polishing job and actually obtain a better finish.

7. If at all possible, try comparing a known original finish, side by side, with the gun you are thinking of buying. This type of comparison, if done carefully, will usually expose some revealing signs that even the untrained eye will detect.

Identifying Damascus Barrels

Damascus barrels consist of a combination of forged iron and steel, which is braided in different forms into a band. This band is then wound around a mandrel and welded. The manufacturing process proceeds little by little by light hammering until all the small rods or wires are joined into a solid piece. The mandrel used as

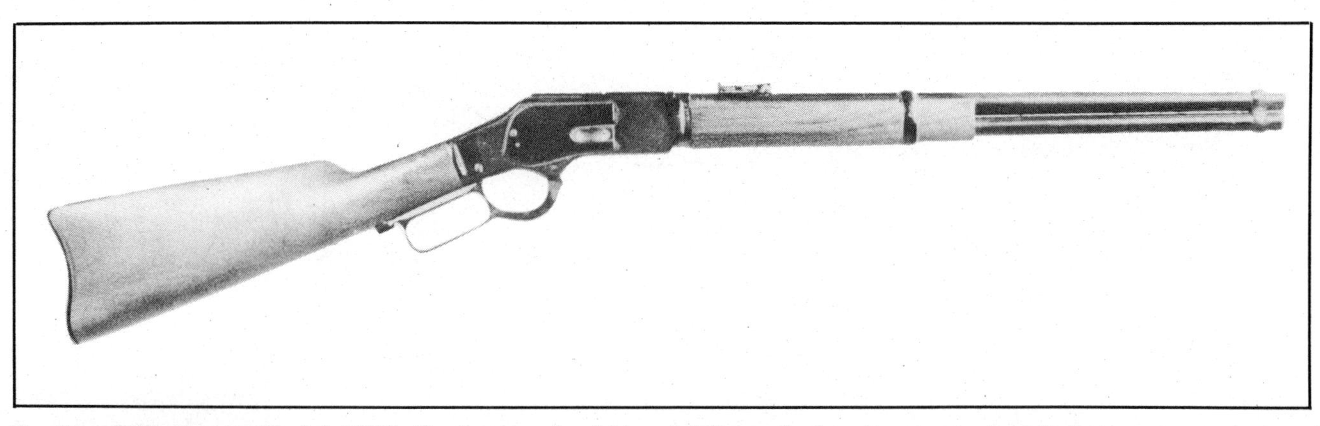

Replica of Winchester Model 1873. Such guns should be plainly marked so they cannot easily be made to fool collectors.

a form is then removed by boring it out. Depending upon how the wires are braided and twisted, on the finished barrel, after browning or bluing, will be a more or less fine Damascus-like figure. The finer and more regular these appear, the greater the worth of the barrel.

Barrels made by this process seem to have originated in the Near East during the 16th century. Through the years they enjoyed great popularity, and confidence in the quality of Damascus barrels became so great that even ordinary steel barrels were either painted or covered with etched designs imitating Damascus patterns. Today the cheapest Damascus barrels are the so-called "band" Damascus barrels. Better-quality types are the so-called "Horseshoe," "Rose," "Bernard," "Crolle," "Moire" and "Laminette." Other fine Damascus barrels include those made in England, known as "Laminated Steel," and the genuine English Damascus produced in Marshall's workshop in Birmingham.

During the manufacture of Damascus barrels, however, grit or coal dust often drifted into the metal during the welding process, causing minor flaws in the steel. These flaws created few problems with the low-pressure black powder loads of the day. But any modern smokeless shotshell fired in these same barrels —even ones that appear to be in good condition—could be disastrous, resulting in the loss of the shooter's fingers or hand, or even his life. The Damascus shotgun barrels are alluring, but so are the markings on a copperhead snake. Both must be treated with respect.

Some owners of shotguns with Damascus barrels are now shooting them with black powder shotshells that once again are available, reasoning that the lower pressure of these shells makes them safe for Damascus steel barrels. I personally will not shoot any shotgun with Damascus barrels using any load, and I'll tell you why: The flaws mentioned in the previous paragraph still exist in the metal of all Damascus shotgun barrels and remember that, in some cases, at least a hundred years have passed since they were manufactured. These flaws are good candidates for rust and deterioration, and after a century or so, it's hard telling just what condition the barrels may be in. Even if test-fired several times, the very next load could cause a barrel to look exactly like a coiled magazine spring—with gaps and all! Shoot Damascus steel shotgun barrels if you like, but consider yourself warned. As for me, I'll pass.

From the foregoing, one would obviously not purchase a shotgun with Damascus barrels for hunting. They are purely wall hangers or to complete collections only, and most are priced accordingly.

Unless the barrel is covered with thick rust, most Damascus barrels are detected by the rings or speckled patterns which normally show through the browning or bluing. However, some will not, but by removing the forearm and dabbing a small amount of Rust and Blue Remover on the barrel beneath the forearm (so it's not noticed later), the pattern can usually be seen on the metal—especially if oil is applied and the barrel lightly polished. Should you not want to remove any of the finish, you might try removing the barrels from the receiver, along with the forearm, and boiling them in a tank of water for about 10 minutes. When the barrels are removed from the boiling water, they should dry almost immediately from the heat, and if the barrels are Damascus, the rings should show up for at least a minute or two at this time. However, be sure to dry and oil the barrels thoroughly before reassembling the gun. If you're still in doubt, have a competent gunsmith check the arm for you.

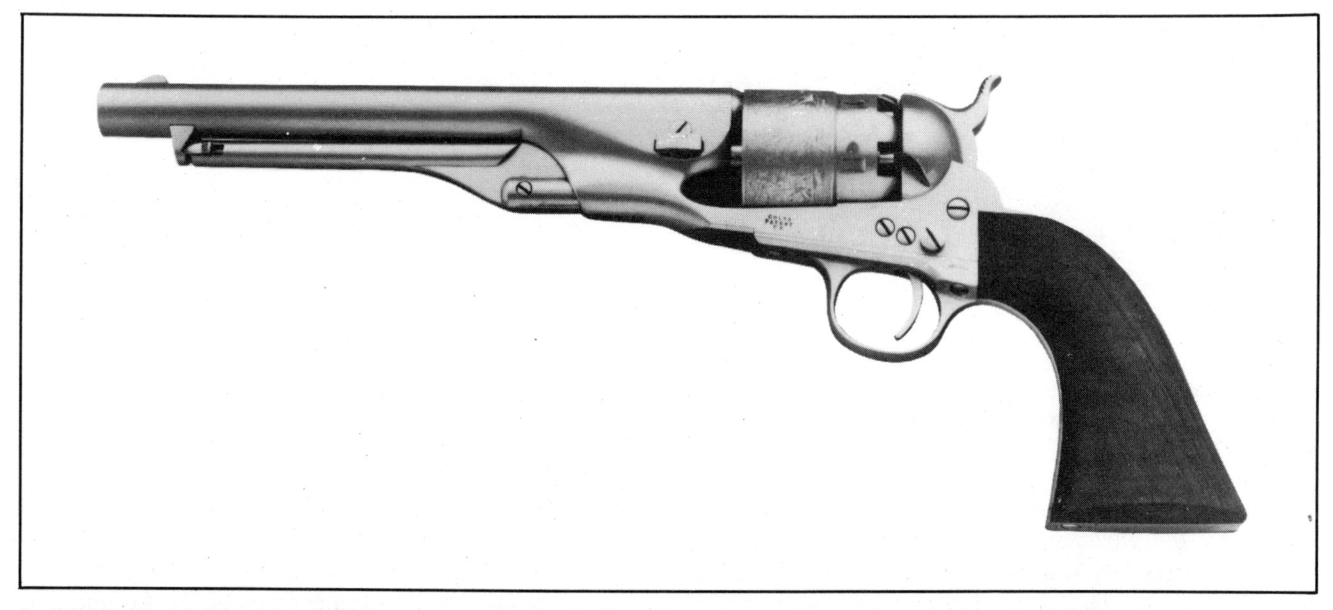

Is this Colt revolver an original or a reproduction? Checking the serial numbers and other features should tell you immediately that it's the latter.

Detecting Fakes

Firearms that are now obsolete are very much in demand by both shooters and collectors alike. Eventually, when the demand for a certain model exceeds the supply and prices are driven exorbitantly high, there are always some individuals who are tempted to fake these high-priced weapons to be sold to some unknowing collector. The collector, unfortunately, who sooner or later learns of the fraud, in discouragement may dump his entire gun collection and turn to collecting something like coins.

The shooting world is well aware of the reproductions of antique weapons that have appeared on the market over the past 20 years or so. These are perfectly legitimate, because most are clearly marked as reproductions. The only trouble is with the fakers. With the groundwork laid, it is a very easy matter to grind off the markings or lettering indicating a reproduction and artificially age the wood and metal. These will eventually become the possession of a beginning collector, having been sold as the authentic thing. Fortunately, many of these reproductions have been changed slightly to discourage the practice of faking.

Fraudulent firearms take many forms, but most represent rare or desirable firearms—those commanding the highest dollars. And, interestingly enough, many of these fakes are ingeniously done. Take, for example, the rare Winchester Model 1873 "One of One Thousand." The last one I heard of being sold brought $35,000 at auction. It is possible for a knowledgeable firearm expert to obtain an authentic Winchester Model 73, copy the One of One Thousand engraving, scroll work and other characteristics of the rare model and pass it off to a trusting collector for a good sum of money. If there is any doubt in your mind, obtain the serial number of the weapon and contact Winchester or U.S. Repeating Arms to determine if the serial number corresponds to what they have on record as being an authentic One of One Thousand. You must provide a number; they won't give out serial numbers, for obvious reasons. If I were new at the game, I'd certainly want a firearm in the five-figure bracket appraised by an expert before I'd assume ownership.

Another form of fraud in firearm dealing is to engrave plain guns of a period to look like special "presentation" models, which are usually worth several thousand dollars more than the plain version. Again, an expert can usually tell the fakes from the original factory presentation models, and most manufacturers will have the history of the firearm recorded; a letter to them with a serial number and description of the firearm will usually bring an accurate identification.

The name of a famous person engraved on a firearm

to represent a rare historical weapon is another form of fraudulent dealing. And this is just for starters; there are dozens of ways firearms are falsified to inflate their value.

The first thing a new collector can do to prevent being "taken" is to educate himself by reading authoritative books, visiting museums and attending lectures given by knowledgeable experts. Also, to frequent as many gun shows as possible. Once you become thoroughly familiar with the real thing, a fake will be easier to detect.

On the rarer models—those demanding the highest prices—the seller is usually required to furnish the necessary proof that a firearm is authentic. If he knows enough about a particular gun to know its value, he should certainly know enough to be able to offer reasonable proof of its authenticity. If not, he should have no objections to your having an expert or two of your choice examine the gun. If he does object, leave the gun alone.

Beware of those sellers who want to complete a transaction hurriedly, particularly the guns valued in the $30,000 to $100,000 bracket, not the run-of-the-mill $300 weapons. Gun dealers must do a certain volume of business to make a buck and most do not want to spend all day on a $100 sale; so out of necessity, a dealer's going to try to push the sale right along so he can get to the next customer waiting in line. Just be cautious of those people who want to meet you on a street corner, hand you a gun and expect a bag of cash in return.

The most common firearm transaction will be with the less valuable weapons that sell in the $500 to $2,000 range. The condition of any weapon determines the value, and the price of a gun in mint condition can vary considerably from one in, say, very good condition. For this reason, some people try to upgrade the condition slightly to obtain several hundred dollars more for a particular weapon.

When a firearm appears to be in mint condition, always check the bore first. If the bore is rusted and pitted or shows signs of hard use, it's highly unlikely that the "mint" outside finish is original. You might find another gun that could be classified as "very good," but in examining the bore, you can tell that it has seen some hard shooting—although still in relatively good shape. Examine the muzzle; if it looks unfired, you can bet the gun has been refinished or at least touched up. A centerfire rifle that has seen much use—although well taken care of—will usually show signs of wear in general and on the muzzle in particular from escaping gas.

Reference books are available on almost any firearm, and I've never seen one yet that I didn't get something of value from. Most offer a wealth of information that can be of help identifying variations, serial numbers, and the like. See Appendix IV for a list of recommended reference books.

Welding is one means of changing the dimensions of a firearm to appear to be something it is not. This technique has been used for years by fakers. To determine if a gun has been faked by welding, there is a relatively simple method used to detect the addition of steel to the original arm. However, the method does require some practice to become proficient in evaluating the results. Ammonium persulfate is a rapid surface oxidiz-

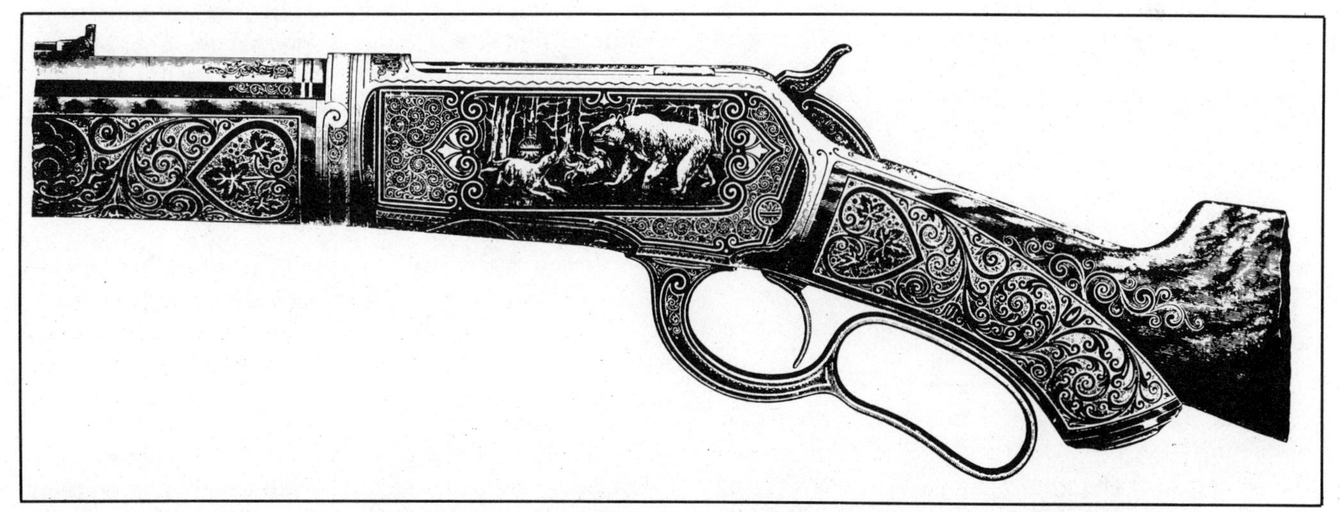

An elaborately engraved Winchester firearm like this Model 1886 can be worth a small fortune if it is in good condition. But be careful of newly engraved versions made to look like the original.

ing agent when dissolved with water at about 5 parts water to 1 part persulfate. The surface to be checked must be polished or at least be relatively clean. The solution can then be applied with a piece of clean cotton and allowed to remain on the gun's surface for about 15 seconds. The difference in the surface color will be readily noted if heat from welding has been applied or metal added at some earlier date. Even the addition of similar metal—not visible to the naked eye—will be discernible when the persulfate solution is applied.

Obviously, the above method requires that the finish be removed. If you're wrong, the value of the arm is going to be lowered. So before using this method, you'd better have some strong suspicions that warrant this type of probing.

The following is an abbreviated list of certain popular collector guns compiled by Dixie Gun Works. The descriptions and serial numbers should help you determine whether you have a fake or not.

Handguns

Colt Bisley Model. Serial numbers between 159000 and 325000. Original barrels will be stamped "Bisley Model" on left side of barrel. 7½-inch barrel length is scarcest and most desirable.

Colt 2nd Model Dragoon. Rarest of 2nd Models between serial numbers 8000 and 10000. Has "V" hammer spring and no hammer-bearing wheel.

Colt 3rd Model Dragoon. 8-inch barrel models, usually in 18000 serial range. 7½-inch barrel models cut for a stock, serial numbers between 16620 and 17940, iron backstrap.

Colt 1851 Navy Model. Cut for stock. Usually 4-screw frame, iron backstrap (few transition models with brass backstrap observed between 164000 and 166000). Standard serial number ranges: 67000–79000; 90000–93000; 128000's.

Colt Percussion 1851 Square Back Navy Model. Under serial number 3000, small cut-out lug, lever screw enters from right side.

Colt Percussion 1860 Fluted Cylinder Army Model. Serial numbers under 6000. Left-twist rifling, opposite to the right twist of the standard 1860 Army Model.

Colt 1849 Pocket Model. Scarce variation has the Hartford address with iron backstrap and trigger guard.

Colt Single Action Army Models. Possible Gen. Custer guns—between 11500 and 14500. Eagle grips—1882 to 1896 or serial numbers 73000 to 168001. Long fluted cylinders—1915 or serial numbers 330000 to 331380.

Smokeless powder models—1896 or serial numbers after 16500. Wells Fargo & Company factory marked—1906 or serial numbers 287000 to 311525.

.357 Magnum caliber—1935, serial numbers 356000 to present.

Script barrel markings—any under serial number 15000.

Round ejector heads—serial number 85000.

Flat-top target models—1888, or after serial numbers 12500.

Factory change to stamping number on frame only and under the grip (right side)—1920, or after serial number 338000.

Colt "Wells Fargo" Hammerless Model. Either big or small trigger guard with two-line address (out of character with one-line address). This model should be verified by a gammagram, X-ray or written guarantee by a reputable seller.

Colt Cartridge Conversions. Rarest of the Colt factory conversions is the Richards-Mason type *without* loading cut out and standard Mason ejector.

Columbus Percussion Revolver. Highly prized model, serial numbers under 100. Marked in two lines "Columbus Firearms Manufacturing Co., Columbus, Ga." on barrel and cylinder.

Dance Brothers Percussion Revolver. Caution on this big frame .44 caliber that resembles a Colt Dragoon, because some clever fakes from England have turned up at U.S. gun shows. An obvious distinguishing feature of the Dance revolver is absence of recoil shields, making a *flat frame.*

Griswold "Marked" Percussion Revolver. 7 3/16-inch to 7½-inch barrel length, with the last 5 inches or more turned round (rather than octagonal), serial numbers under 4000. A cryptic letter proof on frame, cylinder and barrel. Brass frame. Several replica percussions are presently being aged and represented as the "Griswold and Gunnison." Inasmuch as the originals were both red and yellow brass and had unmarked barrels, this is a simple "fake."

Leech & Rigdon Percussion Revolver. Scarce variation of Navy-type revolver, marked atop barrel "Leech & Rigdon Novelty Works, C.S.A." Pin and ball loading lever catch common on this model, also on those marked "Augusta, Ga. C.S.A." that have 12 locking-notch cylinders, termed "Rigdon & Ansley" revolvers.

Le Mat "Grapeshot" Percussion Revolver. Very few enthusiasts can recognize the three basic types of this rare and desirable Civil War arm.

1st Type—Serial numbers 1 to 450. Barrel part octagon and part round; trigger spur, swivel lanyard ring, loading lever on *right* side.

2nd Type—Serial numbers 451 to 951. Lever changed to *left* side; octagon barrel, trigger spur, swivel lanyard ring.

3rd Type—Serial numbers 951 to highest number 8448 reported by a reputable dealer. Octagon barrel, solid lanyard ring with hole, no trigger spur, lever on *left* side. Original barrel length was 7.3 inches.

Manhattan Navy Percussion Revolver. Easily recognized. 6-inch barrel is considered scarcer than the 6½-inch and usually commands a premium price; therefore, careful examination should be made of 6-inch models.

Metropolitan Navy Percussion Revolver. Rolled-on cylinder seen after serial number 1800. Revolvers marked for distribution by "H.E. DIMICK–ST. LOUIS" were in the serial number range 1100 to 1800.

Metropolitan Pocket Police Model. In appearance almost an exact copy of the 1862 Colt Police Model, except loading lever is held by a small visible screw and no ratchet, as is characteristic with the Colt. Fifty percent of the total 3000 were *unmarked*; therefore, a premium price is usually attached to marked specimens.

Remington Big Frame Cartridge Models. 1875 Single Action, 7½-inch barrel—serial numbers 1 to 25000. 1890 Single Action, 5½-inch and 7½-inch barrels—serial numbers 1 to 2000.

Remington Big Frame Percussion Models. Army 1861 Model—6494 to 10446; Navy 1861 Models—2044 to 21533; New Model Navy—24246 to 44944. These serial number ranges are for the early-type Remingtons, listed to prevent the buyer from being confused with the later type.

Spiller & Burr Percussion Revolver. A very close kin to the Whitney Navy revolver, known by most collectors and not rare or difficult to recognize. The problem results from a worn or abused Whitney minus marking being passed as a "Spiller & Burr." Remember —the *frame is brass.*

Tucker, Sherrard & Company Percussion Revolver. Tucker & Sherrard revolvers come in the image of Colt Dragoon 44's and 1851 Navy Models with either round or square guards, the most obvious difference being *no cut out* lug for loading. Beware of the acid-etched, *crude* barrel markings "L.E. Tucker & Sons."

Long Arms

Winchester Lever-Action Rifles. Excluding minor variations and differences that appeal to the advanced Winchester student, an effort has been made to catalog the more important points the average Winchester fan

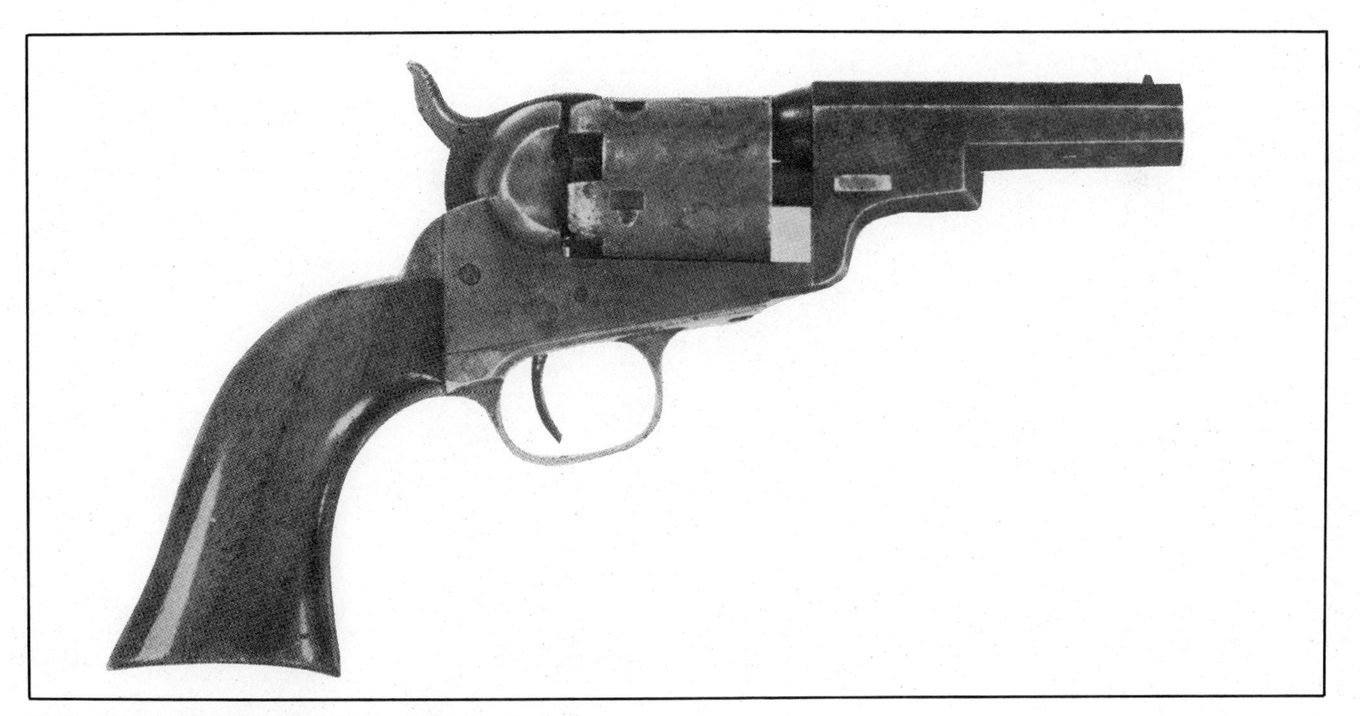

Wells Fargo Colt with three-inch octagonal barrel.

would do well to remember.

Henry Rifles. Purchased by the U.S. Army, marked C.G.C. on barrel and frame, serial numbers 3000 to 4200.

Model 1866. Round barrel rifles were made after 1876—over serial number 130000; total production 1779. Octagon barrel carbines are found over serial number 150000; total production 791. Transition models are found between serial numbers 104000 and 118000 and 81000 through 96000.

Model 1873. Barrel lengths over 24 inches are scarce. Also scarce are heavier barrels measuring over 23/32 inches across the flats at the muzzle.

Model 1876. Saddle ring carbines; standard barrel length, 22 inches with a rapid taper. North West Mounted Police Guns are generally marked N.W.M.P. on right side of stock in a semi-half-moon pattern. Serial numbers 12000, 23801 to 33000, and 43900 to 66000. Muskets have 32-inch round barrels with a rapid taper.

High Wall, Single Shot. Serial numbers under 600 can be considered scarce and rare, and must have *flat-side* receivers.

Model 1886. Octagon barrels, found both tapered and untapered; tapered octagon barrel with lightweight stock is scarcer. Saddle ring carbines—very scarce in this model; barrel length, 22 inches. Barrels over 28 inches should have two magazine bands. The 1886 musket is the rarest of the lever-action muskets; barrel length, 30 inches.

Model 71 (1886-type actions). Made in two barrel lengths, 24 and 20 inches.

Model 1892. Muskets; barrel length, 30 inches.

Model 53. Extremely scarce. 22-inch barrel, button magazine, shotgun butt plate. Marked "Model 53" on left side of barrel. Watch for rebuilt Model 92's with Model 53-marked barrels.

Model 65 (1892 action). Extremely scarce. 22- and 24-inch rapid taper barrels. Marked "Model 65" on right side of barrel. Watch for rebuilt Model 92's with Model 65-marked barrels.

Model 1895 Flat Side. Can be considered rare and desirable; also has one-piece lever instead of two-piece as on later rifles. A further premium could be expected from an 1895 Flat Side with one-piece lever and a *pistol-grip* original stock.

3. Firearm Identification

Before a fair firearm buy or sale can be made, at least one of the parties—and preferably both—must be able to identify the firearm and its variations, if any. For example, let's assume that you walked into a used gun shop and saw a Colt Government Model 1911A1 Pistol in excellent condition for sale. The price tag shows a price of $850. You have seen similar pistols in the same condition offered for $250, so you don't purchase that one. Had you looked closer, you would have noticed that the pistol was manufactured by Singer, who was one of the manufacturers licensed by Colt during World War II to make these pistols. In this case, the pistol has a collector's value of about $2,500, due to the rarity of this particular model. So, had you, the potential buyer, taken the time to identify the pistol correctly, you would have had a good deal at $850.

Old Gun Catalogs

Old gun catalogs are one of the best sources of information for identifying used guns, and every serious collector should purchase every one he can find. These catalogs don't have to be originals. There are many reprints on the market at reasonable prices that will suffice just as well. Besides helping to identify the older firearms, you'll drool at the prices asked at the time for a genuine hand-engraved receiver and fancy stock carving. In fact, collecting old gun catalogs is a hobby in itself and a fine way to educate yourself prior to and during your evolution as a serious gun collector.

Not long ago, a widow of a local gun enthusiast called on me to appraise her husband's gun collection, reloading tools and gunsmithing equipment, which were stored in the basement of her home. After finishing the appraisal, she said that one corner of the basement was filled with old shooting magazines and perhaps I could use them. If I'd move them out of her way, she would be glad to give them to me. Upon investigating the pile, I came across dozens of old gun catalogs, including copies of the 1932 SHOOTER'S BIBLE. Realizing the value of the find, I offered her a check for the numerous books, plus I didn't charge her anything for the appraisal. Although she accepted my offer not to charge her for the appraisal, she refused any further money. Needless to say, this was my lucky day. These dozens of old catalogs have proved invaluable in my work, and I wouldn't part with them for love nor money.

I've also had reasonably good luck advertising for old gun catalogs and shooting publications in small-town weekly newspapers. Besides turning up several old and valuable gun catalogs, I have been able to obtain a copy of nearly every hunting, fishing and shooting magazine published—many dating back to as far as 1913.

Rare gun catalogs are available through used book

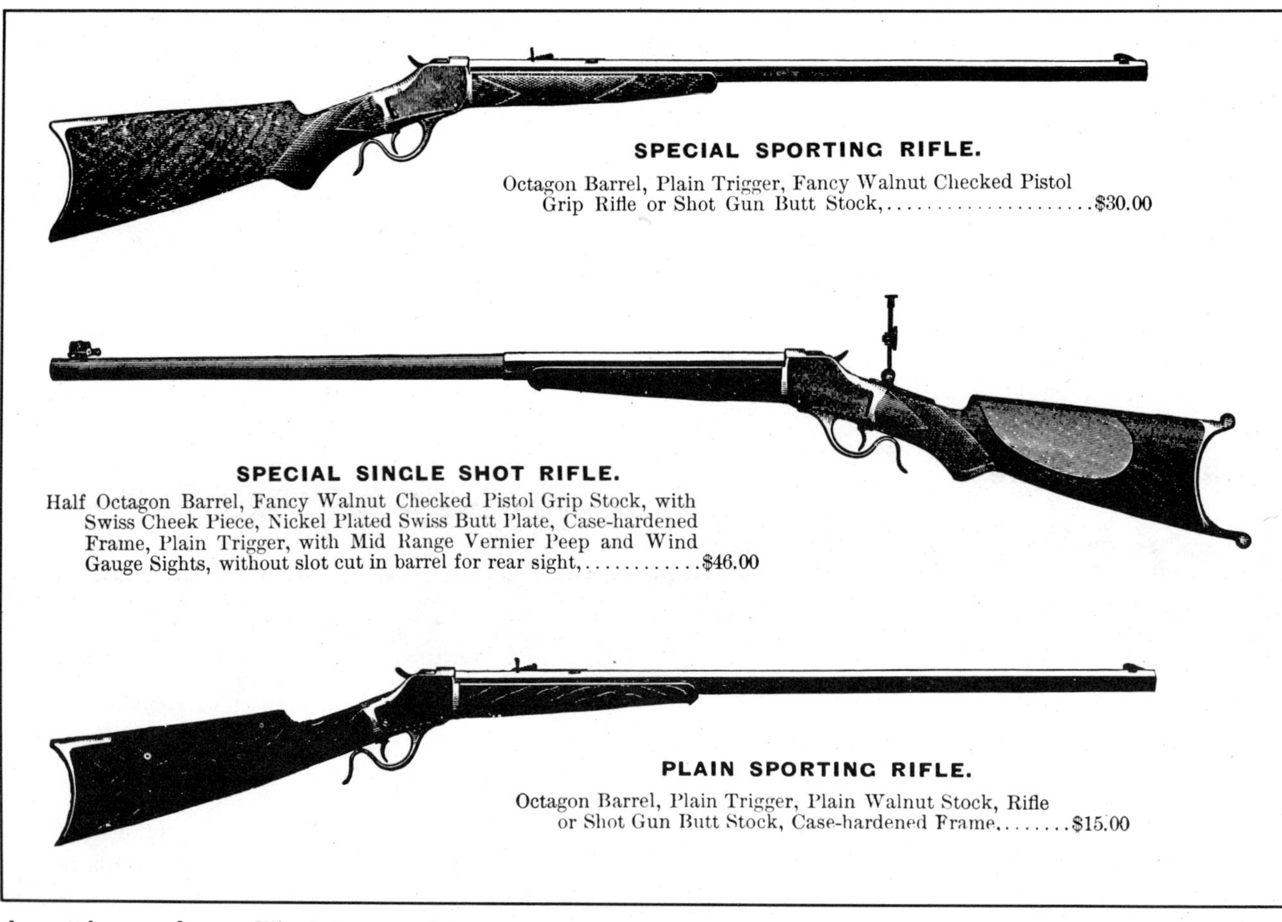

A sample page from a Winchester catalog, dated 1896, shows that their single-shot rifle came in three regular versions. Many old gun catalogs also illustrate sectional views of the various weapons, which are invaluable for assembly and repairs.

dealers and ads in *Shotgun News, The American Rifleman* and other periodicals, but you are going to pay a pretty penny for the original copies—oftentimes more than I'm willing to pay. However, reprints are available from Ray Riling Arms Books Co. and Dixie Gun Works (see Appendix IV for addresses). Write for their current catalogs for a complete description of their offerings and prices.

General Characteristics of Typical Firearms

The matchlock, which came into use about A.D. 1450, was one of the first practical locks and consisted of a semicircular-shaped piece of metal pivoted to the side of the gun. At the end opposite the pivot was a slow match, a device to hold a cord treated with saltpeter to make it burn slowly. The tip of this cord was gripped in the holder at one end of a C-shaped piece of metal and pushed with a finger to contact the priming powder, which fired the weapon.

Around A.D. 1500 the matchlock was greatly improved with the invention of the serpentine match holder which consisted of a piece of metal bent to resemble an "S". The bottom portion of the S became the trigger initially; but a short time later a sear was added, allowing the shooter to pull back the matchlock and hold it, preventing firing until the shooter was ready. This led to the introduction of gun sights, and aim became more accurate.

Rifling was also introduced about the same time, as were efforts to make a multishot gun. Some firearms featured revolving cylinders, similar to the revolvers in use today, while others employed multiload barrels as well as double, triple and other combinations of barrels.

86 A. F. STOEGER, INC., 507 FIFTH AVE., NEW YORK. N. Y.

GENUINE LUGER PISTOLS

AVAILABLE AGAIN FOR THE FIRST TIME SINCE 1914 IN 9 M/M

RANGE 1800 YARDS
ACCURATE—SAFE
POWERFUL

Genuine Luger 7.65 m/m With 4½" Tapered Barrel, Price $100

LOOK FOR THE NAME "STOEGER"

The new Lugers we are now offering can be readily distinguished from the cheap post-war models by their fine finish and unmistakeable "quality" appearance. The stocks are of selected first quality grained dark walnut, finely checkered. To insure identification, all of our Lugers are stamped on the right forward side of the receiver: "A. F. Stoeger, Inc., New York." They are also plainly stamped with the American Eagle on the breech block.

AN ARM YOU WILL BE PROUD TO OWN!

Here is the real Luger—the same high-grade pistol that was turned out by the famous Luger factory before the war—an arm that is built to the highest standard in every detail! And one that you may well be proud to possess! To own a real Luger is to own an automatic that has earned a world-wide reputation for its all around shooting qualities.

Do not confuse this Luger with the rebuilt army Lugers—or with the crude models that flooded the market immediately after the war. The new Luger, as pictured above, with its long slender barrel, fine workmanship and beautiful finish, is an altogether different class from these spurious models. Even a novice could instantly perceive the difference between them.

Genuine Luger 9 m/m With 4" Barrel, Price $100

After the war, the Luger was made up only in 7.65 m/m with stubby 3⅝-inch barrel and it has only been during the last few years that, due to popular demand, the factory has again resumed the manufacture of the 4½ inch, 7.65 m/m tapered barrel, built to absolute pre-war standards. The present day Lugers are built entirely at the Mauser factory in Oberndorf, whence all the dies, jigs, and special tools were removed from the D. W. M. Arms Factory in Berlin where all genuine Lugers were made until that factory discontinued the manufacture of arms a few years ago. The Mauser Factory, affiliated with the D. W. M., manufactures the Luger to the very highest standards.

In 1934 the manufacture of the 9 m/m model, with 3⅝-inch and 8-inch barrel was resumed, and we are able to offer for the first time since 1914, the *genuine* 100 per cent factory built Luger in this caliber and lengths. New Luger pistols caliber 9 m/m hitherto offered by us have had to employ barrels made by outside German manufacturers, and while these were good, we are now discontinuing everything but 100 per cent Luger (Mauser) factory built barrels, and can thus guarantee positive full satisfaction to all purchasers of these genuine Luger pistols.

In considering the price of these Genuine Luger Pistols, it should be borne in mind that the models we offer are the only ones built to pre-war standards and specifications, and cost considerably more at the factory than before the war; they pay a duty of 55 per cent of their factory cost in addition to a special duty of $3.50 and then have to pay a U. S. excise tax of 10 per cent of their selling price. Added to this is the present low dollar value, the dollar being worth only 59 cents in Europe compared to its former purchasing power. In view of the foregoing, it can be understood that the present prices, while appearing exorbitant, are really held just as low as possible.

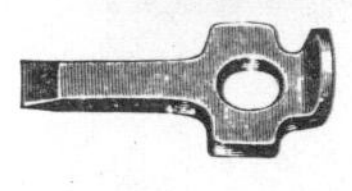

Illustration shows special tool supplied with each genuine Luger. It is used as a screwdriver for removing grip or breech block end piece and also facilitates loading of the magazine. The circular hole fits the magazine button, and the loading platform is then easily held down.

Genuine Luger 9 m/m With 8" Barrel, Price $115.00

Illustration shows special cleaning rod supplied with each 8" Luger.

MECHANICAL FEATURES

The Luger belongs to the recoil type of firearms, with breech lock remaining fixed during the passage of the projectile through the barrel. This form of construction, by preventing the escape of gas, insures full and uniform pressure on the projectile, with resulting maximum power.

Safety is insured by the unique toggle joint construction of the lever mechanism, providing an absolutely secure lock.

Simplicity and ease of operation are outstanding characteristics of the Luger. There are no complicated parts to cause confusion. A novice in the handling of firearms can quickly learn how to use it. The magazine may be emptied by the simple pressure of a button. When the last shot is fired, the breech remains open showing that the gun is empty.

One of the many features of this splendid arm is the construction of the extractor, which enables the shooter to see and feel, from the outside, whether a cartridge is in the chamber.

The "squeezer" grip safety has been eliminated because it often pinched the fleshy part of the hand, and thus prevented firing the pistol, which represented a serious draw-back in an emergency. Since this was never an independent safety, its removal does not make the pistol less safe.

Since 1900 the Luger Automatic, by its consistently excellent performance, has won the approval of firearm experts of all nationalities, as an ordnance, sporting and police arm. It has been accepted as a standard military arm by Germany, Portugal and Switzerland. Large numbers have been purchased by Canada, Russia, Holland, Bulgaria and Brazil for army use. In the World War, the Luger was extensively used by both sides. Ask any war veteran what he thinks of the Luger. Because of its long range, accuracy and power of penetration (1/3 inch sheet steel), the Luger has become a great favorite with motorcycle policemen in rounding up automobile bandits.

©

CAREFUL ATTENTION AND SAFE DELIVERY OF YOUR ORDER

Excerpt from an old A.F. Stoeger catalog showing versions of the Stoeger Luger pistol. Note the prices. Today, this gun is worth over $5,000.

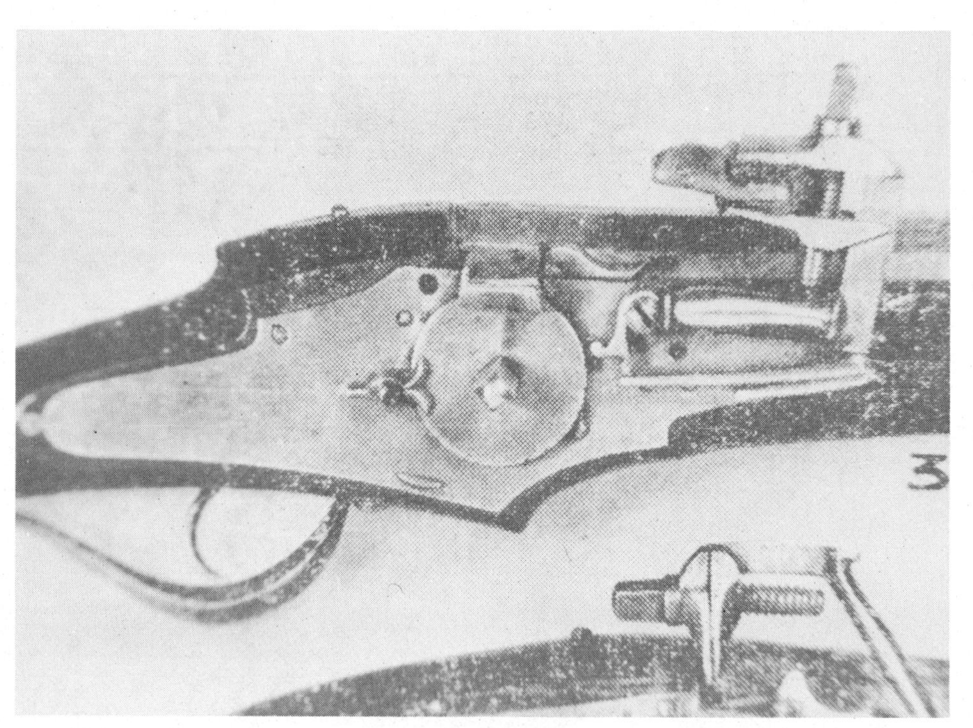

The wheel lock, used on early firearms, operated in much the same way as our modern cigarette lighter.

However, all of these inventions suffered from lack of a good ignition system.

The wheel lock came next and this ignition system operated in much the same way that our modern cigarette lighters work; that is, a serrated steel wheel rotated against a flint which threw sparks down into a priming pan to ignite the charge in the barrel. To fire the wheel lock, a heavy spring was wound, the cock pulled which held a piece of flint until it came in contact with the serrated wheel. This was the "ready" position. The arm was then aimed and the trigger pulled; that started the wheel spinning, throwing sparks meant primarily for the priming pan in all directions.

In the mid-1500's the "snaphaunce" came about. This lock consisted of a hammer which held a piece of flint—just like the flintlocks of nearly a hundred years later. When the hammer was released by the trigger, it fell forward and struck near the touch hole, causing sparks to fly and enter the priming pan, igniting the charge and discharging the firearm, similar to the later flintlocks. In fact, the development of the snaphaunce was the forerunner of firearms used up until about the time of the Civil War.

During the early 1600's, the flintlock system was developed and was basically a snaphaunce with the addition of an angled steel pan that covered the priming pan by use of a hinge at either the front or the back. As the hammer was released, it struck the angled surface

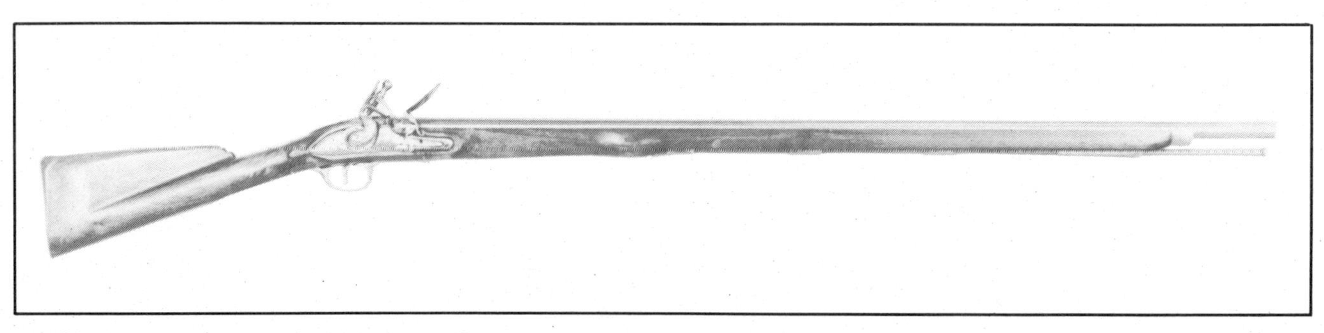

The flintlock system was used in both rifles and pistols and was the U.S. Military type of lock until 1842.

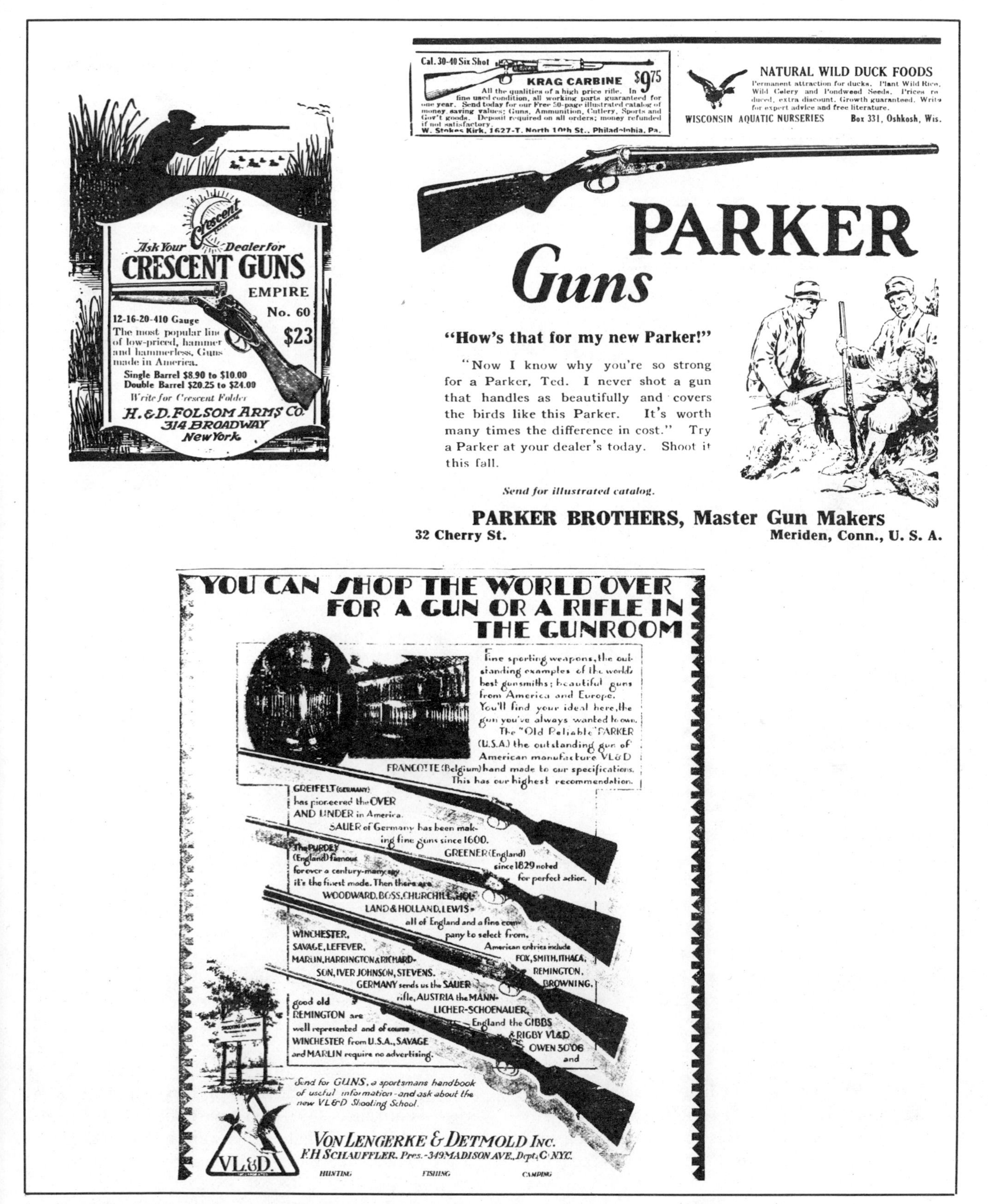

Sample advertisements from old sporting magazines. By checking the dates of the magazines, you can determine the approximate date that a firearm was manufactured.

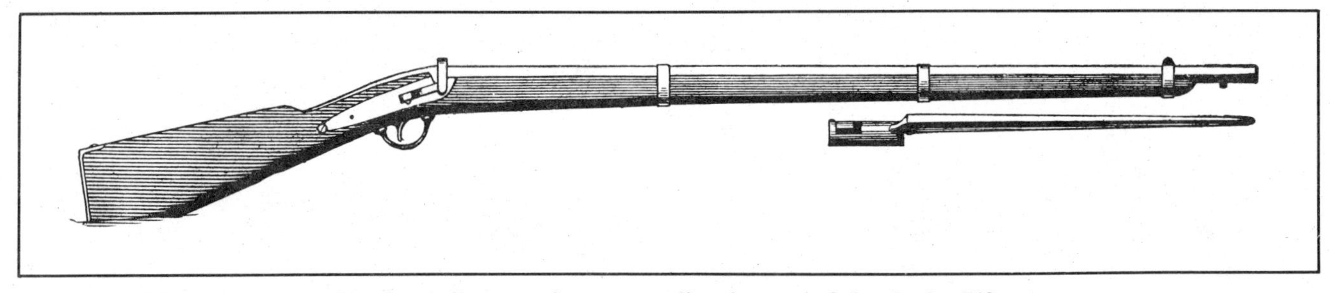

The hammer, which operated horizontally, was the outstanding feature of the Jenks Rifle.

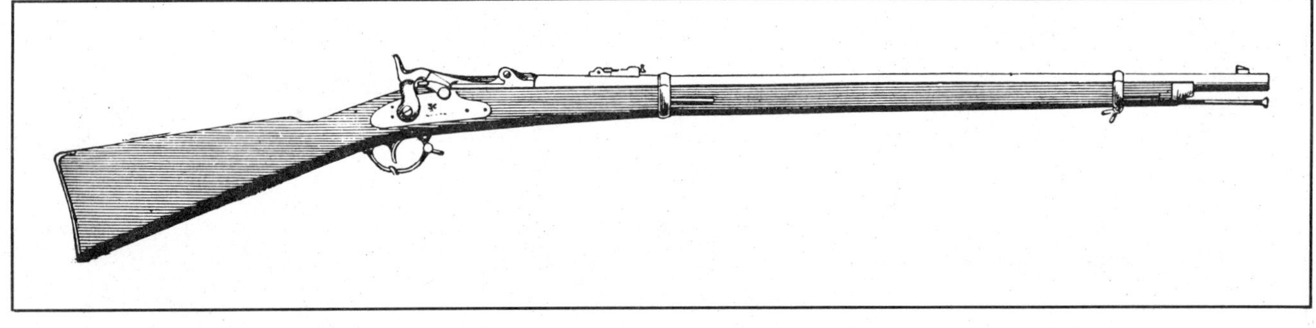

The most popular early breechloader was the Trapdoor Springfield. This rifle was manufactured in both .50-70 and .45-70 calibers.

of this hinged pan called a "frizzen." The striking of the hammer containing flint against the frizzen threw back the cover, exposing the priming powder contained in the pan. It also showered sparks into the priming powder to fire the weapon.

The flintlock was used in both rifles and pistols and was the type used by the U.S. military until 1842. During this same period, paper cartridges were developed and breechloading firearms were put to practical use, although sparingly. The Hall Rifle was the first breechloader adopted by the U.S. Government. It was a flintlock with a tip-up action. Upon releasing a lever, the front end of the breech section tips up, loads and pushes back down into alignment with the barrel. The U.S. Army model was .52 caliber and was used to some extent in the Seminole War in Florida.

The Jenks Rifle, invented by William Jenks in 1838, was the forerunner of the Merrill Rifle and was used in Florida in 1841 by U.S. troops. The hammer, which operated horizontally, was the outstanding feature of these arms.

The Greene Rifle was the first bolt-action gun used by U.S. troops (late 1850's). The bolt handle was in the rear and was released by pressing down a spring catch on the tang. It was a percussion arm and had the nipple underneath with a ring-shaped hammer. The .535 cartridge had the bullet in the rear so there were always two in the gun when loaded; the rear one was intended to act as a gas check. About 900 of these rifles were used in the Civil War.

Breechloaders that followed included the Sharps and Hankins Rifle, the Ballard Rifle, the Merrill alteration of the Model 1842 musket and the Peabody alteration of the Model 1861 Springfield rifled musket. No less than a dozen other experimental breechloaders and variations were used up to the turn of the century—the most popular being the Trapdoor Springfields in .50-70 and .45-70 calibers.

Repeating U.S. handguns followed the same general pattern as the rifles, except were used more extensively by officers and NCO's. The accompanying illustrations show most of the pistols and revolvers used by the U.S. Government, from the Rappahannock Forge flintlock pistol to the Model 1911 Colt Automatic.

The shotgun was born as a reaction to the horrible accuracy of the early firearms. A target had to be hit with multiball loads. Small shot, however, was not invented until about 1750—about the same time that single- and double-barreled shotguns were made in England. They were all matchlock muzzleloaders. By 1850, single-

On the following pages are representative samples of the pistols and revolvers used by the U.S. Government, from the earliest flintlock pistols to the Colt Model 1911 semiautomatic.

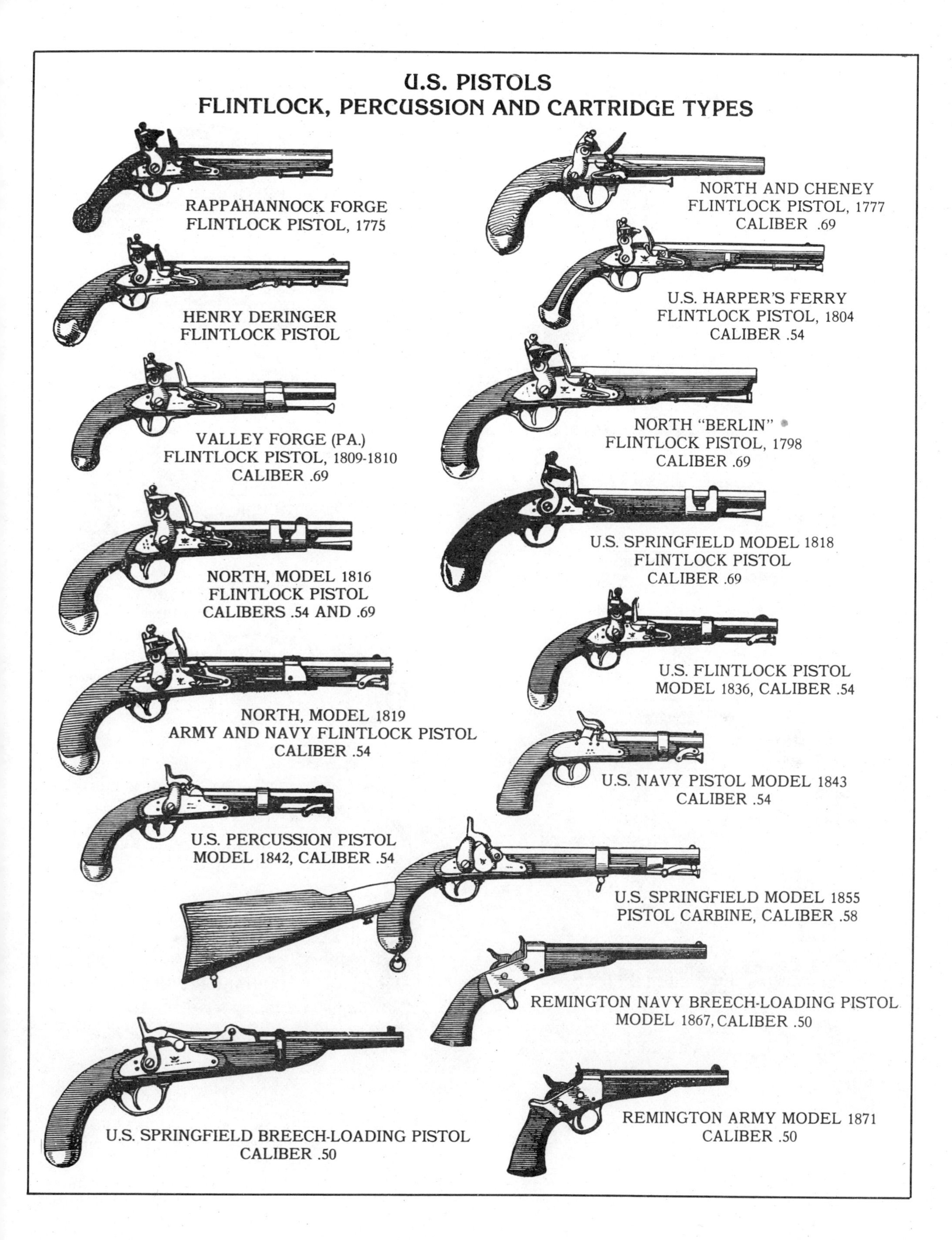
U.S. PISTOLS
FLINTLOCK, PERCUSSION AND CARTRIDGE TYPES
RAPPAHANNOCK FORGE
FLINTLOCK PISTOL, 1775
NORTH AND CHENEY
FLINTLOCK PISTOL, 1777
CALIBER .69
HENRY DERINGER
FLINTLOCK PISTOL
U.S. HARPER'S FERRY
FLINTLOCK PISTOL, 1804
CALIBER .54
VALLEY FORGE (PA.)
FLINTLOCK PISTOL, 1809-1810
CALIBER .69
NORTH "BERLIN"
FLINTLOCK PISTOL, 1798
CALIBER .69
NORTH, MODEL 1816
FLINTLOCK PISTOL
CALIBERS .54 AND .69
U.S. SPRINGFIELD MODEL 1818
FLINTLOCK PISTOL
CALIBER .69
NORTH, MODEL 1819
ARMY AND NAVY FLINTLOCK PISTOL
CALIBER .54
U.S. FLINTLOCK PISTOL
MODEL 1836, CALIBER .54
U.S. PERCUSSION PISTOL
MODEL 1842, CALIBER .54
U.S. NAVY PISTOL MODEL 1843
CALIBER .54
U.S. SPRINGFIELD MODEL 1855
PISTOL CARBINE, CALIBER .58
REMINGTON NAVY BREECH-LOADING PISTOL
MODEL 1867, CALIBER .50
U.S. SPRINGFIELD BREECH-LOADING PISTOL
CALIBER .50
REMINGTON ARMY MODEL 1871
CALIBER .50

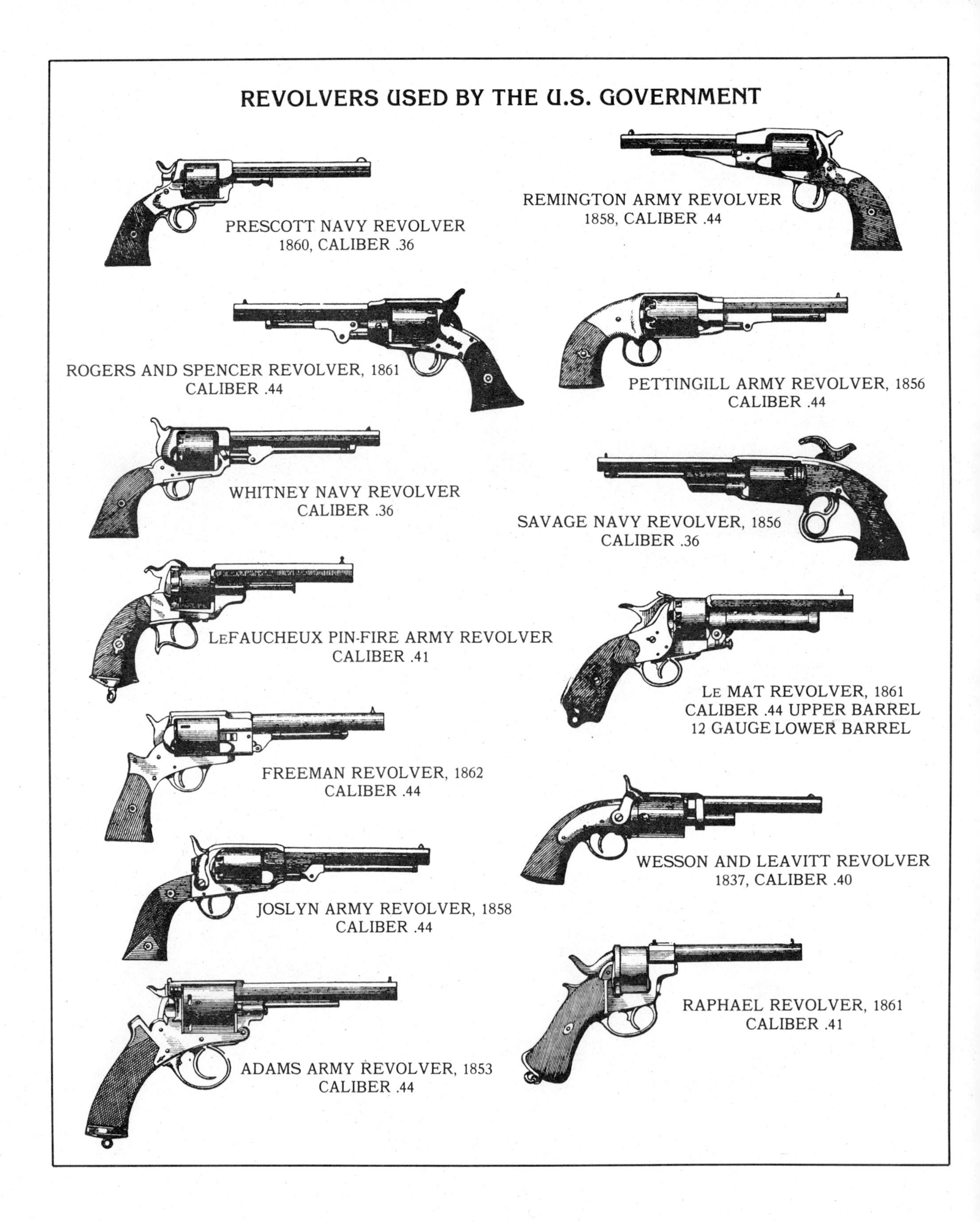
REVOLVERS USED BY THE U.S. GOVERNMENT
PRESCOTT NAVY REVOLVER
1860, CALIBER .36
REMINGTON ARMY REVOLVER
1858, CALIBER .44
ROGERS AND SPENCER REVOLVER, 1861
CALIBER .44
PETTINGILL ARMY REVOLVER, 1856
CALIBER .44
WHITNEY NAVY REVOLVER
CALIBER .36
SAVAGE NAVY REVOLVER, 1856
CALIBER .36
LEFAUCHEUX PIN-FIRE ARMY REVOLVER
CALIBER .41
LE MAT REVOLVER, 1861
CALIBER .44 UPPER BARREL
12 GAUGE LOWER BARREL
FREEMAN REVOLVER, 1862
CALIBER .44
WESSON AND LEAVITT REVOLVER
1837, CALIBER .40
JOSLYN ARMY REVOLVER, 1858
CALIBER .44
RAPHAEL REVOLVER, 1861
CALIBER .41
ADAMS ARMY REVOLVER, 1853
CALIBER .44

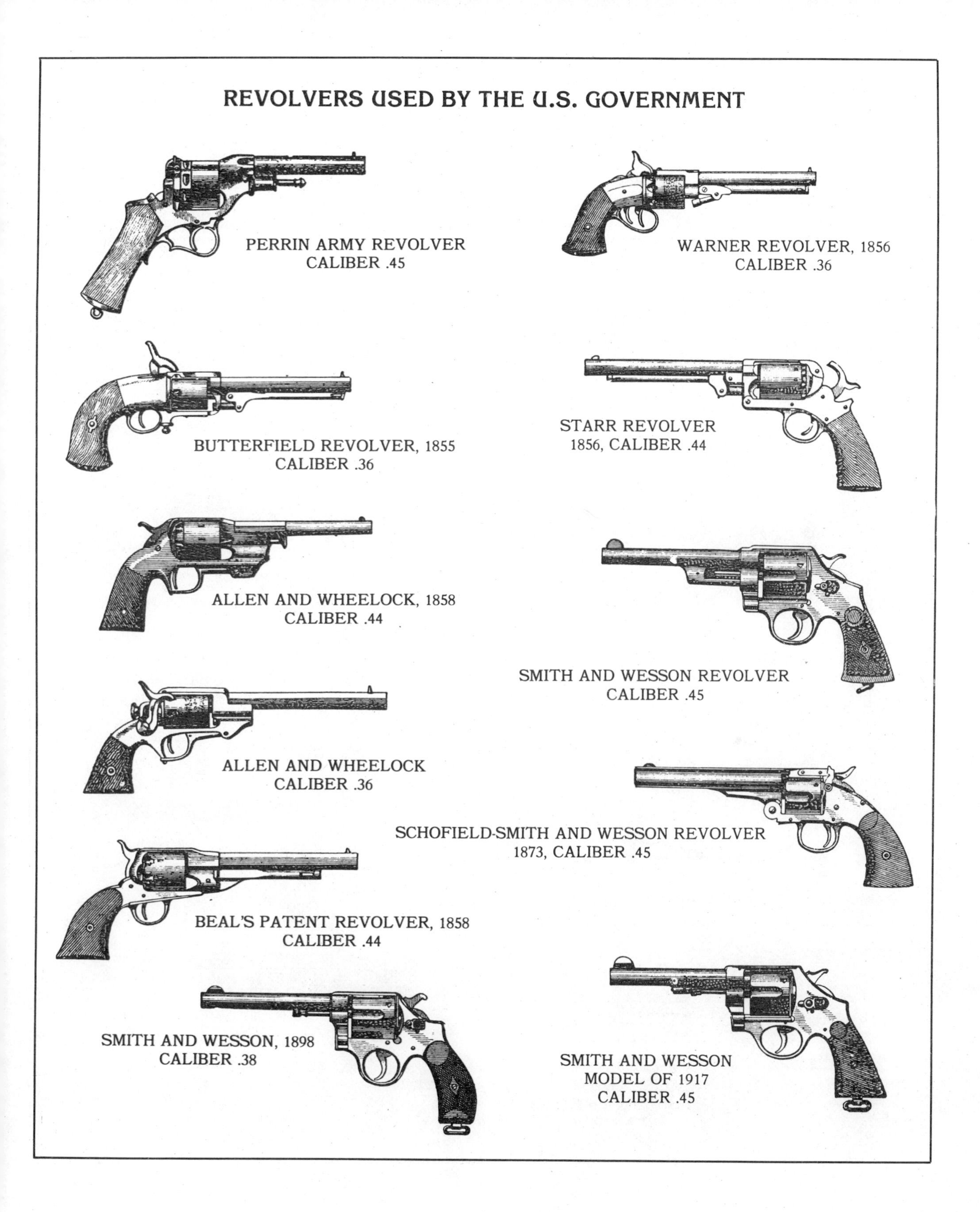
REVOLVERS USED BY THE U.S. GOVERNMENT
PERRIN ARMY REVOLVER
CALIBER .45
WARNER REVOLVER, 1856
CALIBER .36
BUTTERFIELD REVOLVER, 1855
CALIBER .36
STARR REVOLVER
1856, CALIBER .44
ALLEN AND WHEELOCK, 1858
CALIBER .44
SMITH AND WESSON REVOLVER
CALIBER .45
ALLEN AND WHEELOCK
CALIBER .36
SCHOFIELD-SMITH AND WESSON REVOLVER
1873, CALIBER .45
BEAL'S PATENT REVOLVER, 1858
CALIBER .44
SMITH AND WESSON, 1898
CALIBER .38
SMITH AND WESSON
MODEL OF 1917
CALIBER .45

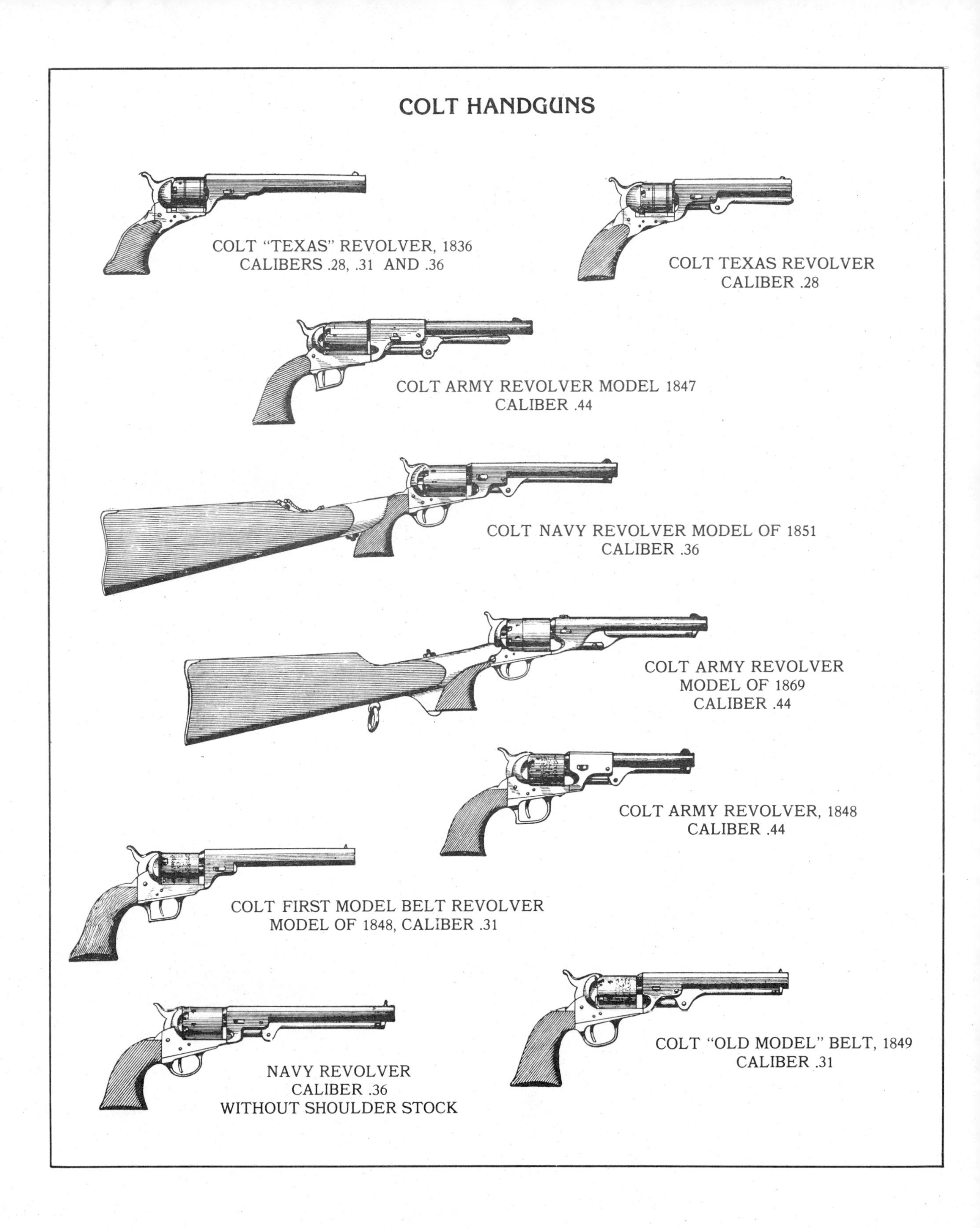
COLT HANDGUNS
COLT "TEXAS" REVOLVER, 1836
CALIBERS .28, .31 AND .36
COLT TEXAS REVOLVER
CALIBER .28
COLT ARMY REVOLVER MODEL 1847
CALIBER .44
COLT NAVY REVOLVER MODEL OF 1851
CALIBER .36
COLT ARMY REVOLVER
MODEL OF 1869
CALIBER .44
COLT ARMY REVOLVER, 1848
CALIBER .44
COLT FIRST MODEL BELT REVOLVER
MODEL OF 1848, CALIBER .31
NAVY REVOLVER
CALIBER .36
WITHOUT SHOULDER STOCK
COLT "OLD MODEL" BELT, 1849
CALIBER .31

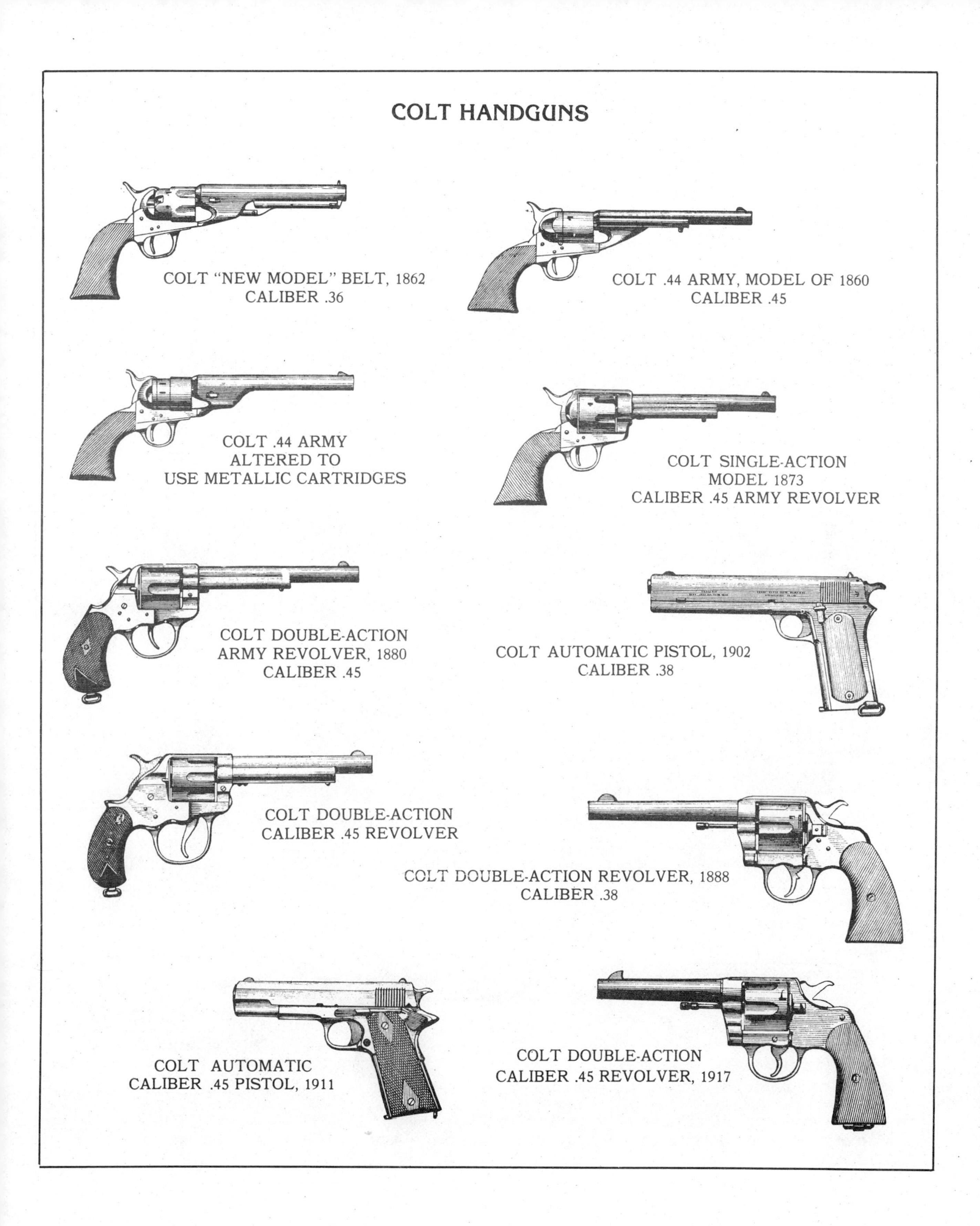

COLT HANDGUNS

COLT "NEW MODEL" BELT, 1862
CALIBER .36

COLT .44 ARMY, MODEL OF 1860
CALIBER .45

COLT .44 ARMY
ALTERED TO
USE METALLIC CARTRIDGES

COLT SINGLE-ACTION
MODEL 1873
CALIBER .45 ARMY REVOLVER

COLT DOUBLE-ACTION
ARMY REVOLVER, 1880
CALIBER .45

COLT AUTOMATIC PISTOL, 1902
CALIBER .38

COLT DOUBLE-ACTION
CALIBER .45 REVOLVER

COLT DOUBLE-ACTION REVOLVER, 1888
CALIBER .38

COLT AUTOMATIC
CALIBER .45 PISTOL, 1911

COLT DOUBLE-ACTION
CALIBER .45 REVOLVER, 1917

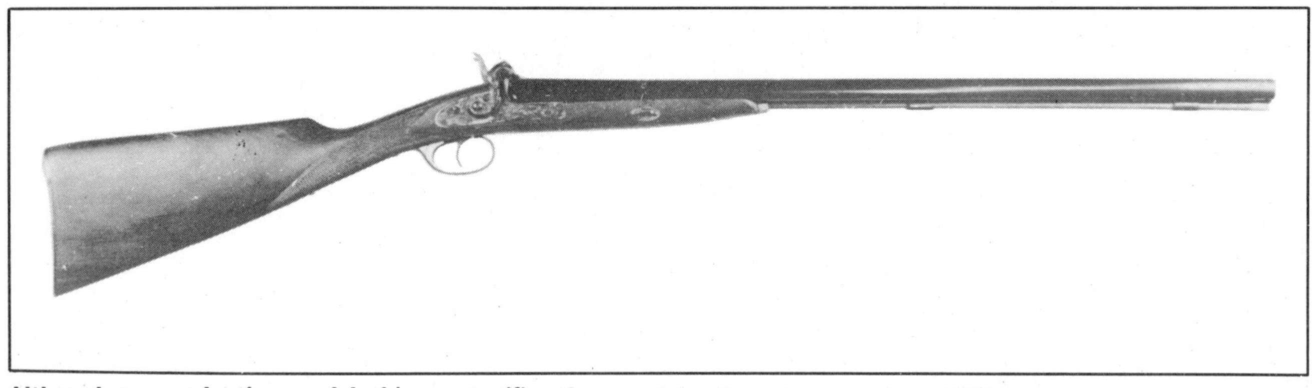

Although a reproduction model, this gun typifies the muzzleloading shotgun, circa 1850.

and double-barreled shotguns were commonplace in the United States. Most were percussion-primed muzzle-loaders, sidelocks with exposed hammers. By 1860, a number of breechloading shotguns, using pinfire and centerfire cartridges, were on the market.

Basically two types of actions were used in early double-barreled shotguns: the box lock and the side lock. Both are still in use today. Of the two, however, the famous L.C. Smith firearms are the only American-made ones that utilized the side lock. The box lock was usually less expensive to manufacture and proved to be strong and reliable.

The first successful American repeating shotgun was the Winchester Model 1887—a lever-action black powder repeating shotgun available in 10 and 12 gauges. Neither version of this lever-action ever gained much popularity, because the slide-action shotguns were slimmer and faster to operate. The Winchester Model 1893 and the Marlin Model 1898 were popular among those hunters who preferred repeaters over the traditional side-by-side doubles. Double-barreled shotguns were still the most popular arms far into the 20th century, mainly because the repeaters were heavier than the doubles and did not "point" so well.

To give characteristics of every gun manufactured from A.D. 1450 to date would take several volumes, but we have touched the subject here—mainly to give the "feel" of the general types of guns. Most of the firearms manufactured since 1900 are listed in Paul Wahl's GUN TRADER'S GUIDE—all persons interested in buying and selling used guns should have it.

Proof Marks

The best reference I know of on proof marks is a book entitled *Gunmarks* by David Byron. In its 185 pages are over 3,000 tradenames, codemarks, logos and proof marks used by the world's firearms makers to identify their products. The book covers most firearms from 1870 to the present. Entries are arranged by basic structure; that is, letter, initial, monogram, and the like. Subdivisions are by general shape and, in addition, an alphabetical list of the world's firearms manufacturers is included and cross-referenced to the many illustrations. This is a very important working tool for collectors, dealers, hobbyists and aficionados.

Another good source is the *Standard Directory of Proof Marks* by R.A. Steindler. This book fully describes the proof laws of each country and lists the changes in

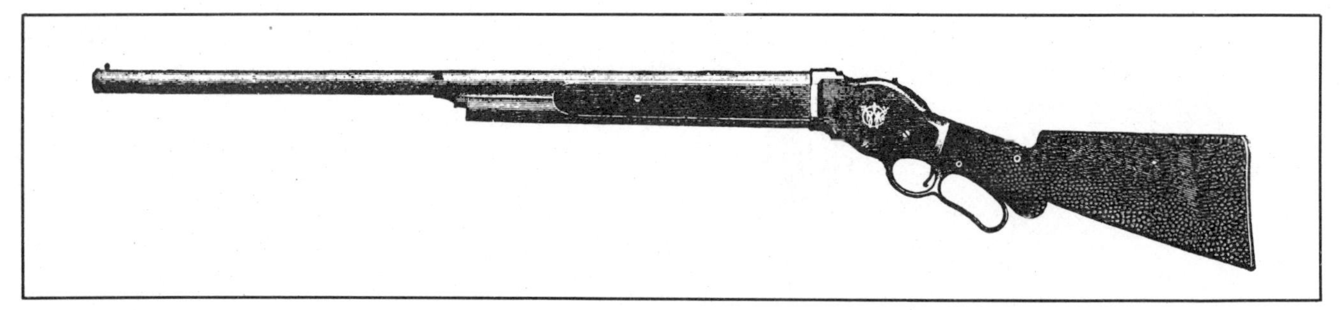

The first successful American repeating shotgun was the Winchester Model 1887—available in 10 and 12 gauges.

those laws; the text covers illustrated proof marks from about 1900 to date.

Practically all foreign guns carry certain proof marks, indicating that the weapon has been tested. These marks can also be used as a guide in identifying the gun; that is, they can tell you the country of origin, the caliber or gauge and the type of tests carried out. This is why it is extremely necessary to obtain a good proof-mark reference and know how to use it if you are dealing in foreign arms.

Tests are made at various stages during the manufacture of firearms, such as when the barrels are turned and bored. The final test for shotguns and rifles is made when the barrels have been fitted to the receiver or when the firearm is completely finished. During this final testing, an exact examination of lands and grooves is also made to ascertain the precise dimensions so the caliber is maintained.

The accompanying illustration shows how proof marks are helpful in identifying foreign firearms. A customer who wanted to know more about his gun came into my shop with an unidentified shotgun bearing the following proof marks. These marks were on the underside of the barrels under the forearm; the marks on other weapons are usually in a similar location, and as a rule of thumb are found on all arms produced in Europe and the British Isles.

A marking on top of the barrels and on the rib indicated that the barrels were "Belgium Laminated Steel," so Belgian references were the obvious place to begin looking. Taking the marking from left to right, it was found that #1 (ELG) was the definitive proof mark in use from July 11, 1893 to the present. From this, we know that the shotgun had to be manufactured after 1893. The #2 marking is the gauge mark and indicates that it is 12 gauge. This mark was in use from October 4, 1898 to June 30, 1924, so we know that the shotgun was manufactured between 1898 and 1924. Mark #3 indicates acceptance after inspection following definitive proof. The "S" with the asterisk is the individual inspector's countermark; mark #5 is an additional inspector's mark; and the 18.0 is the choke designation, used until 1924. We also know that a recessed choke was marked with the muzzle diameter only, but as a fraction with both numbers the same—in our example, 18.0/18.0.

Although the above shotgun has not yet been fully identified, we do know that the barrels were manufactured in Belgium between 1898 and 1924. They are Damascus steel (laminated steel) and are not safe with modern smokeless loads. We also found that the bore is 12 gauge. The sidelocks had the inscription "WM. Parkhurst," so apparently this was the maker. Such shotguns were common during the early part of the 20th century and are valued from $75 to $150, depending upon condition. Due to the Damascus barrels, this shotgun's only use is as a wall hanger or as a complement to a collection.

Tips for Identifying Foreign Firearms

The first item to consider when trying to identify a foreign oddity is to establish the country or place of origin. We mentioned previously that proof marks are usually found on all arms manufactured in England and Europe, and a knowledge of these (along with a good reference book) will help tremendously in pinpointing the origin of a particular weapon.

Firearms that originate from countries other than Europe and England, or those early weapons manufactured prior to proof marks, are not quite as easily identified. It takes much study and experience to identify some of them. However, almost every firearm made will have some markings other than proof marks and the collector or dealer should become acquainted with the more conventional ones.

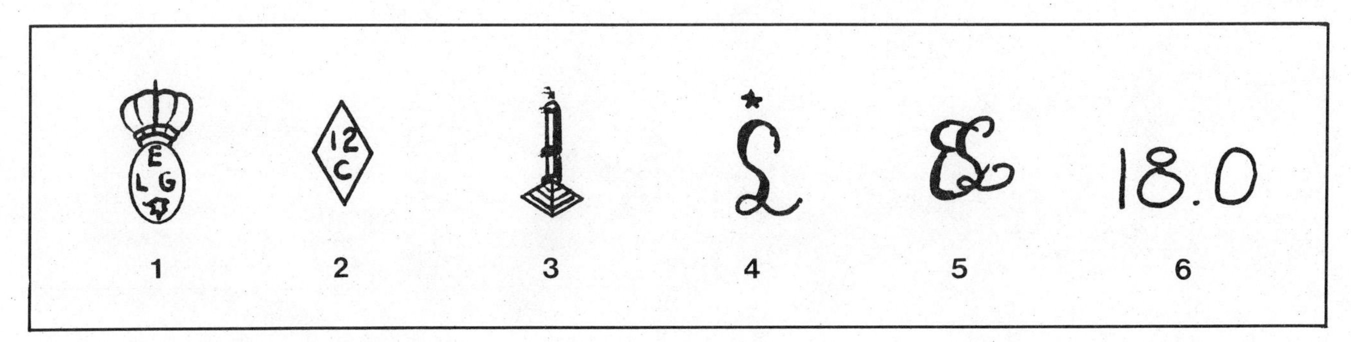

Proof marks on Belgian-made shotgun.

Learning the characteristics of various languages is one way to help pinpoint the origin of a particular weapon. This may seem like a difficult task, but I didn't say you had to learn to understand all languages—just the characteristics of each. For example, most of us can easily recognize the characters of oriental languages. Chinese and Japanese are very similar and look almost identical to the inexperienced person. However, when compared side by side, it doesn't take long to see the difference between Korean and Japanese or Chinese characters. The same is true for Western languages. German and Austrian words look much the same, while French and Spanish have their similarities, too.

Therefore, if the gun dealer learns the basic characteristics of, say, Spanish, German, Arabic, etc., he will at least have a good basis for starting an I.D. search of a particular weapon.

Once the approximate area of the gun's origin is known, reference books will be of endless value and more than likely will describe the gun in question.

Making Chamber Casts and Measuring Bore

There are numerous occasions when a chamber cast will prove beneficial for categorizing and identifying guns. Besides enabling you to determine the exact dimensions of a chamber, such casts are also helpful in measuring the amount of free bore and the bore and groove diameters. Obviously, when running across an oddity—and no markings are available on the gun to help indicate the caliber or gauge—this is one of the quickest ways to acquire the desired information.

Choosing a suitable casting material requires a substance that has a low melting point to prevent possible changes or damage to the metal; once hardened, it should undergo a minimum of shrinkage or expansion; it should not absorb moisture; and it should be safe for home use. Brownells, Inc. sells a special casting alloy called Cerrosafe that is ideal for making chamber and bore castings.

(If you are unable to locate Cerrosafe, other materials, although inferior, may be substituted. A box of children's crayons, from which the paper has been removed, may be melted and poured into the bore. Watch the heat, though, as some crayons contain flammable materials. Sulfur is the old standby, but the stench of heated sulfur means you must have good ventilation or must take your melting pot to the woods, away from everyone. There are other materials that can be used, but these are the only ones recommended outside of the professional gunshop.)

Available in half-pound ingots, Cerrosafe has a low

Although not highly recommended, a box of children's crayons can be melted and poured into the bore to make a chamber cast.

Chamber cast made of a .30 JET wildcat cartridge, designed by the author to enable forming and reloading dies to be made.

melting point (about 150°F.) and may be reused repeatedly. To use, you would melt a sufficient amount in a ladle or a lead melting pot over some source of heat—the kitchen stove will suffice. While the alloy is melting, mount the rifle or shotgun in a vertical position in a padded vise; have the muzzle pointed downward, which means the breech or chamber end will be up.

Use a cleaning rod to drive a couple of tight-fitting cleaning patches down from the breech to a point about two inches into the rifling (or bore in the case of a shotgun). These patches will serve as a seal to contain the Cerrosafe in the chamber area and keep it from dripping down further into the bore. Make sure the wood from the gun is removed, and just before pouring the melted Cerrosafe into the chamber, heat the chamber area slightly—just hot enough so you can't touch it. This heating will help eliminate air bubbles in the casting. You will also want to coat the chamber walls with a light coat of oil. I merely spray a quick shot of WD-40 into the chamber and leave it at that. The molten Cerrosafe is then ladled into the chamber until the chamber is filled. If it should overflow, don't worry about it; after it cools it's easy to peel off of almost any substance.

Let the cast set in the chamber for a few minutes, then rearrange the gun in the vise so it is now in a horizontal position. Use an old piece of short plastic tip on your cleaning rod, insert the rod with tip into the barrel from the muzzle until it meets the resistance of the cleaning patches in the bore, then lightly tap out the patches and casting.

Obviously, if you want only a bore casting, make the cast from the muzzle end. Just plug the bore as before, with cleaning patches a couple of inches below the muzzle, pour the molten casting material, wait a few minutes, then drive the casting out with the cleaning rod, this time from the chamber end.

Whichever type of cast you make, do not take the measurements right away, since Cerrosafe shrinks somewhat during the first 30 minutes of cooling. However, after that it expands again. Casts are permanent and if you desire may be saved and measured anytime with precision tools, or you can melt them at a later date when you need a new cast.

4.

Determining Current Market Value

Modern collectible firearms is the fastest-growing sector of firearms collecting. Not too long ago, collectors concentrated on only antiques and very expensive firearms, limiting the owning of such collections to people of extraordinary means. Collectible firearms are not considered "cheap," but the prices now are at least within the means of thousands, rather than just a few.

Condition, rarity, demand, special features and historical significance all help in determining the current value of a given firearm. The value of a particular arm is always in relation to the condition of other examples of the same make, model and variation. The condition is determined by the amount of overall original finish remaining on all parts of the firearm as well as the condition of the wood.

Printed Price Listings

Knowing what you are looking for or what you have found is one of the first requirements of the serious gun collector, and there is no better way to learn about guns than through the many reference books and catalogs available on the market. For example, let's take the famous Colt Model 1911 automatic pistol. During the World Wars, Colt licensed other firms to make these pistols under government contract; they included Ithaca Gun Co., North American Arms Co. Ltd., Remington-Rand Co., Remington-UMC, Singer Manufacturing Co., and Union Switch & Signal Co., as well as Springfield Armory. Because of these different manufacturers, Colt Government Model automatic pistols vary in value from about $350 for a U.S. Model 1911 in excellent condition (manufactured by Colt) to more than $3,000 for the same model manufactured by North American Arms Co. Ltd.—with many other prices for the models in between. Then there are variations of this model, including the Colt Service Model Ace Automatic Pistol (chambered for .22 Long Rifle), Colt Gold Cup National Match .45 Auto and the commemoratives, just to name a few. Unless you happen to be a Colt collector, curator or dealer who is constantly keeping up with the demand and prices of Colt handguns, you will have to seek the advice of others to find the current market value of all these weapons.

You have heard it mentioned several times throughout this book, but I'll say it again. Paul Wahl's GUN TRADER'S GUIDE is the best single source, in my opinion, for identifying used guns as well as pricing them. Even so, you don't want to look in this guide, find a price of a particular arm and then say, "That's the current market value." Conditions may have caused a particular arm to have doubled in price since the latest edition was printed, causing you to sell or buy a particular gun at more, or less, than the gun is worth. Any printed price guide or reference book, especially in this period

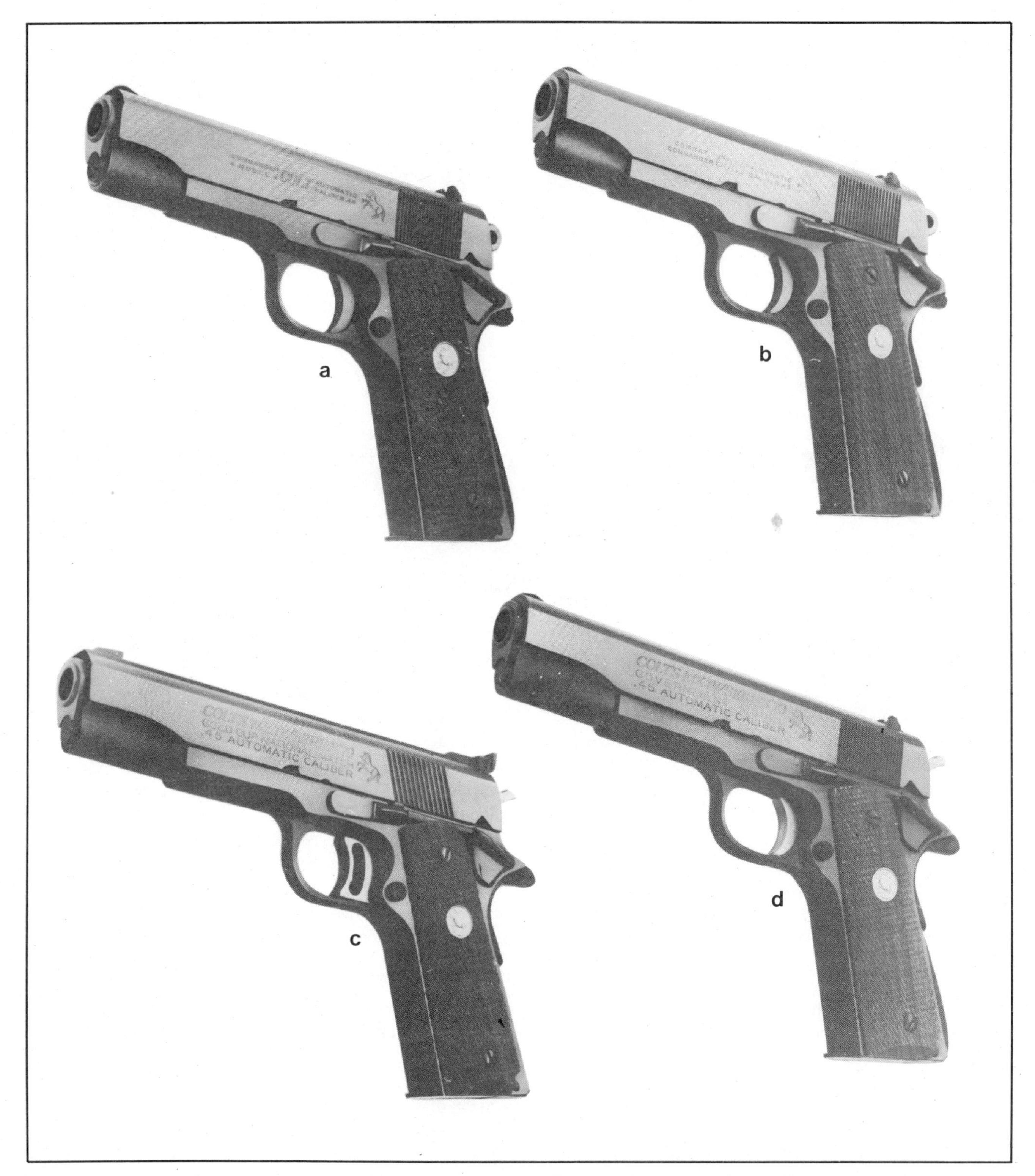

Current variations of the Colt semiautomatic pistol include: (a) Colt Commander Model; (b) Combat Commander; (c) Mark IV Gold Cup National Match; (d) Mark IV Government Model and on next page (e) Colt ACE .22 caliber; and (f) a .22 caliber conversion unit for those chambered for .45 caliber.

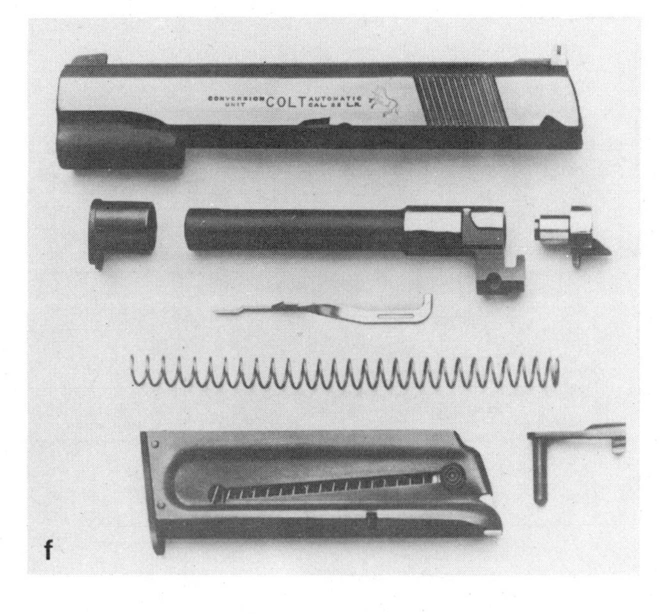

of rampant inflation, can be used only as a guide. Other sources should be consulted before finalizing a deal on any firearm if you aren't sure how the market is doing.

One of the best and most complete publications that lists both new and used guns is *Shotgun News*, published three times a month. What you see in this publication is what you get; that is, the advertisers have actual guns for sale, and their prices are what you can purchase their guns for. A serious dealer, collector or enthusiast will read each issue of *Shotgun News* from cover to cover to keep abreast of new developments in the shooting industry. A person who does this and then practices what he reads by actually trading in firearms will become proficient in a very short time.

You don't want to look at one price in *Shotgun News* and determine that this is the true value of the gun in question. Rather, look through the ads until you find several different guns of the same model offered. Consider the condition of each, then decide what the gun is worth by averaging the prices, unless you have one that is completely out of line; if so, disregard this one price. For example, you may be interested in purchasing a Winchester Model 61 pump rifle in very good to excellent condition. You look through *Shotgun News*, see an ad that lists one in excellent condition for, say, $750, so you buy the firearm. It so happened that this particular ad was taken out by an individual who didn't especially want to part with the gun, so he doubled the normal price and decided if he could get his price, he would sell it anyway. In other words, the price was highly inflated. Had you looked further through the *Shotgun News*, you would have found that this particular model was available from other sources for around $350 in excellent condition.

(For more information regarding *Shotgun News*, please see Appendix IV.)

Traditional Pricing Methods

There was a time when any reputable gun dealer could make a decent living selling firearms. Guns were priced so the dealer could make a reasonable percentage profit on each sale, and that was that. No discounts were allowed. In fact, many of the better manufacturers required that each dealer sign an agreement not to cut prices on their guns—not even one penny. If the dealer was caught doing so, the manufacturer lifted his license to sell that particular brand of firearm. When this manner of gun pricing was in effect, the dealer who sold the most guns usually did so by providing the best service—not the lowest prices—to his customers. Of course, the dealer was allowed to give a reasonable price on trade-ins, and this practice also allowed room for negotiation.

Today, such price fixing is unlawful because of recent federal regulations. Manufacturers can only *suggest* a selling price; they can no longer insist that a retail price be maintained. In fact, at this writing few guns sell for the full suggested retail price, with the possible exception of certain Smith & Wesson handguns. Let's look at some of the reasons why.

Chain store competition. Back when the larger

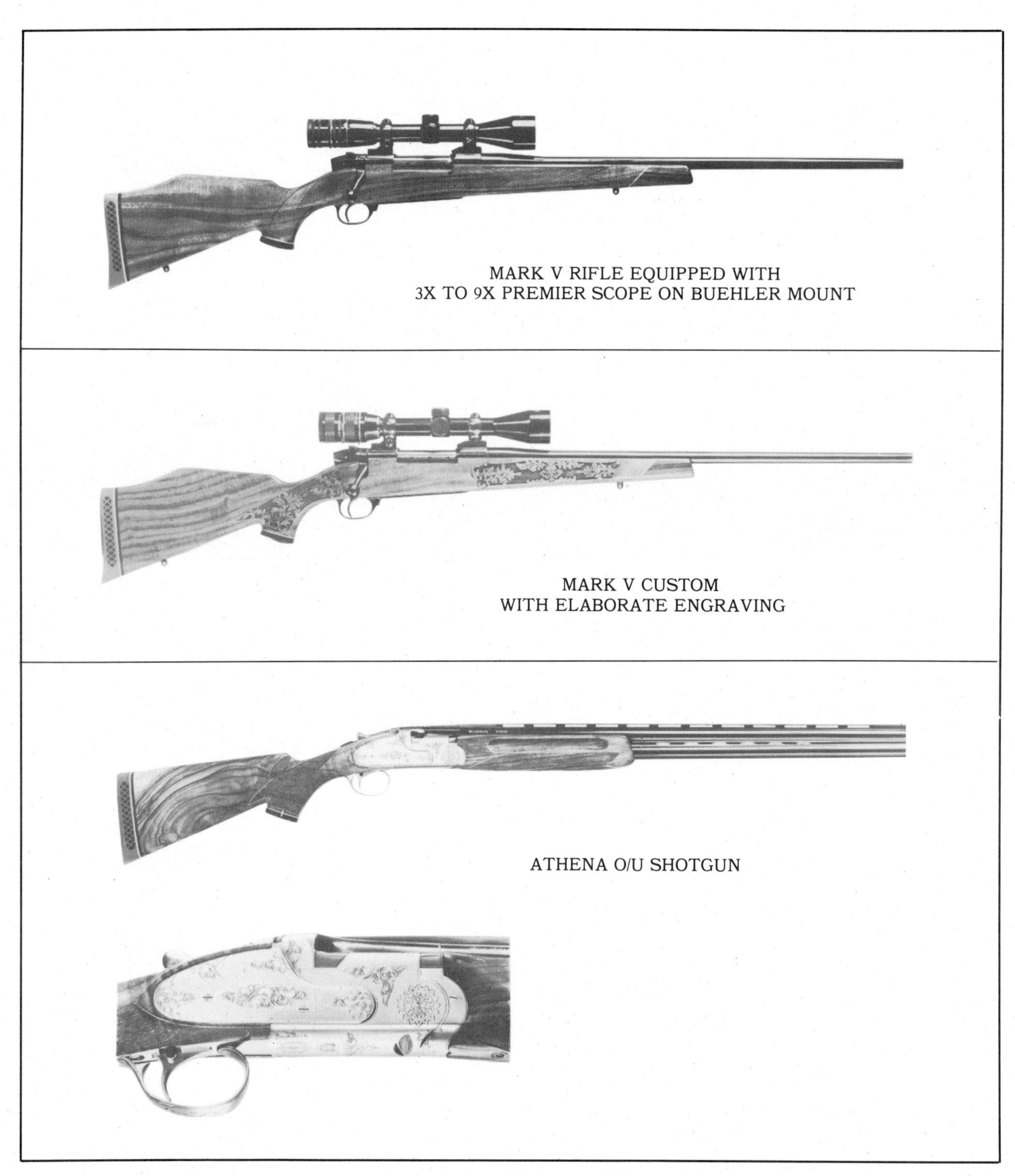
MARK V RIFLE EQUIPPED WITH
3X TO 9X PREMIER SCOPE ON BUEHLER MOUNT

MARK V CUSTOM
WITH ELABORATE ENGRAVING

ATHENA O/U SHOTGUN

Weatherby has traditionally not sold their firearms to the discount houses. Although Weatherby firearms do not sell in the quantities that lower-priced arms do, a dealer can expect to make a reasonable profit on those he does sell. Here are some of Weatherby's latest offerings.

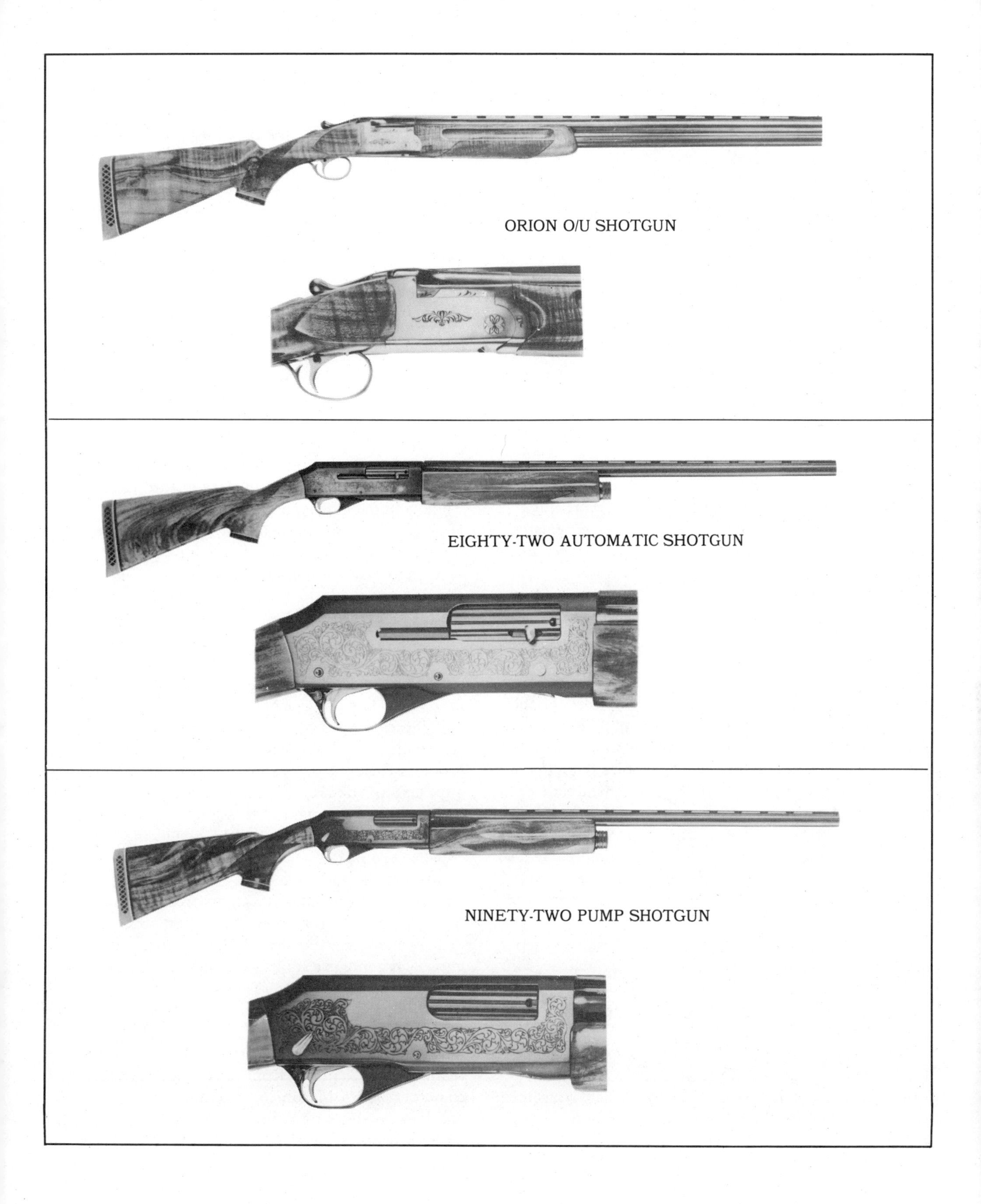
ORION O/U SHOTGUN
EIGHTY-TWO AUTOMATIC SHOTGUN
NINETY-TWO PUMP SHOTGUN

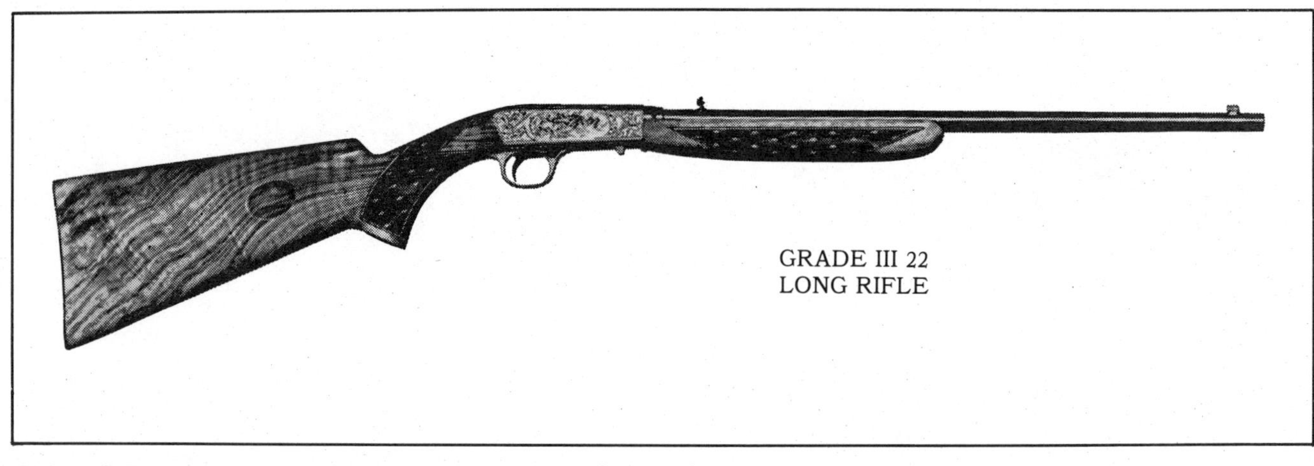

Although Browning arms have been listed in some of the mail-order catalogs, they are usually priced nearer the full retail price.

gun manufacturers insisted that a retail price on their firearms be maintained, even the big mail-order firms of Sears, Roebuck and Montgomery Ward were not allowed to cut prices. The Winchester arms, especially, were listed in these catalogs at full retail price. But today, once the merchandise is shipped from the factory, the manufacturer has no control over the selling price. For this reason, it seems that every chain store tries to cut prices more than the next, resulting in sales of most modern firearms at around dealer cost, or somewhat below retail.

This practice of price cutting may be fine for the consumer, but the small gun dealer is not able to make enough profit for the effort to be worthwhile. The large chain stores buy in quantity, which enables them to obtain the best prices possible. They also buy direct from the factory, whereas a smaller dealer must go through a jobber or distributor. If you will shop around, oftentimes firearms can be purchased at chain stores by an individual for less than the dealer's cost from a supplier. From this, it would seem that there is no way small dealers can compete, or is there?

Some manufacturers of firearms refuse to accept orders from discount and chain stores. Weatherby, for example, reportedly never sells to discount houses. Custom gun shops and sporting goods stores are their prime outlets, and if Weatherby sold to the discount houses, they could forget about getting much business from the smaller dealers. Browning Arms is another example. Although I have seen their models listed in some mail-order catalogs, they were listed at full (or nearly so) retail price.

So the gun dealers who specialize only in guns that are not available through the discount stores are smart. They won't sell a huge amount of these higher-priced guns, but the ones they do sell will net them a profit, plus they won't have a large amount of money tied up in inventory. Continuing on this same route—selling guns not available to discount stores—let's pursue the matter further.

Gun dealers who accept used guns as partial payment for new ones are on the right track. I know of no discount store that will accept trade-ins, nor will it sell used guns. The practice of dealing in used guns will not only increase the dealer's firearms business, but will increase his overall business as well. Many collectors and shooters frequently drop in on shops that handle used guns just to look around. If they don't find what they're looking for, they might at least buy a box of ammo or other sporting goods item while they're there.

The profits derived from used gun sales can also be rewarding. As mentioned previously, it is difficult for any gun dealer to make a high percentage profit any more on a new gun sale. On the other hand, many dealers make an average of 30 to 40 percent on used guns, and some profits go even higher. For example, a recent customer was interested in a new pump centerfire rifle retailing for approximately $300 and costing me about $225. If I had been able to sell the rifle at full retail—which is very doubtful—I would have obviously realized a $75 profit from this sale. However, this customer had a Marlin lever-action rifle with a sling and inexpensive 4-power telescope sight. I offered him $115 for his rifle and closed the deal for $185 difference.

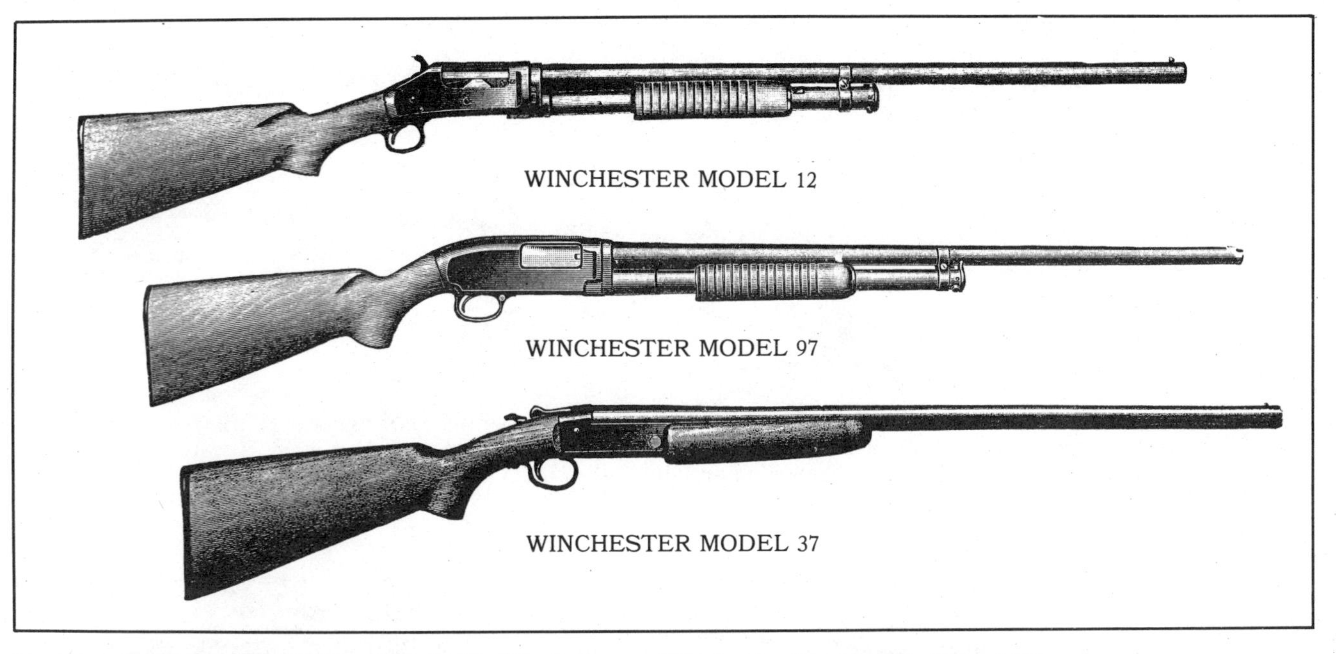

In areas where shooting matches are held with shotguns, Winchester Models 12, 97 and 37 are very popular and command the highest prices. A Winchester Model 37, for example, has been known to bring as high as $600 if it is patterned just right.

Since the new rifle cost me $225, I had, in essence, purchased his rifle for $40 and had sold him the new gun at cost.

Fifteen minutes later the used gun was cleaned, test-fired and on the shelf for sale for $185. That same day another customer bought the gun for $175 (I gave him $10 off since he didn't have a trade-in). So since the used gun had cost me $40, I made about $145 from the two gun sales—much more than I could have ever hoped for on new gun sales alone.

Granted, you don't make a good deal like the one mentioned above every 10 minutes, but I've found such deals are more frequent than similar deals on new firearms.

On the other hand, I've made some bad deals also. Not too long ago, I accepted a foreign-manufactured side-by-side shotgun as a trade-in on a new gun. I figured that I could resell the shotgun for about $160, so I offered the customer $90 for the gun and closed the deal. It was some time before I got around to testing the gun more thoroughly. When I did, I found that both barrels fired simultaneously—a common problem with older double-barreled shotguns. Also, the hammer spring for the right barrel had been brazed together—destroying its temper—and had to be replaced. The stock, I also discovered, had been replaced and didn't fit properly, making the gun unsafe to fire in its present condition. Correcting these problems cost approximately $75 besides my time, and then I got only $150 for the shotgun! So this was a complete loss for me. The problem could probably have been avoided had I taken the time to check the gun more thoroughly before making my offer.

A person dealing in used guns should also have the facilities (and the capabilities) to check and repair used guns. You'd certainly not want to sell a used gun whose defects you were conscious of, especially if it resulted in injury to someone. Therefore, all used guns should be checked thoroughly before reselling them. If the dealer himself does not have the time or skill to do this, a gunsmith should be hired to do the work. Once checked, a complete cleaning, perhaps a little touch-up blue and a stock refinishing kit can do wonders for a rough-looking gun. The small amount of time spent in putting the gun in better condition will pay off in dividends when it comes to getting top dollar for it and keeping your integrity intact, too.

The location of the gun shop will also determine the price that can be had for certain used guns. For example, shooting matches are quite popular in my area. Therefore, tight-choked shotguns that pattern No. 9 and No. 10 shot well are much in demand. Winchester Model

SOME MILITARY ARMS WITH HIGH COLLECTOR VALUE

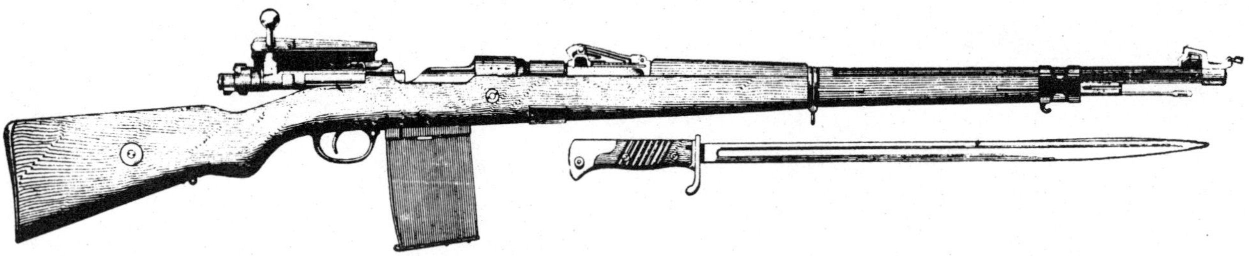

Mauser Rifle—infantry arm of the German Army, .31 caliber with 5-shot magazine. "GEW 98" stamped on left side of receiver for the year 1898. Extra magazine, attached, held 20 cartridges. Equipped with breech cover to keep wind and dirt out of mechanism during trench warfare.

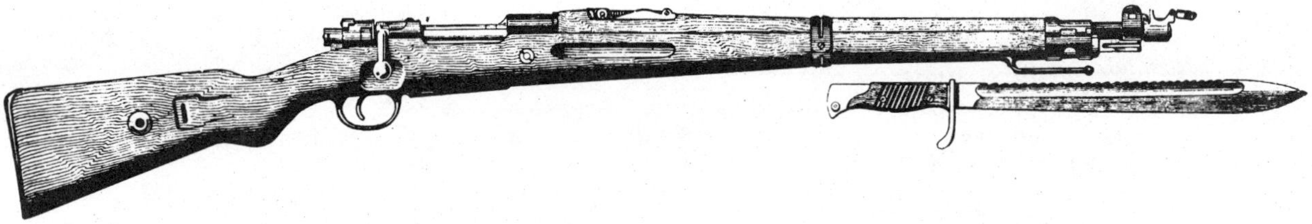

Carbine or Short Rifle, 1898, .31 caliber with bayonet and hook on end for stacking. Bolt handle is turned down similar to the U.S. Springfield. No sling swivels; rather, the sling passes through a loop left of the lower band and is fastened on right side of buttstock after passing through recess just back of pistol grip.

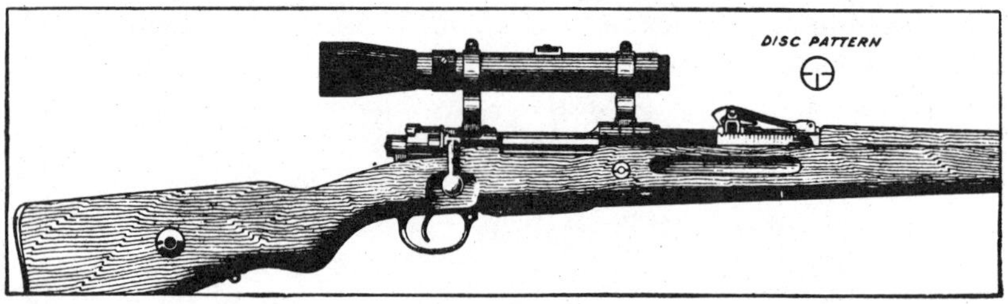

DISC PATTERN

"Sniper" Model of the rifle shown above. Notice that the arm has a telescope with the bolt of the rifle turned down.

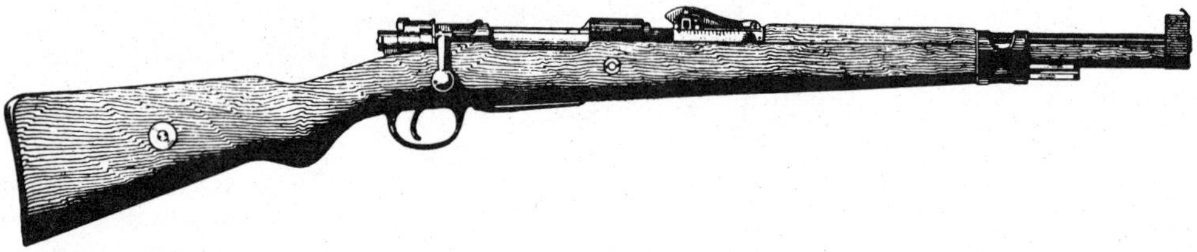

"Real" Carbine of Model 1898, .31 caliber with 5-shot magazine. Barrel is 18½ inches; rear sight is smaller.

Gas-operated 7mm Mondragon Automatic Rifle with 10-shot magazine. Based on same general principle as the Mauser; trigger must be pulled for each shot.

Mannlicher Magazine Rifle of the Model of 1888, .31 caliber with 5-shot magazine and bayonet. Unlike the Mauser, this needed both clip and cartridges (round pointed) to operate. When last shot was fired, empty clip fell out bottom of magazine. Near the end of WWI, rifle was altered to load with Mauser clip, and aperture at bottom was closed.

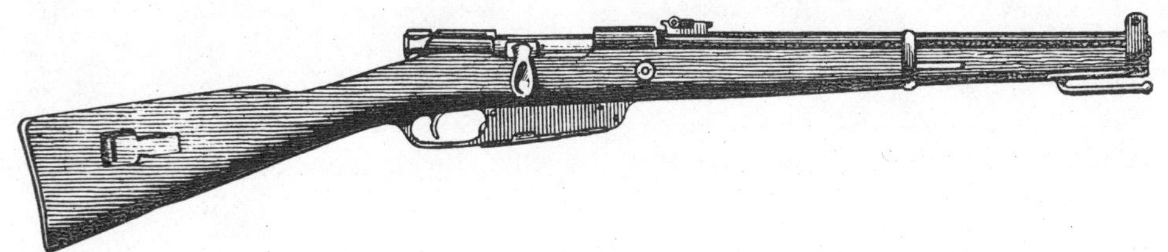

Carbine of 1888, with same sling arrangement and stacking hook as Model of 1898. Notice the front sight protector. This is peculiarly German, as they used this device on the old "Needle"—the carbine of the early 1870's.

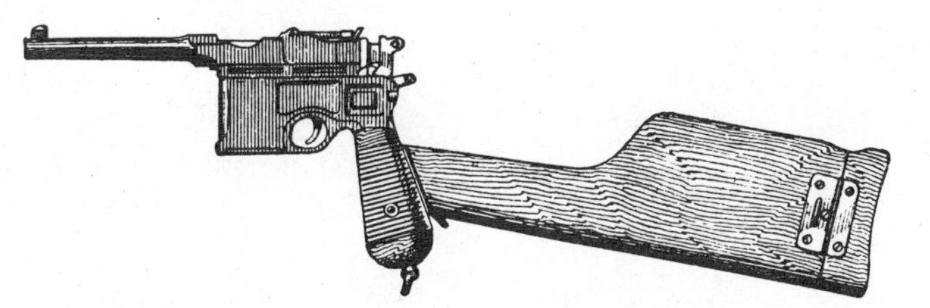

Mauser Automatic Pistol with detachable shoulder, favorite pistol used during the Great War. Held 10 shots, clip-loaded, with magazine in front of trigger guard.

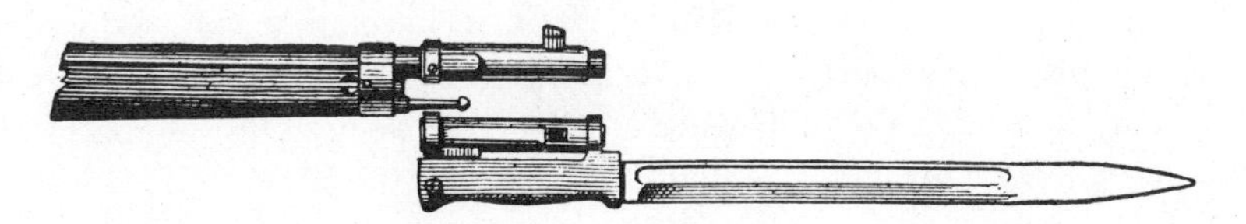

To utilize every possible weapon, the Germans adapted their equipment for use on arms captured from the French, Russians and Belgians. For example, they devised a sleeve just the length of a bayonet handle to slip over the muzzle end of a gun, with a lug on the right side. This enabled them to use their own knife bayonets on foreign rifles.

The majority of the guns seen in this shop have been used—selling much better than their new counterparts.

12's, 97's and 37's are especially popular and we can normally expect to get higher prices for these weapons than the national average. Different, but similar, conditions probably prevail in practically every area throughout the U.S.; a smart dealer will find out what they are.

So there are ways to beat the discount houses. It just takes a little extra effort on the dealer's part.

Pricing Collector Guns

The various catalogs and price sheets provide a fairly accurate guide for pricing used guns. Merely obtain the retail price, determine the gun's condition, then multiply the retail price by an appropriate factor such as .6, .55, etc., to obtain a fair price for the used gun.

Pricing guides usually provide a fairly accurate yardstick for older guns, but not always. Current market values of many antique or obsolete guns are best determined by consulting such publications as *Shotgun News* and *Gun Week* (a weekly publication). Anyone who does much trading should keep these on hand at all times; they should be studied, not just looked at.

Any published listing, however, should be used only as a guide and not the absolute "word." Most of the prices in publications are based on comparative rarity and demand. These factors may vary from one part of the country to another. The best way to determine the price of collectibles is to visit the trade shows or antique gun shows that are held weekly in most parts of the country. Talk to the experienced traders. Here you'll see guns actually being sold, not just what the asking prices are. If a certain gun is bringing, say, $500, and you see several of these sold for around this price, then you can usually be assured that this is the true current value of the particular gun. You'll also have a chance to see if the theoretical published prices conform to the actual buy-and-sell figures.

There are certain arms that are rarely listed in the pricing guides. Included here are custom-built sporting rifles based on military barreled actions, converted factory rifles to wildcat calibers and certain handmade weapons. Determining the value of a custom-built rifle can be downright difficult, if not impossible, if you don't know what you are doing. The reason? They vary widely in workmanship and value.

The fair value for a custom-built rifle depends on the condition, caliber, popularity, type of action and

1982 VALMET RETAIL PRICE LIST

GUNS

	MODEL	MODEL NUMBER	GAUGE	CHAMBER	BARREL LENGTH	CHOKE	SUGGESTED RETAIL
NEW FOR 1982	412 K Extractor O/U Field Shotgun	40266	12	3	36	FULL/FULL	$ 669.00
	412 KE Automatic Ejection O/U Field Shotguns	41261	12	2¾	26	IC/MOD	$ 699.00
		41282	12	2¾	28	MOD/FULL	$ 699.00
		41202	12	3	30	MOD/FULL	$ 709.00
		41061	20	3	26	IC/MOD	$ 699.00
		41082	20	3	28	MOD/FULL	$ 699.00
	412 KE Trap	42204	12	2¾	30	IM/FULL	$ 709.00
	412 KE Automatic Ejection O/U Skeet	43265	12	2¾	26	C/IC	$ 704.00
		43285	12	2¾	28	SK/SK	$ 704.00
		43065	20	2¾	26	SK/SK	$ 704.00
NEW FOR 1982	412 K Extractor Shotgun/Rifle Combination	44222	12	3/.222 cal.	24	IMP/MOD	$ 779.00
		44223	12	3/.223 cal.	24	IMP/MOD	$ 779.00
		44243	12	3/.243 cal.	24	IMP/MOD	$ 779.00
		44306	12	3/30.06 cal.	24	IMP/MOD	$ 779.00
		44308	12	3/.308 cal.	24	IMP/MOD	$ 779.00
	412 K Extractor Double Rifle	45243		.243/.243 cal.	24		$ 999.00
		45306		30.06/30.06 cal.	24		$ 999.00
		45308		.308/.308 cal.	24		$ 999.00
NEW FOR 1982	412 KE Automatic Ejection Double Rifle	46375		.375 WIN/.375 WIN	24		$1,069.00
		46930		9.3x74R/9.3x74R	24		$1,069.00

BARRELS

	MODEL	MODEL NUMBER	GAUGE	CHAMBER	BARREL LENGTH	CHOKE	SUGGESTED RETAIL
NEW FOR 1982	412 K Extractor Barrel	20266	12	3	36	FULL/FULL	$ 304.00
	412 KE Automatic Ejection O/U Field Barrels	21261	12	2¾	26	IC/MOD	$ 334.00
		21282	12	2¾	28	MOD/FULL	$ 334.00
		21202	12	3	30	MOD/FULL	$ 344.00
		21061	20	3	26	IC/MOD	$ 334.00
		21082	20	3	28	MOD/FULL	$ 334.00
	412 KE Trap	22204	12	2¾	30	IM/FULL	$ 344.00
	412 KE Automatic Ejection O/U Skeet	23265	12	2¾	26	C/IC	$ 339.00
		23285	12	2¾	28	SK/SK	$ 339.00
		23065	20	2¾	26	SK/SK	$ 339.00
NEW FOR 1982	412 K Extractor Shotgun/Rifle Combination Barrels	24222	12	3/.222 cal.	24	IMP/MOD	$ 379.00
		24223	12	3/.223 cal.	24	IMP/MOD	$ 379.00
		24243	12	3/.243 cal.	24	IMP/MOD	$ 379.00
		24306	12	3/30.06 cal.	24	IMP/MOD	$ 379.00
		24308	12	3/.308 cal.	24	IMP/MOD	$ 379.00
	412 K Extractor Double Rifle Barrels	25243		.243/.243 cal.	24		$ 544.00
		25306		30.06/30.06 cal.	24		$ 544.00
		25308		.308/.308 cal.	24		$ 544.00

ACCESSORIES

MODEL	MODEL NUMBER	SUGG. RETAIL
Scope Mount	35000	$ 75.00
Gun Case	31000	$125.00

A manufacturer's price sheet can be used to price used guns that are currently manufactured, like this Valmet price list for long guns and accessories.

barrel, quality of stock and checkering, carving and engraving, and several other factors. A stocked Winchester Model 70 rifle by Alvin Linden will bring a premium price over the same rifle stocked by another gunsmith, even though the workmanship appears equal. The same is true for a rifle built by Griffin & Howe. A Paul Jaeger rifle is just as good, in my opinion, but usually will not bring the price that a post-war Griffin & Howe will bring. Therefore, the person dealing in custom-built guns must obtain a very good education before becoming too involved, or he or she will more than likely get "stung."

The value of antique guns has risen astronomically over the past decade or so. Some Winchesters and Colts that could be purchased for a hundred bucks or so a few years ago are now demanding several hundred, if not thousands, of dollars each. The best source of up-to-date values on antique arms is specialized collectors' listings and bulletins. All such publications should be subscribed to, kept on hand and studied frequently.

Older military arms are also gaining in value. Such guns as the Trapdoor Springfield in its variations, and subsequent U.S. Military rifles like the Ward-Burton, Hotchkiss, Lee and Krag-Jorgensen, are all martial collectors' pieces and should be priced and sold accordingly. Again, value can only be determined by consulting current and authoritative listings or by attending shows where such weapons are regularly sold.

The value of all antique guns depends a great deal on their condition. Even though a particular antique gun will never be fired, it must be capable of firing to bring top dollar. An old gun with missing parts is not worth near the value of one that is functional. Even if replacement parts are available, they may not be original and the gun therefore should not be sold as such. Sometimes, if you can buy an old gun that has parts missing (depending on the extent of the missing parts), you would be better off keeping it for replacement parts for another gun of the same model. Another gun may be found that's, say, missing a dust cover (Winchester Model 73), and your gun has one—even though it may be missing several other critical parts. The last original dust cover that I purchased for a Winchester Model 1873 cost about $25, so a half dozen parts from such weapons should more than cover the cost of it provided you can sell them, or use them on weapons of your own. One "junker" can often be used to revive or restore two or three later arrivals to working condition by providing needed spare parts for each.

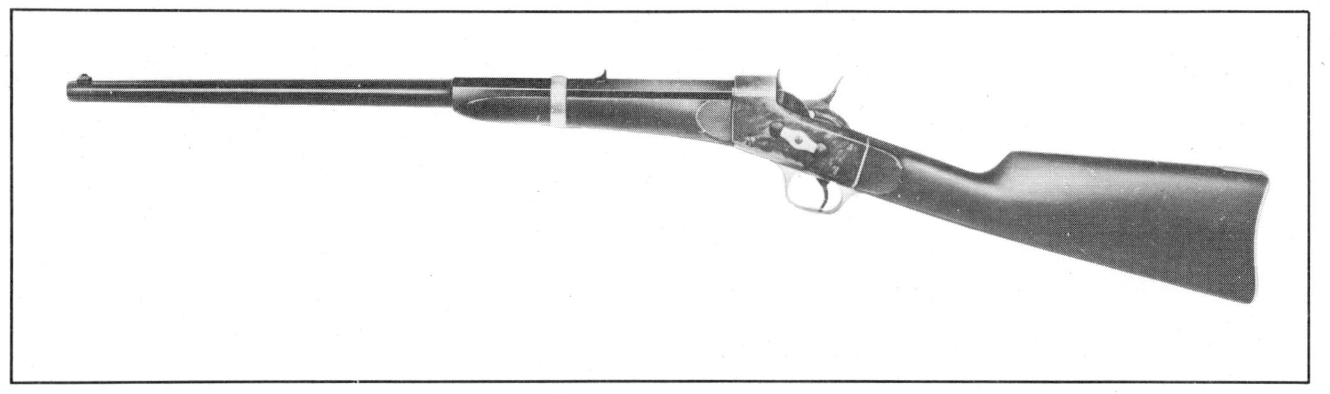

The value of all antique guns depends a great deal on their condition. This Remington Rolling Block breechloading rifle, for example, is in perfect condition and will command a higher price than if parts are missing.

5.

Collecting and Trading for Investment

In 1941, a 28-gauge Parker A-1 Special side-by-side shotgun sold for $898.01, according to *Stoeger's Gun Catalog & Handbook No. 34*. In 1981, some 40 years later, the same gun brought $95,000 at a New York auction. It doesn't take an expert mathematician to calculate that this particular gun increased in value nearly 100 times during that 40-year period. A good investment in anyone's book.

Of course, $898 was one large pile of money back in 1941. In fact, it was about 15 weeks' pay for my father at the time, so let's use a little more practical example. I can still remember the long hours I spent after school working in a local drug store in a small Texas town to earn enough money to purchase a Winchester Model 94 "thutty-thutty" carbine. This was about 1953 and, as I recall, the total price for the rifle was about $65, including a box of 170-grain cartridges that the shop owner threw in at no charge. This same rifle today is worth between $250 and $325, giving me a return on my investment of more than 10 percent a year, plus I enjoyed many hours using the carbine as well.

From the above, it would seem that gun collecting is more profitable than the average mutual fund. It is for some people, but, just like playing the stock market, the practice is best left alone by some investors—particularly if it is done solely for the purpose of making money in a hurry.

Since 1950—about the time I became a full-fledged gun "nut"—collector guns have returned an investment of more than 10 percent a year, and each day more and more models are being added to this "collector" status. However, before a person can be reasonably assured of obtaining such a return, he or she must know the art of gun trading—which sometimes requires many years of training and experience to acquire. For example, if you pay, say, $500 for a firearm that is currently worth only $400, years will go by before you catch up and obviously you won't be getting any return on your investment during that time. By the same token, you may purchase an unpopular weapon, such as a J.C. Higgins shotgun, and chances are you'll lose on your investment or make sparsely little. In other words, if you don't know what you're doing, either learn about it or leave it alone, because it doesn't take many bad buys to put yourself into a lamentable, losing situation.

What Constitutes a Collector Gun?

When collecting guns for investment, certain basic points should be considered. Some have been covered in previous chapters; that is, how to detect fakes, recognizing guns that have been refinished, and the like. As a buyer or seller you should also be aware that a complete and specialized collection will always bring more money than a general one. Also, arms that are part of a

PARKER A-1 SPECIAL

Made to order individually. Finest obtainable specially selected curly walnut stock and fore-end. Elaborate hand checkering. Any stock dimensions, including Monte Carlo, cheek piece or cast off, and any style of grip desired. Choice of recoil pad or engraved skeleton steel butt plate. Barrels and frame extensively engraved. Gold inlay if desired. Triggers gold plated. Hinged front trigger. Solid gold name plate inlaid in pistol grip cap or in stock with owner's name or monogram. Ivory sights if desired. Automatic ejectors. Made in 10, 12, 16, 20, 28, and .410 gauges. Any boring of barrels.

"A. 1. SPECIAL" Grade with double triggers	$898.01
"A. 1. SPECIAL" Grade with selective single trigger	950.48
Raised ventilated rib, extra	46.41
Extra set of interchangeable barrels	393.51

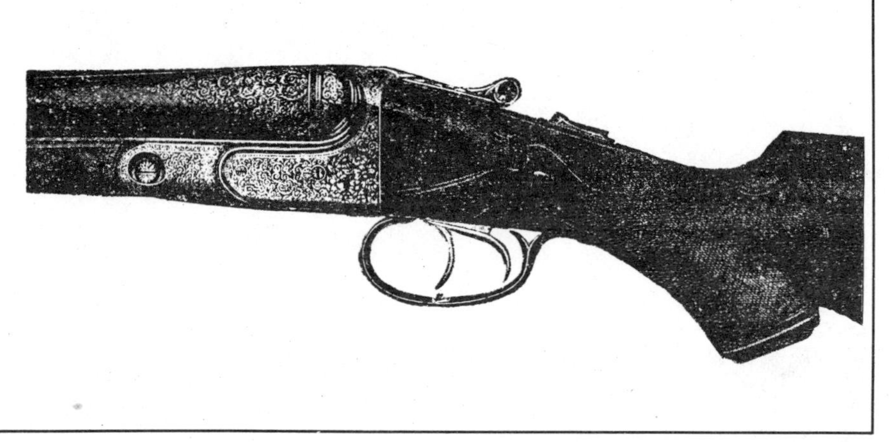

In 1941, the Parker A-1 Special sold for less than $1,000; in 1981, this same gun brought $95,000 at a New York auction.

series, such as variations of the Winchester High Wall single-shot rifle, are desirable. The same is true for guns that are rare and in extremely fine condition. To illustrate, if you happen to own a Winchester single-shot rifle in any model, you've got a gun that's worth some money. However, if you happen to have a set of three, such as the plain sporting rifle with octagon barrel, plain trigger, plain walnut stock, rifle buttstock and case-hardened frame; the special sporting rifle with fancy walnut checkered pistol-grip stock; and the special single-shot rifle with half-octagon barrel, fancy walnut checkered stock with Swiss cheekpiece, nickel-plated Swiss butt plate, case-hardened frame and vernier peep sights, you'd have a gold mine. You'd realize at least 20 percent more on each rifle if you sold them in a set than if you sold them individually.

Almost any gun of historic value is a good investment. The traditional standbys have been firearms used in wars such as the American Revolutionary War and the Civil War, but in recent years, most military arms have spiraled in value. In fact, many military arms that were "sporterized" a decade or so ago are now being restored to their original "as issued" condition. Owners are frantically trying to buy stocks and hardware for Springfields, Krags, and the like, since they are bringing more money in their original condition than in their sporterized versions. Of course, there are exceptions. If you happen to own a sporterized or custom-built rifle by Griffin & Howe, leave it alone; you've probably got a $5,000 rifle!

Any gun used to "win" the West, fight wars or change the course of history is an arm commanding a premium of between 25 and 100 percent or more—far more than any standard arm of the same model and condition. Of course, proof must be substantiated that a particular model was used in such a campaign. Just because your great-granddaddy told you exciting stories about how "Ole Betsy" helped fight back the Spanish at San Juan Hill doesn't mean another collector is going to buy the story . . . or the gun. Usually, some documentation is necessary to establish, beyond a reasonable doubt, that a particular arm was used by a certain person in a certain conflict, etc. Guns without this documentation—although they may be exactly as claimed—will not bring top dollar.

Presentation guns are of particular interest to collectors, historians and museums. Today, presentation Colts and Winchesters are probably the most sought-after American firearms and increase in value almost immediately after manufacture. The gold-inlaid Colt revolver given by Sam Colt to the Sultan of Turkey, for instance, appreciated nearly 500 percent during the past five years. A modest Henry rifle with a presentation inscription to a soldier in General Sherman's Army, and worn by him on his march to the sea, has also appreciated from $525 in 1964 to more than $5,000 today. Winchester One of One Thousand guns that a decade ago were selling for $10,000 to $15,000 are now bringing from $35,000 to $50,000 or more, depending upon their condition and style of engraving. The immutable law of supply and demand is an influential factor in the economics of gun collecting. Because there are fewer presentation pieces than standard models, and because people are interested in other people and in history,

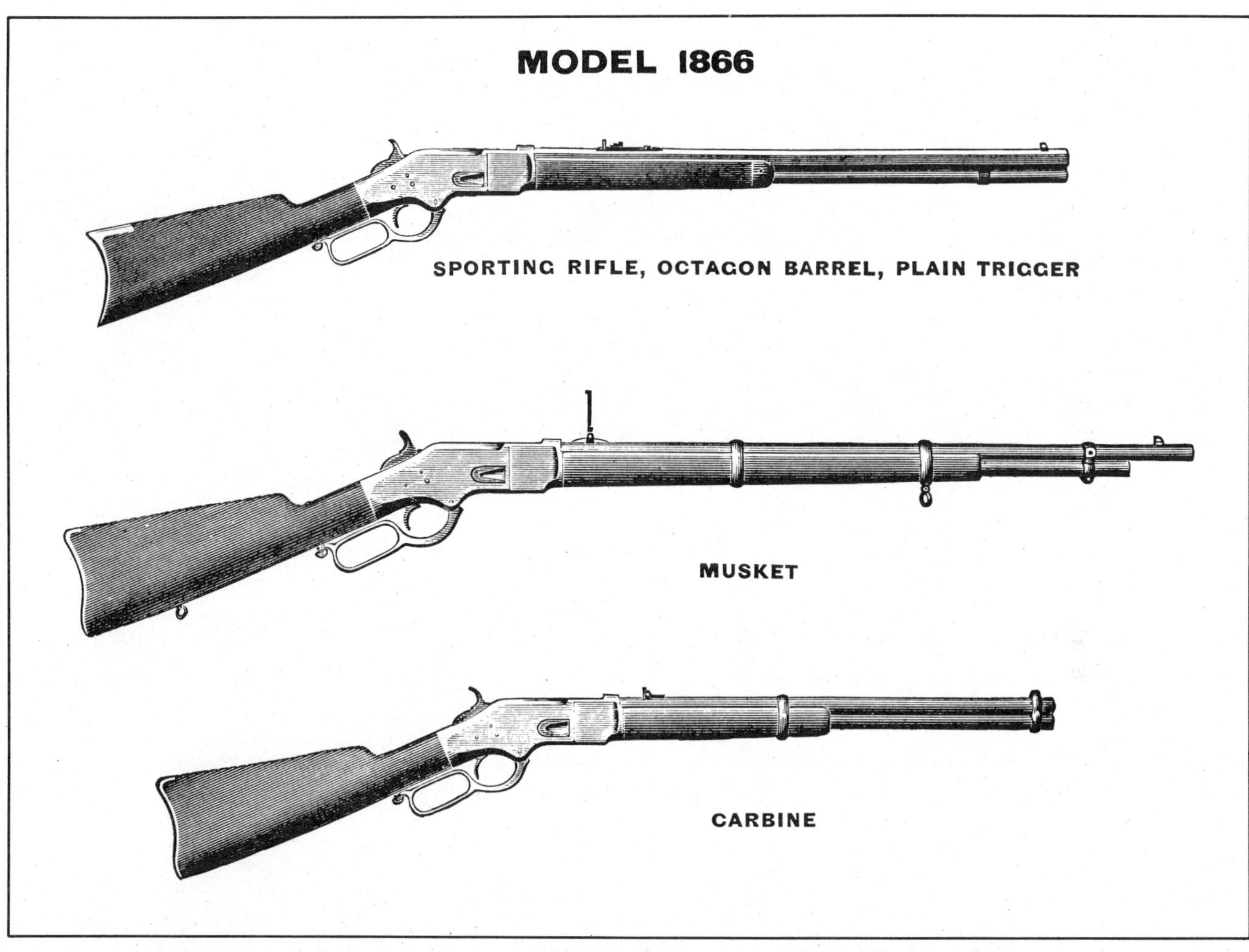

The three variations of the Winchester Model 1866 Rifle sold as a set would bring a premium price over the guns being sold separately.

they are willing to pay for these rare models.

Other arms of investment interest include all of the Colt handguns manufactured prior to World War II, especially the single actions and black powder models. Some of the Colt Peacemakers that could be purchased for a couple hundred dollars a few years back are now approaching the $1,000 mark. A pair of mint-condition Texas Paterson Colts went from $30,000 (about 10 years ago) to $250,000 as they were sold from collector to collector. Today, they would probably bring close to a half-million dollars if they were put on the market! Similarly, a mint Winchester Model 94 that in the late 50's and early 60's was selling for less than $75 will now command $300 or more; a Winchester Model 92, as high as $2,000. Try doing this with your General Motors stock.

Certain firearms made by famous makers, such as Griffin & Howe, Holland & Holland, H.M. Pope and Westley Richards, are valuable because of their superb craftsmanship. Most of these arms are as much works of art as they are firearms. Like presentation guns and guns of historic interest, any firearm containing the unusually fine workmanship of long ago represents an ideal investment. The same is true, to a certain extent, of arms made today. Eventually, these arms will become of interest to collectors, and you can bet your bottom dollar that the Belgian-made Brownings, for example, are going to bring much more than the ones made in Japan; the American-made Model 21's will bring more than the Model 101's, etc. Of course, all of these arms are somewhat in the collector's category

WINCHESTER COMMEMORATIVES MANUFACTURED IN RECENT YEARS

YEAR	MODEL	MATCHED SETS	PRODUCTION	ORIGINAL RTL.
1964	Wyoming Daimond Jubilee	No	1,500	$99.95
1966	Nebraska Centennial	No	2,500	$100.00
1966	66 Centennial	N/A	102,039	$125.00
1967++	M/67 Canadian Centennial	N/A	90,301	$125.00
1967	Alaska Purchase Centennial	No	1,500	$125.00
1968	Illinois Sesquicentennial	No	37,468	$110.00
1968	Buffalo Bill	10,400 x	112,923	$130.00
1968	Buffalo Bill Museum Pres.	No	300	$1000.00
1969	Theodore Roosevelt	5,000 x	52,386	$134.95
1969	Golden Spike	N/A	69,996	$120.00
1970 C	North West Territories	No	2,500	$149.95
1970 C	North West Territories Dlx.	No	500	N/A
1970	Cowboy	3,000 x	27,549	$125.00
1970	Cowboy Hall of Fame Pres.	No	300	$1000.00
1970	Lone Star	3,800 x	38,385	$140.00
1971-72	"NRA" Musket	4,600 x	23,400	$150.00
" "	" Rifle		21,000	" "
1972 E	Yellow Boy	No	5,500	$149.95
1973 C	R.C.M.P.	No	9,500	$189.95
1973 C	M.P. (Mounted Police) *	No	5,100	$189.95
1973	M.P.X. **	No	32	N/A
1973	Texas Ranger	No	4,850	$134.95
1973	Texas Ranger Pres.	No	150	$1000.oo
1974 C	Apache	No	8,600	$149.95
1975 C	Klondike Gold Rush	No	10,500	$239.95
1975 C	K.G.R. (Dawson City Issue)	No	25	N/A
1975 C	Commanche	No	11,500	$229.95
1976	U. S. Bicentennial	No	19,999	$325.00
1976 C	Sioux	No	10,000	$279.95
1976 C	Little Big Horn	No	11,000	$299.95
1977	Wells Fargo	No	19,999	$350.00
1977 C	Cheyenne 44/40	N/A	11,225	$300.00
1977 C	Cheyenne .22	"	3,950	$319.95
1978	Limited Edition I	No	1,500	$1500.00
1978	Antlered Game	No	19,999	$375.00
1978 C	Cherokee 30/30	N/A	9,000	$384.95
1978 C	Cherokee .22	"	3,950	$384.95
1978 E	One of One Thousand	No	1,000	$3000.00
1978	Legendary Lawmen (16-in. bbl.)	No	19,999	$375.00
1979	Limited Edition II	No	1,500	$1750.00
1979	Legendary Frontiersman	No	19,999	$425.00
1979 C	Bat Masterson	No	8,000	$650.00
1979	Matched Set of One Thousand	ALL	1,000	$3000.00 set
1980	Oliver F. Winchester	No	19,999	$520.00
1981 C	Alberta Diamond Jubilee	No	3,000	$650.00
1981 C	A.D.J. Deluxe Pres.	No	300	$1900.00
1981 C	Calgary Stampede	No	1,000	$2200.00
1981 C	Saskatchewan Diamond Jubilee	No	2,700	$695.00
1981 C	S.D.J. Deluxe Pres.	No	300	$1995.00
1981 C	Canadian Pacific Cent.	No	2,700	$800.00
1981 C	C.P.C. Pres.	No	300	$2200.00
1981 C	Canadian Pacific (Empl.)	No	2,000	$800.00
1982	John Wayne (Standard)	No	50,000	$600.00
1982	John Wayne (Duke)	No	1,000	$2250.00
1982	John Wayne (Matched Set)	300	- - - -	N/A
1982 C	John Wayne	No	1,000	$995.00
1982	U.S. Border Patrol (Mbr.)	No	800	
1982 C	Border Patrol (Civilian)	No	1,000	$1195.00

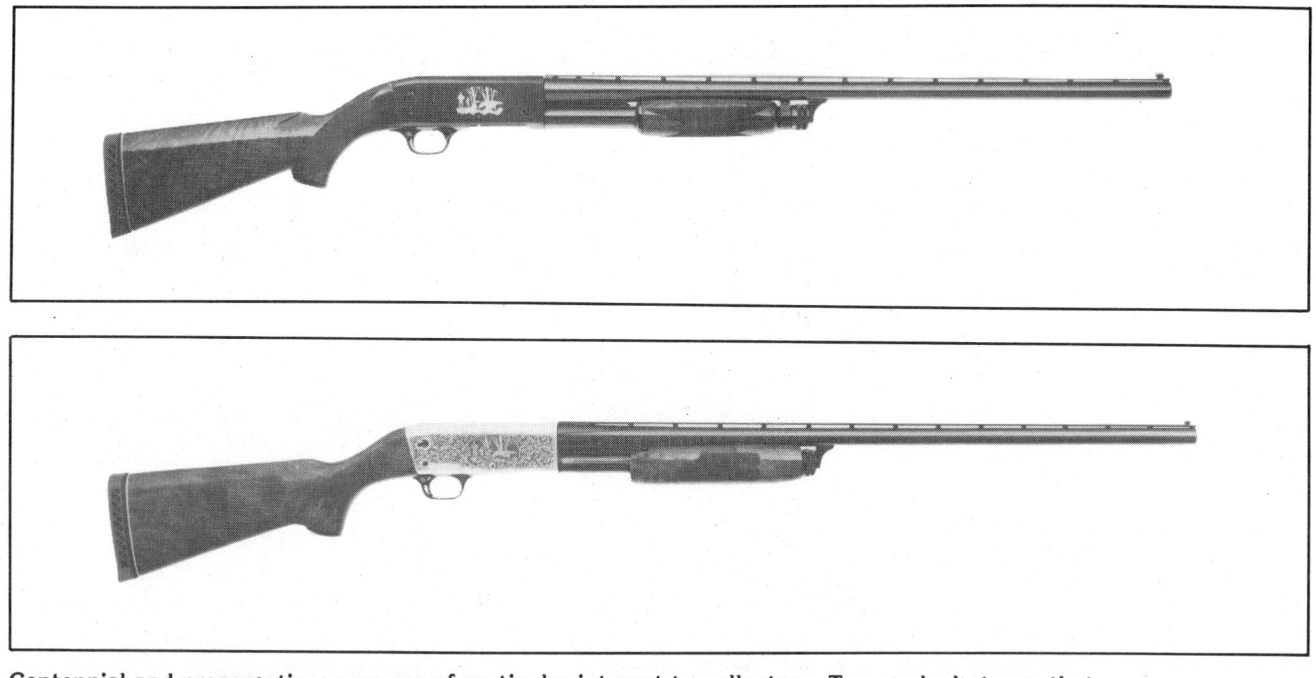

Centennial and presentation guns are of particular interest to collectors. Two such shotguns that fit into these categories are the Ithaca Model 37 Centennial Presentation (above) and the Ithaca Model 37 Centennial 2500 Series (below).

right now, and they will increase in value in the coming years.

From an investment point of view, you can buy a Winchester Model 21 shotgun in standard grade and in good condition for only a little more than you'd pay for a Winchester Model 23 Pigeon Grade and, for my money, the Model 21 is the better investment. Even though the Model 23 is new and in the box, the chances of it surpassing the Model 21 in value over the years is doubtful. Most Winchester Model 21's have been made only in 12 gauge, but recently one made in .410 gauge was auctioned by Winchester at a gun show. This gun has more than doubled in value over the past few years. It stands to reason that the purchaser of this firearm made an exceptionally good investment, increasing his net worth by several thousand dollars. Should he need money, or wish to otherwise sell the gun, he is assured of a nice profit.

Sure, stocks have doubled in value overnight, so has some real estate; but if you're "into" guns, investing in them is one way to double your pleasure. You not only stand to gain financially, but you will also derive much enjoyment from handling firearms of high quality or of historical value. As you continue with your collection, and if you make the right deals most of the time, you will run into duplicates that will enable you to keep the select ones for yourself and sell the less desirable ones to other collectors. This way, you will upgrade the status of your collection while simultaneously making some profit from the sales.

Where to Find Good Values

Here are some of the most popular and reliable sources of good gun buys that should get you headed in the right direction toward investment success.

If you're new at the game, seek the advice of a reputable dealer or collector before purchasing any high-priced gun. A good dealer should be well versed in the interrelation of inflation and investment. And the wise investor buys on the basis of his own and his dealer's estimation of what future collectors will want. Then, if you decide to sell, your firearms will be in great demand and will command a handsome price. Also, an established dealer will usually be willing to offer a guarantee naming him responsible for repayment of the purchase price if the firearm he sells you is actually a fake or a reproduction. If you do not buy through a dealer, do obtain two or even more expert opinions before you purchase a firearm, because once you've bought from an individual or unknown auctioneer, you usually have no legal recourse.

In addition to seeking out knowledgeable gun dealers and other fellow collectors, organizations of collectors and service magazines will be helpful to you in forming your collection. Here are some organizations that you may wish to contact for more details:

American Society of Arms Collectors

c/o Robert F. Rubendunst, Sec.-Treas.
6550 Baywood Lane
Cincinnati, Ohio 45224
Phone: (513) 931-5689
Founded 1953; members, 240

Membership, by invitation only, includes advanced arms collectors, researchers, authors and museum directors interested in antique arms and weapons. This society engages in research on arms makers, exchanges specimens in collections and acquires new specimens, bestows grants toward publication of educational material in the field of arms collecting, maintains a 100-volume library on arms and armour and presents awards. Committees: Investment; Nominating. Publications: semiannual bulletin; annual Membership Directory; monographs. Affiliated with National Rifle Association of America. Semiannual meeting.

Brigade of the American Revolution

The New Windsor Cantonment
P.O. Box 207
Vails Gate, New York 12584
Phone: (914) 561-1765
George Woodbridge, Commander
Founded 1962; members, 1000; units, 80

The men and women of the Brigade are dedicated to the authentic re-creation of soldier life during the American Revolutionary period. The Brigade fosters and encourages the exhibition and display of crafts and skills of the 18th century in general and specifically those closely related to the life of the armies of the time. Each member regiment assumes the identity and organization of an original unit known to have participated in the Revolutionary War. All clothing, arms and equipment are researched for historical accuracy and no substitutions or modern materials are permitted. Various performances of a pageant-like nature are staged, usually at some historic site, involving military drills and exercises, demonstrations of camp life and craft skills, all designed to educate and entertain. Publications: quarterly journal, *The Brigade Dispatch*; monthly newsletter. Meetings: Brigade events commence in March and generally take place every other weekend through November.

Company of Military Historians

North Main Street
Westbrook, Connecticut 06498
Phone: (203) 399-9460
Major William R. Reid, Administrator
Founded 1951; members, 2,500

This is a professional society of military historians, museologists, artists, writers and private collectors interested in the history of American military units, organization, tactics, uniforms, arms and equipment. Publications: *Military Collector and Historian*, quarterly; *Military Uniforms in America*, quarterly; Military Music in America (records), irregular. Formerly Company of Military Collectors and Historians. Annual meeting.

Firearms Research and Identification Association

18638 Alderbury Drive
Rowland Heights, California 91748
Phone: (213) 964-7885
John Armand Caudron, President
Founded 1978; members, 12

Membership includes engineers, curators, safety professionals, insurance, finance and business consultants and medical technicians. This association conducts research on the authenticity, history and development and accident analysis of firearms, submits reports on defective weapons, issues firearms certificates of authenticity and identification, is currently developing a certified test for firearms professionals and maintains a small library. Annual May meeting.

National Muzzleloading Rifle Association

Friendship, Indiana 47021
Phone: (812) 667-5131
Maxine Moss, Office Manager-Editor
Founded 1933; members, 25,000; regional groups, 350

For the black powder enthusiast, this group is dedicated to preserving the heritage left to us by our forefathers and to promoting safety in the use of arms. It maintains a National Range located at Friendship, Ind., sponsors a Beef Shoot in January, a Spring Shoot, a National Shoot in the fall and a Turkey Shoot in October. Committees: Long Range Planning; Property; Fund Raising; Range Officers; Ground; Commercial Row; Traffic; Safety; Camping; Memorial; Public Relations; Scoring; Award. Publication: *Muzzle Blasts*, monthly. Semiannual meetings in May and August.

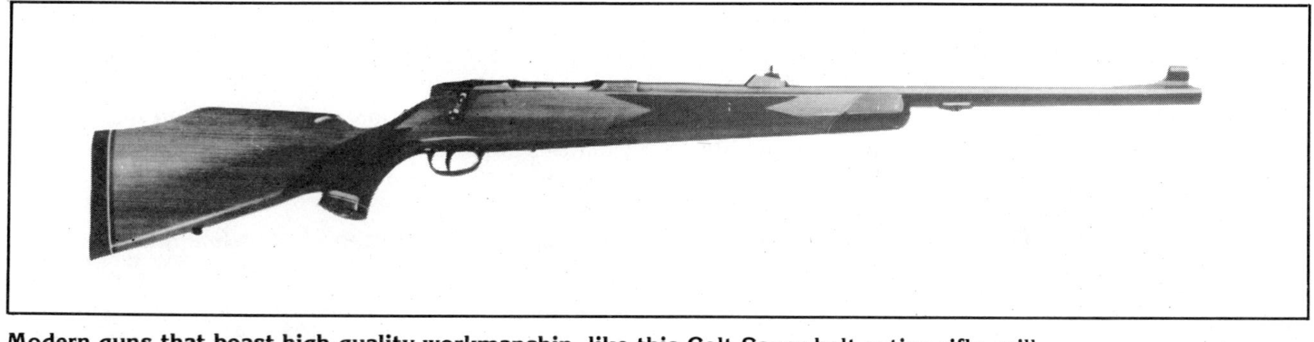

Modern guns that boast high-quality workmanship, like this Colt Sauer bolt-action rifle, will probably yield the highest prices in the future.

National Rifle Association of America
1600 Rhode Island Avenue, NW
Washington, D.C. 20036
Phone: (202) 828-6000
Harlan B. Carter, Executive Vice President
Founded 1871; members, 2,100,000
State groups, 54; local groups, 11,000

Open to target shooters, hunters, gun collectors, gunsmiths, police officers and others interested in firearms, the NRA is involved in many related activities. It promotes rifle, pistol and shotgun shooting, hunting, gun collecting, hunter and home firearm safety, conservation, etc.; encourages civilian marksmanship in interests of national defense; maintains national records of shooting competitions; and sponsors teams to compete in the Olympics and other world championships. Committees: more than 30 standing committees, all with a charter of responsibilities to cover every phase of the shooting sport. Publications: *The American Rifleman*, monthly; *The American Hunter*, monthly; *The American Marksman*, monthly; other publications include a large variety of training, educational and informational pamphlets and brochures. Annual meeting.

Investing in Guns is an excellent service-oriented booklet, supplemented by timely newsletters on profitable buys. The booklet sells for $35 and is available from Matlock Advertising, 4468 Zarahemla Drive, Salt Lake City, Utah 84117.

When you are ready to buy, you must have adequate cash. The places you will find the best buys will not necessarily extend you credit. In fact, this is probably the reason the guns can be had for a low sum in the first place. With adequate cash in hand, here's how I'd go about looking for good gun buys. Of course you will have done your homework; that is, you are familiar with the models you are seeking and you know their approximate value in various conditions.

Ads in small-town weekly newspapers are relatively inexpensive and usually will bring the best results when compared to ads in large city dailies. Few people ever read an entire paper in the cities. On the other hand, the smaller-town weekly papers usually are not very lengthy, and since they only come out once a week, there is a good chance that a large percentage of the local residents will at least look through the entire paper, if not read every word. A small $15 ad will usually suffice, since it will stand out from the classified ads and will be readily noticed. Such ads have worked out well for me. I've been able to acquire hundreds of good salable firearms just this way.

Most of the people answering the ads have been individuals who knew very little about the value of guns but who had a collection of guns in their possession, usually as a result of a death in the family. These people had no use for them, but wanted to get whatever money they could for them. When one of these calls comes in, I usually take my reference books and visit the home, listing each firearm along with the current retail value, or what I think the guns would easily sell for on the open market. I then figure a percentage discount, since I'm a dealer, which enables me to make a profit on the resale. I show the figures to the client and let him or her decide. If I buy the entire collection, I usually discount the price further, especially if there are several undesirable items in the lot. Should the value of the entire collection be more than I want to spend at the time, I usually suggest selling the guns for the person on consignment, charging him from 15 to 20 percent for handling them. Not everyone will go for a gun sale on a consignment basis, but many do.

I've also had good luck at local pawn shops. Most

pawnbrokers are well up on gun prices and know exactly what a particular model is worth, but chances are the pawnbroker did not allow near the value of the firearm when the loan was made and will therefore usually take much less than the actual value of a gun, especially if it is a high-priced piece that he would have to carry for some length of time.

There are also hundreds of small used gun dealers throughout the United States where good guns buys can be had. They are located in service stations, general stores in rural areas, and the like. Many of these dealers purchase firearms from local people who are in need of money. Most are well acquainted with the value of conventional hunting arms and these guns are average priced right along with the national average. However, many are not so well versed on the value of certain collector items, and these arms are frequently priced way below the national average. For example, an EXXON service station near my home also deals in used guns. Recently, a neighbor of mine—durn his hide—found and bought two Winchester Model 1873 rifles in excellent condition for only a fraction of their value. To top this, they had consecutive serial numbers. Had I got there only one hour sooner!

Another friend of mine, who is a gunsmith dealer in the next county, got one up on me by buying nearly 100 Springfield rifles from a military academy that is not 10 miles from my home. This school, like so many others around the country, turned coed and dropped the military program. It had no use for the rifles and was glad to get rid of them for $10 a piece. If there are such schools in your area, you just might be able to take advantage of the situation.

The Springfield rifles mentioned in the above paragraph were not all in excellent condition, but each of them was serviceable. This dealer will realize at least 1000-percent profit on the deal when all are sold.

Because a collection in fine condition increases in value, it's important to take proper care of your firearms. Guns should be cared for as described in Chapter 13 of this book.

Restoration of collector items should only be done by a professional (see Chapter 14), as the process is a highly technical task. An amateur will usually ruin an otherwise very valuable piece if restoration is attempted. However, the collector may clean his guns with mild soap and water to remove years of accumulated grime and oil. Drying should be done with a high-pressure air hose and the firearm then reoiled. Small missing parts may be replaced and items such as screw heads may be gently touched up with abrasive paper or a file. If a gun is rusted, apply a light coat of good machine oil and rub lightly with superfine steel wool (0000) to remove most of the surface rust and prevent further damage or corrosion.

Fine antique guns with original case-hardening should not be exposed either to fluorescent light or sunlight for long periods, because light causes the color to fade. And it's best to keep them in cloth cases . . . never plastic ones. However, storing in a cloth case without proper treatment of the gun beforehand can also cause problems. The arm should be well oiled and inspected at frequent intervals. I prefer a light-tight cabinet because it seems to prevent rusting better.

Investment Tips for the Future

No one can predict the future. All we can do is use sound judgment and try to guess. However, by following the market value of various firearms over the past

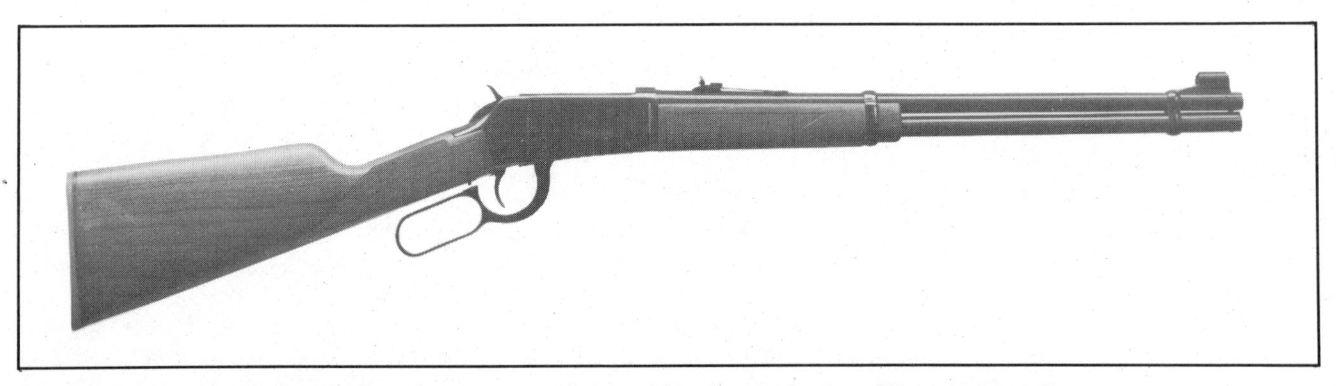

The Winchester Model 94 Big Bore is not presently considered to be in the collector class. However, if this particular model happened to be the last one manufactured by Olin—prior to U.S. Repeating Arms Company taking over—it could be worth a small fortune in the near future.

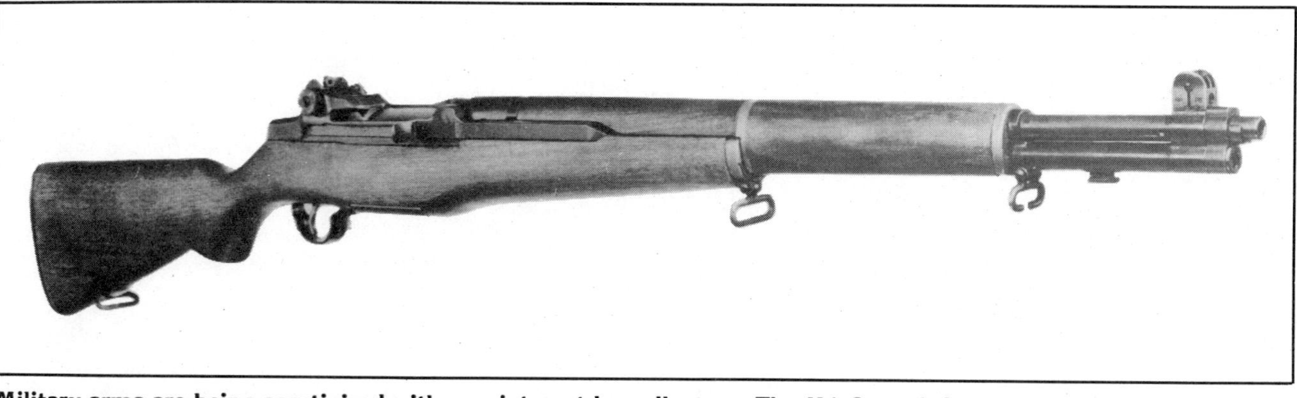

Military arms are being scrutinized with new interest by collectors. The M1 Garand, for example, that sold for only $75 a few years back is now worth nearly $1,000.

decades, certain types of firearms traditionally have been preferred by collectors over other types, and consequently bring the highest prices. Those in this category include guns with high-quality workmanship and weapons with historical value. However, beyond this, the investor must try to establish what will be popular and most in demand in, say, five or ten years.

One item worthy of investigation is the fact that Olin sold the Winchester factory and equipment in New Haven, Conn., to U.S. Repeating Arms Co. Olin also leased the rights for U.S.R.A. Co. to manufacture certain Winchester firearms like the Model 94 and Model 70. In general, they are essentially the same as they were prior to the sale except that the butt plates, I believe, are now supposed to be marked "U.S. Repeating Arms Co." instead of "Winchester." There are also rumors that the barrels may be marked in a similar way. This is really of no concern to the hunter who wants a working gun because to him there is no difference in the design. However, to a collector, it is a different story. Winchester Model 94's manufactured prior to the changeover will more than likely increase in value and, in time, be collector items just like the 94 carbines of pre-1964 are today. The rifles having serial numbers closest to the change should demand a premium, and the last rifle made by Olin should eventually bring a tidy sum of money.

Winchester rifles made by Olin prior to the change are still readily available at reasonable prices. This may be one route to take. But again, I'm not a soothsayer.

On the same order, the first rifles made by U.S. Repeating Arms may eventually spark collector interest. In fact, by the time this book is published, I'm certain that U.S. Repeating Arms will have revived some of the older model Winchesters that are now obsolete. If these guns are priced right, the ones with the lower serial numbers should be a good investment for anyone. I also understand that the quality of current arms produced by this firm shows a marked increase—very closely approaching that of the pre-'64 Winchesters. This is good news . . . if they can hold the price down to within reason.

Military arms, in original condition, seem to be on the rise as collector items, and the cost of them reflects this train of thought. Only a few years ago, a German Model 98 Mauser could be purchased for about $50 in very good condition; today some of them are bringing in $200 or more. Thousands of these and other military arms are collecting dust in basements and closets throughout this country. There is still time to buy many of them for a good price, if you can find them!

Firearms to Avoid

Almost any firearm, regardless of make or model, will usually increase in price as long as everything else does. Some models, however, seem to be slower at gaining in value. Among these include the inexpensive firearms offered by the mail-order firms. There is little, if any, collector interest in these arms at this time, but who knows what the trend may be in 10 years. Still, my advice is to leave these arms alone if you're interested in investing. They are fine as "working" guns and many of them can be recommended if an inexpensive hunting arm is required. But as an investment, no!

Other firearms that I believe will never have very much interest with collectors are the inexpensive imports such as the .22 pistols, better known as "Saturday Night Specials," that sell for $35. In this same category are the inexpensive shotguns that were imported from South America and sold for around $100 a few years back. The marginal quality of these weapons really prevents them from ever increasing much in value.

6. Shotgun Trading

High-quality shotguns—like the Parker, L.C. Smith, and Winchester Model 21, e.g.—have always been in demand by collectors. As these guns become scarcer and the number of collectors multiplies, many people are turning to collecting other types of modern firearms. Especially popular are the shotguns manufactured prior to 1964. By the early 1960's the firearms industry was becoming hard-pressed due to the rising cost of labor. Many manufacturers were losing money on every gun they turned out and a solution had to be found if they were to stay in business. The need for machine-produced guns with a minimum of hand labor seemed to be the only answer; but would the American sportsman buy them?

A survey conducted about that time by the firearms industry revealed that only approximately 10 percent of the market consisted of sportsmen who appreciated and demanded fine craftsmanship. The other 90 percent were satisfied, as long as the firearm was safe, inexpensive, looked fairly decent and was capable of reasonable hunting accuracy. As a result, gun manufacturers began cranking out machine-made guns with burned-in checkering patterns on the stocks, stamping parts out of sheet metal, molding some parts out of plastic and using aluminum and pot metal in castings formerly made of steel. The craftsmanship found in American firearms prior to 1964 is rarely equaled today. Hence, the growing collector demand for these, most of which were considered just "shooters"—and priced accordingly—not too long ago.

There were several models of shotguns, however, that were just not designed for mass production solely by machines and most of these, not surprisingly, have succumbed to the high cost of labor and materials. The Winchester Model 12 tried to hang on, as did the Winchester Model 21, but these finally bit the dust also. Now the Winchester Model 21 is available on special order only, with a starting price of about $10,000.

In 1960 a standard grade Model 12 Winchester shotgun carried a retail tag of about $55. In 1963, the price of the same gun jumped to $110; and in 1968, when the Winchester Model 12 was available only in Super Pigeon Grade, the price was $825—too much for the average hunter.

The Winchester Model 12 is still very much sought after by collectors, and good specimens are bringing upward of $400 in standard grade. The higher grades, of course, demand much more.

Even the lowly single-shot Winchester Model 37 that retailed for about $30 at the time it was discontinued will bring an average price of $125 and as high as $600 or more for the rarer smaller gauges or for the ones that continually win at shooting matches.

Evaluating Condition

Many vintage European and English double-barreled shotguns are not intended to handle Magnum shotshells, even when the barrels are made of fluid steel. Sure, they will take them for a while, but much shooting with high-velocity or Magnum loads will eventually result in a loose action. These guns are fine for upland game shooting with light loads. In fact, I can think of no finer firearm than a light double 12 or 20 gauge for this type of hunting. They handle and point nicely, aren't bulky and most weigh quite a bit less than their autoloading or slide-action counterparts.

To check for looseness in a single- or double-barreled shotgun, hold the gun with one hand on the forearm and the other on the buttstock at the grip. By twisting your hands in opposite directions, you should be able to detect any play that might be present. Headspace can be checked by holding the gun up to the light so you can sight at the gun where the barrel meets the standing receiver. If you can see light through this gap with the action closed, the gun is more than likely dangerous to fire. Further tests may be made by taking a piece of cigarette paper, holding it so it fits between the receiver and the barrel. The action should close tightly on the cigarette paper if headspace is okay. A standard gap gauge (the kind mechanics use to set spark-plug gaps) may also be used to check the gap between the barrel and the standing breech.

If any of the above conditions exist, they will have to be repaired before the gun can be used safely, and of course the gun should be priced accordingly. If the shotgun is an inexpensive piece, you may be able to tighten the action yourself by peening lightly around the semi-circular cutout just behind the edge of it. If done correctly, and looseness is not excessive, the metal will be displaced and moved slightly forward to close the gap. Peen both sides with a block of steel under the lug. When the pivot pin junction is tight, smooth the sides of the lug where the opening has been peened with a pillar file. Only a professional gunsmith should tackle one of the better shotguns.

A loose action can also be caused by a worn pivot pin, requiring the original pin to be replaced with a new one. Since the strength and functioning of the action depends on this pin, care must be exercised during the job and is definitely not for the amateur. You can estimate at least a $35 charge for this installation, so price your shotgun accordingly.

Some older U.S., British and European doubles manufactured between 1910 and 1925 are chambered

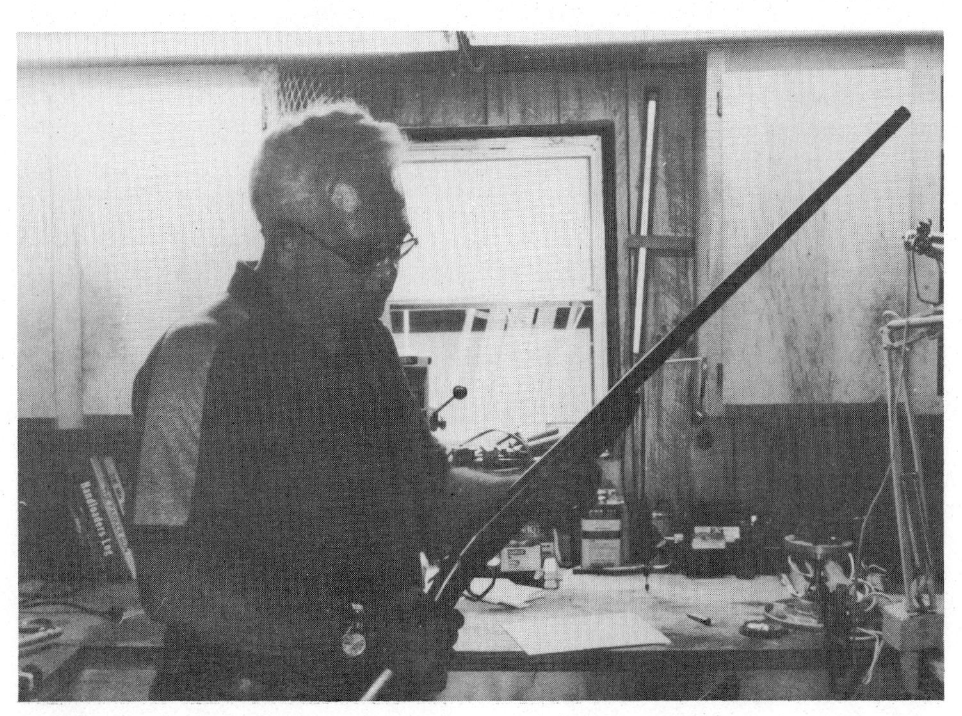

To check for looseness in a shotgun, hold the gun as shown and twist your hands in opposite directions.

Headspace can be determined by holding the gun up to a light source and checking where the barrel meets the standing receiver. If light can be seen through this gap, the gun is too loose.

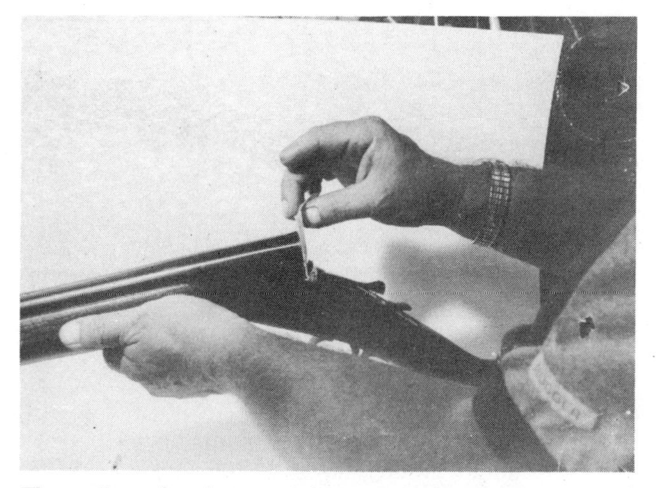

The action of a shotgun with correct headspace should close tightly on a cigarette paper.

for non-standard 2½-inch (12 gauge) shotshells, resulting in high pressures and blown patterns when 2¾-inch shells are used. If you're buying a gun for hunting, you will want to stay away from these models unless you can get an exceptional buy. Then you can have the gun rechambered for standard shells—probably costing anywhere from $50 to $75 for the job.

Buying guns in need of repair is a tricky business, and, unless you're a skilled gunsmith or have the gun checked beforehand by a professional, you're taking a risk when buying such a gun. You may find a gun for sale that doesn't fire and the present owner may think a weak firing pin spring is the only problem. The gun is worth, say, $100 in good condition, so you figure a spring will cost $5 and the labor to install it no more than $15. You offer the guy $80 for the gun ($100 − $5 − $15 = $80) and think you've come out okay. Then you cart the piece to a gunsmith for the minor repair only to find out that the gun has a severe headspace problem requiring that the barrel be removed, rethreaded and set back—an operation costing at least $50 in most shops. When making a deal on a firearm in need of repair, it's always best to have the seller repair the gun before you buy it, or at least guarantee that he will refund an amount equal to what you spend for repairs. Most reputable dealers will offer these accommodations.

Now I'll contradict myself. There are times when buying a non-functioning firearm could pay off. Recently, a customer came into the shop with two obsolete guns for which parts were no longer available to trade on a new gun. He said he wanted only $25 for the two, thinking perhaps they could be cannibalized to repair other guns of the same models; that is, for spare parts. Neither gun functioned properly, but I knew I could get $25 worth of parts from them, so I accepted his offer. Some days later, I got around to checking the guns and found that one of them required only a new 45-cent spring to make it operable; the other required a dent removed from the magazine tube. Both then functioned perfectly and were eventually sold at a substantial profit.

Another time I purchased a .303 British Enfield rifle that had had the chamber welded shut. The high heat necessitated by the welding had ruined all the critical metal parts—action, barrel, etc.—so when I was talked into giving the person $15 for the rifle, I thought I had been taken. A short time later, I traded the stock for $15 worth of goods—so I was even. As time went on, I found uses for nearly all the rifle parts and probably have pocketed as much as $50 for all of them. It took nearly two years, but I got my money back, with a decent profit as well.

I've said it elsewhere in this book, but it's worthy of repeating: Be extremely cautious of shotguns with Damascus barrels. You'll run into lots of them and all are dangerous—very dangerous—when fired with modern smokeless loads.

Models Currently in Demand

For hunting, pumps and autoloaders are currently outselling double-barreled models 10 to 1. The reason may be partly due to firepower, but perhaps the main

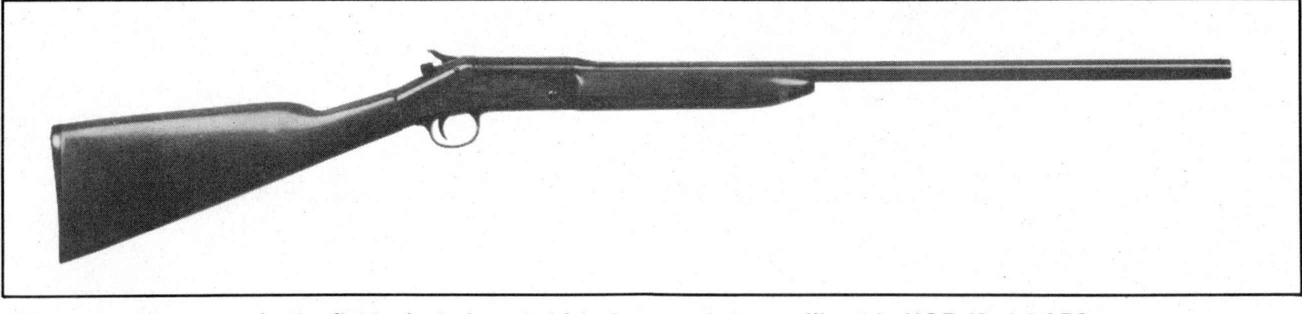

Although seldom seen in the field, single-barreled break-open shotguns like this H&R Model 058 still sell relatively well if the price is right.

reason is the high purchase price of fine double-barreled shotguns. Many grades start at $1,000, and some go for far more.

In my area, single-barreled, break-open shotguns move relatively well if the price is right. Modern H&R Toppers in good condition will bring around $45 to $50; a Winchester Model 37, $125 upward; and an Iver Johnson Champion in good condition will go for around $75. It's hard to get much more than $25 for the cheap mail-order guns that are constantly floating around under various brand names such as "White Powder Wonder," "World's Challenge," etc. These guns have been used as strictly utility guns, for everything from a boat paddle to a fence stretcher. Most are in poor condition with loose actions, and therefore questionable safety. If one is in relatively good condition, I usually offer $20 for it, make the necessary minor repairs and sell it for $30 to $35. Models requiring extensive repairs are disassembled for parts.

Double-barreled shotguns vary greatly in price—from as low as $50 to as high as $100,000—depending on the make, model, condition and the like. Around the turn of the century, many double-barreled hammer breech-loading shotguns were manufactured by various firms for the mail-order houses and local hardware stores, most carrying Damascus barrels. However, they are currently much in demand as wall hangers and the cheaper grades, in relatively good condition, are bringing anywhere from $75 to $150, and as high as $400 for those made by Parker Brothers.

The better grades of these exposed-hammer shotguns include L.C. Smith, Parker Brothers, Ithaca, Baker, Greener, Norwich and Remington No. 3 Grade. When fitted with Damascus barrels, none of these guns will bring much over $200. If equipped with steel barrels, however, and they are shootable, the price usually doubles.

You should also be aware of name similarities during this era. Some "Parker" shotguns were manufactured that were not THE Parker Brothers. Baker shotguns include those made by Baker Gun & Forging Co., Batavia, N.Y., in business from 1886 and purchased by Folsom Arms Co. in 1919; W.H. Baker & Co. of Marathon, N.Y., (1878–1886); and Baker Gun Co. Shotguns made by this latter firm were manufactured in Belgium for the H&D Folsom Arms Co.

The double-barreled shotguns with modern steel barrels, such as the American-made Parker, Fox, L.C. Smith and Lefever, are currently much in demand and, if in very good to excellent condition, bring top dollar.

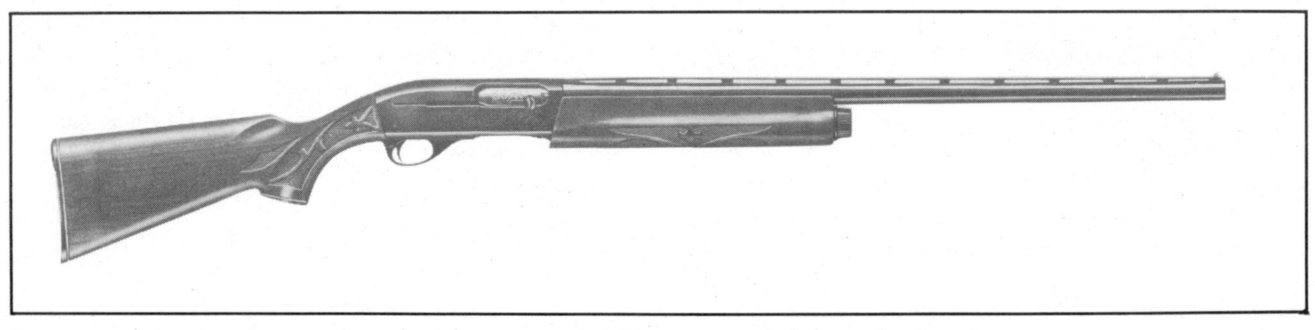

The autoloading Remington Model 1100 seems to be the most-used shotgun for hunting.

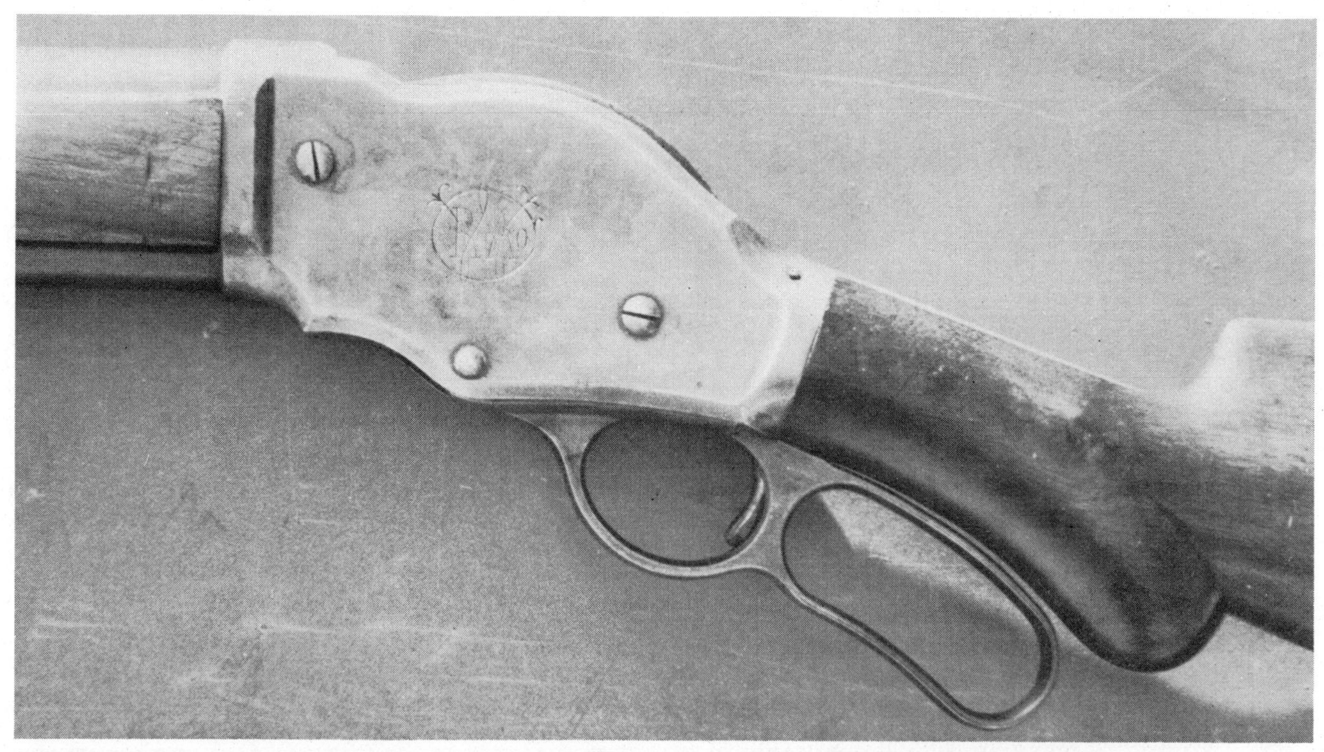

Because the Winchester Model 1887 Lever Action Shotgun is thought of as being the first successful repeating shotgun, it ranks high today with collectors.

The Winchester Model 1901 Lever Action Shotgun is quite similar to the earlier Model 1887. Note the absence of the left-hand carrier stop screw on the Model 1901 and the most interesting difference—the two-piece lever on the Model 1901 which contains a spring and plunger that acts as a shock absorber when the lever is actuated.

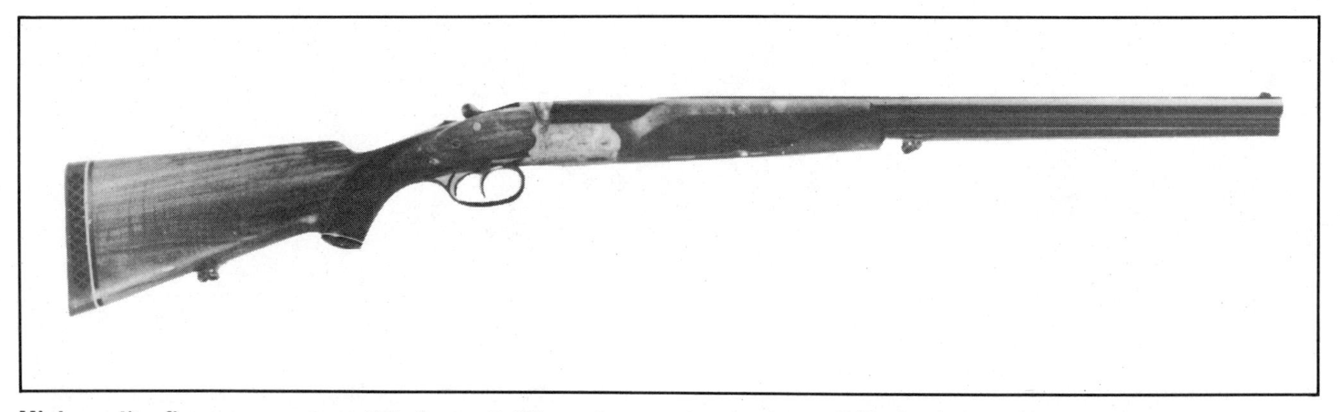

High-quality firearms, such as this Sauer Drilling, always command top dollar in the used-gun market.

Foreign-manufactured varieties in the same category include Holland & Holland, J.P. Sauer, Krieghoff, Webley & Scott and Westley Richards. Most of these shotguns in excellent condition, in the better grades, start at $10,000 and go nowhere but up.

With the exception of Belgian Brownings and some pre-'64 Winchesters, few American-made pumps and autoloaders have reached collector status. Most are used strictly as "working guns" for hunting or competitive shooting (trap, skeet, etc.). Of these, the Remington Model 1100 seems to be the most popular, both as a hunting and skeet gun. On the contrary, the Remington Model 870 pump shotgun is a slow mover, and I find it hard to sell for even $150 at any time other than during the hunting season.

Price Trends in Shotgun Trading

No one can predict the future . . . exactly, but by gathering and analyzing certain statistics, one can come close to guessing the outcome of an event. The same is true with firearms.

To give you an idea of how the trend in gun prices has been going, I've compared the average retail price of a used gun in excellent condition 10 years ago to the price of the same gun today. Below are the results of these findings, along with the percentage of increase. This information should certainly be sufficient to whet your interest and lead you to some predictions of your own.

Shotgun	Price in 1972	Price in 1982	Percent Increase
American Browning Special	$ 95	$ 400	321
AyA			
Matador II	150	375	150
Model 37 Super O/U	800	1,800	125
Baker Batavia Leader, Double Barrel	$ 100	$ 325	225
Beretta			
Silver Hawk, Double Barrel	135	550	307
SO-3EL	850	3,400	300
Bernardelli V.B. Holland	550	4,560	729
Boss Hammerless O/U	3,250	15,000	361
Breda Autoloading	125	250	100
Browning			
Auto-5	150	525	250
Superposed Grade I	300	1,300	333
Churchill Premiere	2,000	10,000	400
Cogswell & Harrison Best Quality	2,000	6,000	200
Colt, Double Barrel	150	320	113
Charles Daly Regent Diamond	1,200	5,000	317
Darne Quail Hunter	315	1,950	519
Davidson 63B, Double Barrel	80	200	150
Fox B-ST	115	230	100
Fox Sterlingworth, Double Barrel	165	550	233
Franchi Side Lock, Double Barrel	415	6,000	1,345
Francotte, Double Barrel	1,200	6,450	437
Greener Ejector, Double Barrel	1,000	3,700	270
Greifelt			
103, Double Barrel	300	1,400	367
Over-And-Under Combination	900	4,800	433

Shotgun	Price in 1972	Price in 1982	Percent Increase
Harrington & Richardson			
No. 8	$ 20	$ 75	275
Model 403	90	210	133
High Standard			
Supermatic Special	105	170	62
Flite-King Special	70	140	100
Holland & Holland Over-And-Under	3,500	14,000	300
Hunter Special, Double Barrel	140	375	168
Ithaca Model 37D Deluxe	95	225	137
Ithaca-SKB Model 100, Side-By-Side	145	300	107
Iver Johnson Hercules Grade	120	375	213
Kessler Lever-Matic	35	75	114
Lefever Nitro Special	125	500	300
Marlin Model 44A Repeater	75	240	220
Merkel			
Model 100 Over-And-Under	300	700	133
Model 304E Over-And-Under	2,500	7,200	188
Mossberg			
Model 85D Repeater	25	65	160
Model 500 Super Grade	85	210	147
Noble Model 50	40	105	163
Parker Trap Gun, Single Barrel	475	2,000	321
Purdey Over-And-Under	3,000	15,000	400
Remington			
Model 1882, Double Barrel	75	385	413
Sportsman Skeet Gun	95	310	226
Model 870 Wingmaster Field Gun	90	190	111
Model 1100TB Trap Gun	175	300	74
Richland Model 202 All-Purpose Field Gun	135	265	96
Rigby Side Lock, Double Barrel	$ 2,250	$ 17,000	655
Sarasqueta Box Lock, Double Barrel	100	400	300
Sauer			
"Artemis," Double Barrel	1,400	4,000	186
Model 66 Over-And-Under Trap Gun	530	1,400	164
Savage			
Model 30ACL	75	120	60
Model 430	115	370	222
Model 745 Lightweight Autoloader	90	200	122
L.C. Smith			
Olympic	465	1,275	174
Premier	2,700	9,000	233

Side-by-side double-barreled shotguns have lost some popularity to the over/under shotguns like the Ruger (above) and the Remington 3200 (below).

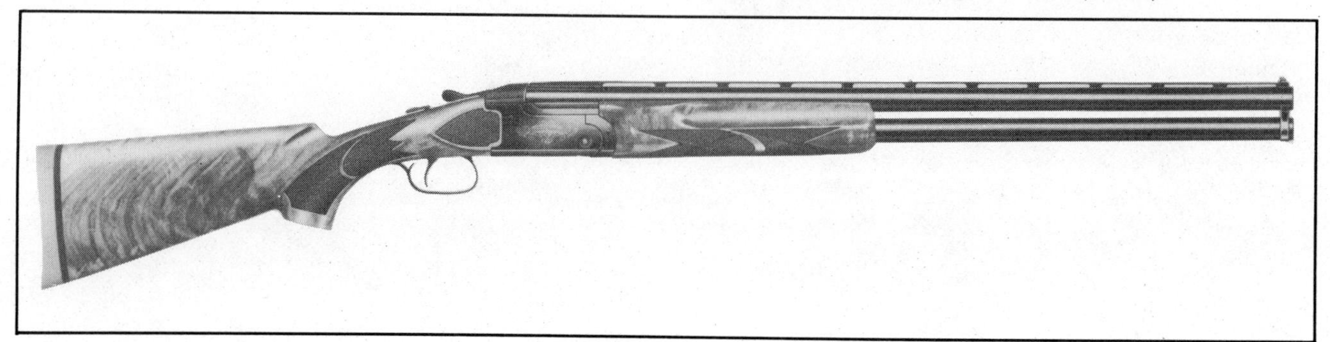

CHRONOLOGY
REMINGTON MODEL 3200 OVER/UNDER SHOTGUN

1973: Introduction of M 3200 in Field grade with 26-, 28- and 30-inch barrels; Skeet grade with 26- and 28-inch barrels; regular Trap grade and "Special" Trap grade and "One of 1,000" Trap grade.

1974: Announcement of M 3200 "One of 1,000" Skeet with 26- or 28-inch barrels.

1975: Introduction of M 3200 3-inch Magnum with 30-inch barrels. Addition of 32-inch barrels to Trap and Special Trap grades.

1976: Addition of M 3200 Competition Skeet grade with 26- and 28-inch barrels. Addition of M 3200 Competition Trap with 30- and 32-inch barrels. Deletion of M 3200 Special Trap grades.

1977: Reintroduction of M 3200 Special Trap grade.

1978: Deletion of M 3200 Field and Magnum grades. Deletion of regular Trap grades.

1979: Introduction of M 3200 Pigeon grade with 28-inch Imp. Modified and Full barrels.

1980: Introduction of M 3200 4-barrel skeet set composed of 12-gauge Competition Skeet and three sets of extra barrels in 20, 28 and .410 gauges, supplied in foam-lined, hard carrying case.

1981: Deletion of M 3200 regular Skeet and Special Trap grades.

To help identify used guns and the dates they were made, some manufacturers will supply data concerning their products, such as the chronology Remington has provided for its Model 3200 shotgun.

Shotgun	Price in 1972	Price in 1982	Percent Increase
Stevens			
Model 124 Cross-bolt Repeater	$ 35	$ 85	143
Model 530 Double Shotgun	75	160	113
No. 22-410 Over-And-Under Combination	45	115	155
Western Long Range, Double Barrel	100	175	75
Westley Richards			
Best Quality, Double Barrel	2,000	7,000	250
Ovundo (O/U)	3,500	14,000	300
Winchester			
Model 21 Skeet Gun	$ 600	$ 2,300	283
Model 59 Autoloading	110	400	264
Model 97 Trench Gun	100	450	350
Model 1400 Deer Gun	105	210	100
Model 1887 Lever-action Repeater	135	475	252
Woodward Best Quality Over-And-Under	5,000	20,000	300

7. Centerfire Rifle Trading

Second only to high-quality shotguns in price increases over the past decade are centerfire rifles. Other than some of the cheap military models, it is difficult indeed to obtain any centerfire rifle these days for under $200. Even the Winchester Model 94 carbine (post-1964 version) that retailed only a few years ago for less than $100 is bringing $125 or so when sold as a used gun.

Models Currently in Demand

Any centerfire rifle in good shooting condition will demand top dollar around the fall of the year when deer hunting seasons open throughout the country. If you have what might be classified as a "working" rifle—one that more than likely will be used for hunting—the best time to sell is from around the middle of October until mid-December. This time, of course, is not the time to shop for good buys if you happen to be in the market for one.

Although a lot depends on the locale, most of the better buys on centerfire rifles can be obtained from January to March of each year. The reasons are many.

First of all, dealers know that non-collectible rifles will move very slowly for the next nine months, and many will be willing to lower their prices at this time of year.

Then there's the construction worker who lives in a rural area and commutes back and forth to the city to work. This person and his coworkers—especially those contracted for residential projects—are sometimes laid off from their jobs during the winter months when adverse weather conditions prevail. They eventually become short of cash before the work picks up again in the spring and they know that firearms will put them in the money; the hunting season is over and they have plenty of time to buy more guns before the next season. Each year from about January 15 through March or the first of April, I receive dozens of phone calls and visits to my shop from such workers who want to sell their firearms for ready cash. Few guns are in the collector status; most are modern arms, such as the Marlin Model 336, the Mossberg bolt action in .243 caliber, the Sears "Special " or similar items.

Since this is a bad time of year to sell centerfire rifles, I can't pay top dollar for them; they are usually discounted about 40 percent because I know I will have to "carry" most of them until the next hunting season. This means interest on borrowed money and, at today's rates, this can add up. However, by the same token, if a customer is interested in buying a used centerfire rifle during this time, he can be assured of getting a good price, something in the neighborhood of 20 percent less than he would have to pay for the same rifle come autumn.

In the hunting classification, Remington centerfire

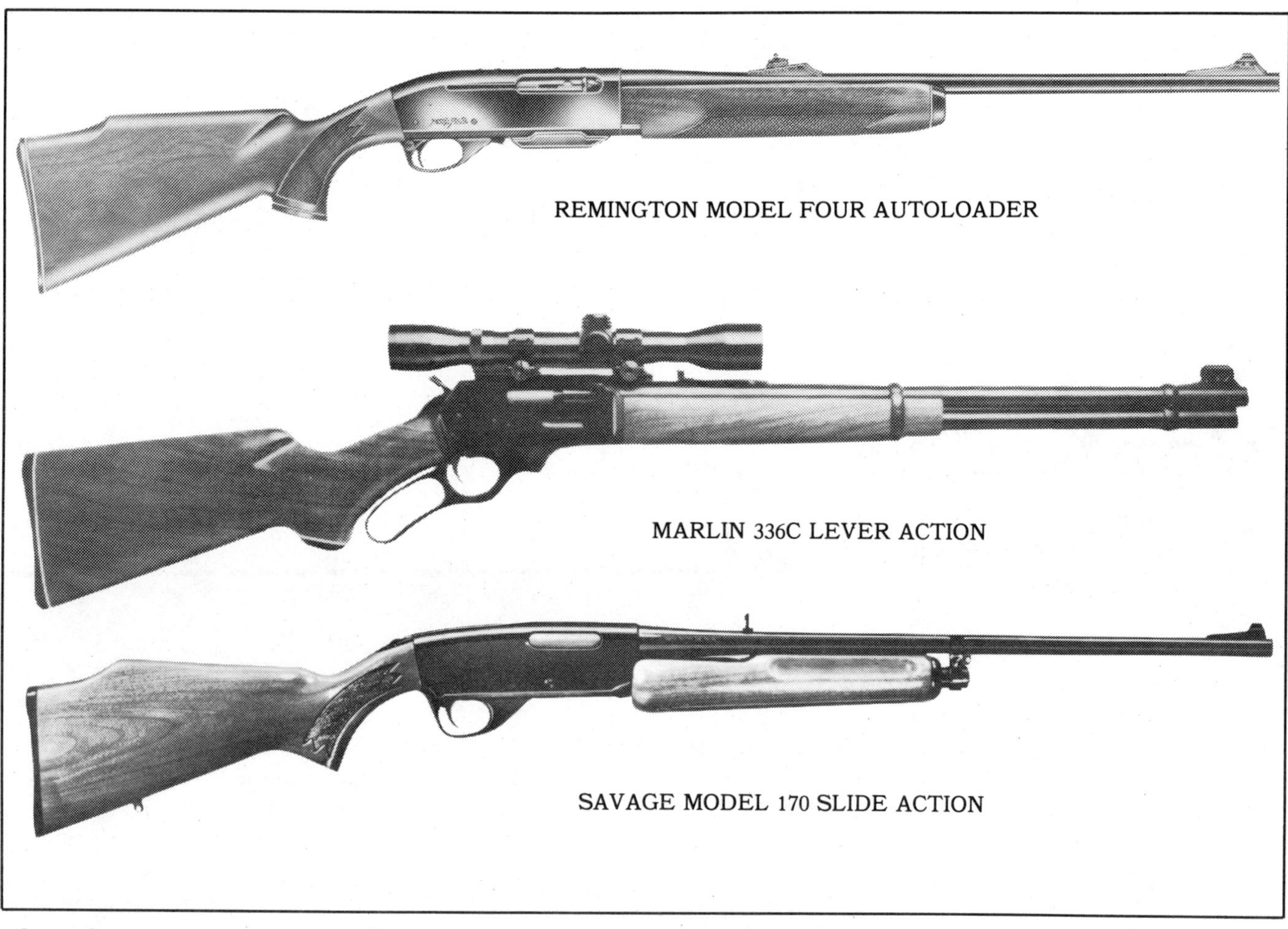

Centerfire rifles popular for hunting in the eastern United States include semiautomatics, lever actions and slide actions.

slide actions and semiautomatics are the most popular for woods hunting in the East, followed very closely by the lever actions. The Marlin 336 seems to outnumber the Winchester Model 94 about 3 to 1 in my area mainly because of its side ejection, which allows a scope sight to be mounted directly over and in line with the bore. On the Winchester Model 94, the scope must be offset to allow for the cartridge ejection out of the top of the receiver.

Hunters in the western part of the country stick with the bolt actions for greater accuracy on the longer shots so often necessary in flat country, or where shooting across a canyon is commonplace.

From the above, it would seem that different locations would have varied prices on certain types of firearms. This is true to a certain extent, but there's not enough difference in price to justify driving or flying two thousand miles just to buy one gun.

For collectors, again Winchester arms are right on top, and any of those that bear factory engraving, deluxe stocking or a presentation inscription command a substantial premium. The best known Winchester inscriptions, of course, are the "One of One Thousand," "1 of 1000" and "One of One Hundred" on premium grade Models 1873 and 1876 rifles. If such a gun can be authenticated as a premium-grade factory issue with any of the above inscriptions, and, if it is in good condition, you have a firearm worth in the neighborhood of $35,000 or more. But be cautious when purchasing such an arm. It is very easy to have an engraver do inscriptions on any rifle, and the practice has been done more than once.

Side-by-side double-barreled rifles are very costly, especially those made by Holland & Holland, Westley

Richards and similar English gunmakers. Sporting rifles manufactured by Mauser are now bringing top dollar, as are the Mannlicher-Schoenauer models.

Evaluating Condition

Centerfire rifles are evaluated just like any other firearm—usually by the percentage of bluing remaining on the gun; that is, 100 percent, 95 percent, etc. The stock and bore also play important roles in determining final price, but the general condition is usually evaluated on the basis of original bluing. Note that I said "original." A refinished firearm will bring less money than one in original factory condition if it is in the collector status. However, a modern centerfire rifle that has no collector value will usually bring more money if it is professionally refinished rather than if it is rusty and in poor shape.

Bolt-action centerfire rifles seldom give trouble even if misused, but occasionally a problem will develop that requires the attention of an expert. Some of the problems to look for include poor accuracy, binding breech bolt, improper feeding, misfiring, defective safety, failure to extract and failure to eject. Too much headspace is also common in some military arms.

Of the problems mentioned in the previous paragraph, the headspace problem is the most serious. The other malfunctions will prevent the gun from operating, but are seldom dangerous to the shooter. Excessive headspace, on the other hand, can endanger the life of the shooter as well as bystanders.

Bolt-action rifles have been the standard military arm for many countries for nearly 100 years. Many of them were imported to the United States, distributed through gun dealers and have since fallen into the hands of many individuals. The majority of these guns were checked by the distributors, and the bad ones were rejected and dismantled for spare parts. The better ones were sold for shooting. However, some of the rejects happened to get through and many have excessive headspace. Some of them have "let go," to the dismay of the shooter, sending hot gas and flying brass particles back into the shooter's face. Therefore, before firing any foreign military weapon, have the headspace checked by a competent gunsmith. Better yet, check it before buying the gun. If the headspace does need to be corrected, you're better off not buying the rifle. Occasionally, a headspace problem can be corrected by installing a slightly over-long bolt; otherwise, the problem must be solved by setting the barrel back.

A defective safety should also be corrected immediately. In most cases, this problem can be traced to a worn or altered cam on the firing pin. If the safety binds, try filing the bearing point on the firing pin, taking only a small amount of metal away at a time until the problem is corrected. If the safety is tight in the bolt sleeve, it may be fitted, but usually a new safety is suggested. When such problems are found, an adjustment in the selling price of the gun is warranted.

Centerfire single-shot rifles are in great demand. Most use the falling-block design, and some have very complex mechanisms, requiring a professional to make any necessary repairs. So check them out thoroughly

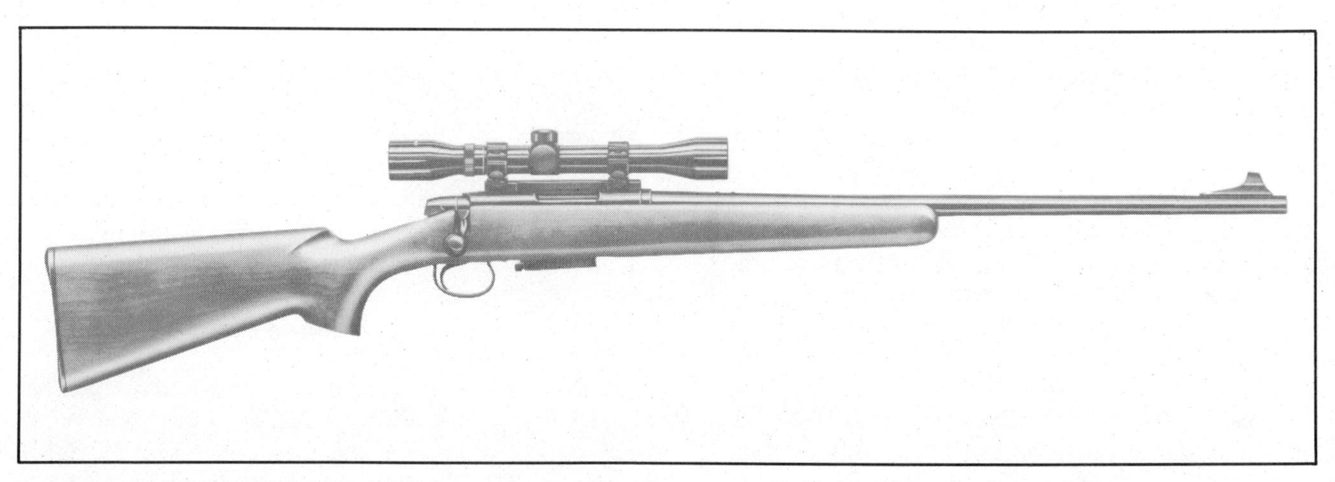

Bolt-action rifles, such as this Remington Model 788, are the most popular in the western United States for long shots over flat terrain.

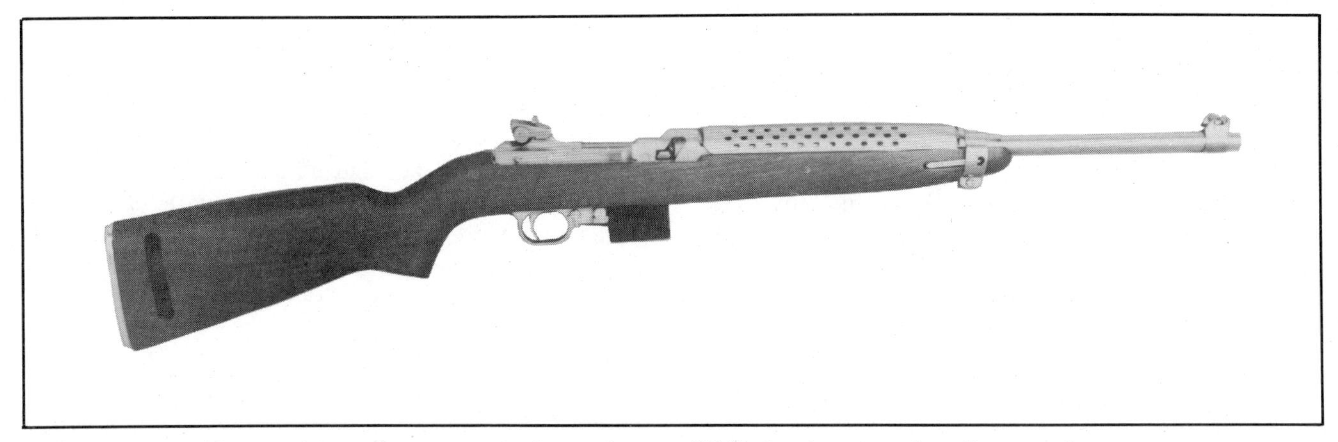

Stainless steel rifles are becoming more popular each year. While few have much collector value as yet, they are being purchased by shooters who need ultimate protection from adverse weather conditions.

before you reach a deal. Even the replacement of a minor part in some of these single-shot models can cost a small fortune.

Although a collector's item, the Remington Rolling Block single-shot rifle is low on the list when it comes to value. Most of these should be retired to the wall rack and not fired; however, they can be made to shoot cartridges of moderate pressure by using one or more of the following suggestions. Bush the firing pin, i.e., add bushings to make the firing pin hole smaller, reface the breech blocks or adjust the trigger pull. You will also want to give them a very close examination to detect any hairline cracks that may be present in the action or parts.

The worst, and most common, problem that occurs in the older centerfire lever-action rifles is looseness caused by wear of moving parts. You will find that some original round holes in parts have become egg-shaped, mortises in the receiver are worn and metal has been shed from mating surfaces. Any of these defects can lead to malfunctions, making the gun unsafe.

Feeding problems are often encountered that are caused by dented, dirty or corroded magazine tubes and/or weak magazine springs. Recesses in the receivers are prone to collect bits of debris and foreign matter which, when combined with gun oil and grease, cake and gum up the action, causing feeding, extraction and ejection problems.

The third most common problem in older lever-actions is excessive headspace. These rifles lock up at the rear of the sliding breech bolt and, after much firing, stretching occurs which causes excessive headspace. If you're paying for one of these rifles, it's best to check it out thoroughly before closing the deal.

Malfunctions in slide-action rifles are second in frequency only to the autoloaders. The biggest cause of problems with both of these action types is the presence of dirt, dust and assorted debris that, when combined with gun grease and oil, prevent proper operation. This is really not a serious problem, since most of these malfunctions can be corrected by giving the gun a consummate cleaning. However, if you find a gun in this condition, you'd better give the bore a going over before buying it. Chances are an owner who has neglected cleaning the receiver has also not kept the bore in good shape, which means a strong probability it may be badly leaded, rusted or pitted—any of which will seriously affect accuracy.

Before purchasing a slide-action rifle for hunting, you'll want to be reasonably sure the gun feeds properly, does not double-feed, retains cartridges in the magazine, action bars do not stick, action locks properly, extracts and ejects as it should, cocks properly, safety functions as it should and the gun does not discharge when the bolt is closed.

Semiautomatic rifles are becoming very popular for deer hunting in the eastern United States. Unfortunately, these guns have more malfunctions than any other type of action made.

Besides feeding problems, you'll find autoloaders that fail to extract fired cases; some that won't eject; some that won't fire; and others that won't lock up properly. It is difficult to detect all of these problems by just looking at a gun, but here are some tips in case you don't have time to test-fire the weapon thoroughly before buying it. Look for marred screw heads. If these are found, chances are the previous owner tried to take the gun apart to fix it for some reason. Operate the bolt. Does it feel free, or does it slide roughly? If the latter is the case, beware.

Price Trends in Centerfire Rifle Trading

A comparison of the price increases of the different centerfire rifles over the past 10 years may be helpful in determining good investments for the future. In most cases, the ones that show the greatest increase will remain the most in demand for many years to come. As these more popular models become scarcer, collectors will turn to other models, but no doubt the highest priced firearms will get even higher. Collectors who buy a Winchester or a good Holland & Holland double-barreled rifle at a good price cannot go wrong; these models will always bring top prices regardless of any new models that may arrive later.

Rifle	Price in 1972	Price in 1982	Percent Increase
Brno			
Hornet	$ 200	$ 635	217
Model 21H	225	635	182
Browning			
High-Power Rifle	200	700	250
High-Power Rifle, Short Action	180	650	261
High-Power Rifle, Medium Action	190	675	255
High-Power Rifle, Medallion Grade	300	1,125	275
High-Power Rifle, Olympian Grade	$ 500	$ 1,700	240
BSA			
Majestic Deluxe Standard	120	240	100
Monarch Deluxe Hunting	120	250	108
Colt			
AR-15 Sporter	165	375	127
Lightning Magazine	165	875	430
Lightning Carbine	175	1,375	685
Lightning Baby Carbine	185	2,800	1,413
Coltsman "Custom," 1957	150	400	166
Coltsman "De Luxe," 1957	125	375	200
Coltsman "Standard," 1957	100	325	225
Coltsman "Custom," 1961	150	440	193
Coltsman "Standard," 1961	100	375	275
Charles Daly Hornet	250	890	256
F.N.			
De Luxe Mauser	200	585	192
Supreme Magnum Mauser	315	595	88
Hämmerli Model Olympia 300	300	750	150
Haenel			
Mauser-Mannlicher	150	300	100
'88 Mauser Sporter	150	300	100
Harrington & Richardson Model 360 Ultra Auto.	130	310	138
High Standard Hi-Power Deluxe	100	250	150

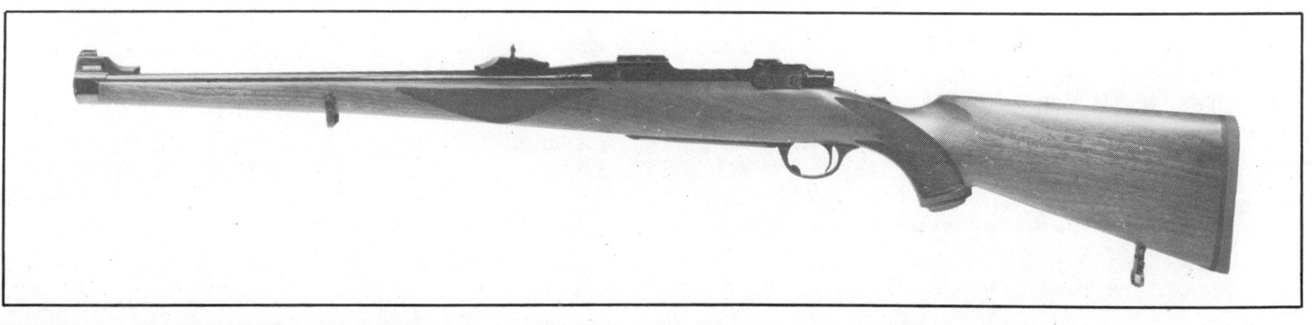

This Ruger Model 77 Rifle with full Mannlicher stock is suitable for any type of hunting. It is compact enough for quick shots in heavy brush, yet has accuracy for open plains shooting. It would be hard to find a better all-around rifle.

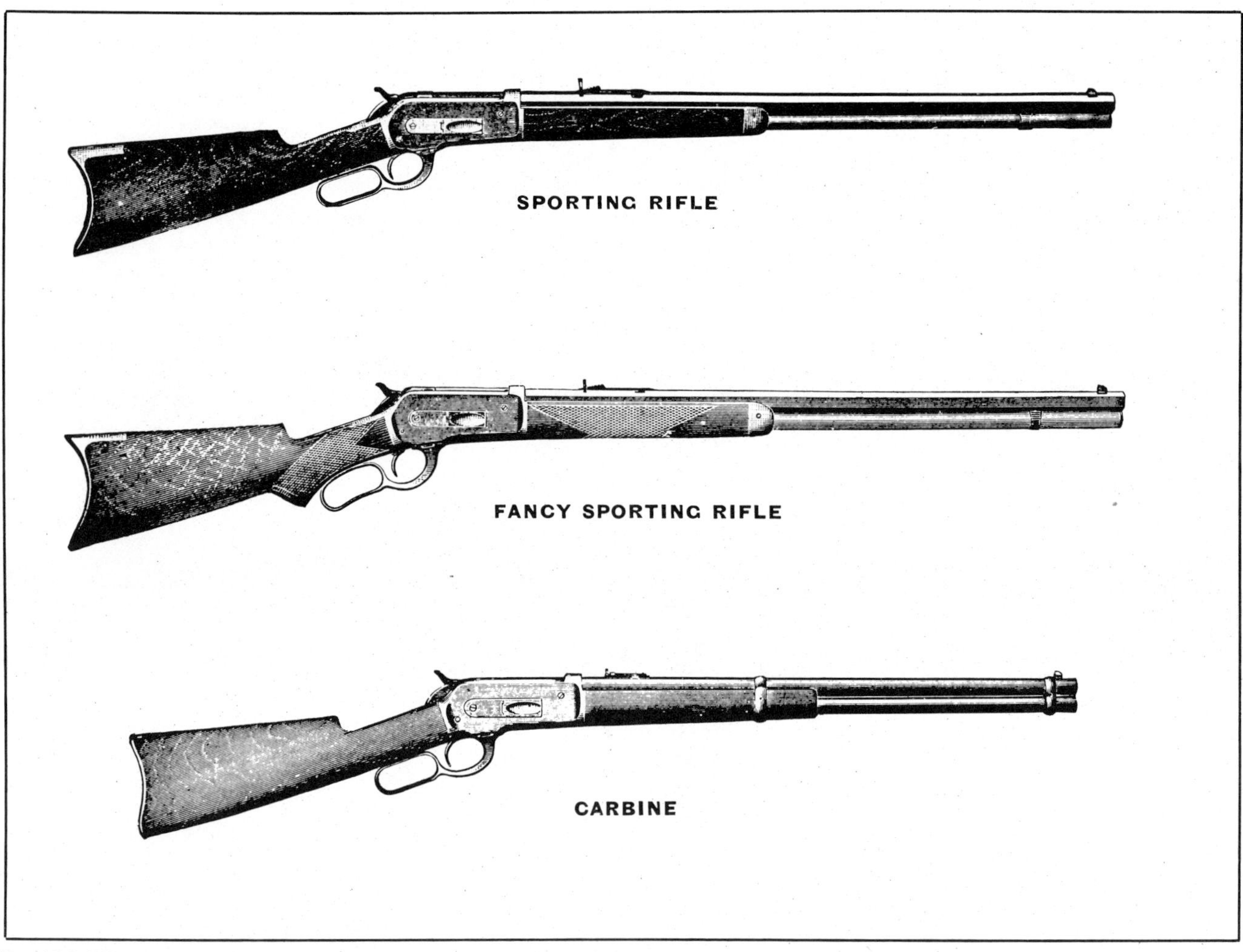

Pre-'64 Winchester rifles rank high on any collector's list. These variations of the Model 1886, for example, all will command prices in excess of $1,000 if in excellent condition.

Rifle	Price in 1972	Price in 1982	Percent Increase
Holland & Holland			
Modele, De Luxe			
Double Barrel	$ 3,000	$ 15,000	400
Best Quality Magazine	500	2,500	400
Husqvarna			
Crown Grade, 3000	135	350	159
Crown Grade, 3100	115	350	204
Lightweight, 4000	125	350	180
Lightweight, 4100	120	325	170
Model 8000	190	450	136
Model 9000	140	325	132
Mannlicher-Schoenauer			
1903	200	750	275

Rifle	Price in 1972	Price in 1982	Percent Increase
Mannlicher-Schoenauer			
1950	$ 200	$ 700	250
Marlin			
Model 27	50	210	320
Model 36	75	295	293
Model 62 Levermatic	55	135	145
Model 93 Rifle	100	375	275
Model 93 Carbine	100	550	450
Model 93 Musket	150	680	353
Model 322	125	350	180
Model 336 "Marauder"	75	275	266
Model 336 Zane			
Grey Century	150	225	50

Rifle	Price in 1972	Price in 1982	Percent Increase
Marlin			
Model 336T "Texan"	$ 75	$ 140	86
Model 444	100	205	105
Model 455	135	370	174
Model 1895	120	530	341
Model 1897	60	300	400
Mauser			
Sporting Rifle	175	475	171
Sporting Carbine	175	480	174
Magnum Rifle, Type "A"	250	600	140
Sporting Rifle, Type "B"	200	475	137
Carbine, Type "M"	225	525	133
Carbine, Type "S"	200	500	150
Standard Model	185	450	143
Musketeer Mauser Sporter	120	230	91
Newton-Mauser Sporting Rifle	150	500	233
Newton Standard—2nd Type	185	575	210
Remington-Lee Sporting Rifle	100	500	400
Remington			
No. 3 High Power	150	425	183
No. 5 Special	100	350	250
Model 8A	100	235	135
Model 14A	60	225	275
Model 14½	60	550	816
Model 30A	100	495	395
Model 141A	85	275	223
Model 600 Carbine	75	220	193
Model 600 Magnum	100	250	150
Model 660 Carbine	85	225	164
Model 660 Magnum	105	275	161
Model 720A	100	245	145
Model 721A	80	190	137
Model 722A	75	275	266
Model 725 "Kodiak"	210	550	161
Model 742	125	280	124
Model 760	100	230	130
Model 740A	110	180	63
Rigby			
"Best Quality" Rifle	2,000	16,000	700
275 Sporting Rifle	500	2,500	400

Rifle	Price in 1972	Price in 1982	Percent Increase
Rigby			
350 Magnum	$ 500	$ 2,500	400
416 Big Game Rifle	525	2,500	376
Ross Model 1910	125	250	100
Ruger Model 44 Carbine	80	180	125
Sako			
Finnbear Sporter	170	400	135
Finnwolf Rifle	185	400	116
Sauer Mauser Rifle	200	475	137
Savage			
Model 99A	90	425	372
Model 99E	95	185	94
Model 99C	115	215	86
Model 110	80	160	100
Savage/Anschutz Model 153	140	370	164
Sedgley Springfield Sporter	150	400	166
Standard Model G Automatic	200	300	50
Stevens Model 325	60	110	83
U.S. Carbine, Caliber 30, M1	100	235	135
Universal Standard 30 Caliber	75	140	86
Weatherby De Luxe Magnum	175	510	191
Westley Richards			
Best Quality Double	1,500	13,000	766
Best Quality Magazine	500	4,000	700
Winchester			
"Centennial '66"	200	425	112
Model 05	80	350	337
Model 07	150	380	153
Model 10	125	350	180
Model 43	60	285	375
Model 54 Rifle	90	475	427
Model 54 Carbine	90	450	400
Model 55	100	625	525
Model 64	135	500	270
Model 86	400	1,250	212
Model 88	115	375	226
Model 92	200	750	275
Model 94 (pre-World War II)	135	475	251
Model 95 Rifle	200	750	275
Model 95 Carbine	300	950	216

8. Rimfire Rifle Trading

There is a good possibility that more .22 rimfire rifles are bought and sold each year than any other type of rifle. While many of these are sought by collectors, most are "working" guns, used for training young shooters, for target work and hunting small game. Since .22 rimfire ammunition is the least expensive of all, it would stand to reason that this rifle group would be the most used for plinking in this country.

Models Currently in Demand

From a collector's point of view, any Winchester pre-'64 rimfire rifles are being hotly pursued, with prices for these models having seen a sharp rise in the past few years. The early Stevens single shots, such as the "Walnut Hill" and the "Armory Model," are also commanding high prices. But the rifles assessed the steepest are the high-quality match rifles like the Winchester Model 75 Target and the Winchester Model 52 in its variations.

For general hunting and plinking, the .22 rimfire semiautomatics outsell all others by a wide margin. I see more Savage-Stevens Model 80 rifles on used gun racks than any other type. To me, this means one thing! As a working gun, the Savage-Stevens seems to be the most popular, but few people are interested in actually collecting this model.

In comparison to the high collector interest in centerfire rifles, veteran collectors have traditionally shown little interest in rimfire rifles, with the only possible exceptions of rimfires manufactured before, say, 1920, such as the Winchester Model 73's, Colt slide-action repeaters and the like. The more conventional rimfire rifles were usually purchased only for hunting, target shooting and plinking. During the past few years, however, the popularity in rimfire rifle collecting has increased tremendously and is still rising at a phenomenal rate.

There are several reasons for this upsurge. First, the increasing costs of all collectible centerfire rifles require some serious thinking on the part of the buyer. Gone are the days when you could purchase 10 pre-'64 Model 94 carbines for $350. Now even one fair piece costs over $150. A Winchester Model 86 will go for about $1,000 in good condition—too much for the average collector to put up, at least not too often.

Second, the mushrooming number of collectors at large has swallowed up an unbelievable quantity of firearms and today's avid collector can easily become frustrated and bored by the dearth of unusual or exciting acquisitions.

The third and most important reason is the availability of rimfire rifles and the opportunity of getting a really good buy—despite these days of high inflation. Few households in this country are without a .22 rim-

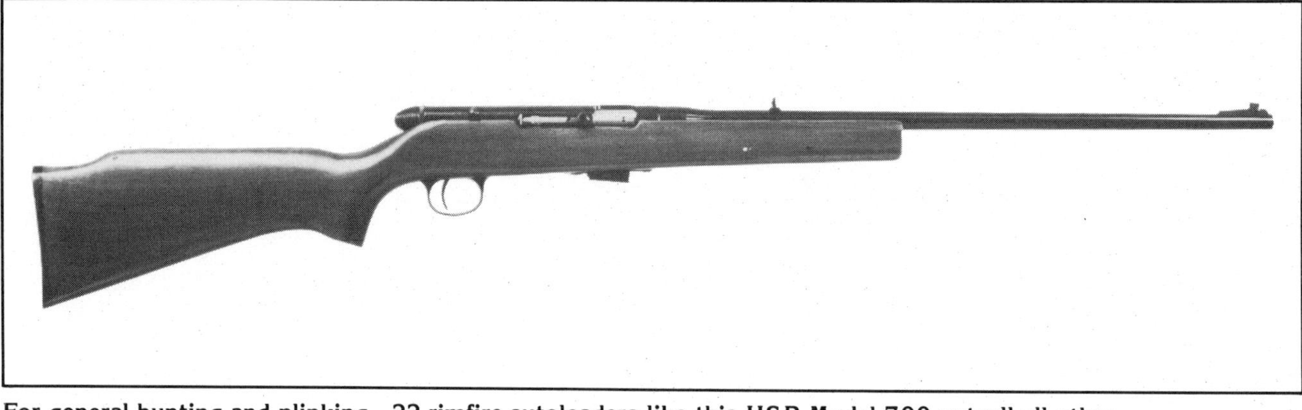

For general hunting and plinking, .22 rimfire autoloaders like this H&R Model 700 outsell all other rifles by a wide margin.

fire rifle, many of which have been around for a long time. Some owners who use these rifles as tools around the farm, or for hunting and shooting pests are interested in trading them for more modern arms that will be more useful. To illustrate, many of the old bolt-action rimfire rifles are not easily adapted to scope sights—the bolt will hit a top-mounted scope when the action is operated; many eject out of the top of the action; and the receiver must be drilled and tapped for scope mounts. Such an installation will cost anywhere from $25 to $35, and rather than pay this amount, the owner would just as soon trade the gun in on a new one. Transactions like these occur daily and a lot of action frequently takes place at the busier gun shops. A collector of .22 rimfire rifles can go into his favorite used gun shop two or three times a week and usually find some new items on the shelves every time.

To demonstrate just how profitable .22 rimfire collecting can be these days, in 1978 I purchased several Winchester Model 67 single-shot rifles for an average of $30 each. I sold most of them a year or two later for $65 each—making over 100 percent profit on each. Today, I could easily get $90 each for them and by the time this book is published, perhaps well over $100. The Model 67 is probably the least expensive of the Winchester line; just think what the others could bring.

As with other types of firearms, the pre-'64 rimfire rifles are the most in demand. Winchester, Remington and Savage-Stevens are your best bets. Rifles such as Noble, J.C. Higgins, High Standard and even the late model Winchesters (Models 250, 270, 150 and 290) have little collector value. All are good shooters, though, and are highly recommended as a first gun or for hunting or plinking in general. However, I've found that all of these models suffer from poor accuracy, and malfunctions are not uncommon. Parts are also hard to come by —particularly for those models that were specially made for the mail-order houses.

Generally speaking, virtually any Winchester rimfire rifle in good condition and manufactured prior to 1964 is in the collector status and should make a good investment . . . if you buy right. The first .22 rimfire repeating rifle was the Model 1873, but this rifle was relatively heavy and expensive and never gained much popularity as a "working" gun. No matter. Rifles such as these demand the highest prices from collectors of rimfires.

You should be aware of some of the other Winchester rimfires that have collector value. The Model 90 rimfire, for example, was light and relatively inexpensive and could hold from 11 to 15 cartridges—depending upon the type used—and nearly one million of these rifles were manufactured. A shorter version of this model, called the Model 06, came out in 1906. Both the Model 06 and Model 90 were popular for gallery use as well as for plinking and hunting small game. In 1932, Winchester came out with an improved version of the Model 90, the Model 62.

Winchester also developed a concealed hammer pump in 1932, the Model 61, which happened to be my first new .22 rimfire rifle.

The first Winchester semiautomatic rifle was invented by Thomas C. Johnson and was called the Model 03. Earlier models were chambered only for the .22 Winchester Automatic cartridge. At this writing, cartridges are still available—at a retail price of about $5 per box.

So if you're in the market for a plinking rifle, this model obviously would not be first choice. In 1933, this rifle was revamped and chambered for the .22 Long Rifle and renamed the Model 63.

A new semiautomatic rifle was introduced in 1939. It was chambered for .22 Shorts in the "Gallery Special" model; and in 1940 the .22 Long Rifle chambering was added for sporting rifles.

The Model 1900 single shot was Winchester's first bolt-action rimfire rifle. Through various improvements, it became known as the Model 02, and then the Model 04. In the later version, a thumb trigger rifle was introduced which had no trigger or trigger guard. Instead, a thumb latch served to release the firing mechanism. This rifle was eventually called the Model 99.

Other Winchester bolt-action rifles include Models 58, 59 and 60. The Model 60 was later revamped to become the Model 67. Then came the Model 52, Model 75 and other models suitable for target work.

The development of Remington products closely paralleled that of Winchester; that is, they too brought out pumps, autoloaders, bolt actions and the like. Many shooters, however, felt that the workmanship of Remington rifles was not quite up to par with the Winchesters. This may or may not be true, but at the present time Winchester arms are still yielding more to collectors than the Remingtons. For example, the Winchester Model 61 slide-action rifle in excellent condition is worth about $350. Remington's Model 12 slide action is valued at around $200.

Rifles of other manufacturers have yet to reach the stature of Winchester and Remington rimfire rifles. However, as the supply of these more desirable arms diminishes, the less pursued ones are certain to increase in value. This might just be the avenue to follow if you are considering a reasonably priced gun collection now, which you hope should pay off in years to come.

How to Evaluate Condition

Chapter 1 of this book covered the NRA method of grading firearms using the terms "Excellent," "Fair," "Good," etc. Since an "antique excellent" is different from an "excellent" modern gun, many professionals now use a different method to grade firearms: namely, the percentage of original factory finish remaining on the gun. Any method you employ will take some practice, but eventually even the novice will be able to tell the approximate amount of bluing remaining on the gun. Of course, the condition of the wood is also taken into consideration when pricing used guns, but most collectors consider the bluing for determining the basic "condition."

After you've acquired some experience, you will soon learn that some types of firearms wear differently than others. Bluing on some arms will wear off first in a particular location, while on others this location varies. Besides the muzzle, these places are usually where the gun is touched most by the hands or body. In a tubular magazine rifle, for example, the bluing will be worn off at the top of the magazine tube where the hand has gripped it to unscrew the magazine tube.

After the outside condition has been examined and evaluated, the bore is the next place to inspect. A rifle that won't shoot accurately is next to worthless. Even if the gun is solely for a collection and will probably never be fired, you won't be expected to pay top dollar for an arm that will not shoot as it should.

When looking for a serviceable rimfire rifle for

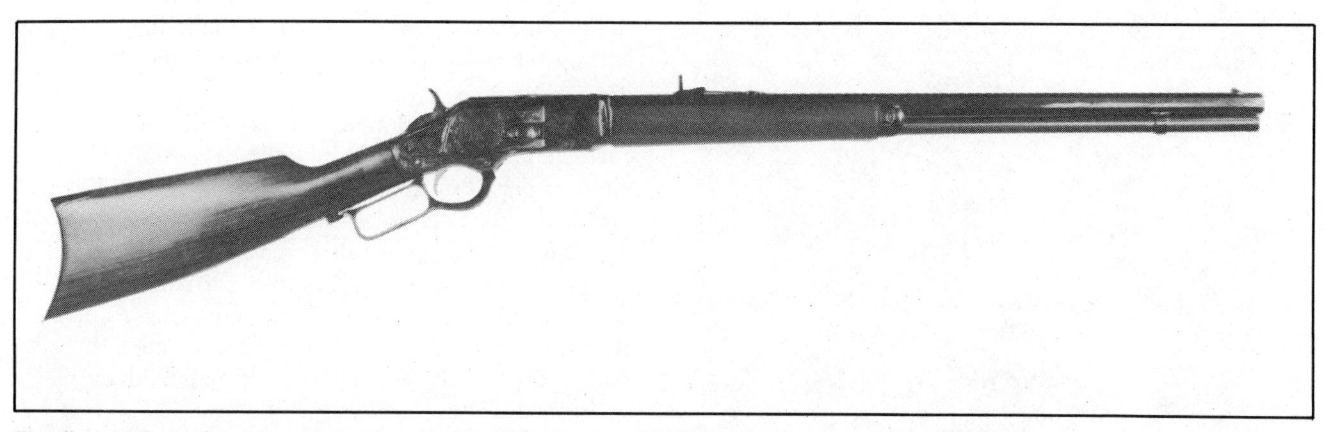

The first .22 rimfire repeating rifle was the Winchester 1873, perhaps tops on the list of collectible rimfires.

Peened muzzles, a common cause of malfunctioning in rimfires, can be shortened. . .
. . . and crowned. The procedure takes some practice, but is usually within the capability of the average handy gun owner.

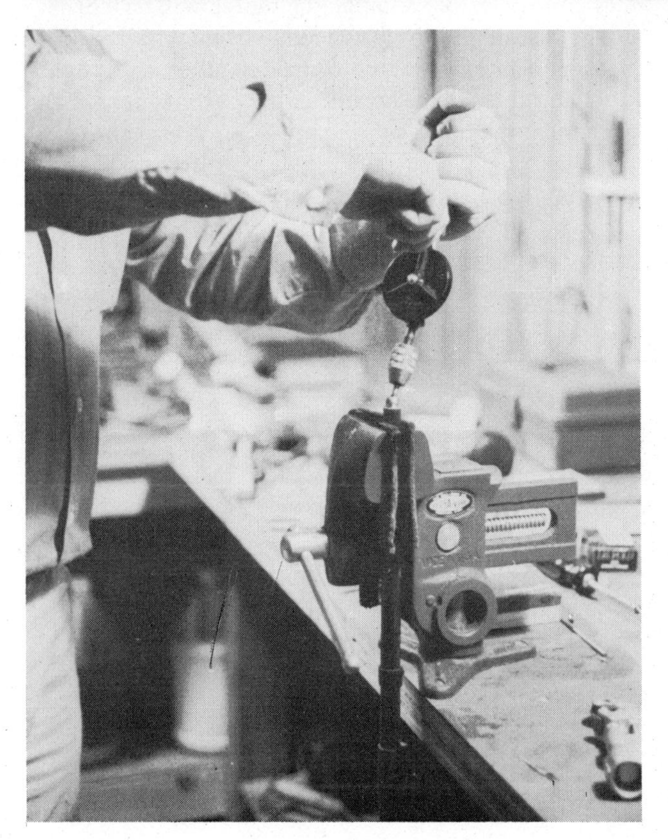

hunting or plinking, you will want to run several tests with it to make sure it is functioning properly. If purchased from a dealer, be sure to get his guarantee that the gun will function properly. If it doesn't, see that he agrees to repair it or will pay to have it repaired.

The most common malfunctions of rimfire rifles include burred or scratched chambers and peened muzzles. Repeating and semiautomatic rifles are subject to misfeeding due to hardened grease and foreign matter in the receiver and extractor recesses. In these areas, the problem is compounded by the lubed ammunition and by the comparatively small size of the various action recesses.

In most cases, ailments in .22 rimfire rifles can be corrected by a good cleaning and/or the replacement of a minor part. But then sometimes they're not. Feeding problems, for example, can be caused by dents or debris in the magazine tube, weak or broken magazine springs, bent, broken or blocked cartridge stops and cutoffs, and worn carriers or carrier cams. Faulty extraction and ejection are most often related to badly fouled or burred chambers or to jammed extractor springs.

As mentioned previously, many problems associated with repeating rifles can be corrected by a thorough cleaning and degreasing, so make this operation your first before having any repair work done on the arm by a professional gunsmith. Strip the gun down to its basic action components and clean and degrease them thoroughly. Once the parts are clean, those requiring replacement or touching up are fairly easy to detect. Then you can show these to your gunsmith should repairs be necessary—saving him time and you money.

Price Trends in Rimfires

Traditionally speaking, the .22 rimfire rifle has been a relatively low-priced firearm with the exception of the higher grade target rifles. Even the better English and European gunmakers who made the finest double shotguns and drillings seldom put forth the same effort when building a .22 rimfire rifle. There were exceptions, of course, but as a general rule, .22's never got the attention that their bigger-bore counterparts did.

To get an idea of how the market trend has gone over the past 10 years, the following comparison should give you a picture of the most popular models. You will generally find that the better quality rifles enjoy the highest interest with collectors, and therefore command the tidiest sums. The prices are for models in excellent condition.

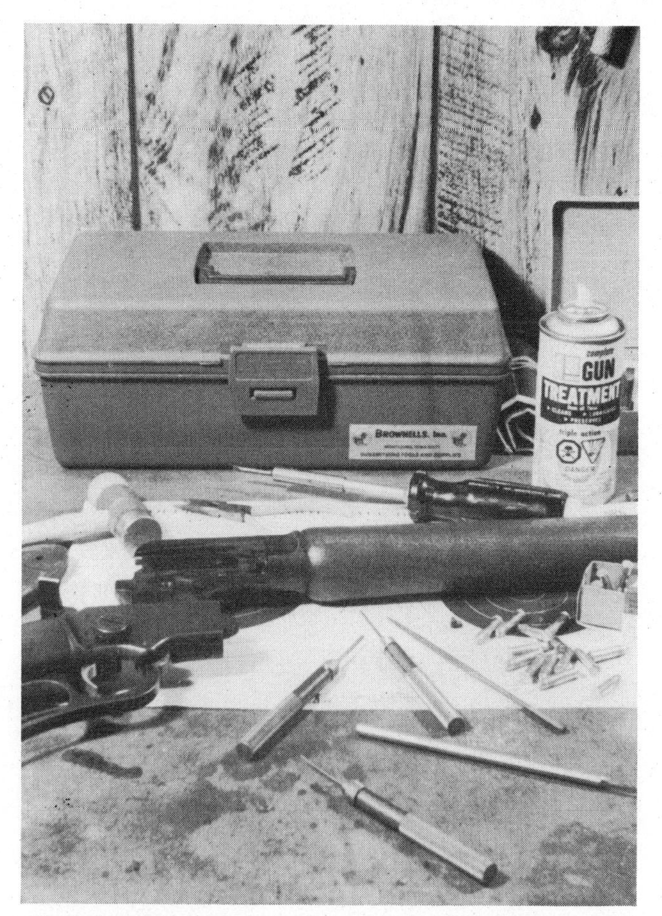

All rimfires, just as most used guns, should be disassembled and thoroughly checked for worn parts and other areas that could cause malfunctions.

Rifle	Price in 1972	Price in 1982	Percent Increase
Anschutz			
M/1411 Match 54	$ 180	$ 495	175
M/1413 Super Match	300	775	158
Armalite			
AR-7 "Explorer"	40	85	112
Custom AR-7	45	125	177
Brno Model 1	100	395	295
Browning			
22 Grade I	70	260	271
22 Grade II	105	360	242
22 Grade III	185	825	345
"T-Bolt" T-2	65	250	284
BSA			
No. 12	100	230	130
Model 15	110	375	240
Centurian Model	125	310	148
Model 12/15	125	305	144
Heavy Model 12/15	135	340	151
No. 13 Martini	100	235	135
Martini- International-Heavy	150	350	133
Martini- International MK II	175	350	100

Rifle	Price in 1972	Price in 1982	Percent Increase
Colt			
22 Lightning Magazine	$ 110	$ 875	695
Stagecoach 22	55	145	163
Coltsman "Custom"	150	400	166
Coltsman "De Luxe"	125	375	200
Colteer 1-22	18	50	177
Colteer 22	45	135	200
Hämmerli Model 45	250	550	120
Harrington & Richardson			
Model 60	185	375	102
Model 65	85	200	135
Model 150 "Leatherneck"	40	100	150
Model 151	50	125	150
Model 165 "Leatherneck"	45	100	122
Model 251	28	50	78

Rifle	Price in 1972	Price in 1982	Percent Increase
H & R			
Model 265 "Reg'lar"	$ 25	$ 50	100
Model 365 "Ace"	18	40	122
Model 422	45	85	88
Model 450	60	125	108
Model 451 "Medalist"	70	150	114
Model 465	40	90	125
Model 750 "Pioneer"	20	40	100
Model 751	25	50	100
Model 755 "Sahara"	20	40	100
Model 760	20	40	100
Model 765 "Pioneer"	15	30	100
Model 800 "Lynx"	35	65	85
Model 852 "Fieldsman"	30	65	116
Model 865 "Plainsman"	30	60	100
Model 866	35	65	85
"Targeteer Jr."	40	85	112
High Standard			
"Field"	30	75	150
"Special"	35	85	142
Autoload Carbine	38	100	163
De Luxe Autoloader	40	95	137
Pump Rifle	42	95	126
Ithaca			
Model X5-C	30	65	116
Model X5-T	30	65	116
Model 49 Saddlegun	25	40	60
Model 49 Youth Saddlegun	25	40	60
Model 49 Magnum Saddlegun	30	45	50
Model 49 Deluxe Saddlegun	30	55	83
Model 49R Saddlegun	35	110	214
Model 49 Presentation	100	175	75
Iver Johnson			
Model X	15	100	566
Model 2X	20	125	525
Marlin			
Model 18	60	190	216
Model 20	50	180	260
Model 25	50	225	350
Model 29	50	200	300
Model 32	50	200	300
Model 38	50	200	300
Model 39	150	275	83
39 Century Ltd.	125	225	77

Rifle	Price in 1972	Price in 1982	Percent Increase
Marlin			
Model 39A	$ 75	$ 135	80
Model 39A "Mountie" Rifle	75	175	133
Model 39 "Mountie" Carbine	75	500	566
39A Article II	135	200	48
39M Article II Carbine	135	200	48
Model 50	25	55	120
Model 57	45	105	133
Model 65	15	35	133
Model 80	20	45	125
Model 80-C	23	55	139
Model 81	24	50	108
Model 88-C	28	60	114
Model 89-C	25	60	140
Model 92	60	430	616
Model 98	28	60	114
Model 99	28	60	114
Model 100	15	35	133
Model 122	20	55	175
Model 980, 22 Magnum	30	85	183
Model 989	30	65	116
Model A-1	25	85	240
Mauser			
Model ES340	90	225	150
Model ES350	150	375	150
Model M410	125	300	140
Model MS420	125	300	140
Model EN310	70	195	178
Model EL320	90	225	250
Model MS350B	175	400	128
Model ES340B	125	300	140
Model MM410B	150	360	140
Model MS420B	150	350	133
Model DSM34	125	330	164
Model KKW	125	350	180
Mossberg			
Model K	25	100	300
Model M	30	115	283
Model L	50	225	350
Model B	12	40	233
Model R	15	45	200
Model 10	12	40	233
Model 14	12	40	233
Model 20	12	40	233
Model 25	12	40	233
Model 25A	12	40	233

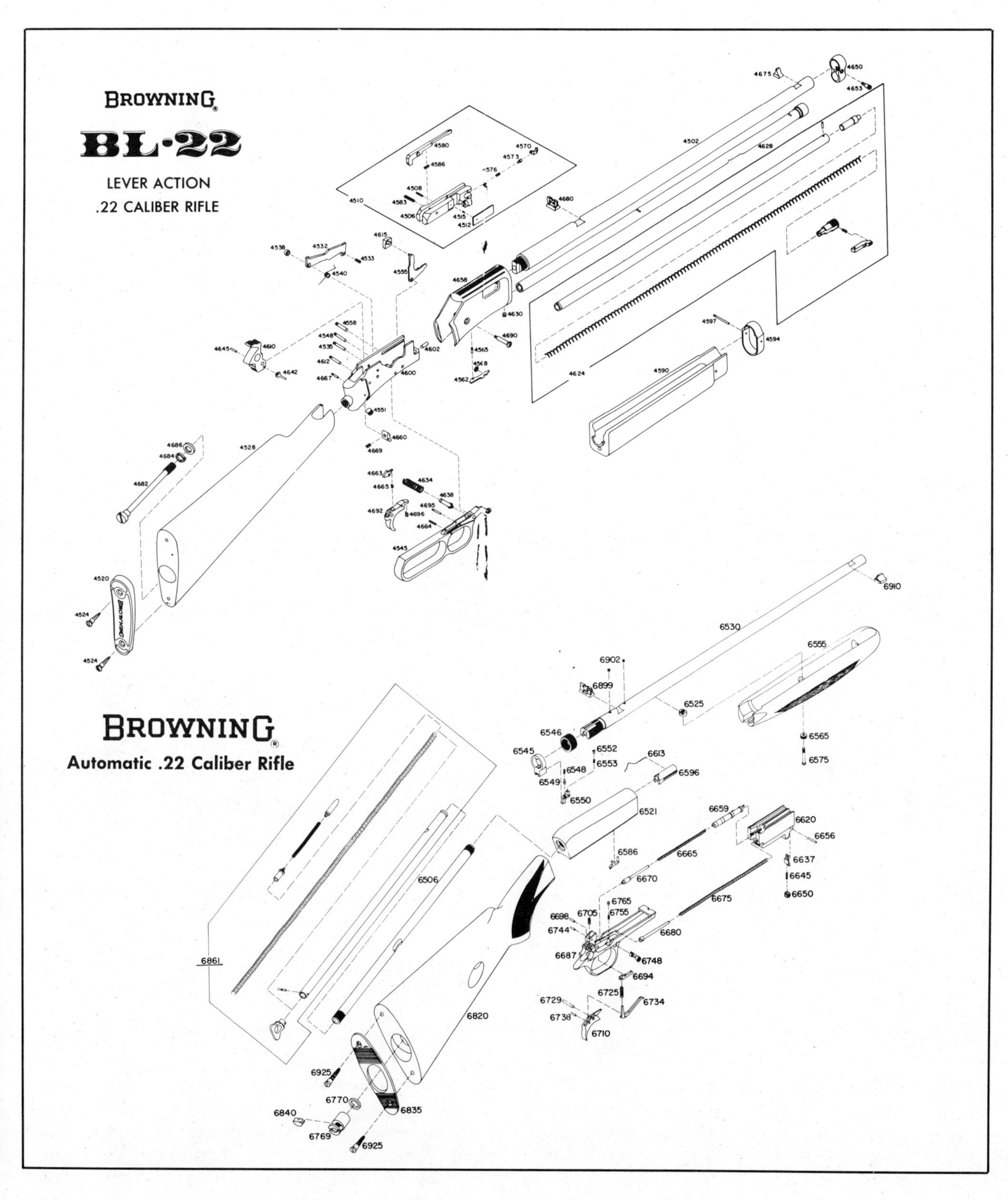

Exploded views can be extremely helpful in getting a diassembled gun back together.

Rifle	Price in 1972	Price in 1982	Percent Increase
Mossberg			
Model 26B	$ 15	$ 45	200
Model 30	12	40	233
Model 34	12	40	233
Model 35	25	90	260
Model 35A	20	60	200
Model 35A-LS	25	75	200
Model 40	15	45	200
Model 42	18	55	205
Model 42A	18	55	205
Model 42B	18	55	205
Model 42M	25	85	240
Model 43	25	75	200
Model 44	18	55	205
Model 44B	30	90	200
Model 44US	30	100	233
Model 45	18	55	205
Model 45A	18	55	205
Model 45B	20	60	200
Model 45C	15	45	200
Model 46	18	55	205
Model 46A	20	60	200
Model 46B	25	60	140
Model 46C	20	60	200
Model 46M	28	70	150
Model 51	30	75	150
Model 140K	27	60	122
Model 142-A	25	60	140
Model 144	35	95	171
Model 146B	30	70	133
Model 152	30	90	200
Model 320B	30	70	133
Model 352K	35	70	100
Model 402	45	90	100
Model 430	40	75	87
Noble			
Model 10	10	30	200
Model 20	10	30	200
Model 33	25	50	100
Model 222	14	35	150
Model 236	28	45	60
Remington			
No. 2 Sporting	50	245	390
No. 4	50	175	250
No. 6	45	150	233
No. 7	150	525	250
Model 12A	50	160	220
Model 16	45	195	333

Rifle	Price in 1972	Price in 1982	Percent Increase
Remington			
Model 24A	$ 60	$ 225	275
Model 33	20	55	175
Model 34	30	95	216
Model 37, 1937	110	425	286
Model 37, 1940	150	350	133
Model 40X Heavyweight	130	300	130
Model 341A	30	60	100
Model 510A	23	75	226
Model 510X	25	55	220
Model 511A	28	65	132
Model 511P	30	65	116
Model 512A	30	65	116
Model 512X	30	75	150
Model 513TR	70	160	128
Model 513S	50	150	200
Model 514	18	90	400
Model 552A	50	95	90
Model 572A	50	100	100
Nylon 66 "Mohawk Brown"	35	75	114
Nylon 76	35	75	114
Nylon 12	25	65	160
Ruger			
Model 10/22 Standard	40	70	75
Model 10/22 Sporter	45	80	77
Savage			
Model 3	18	55	205
Model 4	25	70	180
Model 6	35	90	157
Model 19 N.R.A.	45	175	288
Model 19 Target Rifle	75	180	140
Model 25	35	200	471
Model 29	45	175	288
Model 71	95	125	31
Model 1903	25	145	480
Model 1904	15	55	266
Model 1905	15	55	266
Model 1909	25	175	600
Model 1912	30	325	983
Model 1914	30	200	566
Stevens			
"Favorite" No. 17	30	125	316
"Visible Loading"	30	140	366
"Armory Model"	100	325	225
"Little Scout"	25	85	240
"Jr. Target Model"	25	50	100
"Walnut Hill" No. 417-0	175	500	185
"Walnut Hill" No. 417½	160	500	212

Rifle	Price in 1972	Price in 1982	Percent Increase
Stevens			
"Walnut Hill" No. 418	$ 75	$ 290	286
"Walnut Hill" No. 418½	75	270	260
"Buckhorn" No. 076	20	55	175
"Buckhorn" Model 53	12	40	233
Stevens-Springfield			
Model 15	12	30	150
Model 82	12	30	150
Model 86	25	45	80
Model 87	27	60	122
Model 87-S	27	60	122
Steyr Small Bore Carbine	125	350	180
U.S. Model 1922-MI 22	125	375	100
Walther Olympic	250	700	180
Weatherby Mark XXII			
De Luxe 22	85	175	118
Winchester			
Model 02	25	80	220
Model 04	25	90	260
Model 03	45	300	566
Model 06	45	350	677
Model 52 Sporting	150	895	496
Model 52 Target	75	375	400
Model 57	40	195	387

Rifle	Price in 1972	Price in 1982	Percent Increase
Winchester			
Model 58	$ 15	$ 90	100
Model 59	20	125	525
Model 60	25	90	260
Model 60A	30	145	383
Model 61	75	395	426
Model 61 Magnum	75	425	466
Model 62	60	395	558
Model 63	100	395	295
Model 67	25	110	340
Model 67 Boy's	25	110	340
Model 69	35	125	257
Model 73	300	1,500	400
Model 75	70	250	257
Model 77	30	150	400
Model 250	45	80	77
Model 255	50	90	80
Model 250 De Luxe	60	100	66
Model 255 De Luxe	65	120	84
Model 270	45	80	77
Model 290	45	65	44
Musket	125	395	216
Sporting Rifle	125	1,000	700

9. Handgun Trading

No particular time of year appears to be the best for trading in handguns—the business is good all year long. Manufacturers cannot seem to supply enough handguns to meet the current demand—especially the Smith & Wessons. Most dealers are allotted a certain number each month and they are sold on a first-come basis. In fact, I've been trying to obtain one particular S&W pistol for a customer for more than a year, and I've yet to receive it. Distributors merely say, "Perhaps next month."

Proposed and enacted firearm legislation is one critical factor that boosts handgun sales. Many people are afraid the guns will be banned in their cities over the next few years, and they want to make sure they have a handgun for self-protection before the laws are passed. Also, with crime increasing at a rapid pace, homeowners who have never owned any type of firearm before are finding that they feel safer with a handgun loaded in the drawer of their bedside table.

Regardless of the reasons, you can be certain that handguns will be on the best-seller list for a long time to come, and any workable, safe handgun is certain to rise in value over the years.

Models Currently in Demand

The modern handguns most in demand at this writing are those manufactured by Smith & Wesson. German Walthers are coveted by many and are bringing a good sum. The American Walther, distributed by Interarms, is also becoming very popular, but not commanding the money that its German-made counterpart does. Other than the Single Action Army Model, Colt handguns seem to be losing some of their popularity; perhaps production is keeping up with demand, while Smith & Wesson's is not. I understand that Smith & Wesson has several good contracts with foreign governments to supply their handguns in 9mm, and I would imagine that these contracts are taking first priority.

In looking at the workmanship of Smith & Wesson and Colt handguns, both are top quality when compared to the majority of production firearms manufactured today. In testing a Colt Trooper Mark III in .357 Magnum along with an S&W Model 19 (also in .357 Magnum), both obtained about the same smoothness and accuracy.

The SIG is another modern handgun that has doubled in value (and retail price) over the past few years. It is a well-made pistol, but any handgun that retails for nearly $1,500 is too much money for me. For my money, the Walther—selling for much less—is just as good.

Any of the better handguns are capable of performing the function for which they were intended, and selecting one for yourself boils down to your own preference. For my own use, I want a handgun that is light,

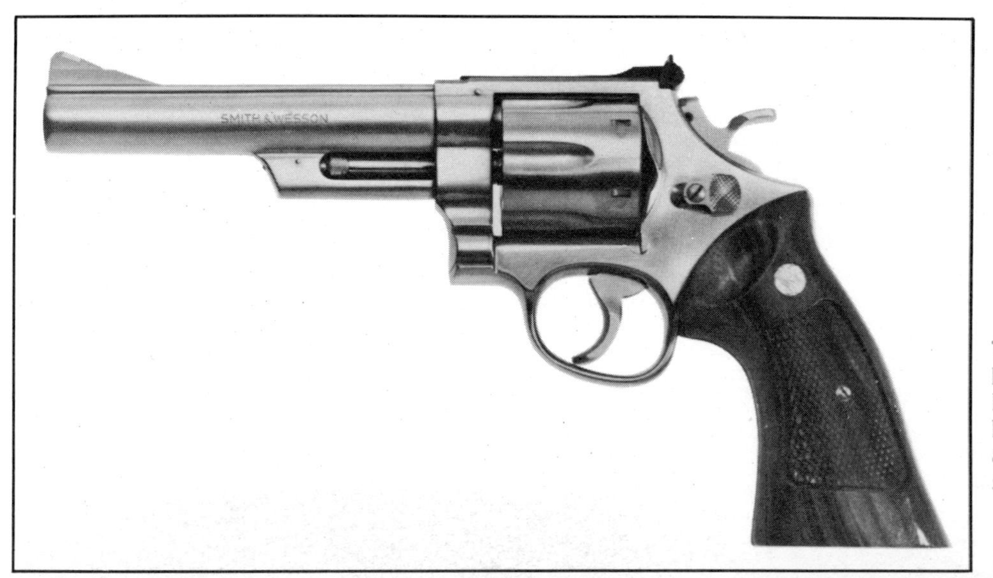

The most popular modern handguns are those made by Smith & Wesson. At left is the S&W Model 629, a .44 Magnum in stainless steel.

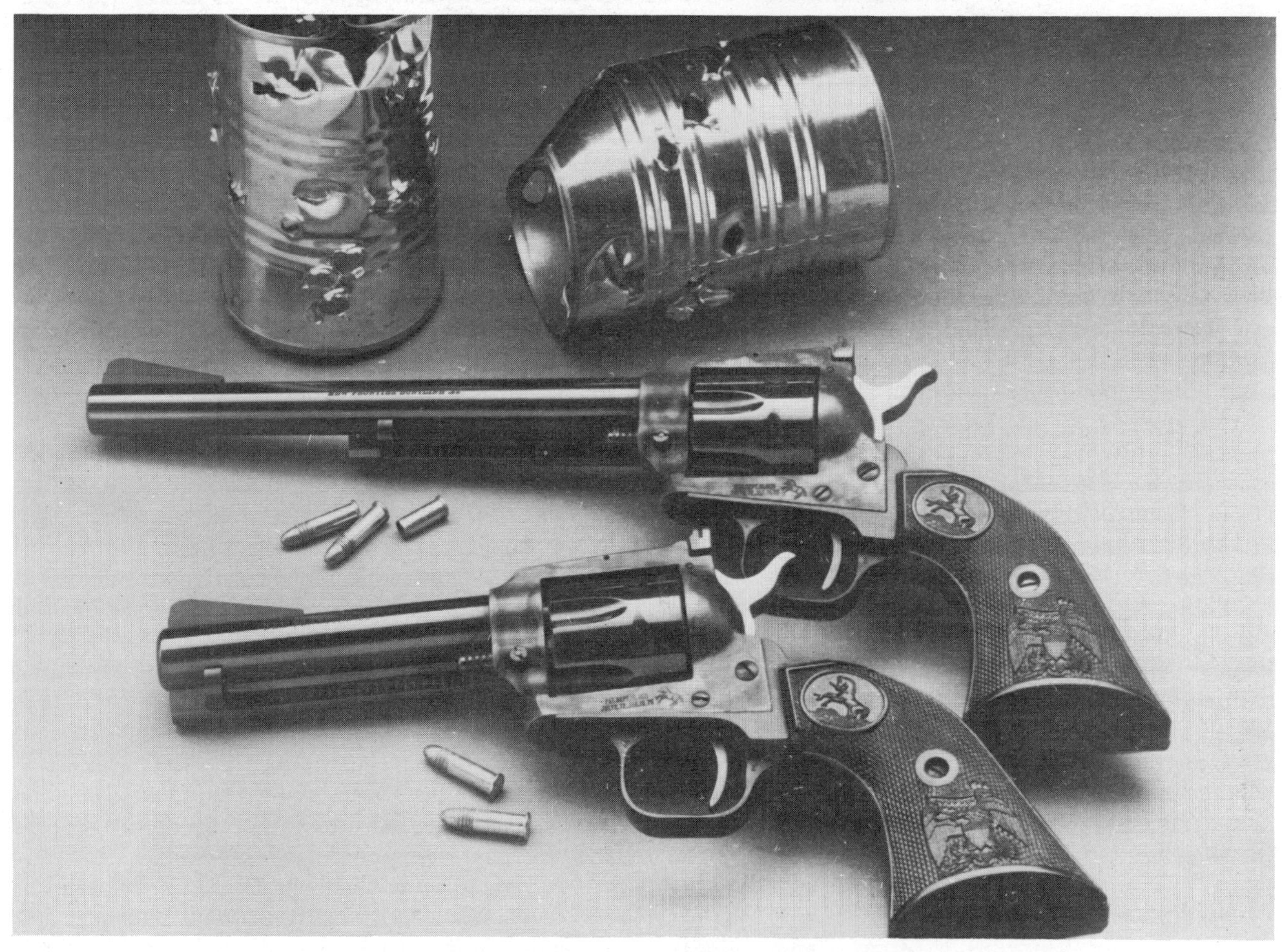

Colt single-action revolvers, shown here in the .22 rimfire version, remain much in demand for plinking and small game hunting, and are among the most trouble-free handguns manufactured today.

compact and, above all, has good accuracy. You can have all the firepower in the world, but if you can't hit anything, what good is it? The handgun I carry and use the most is the S&W Model 19 Combat Magnum, chambered for .357 Magnum. My handgun has a 2½-inch barrel and can be carried all day on my belt without tiring me out. It usually accompanies me on fishing trips where it's loaded with No. 9 shot cartridges for use on snakes; the last three rounds are full-power 160-grain Keith bullets backed by 15 grain of 2400 powder, in case a bear should want to fight over a fishing hole. At 30 yards, I can hit a squirrel every time, firing the revolver with no rest. A deer is "gone" from 100 yards on down. It also offers home protection. Since I don't shoot competition any longer, this is really the only handgun I need. If I were going to buy another, it would be a High Standard .22 rimfire autoloader.

The gun you buy should be one that you are comfortable with and one with which you are able to hit what you aim at. What good is a .44 Magnum if you flinch every time you pull the trigger and can't hit the broad side of a barn door? Both the .41 Magnum and .44 Magnum are difficult to master for beginning handgunners; the .357 Magnum doesn't pack quite as much

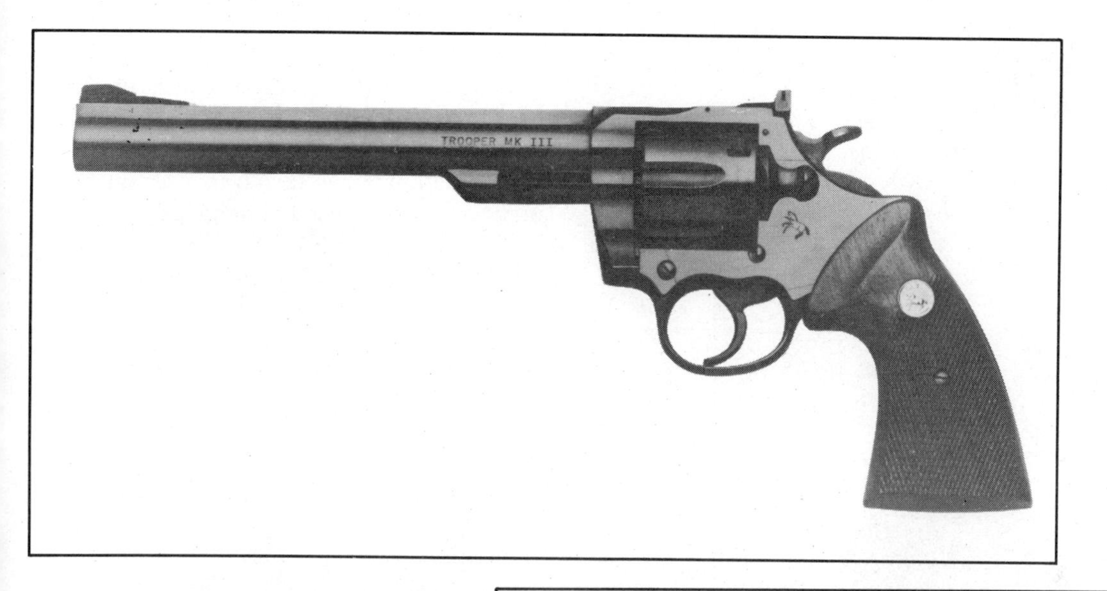

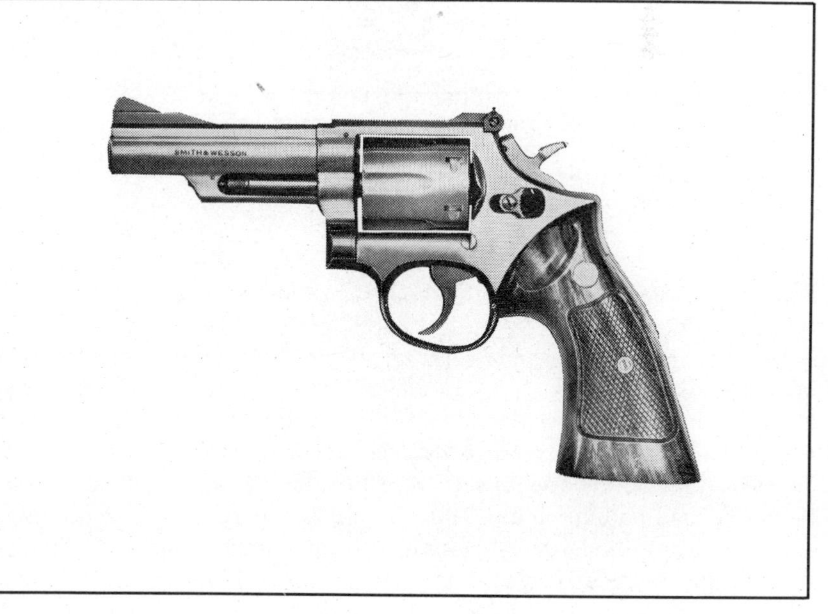

In terms of workmanship and accuracy, the Colts and Smith & Wessons are comparable as top-quality arms. Two examples are the 357 Magnum Colt MK III (above) and the S&W Model 66.

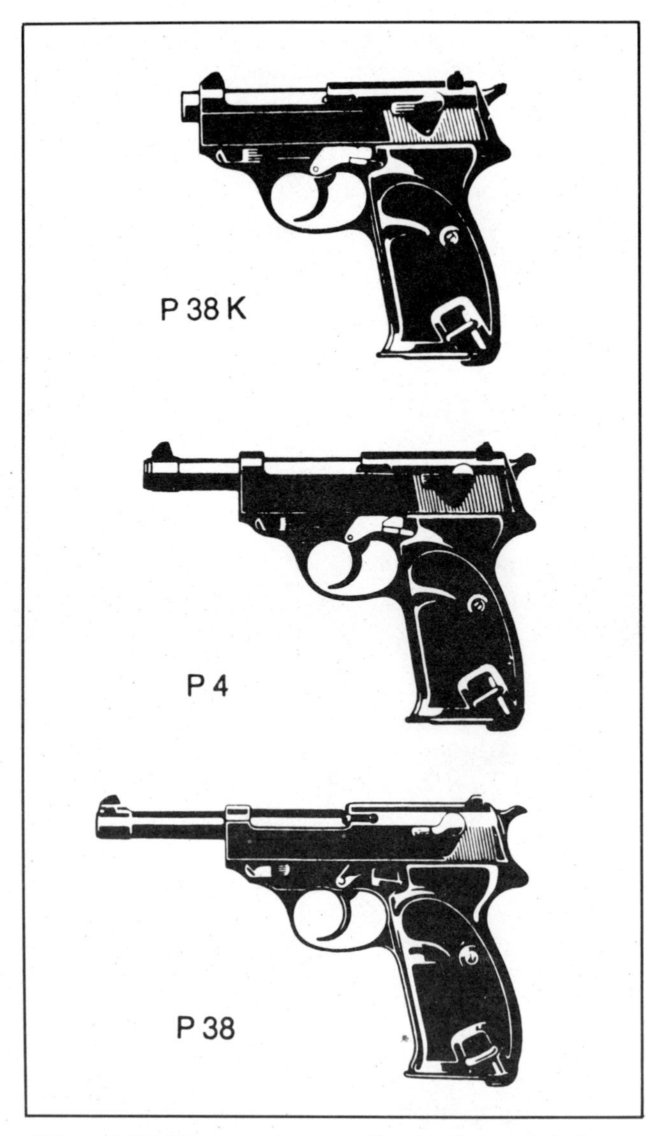

Although Walther semiautomatic pistols seem to be the models preferred by most handgun enthusiasts, they are not always the ones they buy because of lack of availability and exorbitant prices.

punch, and it's easier to learn to shoot than the larger Magnums. You can use .38 Special cartridges for low report and recoil and then work up to the heavier Magnum loads.

Of course, if you just want a handgun to plink with and perhaps pop a squirrel or two, a .22 rimfire is fine. This is not the best choice for self-protection, but it may be better than nothing in a life-threatening situation.

Countless millions of handguns have been manufactured in the past, and it would not surprise me to find that over 50 million of these are currently in the possession of U.S. citizens.

The average handgun is presently purchased in part for home-defense, which means that it is fired very little when compared to those used for competition, plinking and hunting. These seldom-fired handguns remain in the household for generations. Then these guns are sold for various reasons and become part of the massive used gun market. Police departments buy hundreds of thousands of new guns each year; so what becomes of the ones that are replaced? In most instances, they are traded as partial payment for the new ones, or else they are auctioned off—usually allowing law enforcement personnel to have first bid on them. Many of these trade-ins enter the used gun market. Add to this the hundreds of thousands of gun enthusiasts, each of whom buys dozens of new guns each year, and it's no wonder the number of used handguns on the market is overwhelming. The turnover is astonishing!

The condition of these used guns ranges from useless junks to the finest models valued at several hundred dollars, to priceless antiques and objects of art demanding five-figure prices and more.

The autoloading pistols available on the used market may be broken down into several classes. First, there are the rare collector models such as the Lugers, Mausers, etc., which will bring a mid-four-figure price if they are in good condition. The sporting-type .22 rimfire pistols come next; most are manufactured domestically and include the non-target Colt Woodsman models and variations, plus the similar products of High Standard and Ruger.

Pocket pistols are in a category of their own and include such models as the tiny palm-sized pistols in .22 rimfire and .25 ACP, and the larger .32 and .380 ACP pistols by Walther, Llama and Mauser. The military and police types are typified by the 1911 Colt Government Model and the S&W Model 39, as well as the Walther P38 and similar models.

Revolvers may also be classified as inexpensive plinking and hunting models such as manufactured by H&R, Iver Johnson and others. The police versions such as the Colt Trooper Mark III and S&W Model 19 Combat Magnum have now flooded the market. Then comes the competition models that have been customized just for a particular shooter—costing upward of $500 in addition to the original cost of the arm. There are others.

When buying a handgun for practical use, choose one whose original manufacturer is still in business and

This High Standard automatic pistol is hard to beat for plinking and small-game hunting.

from whom parts are still available. If you receive word that a handgun that you own has become obsolete, it would be wise to buy several of the most critical parts (those more than likely to give the most trouble) and save them, should you need them at a later date; a firing pin or two, an extractor and other such parts as one may determine from the design and experience and references might require replacement in the future.

When buying autoloading pistols, one particular class should be avoided. These are the Spanish autos manufactured under innumerable names by countless companies from about 1910 until the mid-1930's. Such guns were quite often crudely made and contained the cheapest materials available at the time. Dimensional control of critical areas—like chambers and bores—was very poor, with the tendency to be oversized to avoid high pressures and to facilitate functioning. The principal problems encountered with these handguns are poor design, soft working parts (which wear rapidly or damage easily), substandard workmanship and consequently poor functioning, short service life and low durability.

Some Spanish makers, however, produced guns of excellent quality. The Astra trademark means a good-quality handgun. So do those marked "Star." Gabilondo y Cia manufactured excellent autoloaders during this era. While the pistols manufactured by this latter firm have appeared under a variety of names, most of them have been made under the name "Llama." Slightly modified and improved since, they are available today exclusively from Stoeger Industries in the United States, and are highly regarded by many shooters.

Evaluating Condition

As with other firearms, handguns are evaluated by either the NRA Method or by the percentage of original bluing remaining on the gun. The former may leave room for debate, since one man's "excellent" may be another man's "very good." With the percentage method, it's difficult to make a mistake unless it's intentional.

Besides the outside condition, you will want to check several items on the inside. As with rifles, you will want to inspect the bore in all handguns prior to purchasing. Many have seen years of neglect, resulting in pitting. While lapping may help solve the problem, it

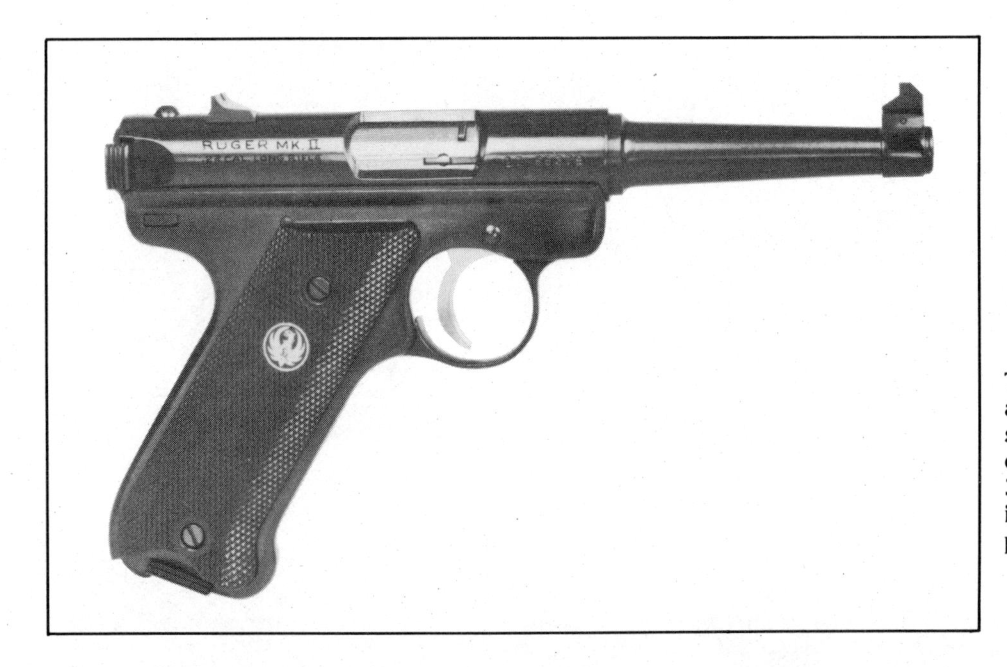

This Ruger MK.II semiautomatic pistol and its several variations have been extremely popular for over 30 years, due to its pleasing lines and relatively low price.

may not; and if the handgun is one for which there are no longer parts available, you may be one disappointed buyer.

When examining a handgun with the possibility of purchasing it, look at the gun's general condition. If it looks as though it has been taken care of, chances are the gun will function properly; most problems occurring with a double-action revolver usually can be traced directly to mistreatment by one of its owners. In some cases, a thorough cleaning of the revolver will solve many of the problems; this gets rid of lead, bullet lubricants and other residue. It also enables the mechanism to be properly lubricated.

Look for signs of tinkering—damaged screw heads, scratches on the frame around screws where a screwdriver slipped off from the slot—all are signs that an amateur has mishandled the job. When these tell-tale signs occur, internal parts may have been damaged during the procedure or perhaps reassembly has been done incorrectly. So check these out thoroughly. If you want to make absolutely sure the gun is okay, first clean it and then completely disassemble the revolver and inspect all parts for wear, damage or for those that may be missing. If you are unfamiliar with the disassembly operation, use printed instructions (if available) such as the NRA Handgun Assembly book, Brownell's *Encyclopedia of Modern Firearms* or the *Gun Digest Book of Exploded Firearms Drawings.*

Other problems to look for include a misaligned cylinder, timing, a broken or weak spring, a bent ejector rod, an improperly fitted cylinder latch, failure of the cylinder to lock, worn locking slots in the cylinder, skipping, and the like.

The most common ailment in single-action revolvers is a broken trigger spring. You'll also find a broken mainspring, a broken bolt, a broken sear, a loading notch cover, etc. This does not mean that the single-action handgun is fragile. On the contrary, it's one of the least troublesome handguns manufactured. Still, these problems can occur and it doesn't take long to check them out before you buy.

Semiautomatic pistols are divided into two systems, based on the method of operating the action. The types that use low-powered centerfire and rimfire cartridges usually utilize a blowback system that doesn't use a locking mechanism to hold the breechblock in place. Instead, the weight of the breechblock and the power of the recoil spring keep the breech in place during firing.

Other types utilize a slide extending over the barrel, or what is called a delayed-blowback system. The .45 Colt Model 1911 is a good example of this system. Of course, you can also have short recoil designs or a combination system of short recoil and blowback.

Unlike the semiautomatic rifles and shotguns, autoloading pistols tend to malfunction less than other types of handguns. Many competitive shooters also prefer autoloading pistols for target work, since a revolver with a chamber hole off center or out of sync will produce poor accuracy.

When examining a semiautomatic pistol, look for

such malfunctions as jamming and failure to feed, extract or eject. These are some of the more common problems that will occur with this type of pistol. In many cases, a good cleaning is all that is required to put an ailing semiautomatic pistol back into proper shooting condition.

Finding the Right Gun or Market

Gun shows are probably the best places to buy, sell or trade. The most prestigious ones will have large displays, enabling you to compare prices easily. You will be able to see all sorts of guns which may help you to narrow down your own interests. Once you have decided what you want to collect—Colts, Lugers, Mausers, Smith & Wessons, or what have you—read everything you can put your hands on concerning that type of weapon. Then keep updating this knowledge. And, by all means, talk to other collectors, investors and dealers who can provide you with knowledge about the models you wish to collect. When you attend gun shows, you will learn which dealers are the most reliable. You will also meet the few collectors and dealers who are not above upgrading a gun and selling it as an original something that it is not. Learn which dealers have a reputation for honesty and avoid the others.

You will want to check the advertisements in local newspapers, *Shotgun News* and other local and national publications. When buying by mail, however, always obtain at least a three-day inspection period, so you can return the firearm for a full refund if you are not completely satisfied. Most reputable dealers will grant this privilege.

To obtain the best deals, shop around and compare prices. Once you have decided on the model you like, and have obtained several prices, you may be able to pick up a bargain at even one of the flea markets or yard sales that are springing up everywhere. But, remember, these sales are usually final. If the handgun you've bought doesn't work, you'll probably have to spend additional money for the repair yourself, whereas a reputable dealer will usually guarantee all firearms sold by him.

Check local pawn shops or some of the smaller rural gun dealers who deal mainly in "working guns" and very little with collector arms. Every now and then a rare collector's model turns up in these shops that the dealer may not be familiar with. The gun may be priced as a common version when, in fact, it is a far more valuable variation, but the opposite may also be true. There is always the chance of your getting a good buy at these small shops.

If you want to start collecting handguns, you should probably join a firearm collecting association—many of which are located in various parts of the country. Then you'll be able to rub elbows with other experienced col-

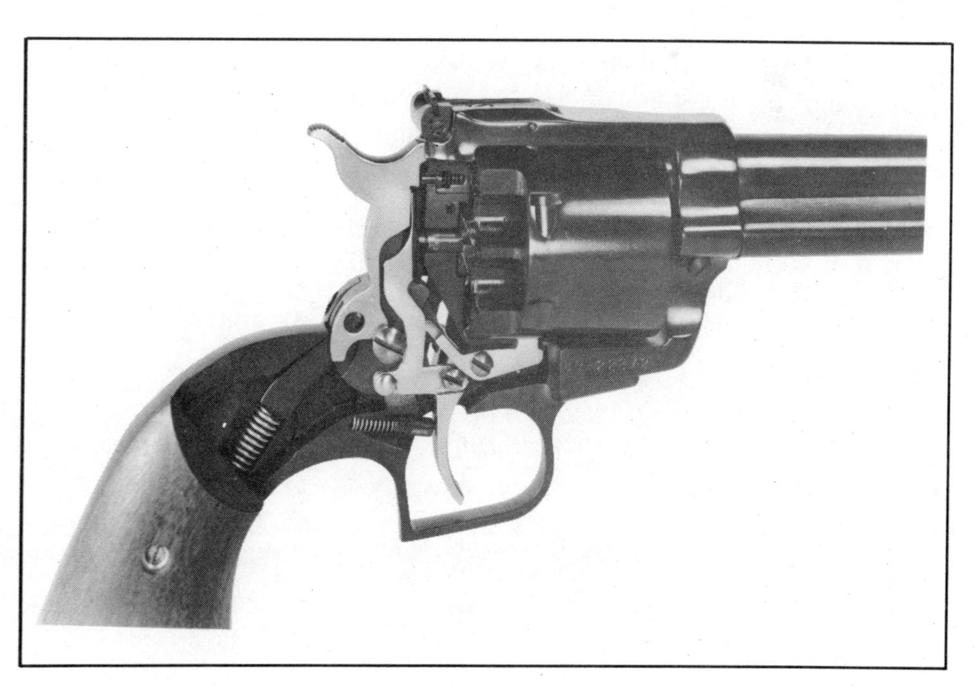

Cut-away views as well as exploded views are extremely useful when disassembling handguns for cleaning and/or repairs.

lectors who will serve as excellent sources of information, and who will often offer guidance.

If you decide to get into collecting rare, expensive models, be especially cautious of frauds. Look closely at what may first appear to be a great bargain, for "great bargains" are hard to come by these days unless someone is trying to swindle you. The greater your knowledge about a certain type of firearm, the greater will be your defense against misrepresentation or outright fraud, so do your homework and learn everything you can about your chosen area of gun collecting.

Now, if you happen to have one or two guns to sell, and they are not in the rare collector status, the best way is to consult pricing guides, and determine a fair "asking" price. Then advertise in your local newspaper. Before doing so, however, always make sure you are aware of all laws governing the sale. You will usually get the most for your gun when you sell to an individual rather than a dealer. The dealer must make a profit and will therefore only give you from 60 to 80 percent of the gun's value . . . perhaps not even that much if he has plenty of the same models in stock.

If you have several guns in the collector status, you may want to consider renting table display space at a trade show. Check the advertisements in *Shotgun News*, then write or call about making an application for table space. Listed in Appendix II are gun shows and some of the organizations that regularly sponsor them. A letter to any one of them should bring a prompt reply.

Price Trends in Handguns

In comparing prices of used handguns sold in the U.S. over the past 10 years, you will find that all have increased to some extent. Some more so than others.

Used handguns are usually valued at about 30 percent below retail price if they are in excellent condition, but new ones of the same model usually can be readily purchased from dealers. Used handguns that are harder to come by—like the Smith & Wessons—often bring more.

Handgun	Price in 1972	Price in 1982	Percent Increase
American 25 Automatic	$ 40	$ 140	250
Astra			
Model 200	50	120	140
Model 400	75	210	180
Model 600	50	350	600
Model 3000	50	175	250
Model Cub	50	165	230

Handgun	Price in 1972	Price in 1982	Percent Increase
Bayard			
Model 1908	$ 50	$ 160	220
Model 1923, 25 Cal.	50	325	550
Model 1923, 32 Cal.	50	150	200
Model 1930	50	150	200
Beretta			
25	50	210	320
32	60	260	333
380	60	230	283
Jaguar Plinker	60	175	195
Jetfire	50	110	120
Minx M2	50	115	130
Minx M4	50	130	160
Olimpionico	150	450	200
Puma	60	185	208
Bernardelli			
Pocket	60	135	125
"Sporter"	65	225	275
Vest Pocket	50	160	220
Browning			
25	50	210	320
380	60	280	366
Challenger	70	210	200
Hi-Power 9mm	95	290	205
Medalist	110	475	331
Nomad	55	225	309
Renaissance Set	600	1,300	116
Charter Arms Undercover	55	135	145
Colt Automatics			
Ace	150	500	233
Challenger	50	175	250
Commander Lightweight	85	275	223
45-22 Conversion	75	150	100
Gold Cup Mark III	130	525	303
Gold Cup Nat'l Match 45	120	450	275
Gov't Model	90	365	305
Huntsman	50	190	280
Junior Colt Pocket Model	50	140	180
Match Target	80	300	275
Match Target "4½"	80	300	275
Military 38	200	450	125
Military Model 45	250	610	144
Model 1900 38 Auto	175	485	177
National Match	200	600	200
Pocket Model 25	100	240	140
Pocket Model 32, 1st	85	210	147
Pocket Model 32, 2nd	85	225	164
Pocket Model 32, 3rd	85	225	164
Pocket 38	125	235	88

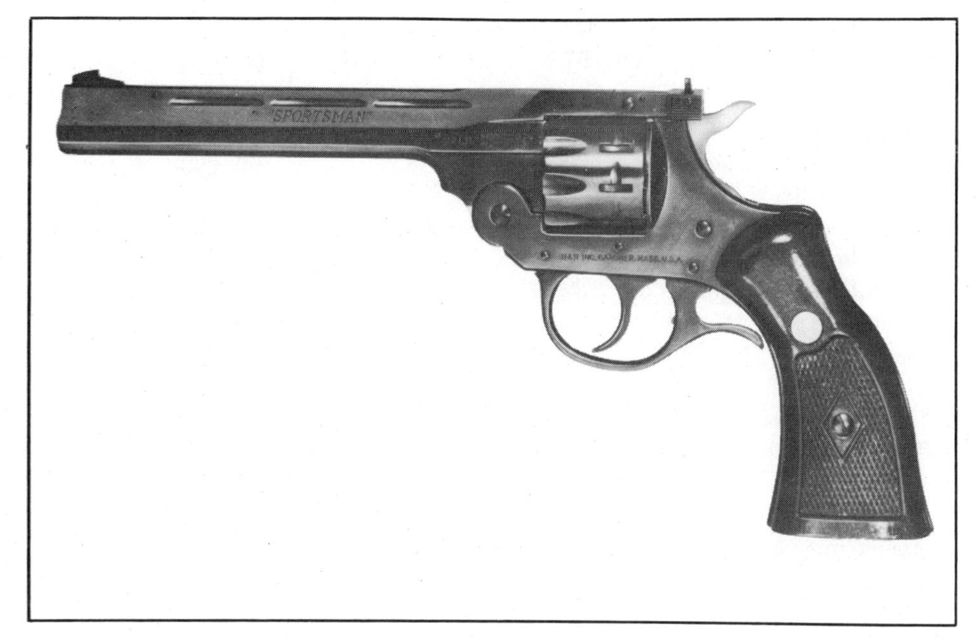

H&R Top Break Model 999 revolvers are highly recommended to purchasers of used guns because of their reliability and ready availability at reasonable prices.

Handgun	Price in 1972	Price in 1982	Percent Increase
Colt Automatics			
Pocket Model 380, 1st	$ 85	$ 225	164
Pocket Model 380, 2nd	85	225	164
Pocket Model 380, 3rd	85	225	164
Service Model Ace	300	550	83
Sporting 38, 1902	150	460	206
Super Match	200	600	200
Super 38	85	365	329
22-45 Conversion	40	95	137
Woodsman Sport Model, 1st	100	325	225
Woodsman Sport Model, 2nd	70	295	321
Woodsman Target, 1st	90	325	261
Woodsman Target, 2nd	100	350	250
Match Target Woodsman, 1st	250	500	100
Woodsman Target Model	70	295	321
Woodsman Targetsman	55	200	263
WWI 50th Anniversary	250	410	64
WWII Commemorative 45	250	475	90
Colt Revolvers			
Agent	70	190	171
Army Revolver	350	2,000	471
Army Special	90	260	188
Bankers' Special	80	320	300
Bisley Model	200	845	322

Handgun	Price in 1972	Price in 1982	Percent Increase
Colt Revolvers			
Buntline Scout	$ 60	$ 160	166
Buntline Special 45	150	480	220
Camp Perry, 1st	250	600	140
Camp Perry, 2nd	300	995	231
Civil War	60	95	58
Cobra Detective	70	300	328
Cobra Police	70	315	350
Deringer No. 4	30	80	166
Deringer No. 4 Commemorative	325	600	84
Detective	65	250	284
Diamondback	95	275	89
Frontier Scout	45	195	333
Marine Corps	200	750	275
New Frontier Army	160	375	134
New Frontier Buntline	175	540	208
New Navy	100	300	200
New Pocket	80	260	225
New Police	80	255	218
New Police Target	80	285	256
New Service	90	335	272
New Service Target	150	540	260
Officers' Model Match	100	255	155
Officers' Model Special	90	255	183
Officers' Target, 1st	125	600	380
Officers' Target, 2nd	150	650	420

Handgun	Price in 1972	Price in 1982	Percent Increase
Colt Revolvers			
Official Police	$ 70	$ 215	207
125th Anniversary Model	325	545	67
Pocket Positive	80	230	187
Police Positive	75	325	333
Police Positive Special	65	215	230
Police Positive Target	100	325	225
Python	130	375	188
Rock Island	125	195	56
Sheriff's Model 45	450	1,200	166
Shooting Master	200	640	220
Three-Fifty-Seven	90	240	166
Trooper	90	235	161
Colt Army Commemoratives			
Abercrombie & Fitch—Chicago	850	2,040	140
Abercrombie & Fitch—N.Y.	850	2,000	135
Abercrombie & Fitch—S.F.	850	2,000	135
Appomattox Centennial	350	600	71
Arizona Territorial	350	600	71
California Gold Rush	500	840	68
Chamizal Treaty	550	1,000	81
Col. Sam Colt Sesquicentennial	400	525	31
General Meade	425	740	74
Lawman Series—Earp	750	1,340	78
Lawman Series—Garrett	350	645	84
Lawman Series—Hickock	350	640	82
Lawman Series—Masterson	375	650	73
Missouri Sesquicentennial	275	555	101
Montana Territorial	375	600	60
NRA Centennial	250	550	120
Nevada "Battle Born"	550	950	72
Nevada Statehood	300	600	100
New Jersey Tercentenary	425	525	23
Old Fort Des Moines	400	700	75
Pony Express Presentation	400	750	87
St. Louis Bicentennial	350	425	21
Texas Ranger	650	1,340	106
W.V. Statehood	350	600	71
Wyatt Earp Buntline	700	1,550	121
Colt Frontier Scout Commemoratives			
Alabama Sesquicentennial	150	275	83

Handgun	Price in 1972	Price in 1982	Percent Increase
Colt Frontier Scout Commemoratives			
Alamo	$ 150	$ 275	83
Appomattox Cent.	200	275	37
Arizona Territorial	175	275	57
Arkansas Territory Sesquicentennial	110	245	122
Battle of Gettysburg	200	275	37
California Bicentennial	135	275	103
California Gold Rush	225	320	42
Carolina Charter Tercentenary	250	350	40
Chamizal Treaty	175	320	82
Colorado Gold Rush	175	275	57
Columbus Sesquicentennial	425	600	41
Dakota Territory	175	275	57
Ft. Findley Sesquicentennial	425	600	41
Ft. Stephenson Sesquicentennial	425	600	41
Forty-Niner Miner	200	275	37
Gen. Forrest	150	275	83
Gen. Hood Centennial	175	275	57
Gen. Meade Campaign	175	275	57
Gen. Morgan Indiana Raid	550	810	47
Golden Spike	150	275	83
Idaho Territory Centennial	250	350	40
Indiana Sesquicent.	150	275	83
Kansas Cowtown Series			
Abilene	200	320	60
Coffeyville	200	320	60
Dodge	200	320	60
Wichita	200	315	57
Kansas Fort Series			
Ft. Hays	130	275	111
Ft. Larned	150	275	83
Ft. Riley	130	275	111
Ft. Scott	130	275	111
Kansas Statehood	200	275	37
Kansas Trail Series			
Chisholm Trail	150	275	83
Pawnee Trail	150	275	83
Shawnee Trail	150	275	83
Lawman Series			
Wyatt Earp	175	350	100
Pat Garrett	200	320	60
Wild Bill Hickock	175	320	82
Bat Masterson	200	320	60
Maine Sesquicentennial	120	275	129

Handgun	Price in 1972	Price in 1982	Percent Increase
Colt Frontier Scout Commemoratives			
Missouri Sesquicentennial	$ 125	$ 275	120
Montana Territorial	200	275	37
Nebraska Centennial	125	275	120
Nevada "Battle Born"	175	275	57
Nevada Statehood Centenary	150	275	83
N.J. Tercentenary	175	275	57
New Mexico Golden Anniversary	225	315	40
Oklahoma Territory	175	275	57
Old Ft. Des Moines	200	315	57
Oregon Trail	150	275	83
Pony Express Centennial	350	490	40
St. Augustine Quadricentennial	200	315	57
St. Louis Bicentennial	175	275	57
W.V. Statehood Centennial	200	250	25
Wyoming Diamond Jub.	175	275	57
CZ			
"Duo"	50	125	150
Model 27	60	170	183
Model 1938	60	180	200
New Model .006	50	185	270
Pocket	60	150	150
Dreyse			
Model 1907	50	395	690
Vest Pocket	50	175	250
DWM Pocket Automatic	65	200	207
Enfield No. 2 Mark I	50	125	150
Erma			
Automatic Target	45	145	222
Luger Conversion	35	145	314
FN Browning			
6.35 mm	85	240	182
Baby	50	140	180
Model 1900	50	160	220
Model 1910	60	155	158
Mil. Mod. 1903	75	180	140
Mil. Model 1935	150	480	220
Pol. & Mil. 1922	65	135	107
Fiala Repeating Pistol	125	375	200
Frommer			
Stop Pocket	45	140	211
Baby Pocket	55	175	218
Galesi Model 9	45	115	155
Glisenti Model 1910	60	220	266

Handgun	Price in 1972	Price in 1982	Percent Increase
Great Western			
Single	$ 75	$ 175	133
Double	35	75	114
Hämmerli			
Model 100	200	805	302
Walther Model 200	200	640	220
Harrington & Richardson			
American	25	60	140
Automatic Ejecting	30	100	233
Bobby	40	105	162
Defender 38	40	110	175
Double Action, Small	35	75	114
Double Action, Large	35	75	114
Expert Model	40	100	150
Hunter Model	35	90	157
Model 4	25	55	120
Model 5	25	60	140
Model 6	25	60	140
Model 622	25	55	120
Model 632 Guardsman	35	60	71
Model 732	35	70	100
Model 900	30	60	100
Model 922	35	75	114
Model 925	40	75	87
Model 929 Side-Kick	35	70	100
Model 939	45	90	100
Model 949	30	70	133
New Defender	60	150	150
No. 199 Sportsman	50	120	140
No. 999 Sportsman	50	115	130
Premier	30	60	100
Self-Loading Pistol	60	230	283
Target Model	35	85	142
Trapper Model	35	75	114
22 Special	40	95	137
Ultra Sportsman	60	160	166
USRA Model	125	390	212
Vest Pocket	25	60	225
Young America	25	60	225
Hartford			
Automatic Target	75	325	333
Repeater	75	290	286
Single Shot	75	290	286
High Standard			
Derringer	90	150	66
Double-Nine	45	110	144
Dura-Matic	40	90	125
Field-King	55	150	172

Handgun	Price in 1972	Price in 1982	Percent Increase
High Standard			
Flite-King, 1st	$ 50	$ 160	220
Flite-King, 2nd	55	125	127
Longhorn	45	125	177
Model A	50	175	250
Model H-A	50	175	250
Model B	40	220	450
Model H-B	40	175	337
Model C	45	190	322
Model D	60	225	275
Model H-D	60	225	275
Model H-DM	65	225	246
Model E	75	270	260
Model H-E	75	250	233
Model G-380	50	255	410
Model G-B	50	180	260
Model G-D	60	220	266
Model G-E	75	275	266
Natchez	45	125	177
Olympic, 1st	85	390	358
Olympic, 2nd	70	220	214
Olympic I.S.U.	95	225	136
Posse	45	100	122
Sentinel	40	90	125
Sentinel Deluxe	45	105	133
Sentinel Imperial	45	105	133
Sentinel Snub	45	120	166
Sport-King, 1st	50	150	200
Sport-King, 2nd	50	125	150
Lightweight Sport-King	50	160	220
Supermatic	60	200	233
Supermatic Citation	65	215	230
Supermatic Tournament	60	200	233
Supermatic Trophy	80	225	181
Iver Johnson			
Armsworth Model 855	40	125	212
Champion 22	45	110	144
Model 50A	30	85	183
Model 55A	30	60	100
Model 55S-A	30	90	200
Model 57A	32	75	134
Model 66	35	85	142
Model 67	40	100	150
Model 67S	40	95	137
Model 1900	20	75	275
Model 1900 Target	30	85	183
Protector Sealed 8	45	125	212
Safety Hammer	30	75	150
Safety Hammerless	35	95	171

Handgun	Price in 1972	Price in 1982	Percent Increase
Iver Johnson			
Supershot Model 844	$ 40	$ 95	137
Supershot Nine-Shot	40	95	137
Supershot Sealed 8	50	125	150
Target 9	30	85	183
Target Sealed 8	35	95	171
Trigger-Cocking	45	110	144
22 Supershot	30	75	150
Japanese Model 14 (1925)	50	190	280
Japanese Model 94 (1934)	40	190	375
Japanese Nambu Model 1914	60	225	275
Lahti Automatic Pistol	150	520	246
Le Francais			
Army	45	110	144
Policeman	45	110	144
Staff Officer	45	105	133
Lignose			
Einhand Model 2A	60	180	200
Einhand Model 3A	60	180	200
Model 2	40	135	237
Llama			
Model III	50	170	240
Model VIII, 38 Cal.	75	210	180
Model IX	55	210	281
Model X	50	170	240
Luger Parabellum	200	350	75
Luna Free Pistol	200	920	360
Mauser			
Auto. Pocket	85	200	135
Military Model	200	1,200	500
Model HSs Pocket	70	325	364
WTP Model, 1st	75	225	200
WTP Model, 2nd	90	250	177
Ortgies			
Pocket, 25 Cal.	50	130	160
Pocket, 32 & 380 Cal.	50	130	160
Radom P-35	60	270	350
Record-Match			
Model 200 Free	250	800	220
Model 210 Free	500	1,100	110
Reising Automatic	100	345	245
Remington			
Model 51	90	350	288
Model 95	100	700	600
New Model	150	900	500
Ruger			
Bearcat	30	185	516
Blackhawk 44 Magnum	75	275	266

Handgun	Price in 1972	Price in 1982	Percent Increase
Ruger			
Blackhawk 357 Magnum	$ 70	$ 150	114
Hawkeye	75	800	966
Mark I	45	120	166
Single-Six	45	110	144
Single-Six Lightweight	45	240	433
Standard	30	280	833
Super Blackhawk	90	275	205
Super-Single Six Convertible	55	170	209
Russian Tokarev Service	70	225	221
Sauer			
Model H	75	225	200
Pocket 25	50	160	220
Pocket, 1913	50	160	220
Pocket, 1930	60	220	266
Savage			
Model 1910	75	145	93
Model 1917	75	175	133
Sedgley Baby	35	130	271
Sheridan Knocabout	20	70	250
Smith & Wesson Automatics			
32 Automatic	350	1,200	242
35 Automatic	150	800	433
Model 39 9mm	350	750	114
Model 41 22	100	300	200
Model 46 22	80	400	400
Model 52 38	150	420	180
Straight Line	250	600	140
Smith & Wesson Revolvers			
32	75	205	173
38	75	650	766
38 Perfected	75	475	533
44 (1881-1913)	135	750	418
44 (1915-1937)	75	430	900
1917	70	400	471
1926 Model 44, Military	100	650	531
1926 Model 44, Target	150	500	233
Combat Masterpiece	70	180	157
22/32	80	450	462
22/32 Kit Gun	80	215	168
K-22 Masterpiece	90	595	561
K-22 Outdoorsman	90	390	333
K-32	85	700	723
K32 and K38	80	175	118
Mil. & Pol.	60	270	350
38 Mil. & Police	85	200	135
Model 10	65	360	453
Smith & Wesson			
Model 12 38	$ 65	$ 170	161
Models 17, 48, 16, 14	80	175	118
Model 19 357 Magnum	100	230	130
Model 20 38/44	95	400	321
Model 21 1950 44	95	360	278
Model 22 1950 Army	70	440	528
Model 23 38/44	110	525	377
Model 24 1950 44	125	490	292
Model 25 1950 45	100	450	350
Model 27 357 Magnum	350	895	155
Model 28	80	230	187
Model 29 44 Magnum	135	345	155
Model 30 32	65	200	207
Model 31 & 33	65	200	207
Model 32 Terrier	65	225	246
Model 34	80	190	137
Model 35	80	300	275
Model 36	65	175	169
Model 37	65	195	200
Model 38 (1899-1902)	75	500	246
Model 38 (1955 to date)	65	200	700
Model 40	65	325	400
Model 42	65	350	438
Model 43	80	300	275
Model 49	65	190	192
Model 51	80	325	306
Model 53 22 Magnum	105	475	352
Model 57 41 Magnum	135	300	122
Model 58 41 M&P	80	270	237
Model 60	85	300	252
Model 1891 Single Action	75	505	573
Model 1891 Single Shot	150	340	126
Model 1891 Single Shot, 2	150	340	126
Model "I"	85	465	447
Model "M"	225	715	217
New Century Model	200	570	185
No. 3 (Frontier)	250	950	280
No. 3 (New Model)	250	1,000	300
No. 3 (Target)	175	1,200	585
Perfected Single Shot	150	400	166
Reg. Police Target	85	215	152
Safety Hammerless	80	340	325
Star			
Military Model A	60	195	225
Military Model M	60	185	208
Model CO	50	135	170
Model F	40	135	237

Handgun	Price in 1972	Price in 1982	Percent Increase
Star			
Model F Sport	$ 50	$ 140	180
Model HN	45	135	200
Model H	45	135	200
Model S	55	190	245
Model SI	55	175	218
Model SI & Super S	60	200	233
Police Model I	45	135	200
Police Model IN	45	135	200
Super Star Automatic	65	230	253
Super Star Target	75	260	246
Stevens			
No. 10	45	180	300
No. 35	90	170	88
Thompson/Center Contender	100	175	75
Universal Enforcer	90	190	111
Walther			
Model 1	60	260	333
Model 2	60	260	333
Model 3	60	260	333
Model 4	70	290	314
Model 5	60	295	391
Model 6	80	375	368
Model 7	60	260	333
Model 8	75	260	246
Model 8 Lightweight	90	295	227
Model 9	75	350	366
Model HP	200	1,000	400
Walther			
Olympia Funfkampf	$ 250	$ 1,250	400
Olympia Hunting	175	675	285
Olympia Rapid Fire	200	1,000	400
Olympia Sport	175	650	271
Model PP	125	445	256
Model PP Lightweight	185	665	259
Pres. Model PP 7.65mm	200	1,350	575
Model PPK	175	700	300
Model PPK Lightweight	260	1,050	303
Pres. Model PPK	200	1,150	475
P-38	80	450	462
Self-Loader	150	600	300
Warner Infallible	45	195	333
Webley			
25 Hammer	45	140	211
25 Hammerless	45	145	222
9mm M&P	50	225	350
Fosbery	85	375	341
Mark III 38	50	150	200
Mark IV 38 M&P	50	150	200
Mark IV 22	60	170	183
Mark VI 22	60	170	183
No. 1 Mark VI 455	50	135	170
Metropolitan Police	50	145	190
"RIC"	50	140	180
"Semiautomatic"	50	200	300
Single Shot	60	225	275

10. Black Powder Trading

Since the Gun Control Act of 1968 came into effect, limiting the sales of firearms through the mails, black powder arms have steadily and rapidly increased in sales because muzzleloading arms may be shipped through the mails without any special permit or license. Also, compared to modern cartridge firearms, most of the black powder arms are very reasonable in cost. Add to this the fact that many states offer special hunting seasons for black powder firearms only, and it is understandable why the black powder guns are experiencing a new popularity.

While black powder antiques are selling very well, the real sales are in the form of reproduction black powder arms, either in finished or kit form. However, it seems that few used guns are available. I can count on my hand all the modern black powder used guns I've seen offered for sale during the past year. In other words, the owners of these guns are holding onto them, and justly so. When someone spends hours assembling one of the black powder kits, carefully attending to every detail of inletting and finishing, he or she is not so apt to part with it when so much personal effort is involved.

About the only time you'll find a used muzzleloader offered for sale is when someone graduates to a different model, and then the gun is usually sold to a friend or to someone in the seller's black powder club who has been waiting in line.

Original antique black powder arms are traded daily, and many varieties, in various conditions, are readily available, but usually for a good price. Dixie Gun Works, one of the largest dealers, probably has the biggest supply of antique black powder arms in the U.S., if not in the entire world. At any time, they will have 1,000 or more original and collector guns in stock. Their turnover in antique arms is tremendous, and they publish an updated antique arms catalog about every six months. Each gun is pictured and thoroughly described, along with any historical information that may be available. Each catalog makes an excellent reference and a fine price guide to antique arms. Write to Dixie Gun Works for complete information (see Appendix IV).

Also listed in their antique catalog are handsome custom muzzleloading rifles that they have on hand at the time of publication. No two of these rifles are alike and each is pictured and described in the catalog. Generally, a nicely styled Kentucky rifle of high quality will demand anywhere from $600 to $1,000. Occasionally, they have rifles built by some of the well-known black powder arms makers and, of course, these will bring a premium—as much as $2,000 or more.

Evaluating Condition

The grading system used for antique arms varies somewhat from the system used to evaluate modern

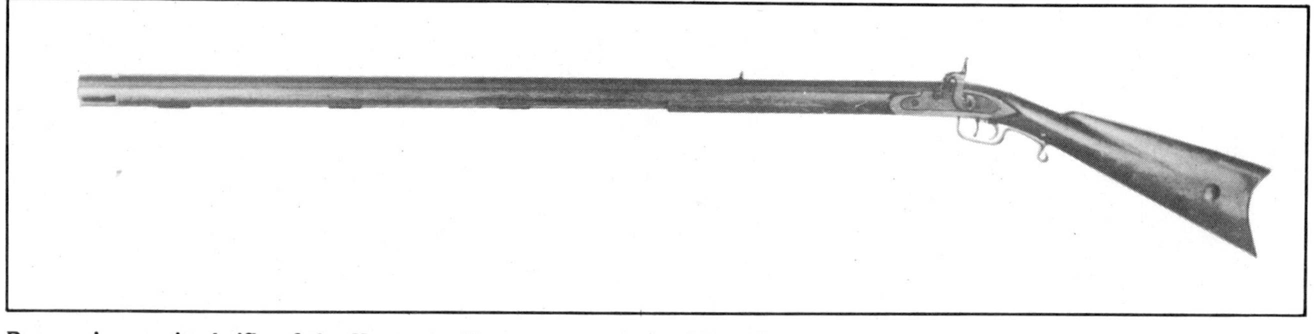

Percussion squirrel rifle of the Kentucky/Tennessee style in .32 caliber.

arms. The official condition standard for antique firearms is as follows:

Factory new: All original parts; 100 percent original finish and in perfect condition in every respect, inside and out.

Excellent: All original parts; over 80 percent original finish; sharp lettering, numerals and design on metal and wood; unmarred wood; fine bore.

Fine: All original parts; over 30 percent original finish; sharp lettering, numerals and design on metal and wood; minor marks in wood; good bore.

Very good: All original parts; none to 30 percent original finish; original metal surfaces smooth with all edges sharp; clear lettering, numerals and design on metal; wood slightly scratched or bruised; bore disregarded for collectors' firearms.

Good: Some minor replacement parts; metal smoothly rusted or lightly pitted in places, cleaned or reblued; principal lettering, numerals and design on metal legible; wood refinished, scratched, bruised or minor cracks repaired; in good working order.

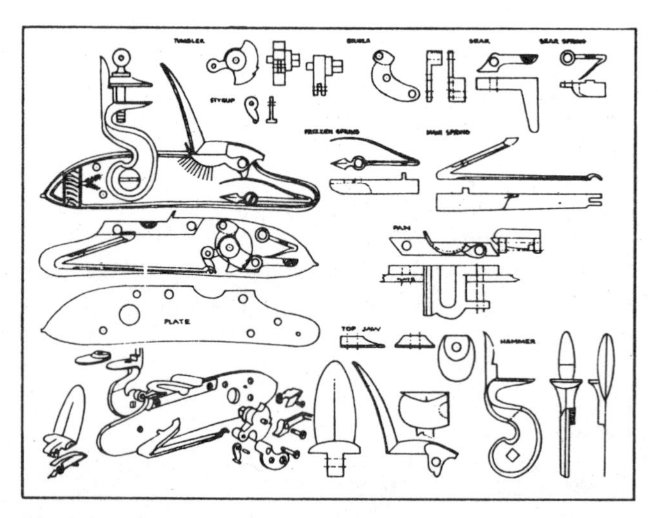

Diagram of the "stirrup-type" lock mechanism used in many Kentucky rifles.

Fair: Some major parts replaced; minor replacement parts may be required; metal rusted, may be lightly pitted all over, vigorously cleaned or reblued; rounded edges or metal partly obliterated; wood scratched, bruised, cracked or repaired where broken; in fair working order or can be easily repaired and put in working order.

Poor: Major and minor parts replaced; major replacement parts required and extensive restoration needed; metal deeply pitted; principal lettering, numerals and design obliterated; wood badly scratched, bruised, cracked or broken; mechanically inoperative; generally undesirable as a collector's firearm.

The appearance of an antique weapon is easy to evaluate—even by the beginner, but detecting worn or broken parts can be rather difficult. First of all, it is very difficult to disassemble many antique firearms without damaging the weapon due to rusted screws and parts. I have seen arms that were so rusted that the parts looked as though they were welded together. However, in all but the worst cases, most of these can be disassembled with the proper tools and a good working knowledge of their use.

There are numerous guides available that will help you to determine the prices for most antique firearms. Attending antique gun shows, talking to the experts and noting the prices asked are probably the best ways to determine the current market value of an antique arm. However, just because a firearm has a certain price tag doesn't necessarily mean the gun will bring this amount. Watch sales being made and see just how much the guns are actually bought for. If several guns

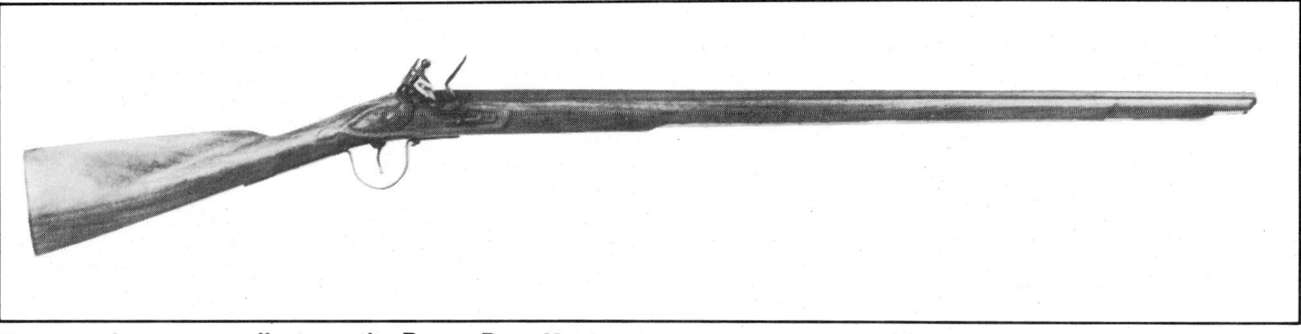

Very popular among collectors, the Brown Bess Musket was used during the Revolutionary War.

of the same model and condition bring similar prices at a gun show, you can be relatively sure this is the going market price at the time.

If you have an antique arm that you think is valuable, but you cannot find out any pricing information from the sources previously mentioned, Turner Kirkland of Dixie Gun Works offers an appraising service. Here are the particulars.

Certification. Dixie Gun Works is a member of the Appraisers Association of America. There is no national or state organization of gun dealers to pass on or certify that an individual is a certified appraiser of antique firearms.

Fees. Their fee is $40 per hour or any fraction thereof while working. This calculated time also includes the time required for their secretary to write and mail or hand you their documents. If an appraisal is made outside of their store, the fee is $45 per hour plus a travel fee of 50 cents per mile, plus necessary telephone calls and overnight accommodations. Compared to doing an appraisal out of town, the cost is at a minimum when done in the store in Union City.

Documentation: The appraisal document you receive from Dixie is in such a form and completeness that it will be good for any legal debate in court or within the offices of an insurance firm. They understand how to describe antique firearms and their accoutrements, and how to put this wording into such language that it is understood by the average layman.

Their evaluation is at the retail level, which means that they will evaluate an item at what they know its average retail value to be. They will not purposely appraise a gun higher than its real value in the case of an insurance claim.

Experience. Turner Kirkland is the Chairman of the Board at Dixie Gun Works and has bought, sold and traded antique guns since 1932. Dixie buys, sells and trades over 1,000 guns per year and, in addition, they attend from 25 to 30 gun shows each year, at which time they examine and view tens of thousands of antique firearms. Since their expertise is in the field of antique firearms or collectors firearms, in special cases of unusually rare antique firearms or those that may be historically oriented, they may need to consult with outside contacts. In appraising strictly modern guns, which they do not study, they may also need to turn to outside con-

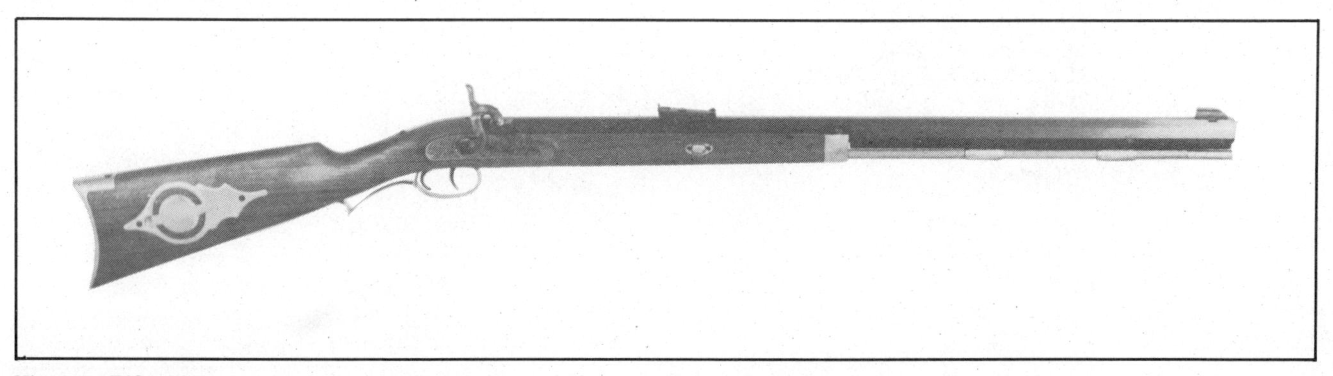

Hawken Rifle kits are extremely popular among black powder enthusiasts and are well worth the effort expended in putting them together.

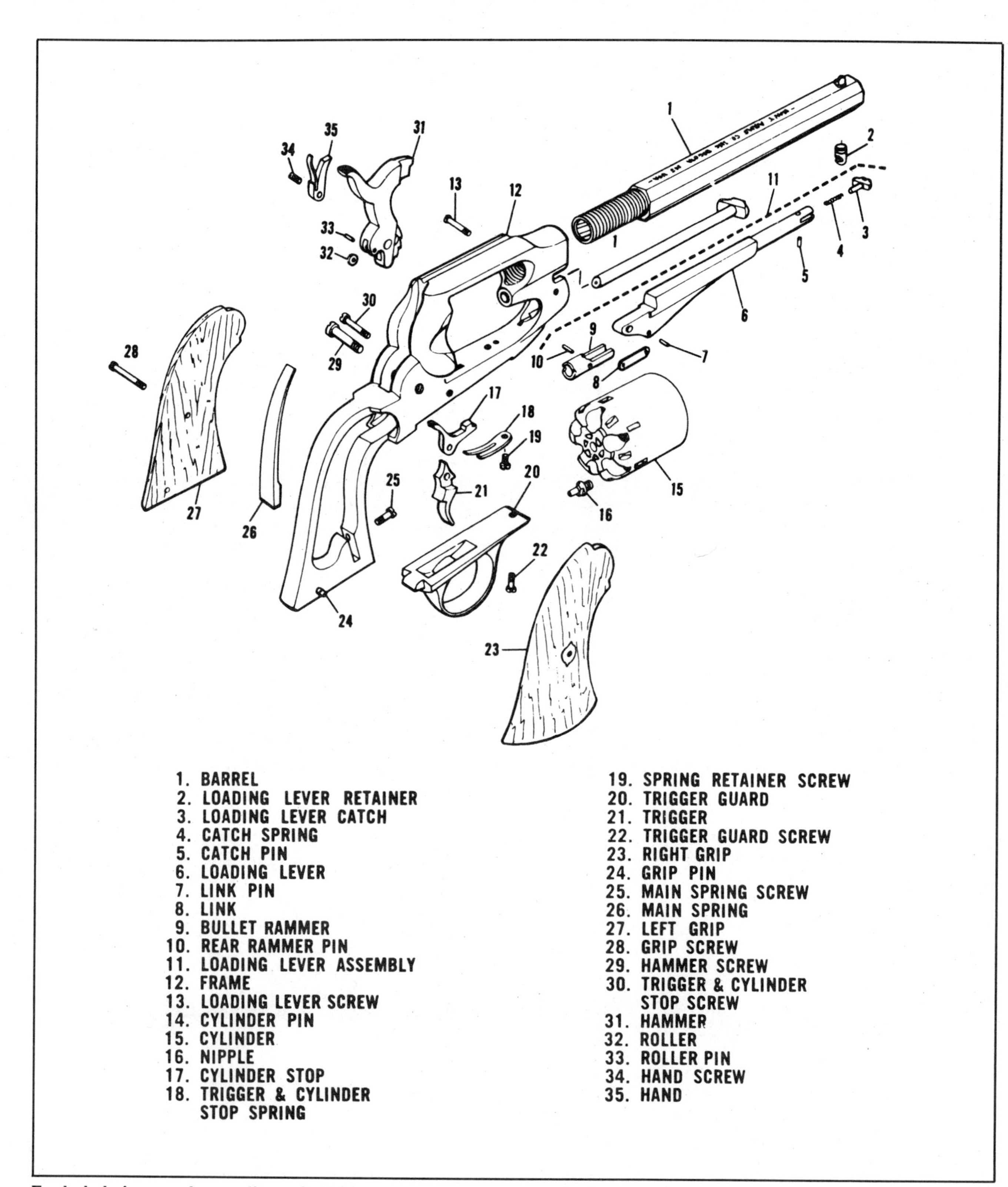

Exploded views and parts lists of old black powder guns are invaluable for use in disassembling arms as well as checking for missing parts.

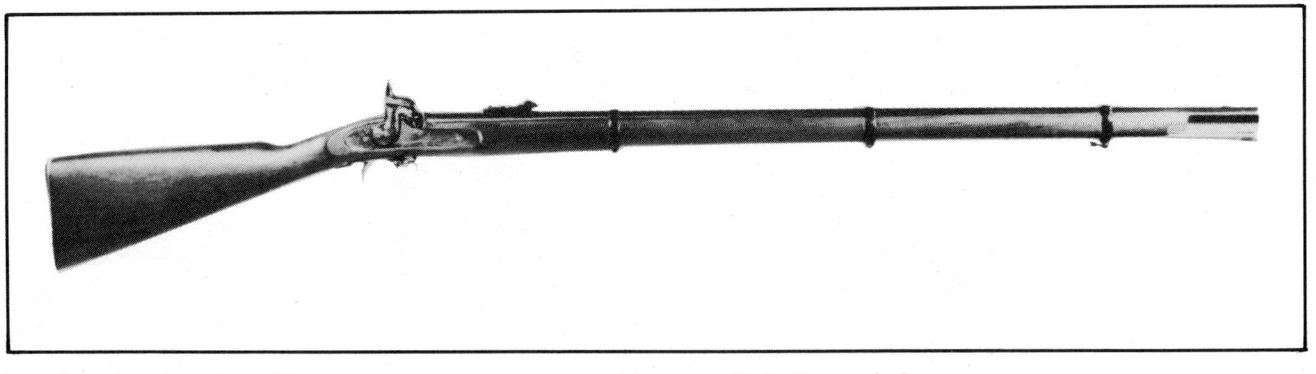

The three-band Enfield Rifle Musket was widely used during the Civil War period.

tacts. These guns would take a little longer to appraise than antiques.

As a general rule, antique black powder arms of collector status should not be fired. Their present condition should be preserved as much as possible. However, there may be times when an owner may desire to fire an arm of questionable condition. Before doing so, however, the arm should be completely disassembled—including the removal of the breech plug—and checked over completely as discussed previously. If there are no signs of cracks in the metal or serious metal deterioration, and the gun seems tight and sound, the next step would be to "proof" the arm.

Proofing is done by firing heavier-than-normal charges in the gun from a rest and with the trigger pulled by an attached cord, with all personnel safely away from the arm and preferably behind some type of protective cover. The arm, pointed in a safe direction, may be secured to an old auto tire and then a string run from the trigger to a safe location away from the gun. After firing an overload several times and the gun holds together, the firearm should be relatively safe to fire with reduced loads. For example, let's assume you have calculated that your black powder arms should hold a load of, say, 60 grains of FFFg powder behind a round ball of the correct size. Five or six loads shot with 100 grains of FFFg black powder behind the ball should be sufficient. I've seen rifles tested in this manner with two balls in front of the powder charge to obtain extra pressure.

This test, of course, does not guarantee that the gun will be safe for future firings. The last proof load may have caused a crack in the barrel that would go unnoticed. Then, on the first firing by hand, the barrel could let go. Therefore, after each proof load—especially after the last one—carefully examine the gun for hairline cracks or other tell-tale signs.

Finding Black Powder Guns

The various antique gun shows held monthly throughout the country are, by far, the best places to see the trading of a lot of antique firearms. You will also have a large variety of weapons to choose from. Furthermore, you'll be able to see just what the arms are selling for, enabling you to determine a fair price for the one you may want to buy. In each issue *Shotgun News* lists dozens of such arms.

Flea markets and yard sales are other good sources of antique arms. Comb your local newspapers, too, for notices of auction sales. Many times an estate will be

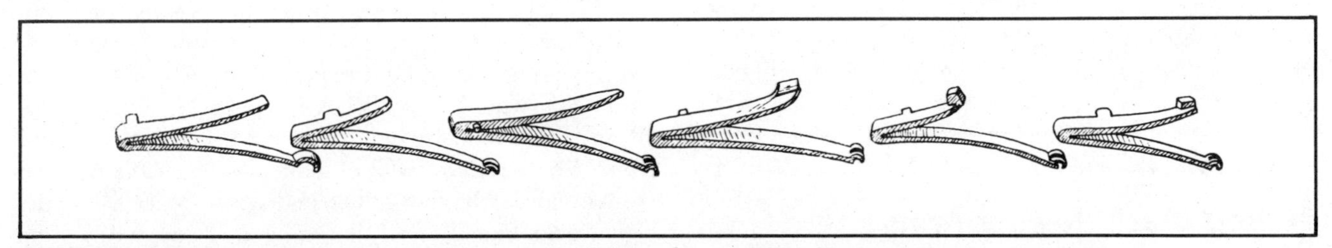

The main spring is a gun part that often requires replacing to make a black powder arm shootable; above is a sampling of different types of main springs you should become familiar with.

Drawing showing one of the better examples of rifling machines of the 18th century.

sold at public auction in which the entire goods from a household will be sold. As these items are being gathered up for sale, all sorts of goodies usually turn up —especially in the attic. Not too long ago, a box of odds and ends at an auction had in its midst a Spencer Carbine in excellent condition!

Since black powder arms are exempt from the Gun Control Act of 1968, much trading in these types of arms is done through the mails. In advertisements, you will most often find the condition listed as "good," and this "good" will vary from poor to just a little less than excellent, so it is always recommended that you have the privilege of returning the gun for a full refund if it is not what you expected.

Selling Black Powder Arms

A person who has one or two antique arms that he wishes to sell, and who is not very knowledgeable about the subject, would do well to let a reputable dealer sell the guns for him. This way, he stands a better chance of getting a fair price and a quicker sale. The usual fee for this service is from 15 to 25 percent of the gun's value. That is, if the gun sells for, say, $200, the dealer would withhold anywhere from $30 to $50 commission and give the balance to the former owner.

Many gun owners balk at this practice, since they think that by selling a gun or two themselves, they will save themselves the commission and, consequently, will receive more for their firearms. But look at the situation this way. You will have advertising fees to pay. You will have many inquiries from people who will not buy. You will have a lot of lookers—those who have no intentions of buying—they just want to see what the gun looks like. Then if the gun is misused, will you be liable? When all of these factors are added together, the commission paid to a dealer is well worth it.

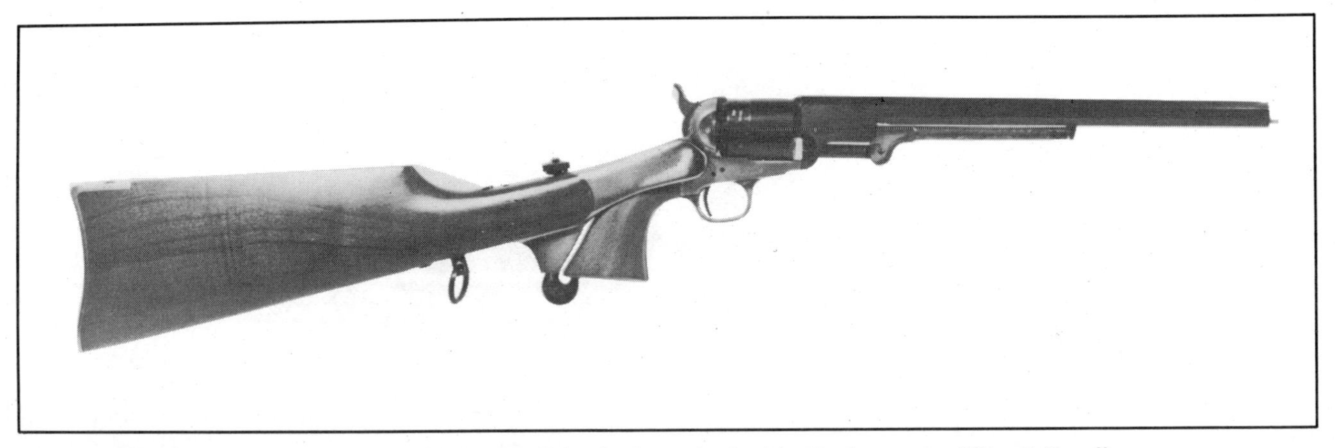

Named after Wyatt Earp (who actually used a Colt single action), this black powder "Wyatt Earp" revolver by Dixie comes with a shoulder stock.

If a person has enough firearms on hand to make it worthwhile, he may consider taking them to a gun show or else advertise in the few publications that cater to gun collectors and then send a list to those who reply. The list should include detailed descriptions of every gun offered for sale, with careful evaluations and listings of the exact condition of each gun.

When an order is received, guns should be shipped only upon receipt of payment, or C.O.D. United Parcel Service (UPS) is an excellent way to send black powder arms. Merely package the firearm according to postal requirements and take it to the nearest UPS office. If you want to send the gun C.O.D., specify if you will accept a check or want cash only. The UPS personnel will comply and send you payment within a short time after the package is delivered.

If the gun has been carefully described and the condition is exactly as stated, the buyer will seldom complain. However, if he does grouse, never argue. Ask him to return the gun and promptly refund his money when the gun is returned in the condition it was sent out. By doing so, you'll maintain a good reputation as a gun dealer, which will pay off in dividends later.

Once a person becomes successful in disposing of a

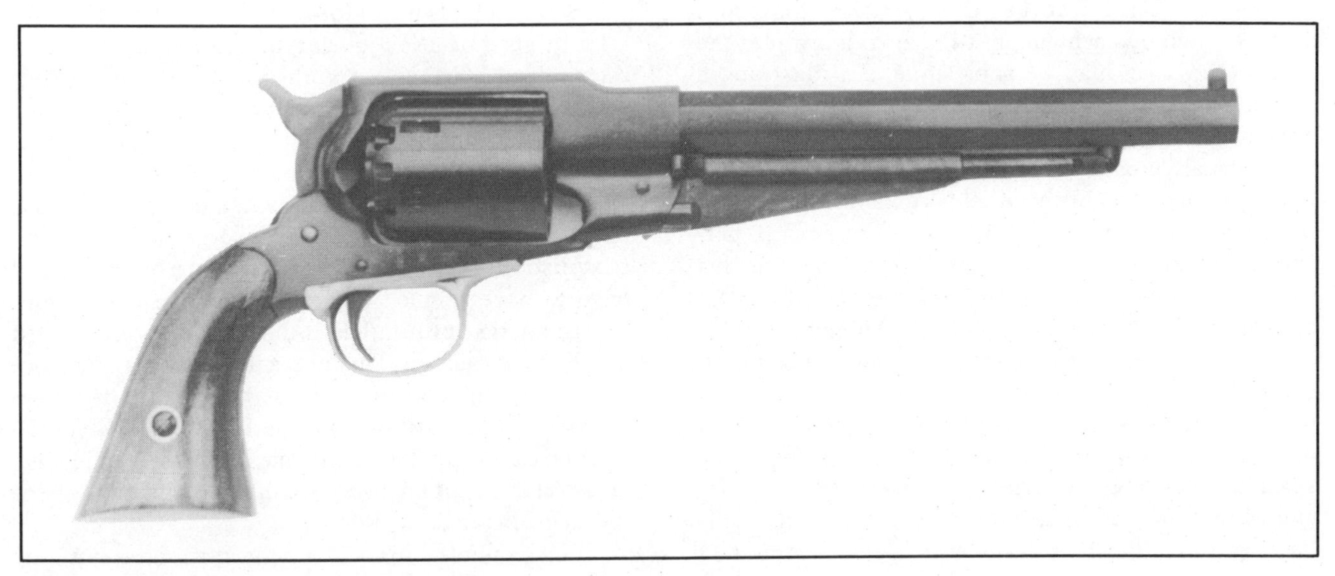

Reproduction of the New Model .44 caliber Remington Army revolver.

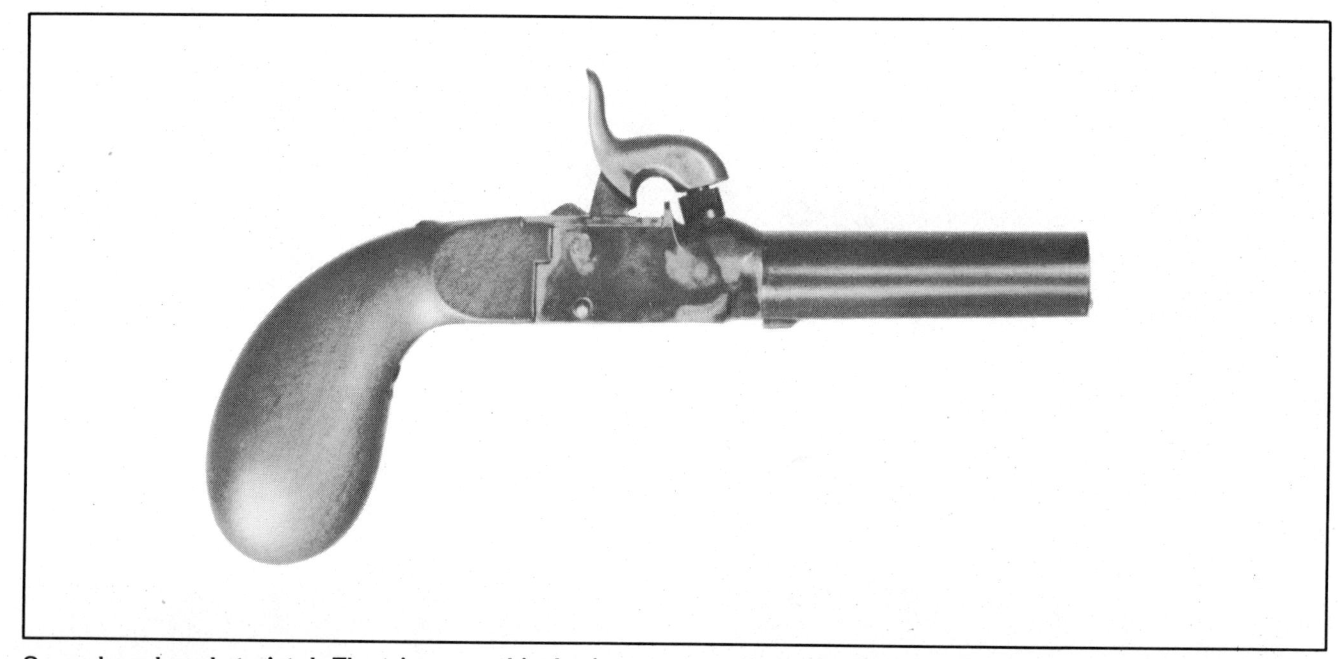

Screw-barrel pocket pistol. The trigger on this derringer automatically folds down when the hammer is cocked back, while when the gun is being carried, it folds up into the frame.

few unwanted firearms, he may decide to deal in guns as a part-time occupation, especially if he wants to try to find good specimens for his private collection. If so, he must decide what profit must be made to make the occupation worthwhile. This decision must be based on several factors, and all should be considered thoroughly before reaching a conclusion.

When firearms can be resold quickly, the profit may be small on each gun, but the overall profit at the end of the year may be substantial. To illustrate, a dealer near my home operates from a garage in back of his house—keeping his overhead to the barest minimum—and usually marks his arms up only 10 percent above cost. He is usually able to resell his guns within 30 days or less after purchase, and therefore makes his 10 percent profit in that period of time. By turning over his capital investment 12 times during the year, the total gross profit on his working capital is 120 percent.

Another dealer, who converted part of his supermarket into a gun shop, looks at the situation differently. The space allotted for his guns occupies about 30 percent of the total area in the building. Therefore, this space must be charged against his overhead, which includes the amount he spends for rent, utilities, insurance, and the like. This dealer lists his guns so that 30 percent profit can be made on each one. However, his turnover is not as fast as the previous dealer's and many of his guns are kept for 90 days or more before they are sold; many have occupied the gun rack for a year or more. From this, it's easy to see that this dealer is turning his capital over not more than four times each year, still he makes 120 percent on his capital investment (4 × 30 percent).

So, it all boils down to whether you want to handle a lot of guns or a few during the period of a year. I'd recommend starting out with a relatively high profit and then adjust it to suit your own personal needs. It's much easier to come down on a price than to go up—if you want to continue to attract customers.

Another factor to consider when dealing in guns is the cost of operation. Obviously, a large store in a high-rent district with all kinds of operating expenses will have to have a much bigger volume of sales, or else charge a larger profit, than if the business were located in a home or garage. The larger the business, the more employees will have to be hired, the rent will be higher on the building, utilities will be higher, etc. If you do your research, you'll find that most successful gun businesses started out on a very small scale, and enlarged as the sales dictated.

For example, Francis Bannerman Sons—at one time *the* largest dealer in antiques and military goods in the world—was started in the 1860's by Francis Bannerman who, by capitalizing on post-Civil War opportunities, became the first seller of surplus war materials. By using sound business practices and shrewd Scottish acumen, he expanded the business to legendary proportions that lasted nearly a century. Turner Kirkland of Dixie Gun Works started out on a small scale in his back yard and is presently one of the largest dealers in black powder guns and parts in the United States.

Many dealers are engaged in other businesses besides dealing in guns. Some may be running a service station, country general store, a hardware store, automotive shop and the like. When one type of retail business is being operated, the addition of a firearms business usually increases the revenue without adding too much to the overhead.

In selecting stock, condition should be emphasized. It's best not to concentrate on low-quality arms. Sure, you'll get a few, but try to have a good stock of the better collector items also. The only time a firearm in poor condition should be purchased is when the arm can be salvaged for parts or else the gun can be repaired and put into good condition. Dealers who sell only junk soon earn a reputation of selling only poor-quality firearms and, although these eventually will be sold, the turnover is usually slow, and the danger of having defective arms on your shelf is ever-present.

Dealers who have become the most successful are those who over the years have worked diligently to establish a reputation of fair dealing. The gun dealer who consistently provides fair values and is astute enough to buy merchandise at competitive prices is the dealer who is going to stay in business, enjoying nice profits.

As a dealer, service should be another important aspect of your business. And, if you're on the other side of the counter as a consumer, don't be lured into buying a product from one retailer simply because his price tag is a few dollars cheaper than another's; you'll only regret that when a problem occurs, the service is poor or even non-existent.

So, for buyer and seller alike, be sure to take these three major considerations into account when making a firearm transaction—product knowledge, value and service.

11. Safety Procedures for You and Your Used Guns

Generally, when new firearms leave the factory, they have been fired and tested for safety and accuracy. Used guns, on the other hand, seldom are tested by an expert before they find their way into the hands of their new owners. And since many used guns are sold because they are already in malfunctioning condition, anyone who purchases a used gun should beware, especially if you don't know the previous owner personally.

There are certain safety rules that apply to everyone who handles any type of firearm—new or used. The chief rule is NEVER point a firearm at anyone or anything unless you intend to hit and/or kill. This applies to loaded and unloaded guns alike. Second, make certain the firearm you intend to shoot is in good operating condition, with the proper ammunition used, and that no obstructions—such as a cleaning brush or patch—are in the chamber or bore.

Before You Use That "New" Gun . . .

Beyond these, anyone who purchases a used firearm and intends to shoot it should observe the following:

Visual inspection. Unless the firearm is a prized collector's item, you should disassemble a used gun shortly after it is purchased and give it a thorough cleaning. At the same time, examine all parts for wear. Carefully inspect questionable parts under a magnifying glass for hairline cracks and excessive wear. If any are found, repair or replace the parts immediately, not when the gun malfunctions on the range or in the field.

Dry firing. Dummy cartridges should be used to test the feeding of repeating rifles and shotguns, along with the safety, trigger pull and the action in general. In recent months, this test alone on several of my firearms has revealed an inoperative safety, a foreign-made double-barreled shotgun that fired both barrels when only one trigger was pulled, a defective sear that allowed the hammer to fall with only a slight bump of the buttstock on the floor, and several other unsafe conditions. Remember, when shopping around pawn shops and other places where used guns can usually be purchased at bargain prices, a good many of these guns will malfunction. This is the reason many of them were put up for sale in the first place. Some previous owners have even taken pains to cover up the flaws so more money could be obtained for the gun.

Check barrel materials. Many double-barreled shotguns manufactured around the turn of the century had Damascus steel barrels which I've said are definitely unsafe with modern smokeless shotshell loads, and questionable even with black powder loads. These are usually detectable by the circular rings or bands around the barrels, although some may require a close inspection by removing the forearm or removing a small spot of bluing or browning to reveal the bare metal underneath.

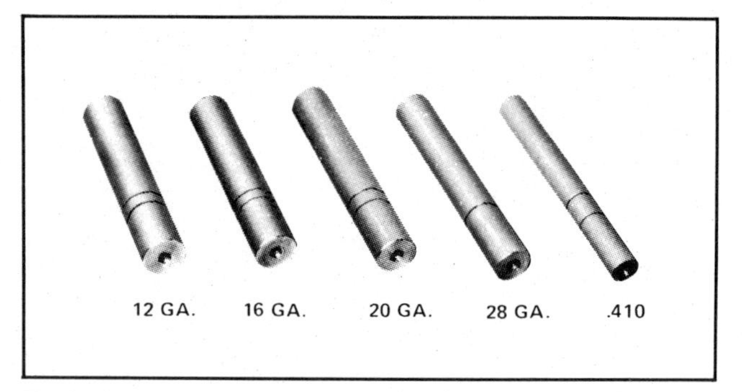

To check the chamber length of a used shotgun, clean the chamber thoroughly, then insert a gauge made especially for this purpose. If the ring (see above) lines up flush with the breech end of the barrel, the chamber is the correct depth. If not, rechambering may be called for.

Check shotgun chambers. Over the years a great variety of "correct depths" have been designated for shells—most of them less than the standard overall 2.760-inch length of the fired cases of today's plastic shells. When a shotshell is fired, the crimp must have room to unfold far enough to allow the shot and wad to pass from the shell to the bore smoothly. Any minute amount of case forced into their path—because of a short chamber—can cause deformed shot, distorted patterns, torn hulls, excessive kicking and pressure.

Although many American-made shotguns have short chambers, most of them will be found in the older (and some not-so-old) foreign shotguns. The simplest way to detect these short chambers is to use a shotgun chamber gauge which you can get for about $5 from a place like Brownells, Inc. To use, merely insert the cylinder-shaped gauge into the chamber—after first thoroughly cleaning it—and observe the marked ring on the gauge. If the ring lines up flush with the breech end of the barrel, the chamber is the correct depth. If the ring is not exactly flush—protruding out from the barrel—then you have a short chamber.

A short shotgun chamber is usually not serious, if detected, and can be corrected by rechambering, which should not cost more than $50.

Check serial numbers of arms. One model of firearm, manufactured between certain dates, may be unsafe to fire, whereas the same model, manufactured at a different time, may be entirely safe. For example, the first 285,000 Model 1903 Springfield rifles manufactured at Rock Island Arsenal had receivers made from very hard carbon steel and are known as "low-numbered" rifles. It is dangerous to shoot one of these rifles with modern loads. Beginning with serial No. 285508, the consistency of the steel was changed to make them safe for use with modern loads. These models are commonly called "high-numbered Springfields."

Check bore diameter. Many rifles of the past experienced a wide variation in bore diameters for the same caliber—especially in some of the foreign military arms. Some of the smaller bores could cause excessive pressure when fired with a bullet larger than the bore diameter. For example, one Mauser action in a 7mm Mauser (7×57) was damaged when a regular factory round was fired. Upon checking the bore, the diameter measured .278 instead of the normal .284. Some stronger actions may hold loads like these, but not this particular receiver.

Check headspace. Excessive headspace not only ruins accuracy in a rifle, but is dangerous. It seems that military rifles are most guilty of this problem—although it can occur in any rifle or shotgun—and it is a good idea to check any military weapon prior to firing it. Headspace guages are available in "Go," "No Go" and "Field" gauges.

To check for headspace, first make sure the chamber and action are clean and free of oil, grease, grit or any other foreign matter, as any of these will interfere with the proper seating of the gauges. Also check to see if the serial numbered parts match; if not, be especially cautious.

A makeshift gauge out of a brass shim stock can be used to test headspace. Here is one in place in the bolt recess, held in position with grease.

Insert the "No Go" gauge in the magazine, not in the barrel, then slowly move the bolt forward, which will pick up the gauge and push it into the chamber. If the bolt will not close, there is no headspace problem. In closing the bolt, never use force; you should feel only a slight resistance when closing the bolt with the gauge in place. If the bolt should close with the "No Go" gauge inserted, and using only moderate pressure, you have excess headspace. The rifle should then be checked with the "Field" gauge. If the bolt closes on this gauge, the rifle is dangerous and should definitely not be fired.

The exact amount of headspace will vary from cartridge to cartridge, but to use an example, let's consider the popular .30-06. If the bolt closes relatively easily with a "No Go" gauge inserted, there is at least .006 of an inch excess headspace. If the bolt closes on the "Field" gauge, this means at least .010 of an inch excess headspace. From this, it would seem that it would be quite simple to construct your own headspace gauges, and this is true if you are capable of taking accurate measurements. In the case of the .30-06, a brass shim stock may be cut to fit the inside of the bolt recess. The thickness should be .006 of an inch for a "No Go" gauge equivalent and .010 of an inch for a "Field" gauge equivalent. Once the shims are in place in the bolt recess (held in place with grease), insert a fired or dummy round in the chamber and try closing the bolt. The results should indicate the conditions previously described. These makeshift headspace gauges, however, are just that—makeshift—and are recommended only in an emergency; it is best to buy the precision-ground gauges, like the ones manufactured by Clymer or Forster.

Check stocks for proper inletting and fitting. Many people overlook the potential danger of an improperly fitted stock. Most are aware that proper bedding is necessary for good accuracy, but few consider it a safety necessity. Some years ago, I was test-firing a 20-gauge double-barreled shotgun and was not aware it had an improperly fitted stock. When the right barrel was fired, I heard a slight crack and felt a "give" in the grip, but I went ahead and fired the second barrel anyway. This shot splintered the stock at the grip, running long splinters deep into the web of my hand. This was

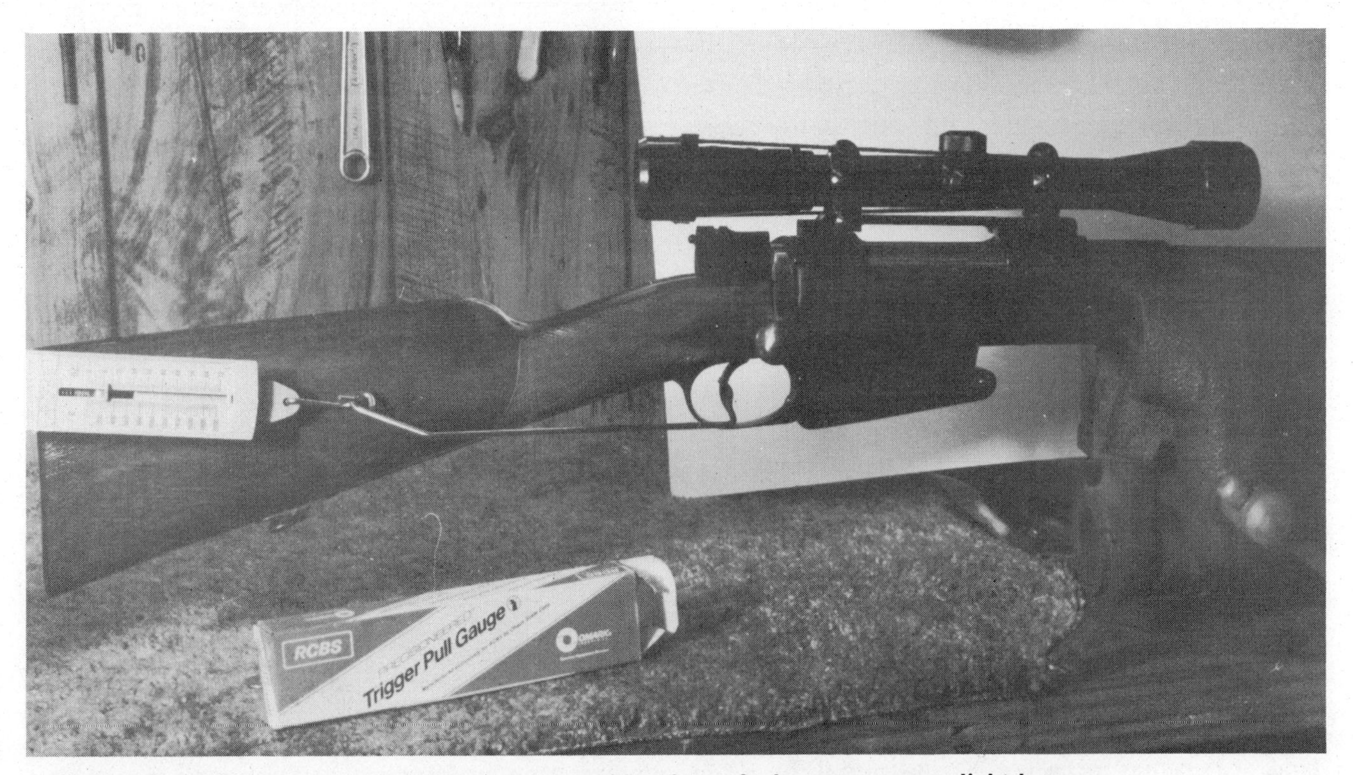

Anything less than a three-pound trigger pull is considered unsafe, because even a slight bump on the buttstock could cause the gun to go off. Check the weight of the trigger pull, a relatively simple procedure, using any of the trigger-pull gauges on the market, like the one shown above.

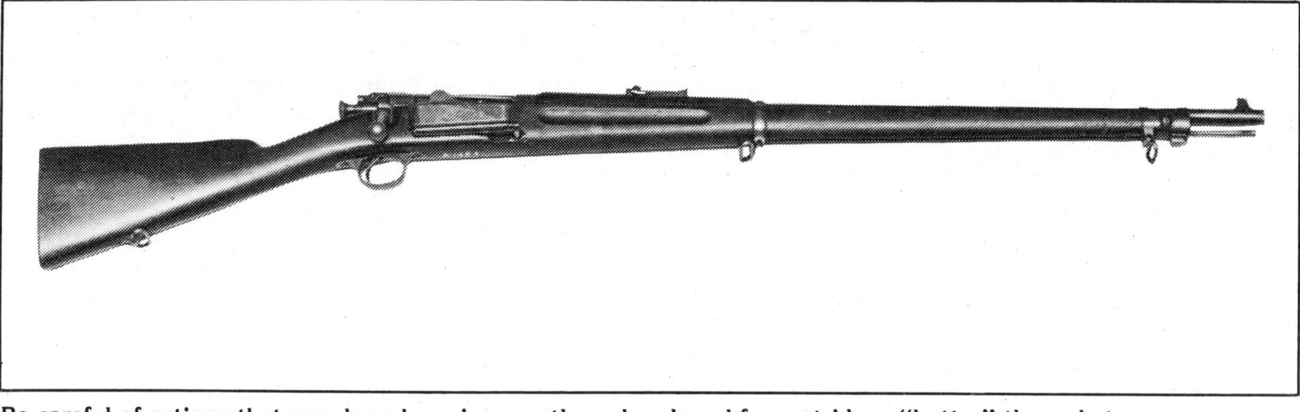

Be careful of actions that may have been incorrectly rechambered for cartridges "hotter" than what they will safely fire. The bolt-action .30-40 caliber Krag Rifle, like the Model 1892 (above), will safely handle loads of up to about 41,000 psi. Any pressure exceeding that can be dangerous.

not exactly a disaster, but I can assure you that the experience was not pleasant. It was enough to make me check, or at least look over, every gunstock before firing the gun. What if the splinters had been shot back into my eye?

Check trigger pulls and safeties. Sears and safeties tend to wear and eventually may become dangerous —especially if either have been tampered with. "Hair triggers" on hunting arms should be avoided; usually anything less than a three-pound pull is considered unsafe, as a slight bump on the buttstock may cause the gun to fire.

Be careful of altered firearms. There has been a tendency among some groups of gun enthusiasts to alter or rechamber firearms. This operation is perfectly safe when done by an expert, but can mean disaster if done incorrectly. Some actions have been rechambered for cartridges "hotter" than what they will safely handle. For example, the 1898 Krag action is safe at around 40,000 to 41,000 pounds per square inch (psi)—the approximate amount of pressure exerted by the .30-40 Krag cartridge. If this action were chambered for one of the Krag wildcats, say, the .25 Short Krag, the chamber pressure would be from 48,000 to over 50,000 psi—way too much for the action to handle. Learn the strength of the more common actions, and then the approximate pressure of the cartridges they may be chambered for. This does not mean that you have to memorize all the figures, but you should know where you can put your hands on the figures (usually through a good reference book or reloading manual) when you need them.

If you plan to do any work on a firearm, never apply heat to any part of a firearm unless you know precisely what you are doing; even then, proceed with caution. Also, never remove excessive amounts of metal from a rifle, shotgun or handgun at points of stress, such as the receiver ring, locking lugs, etc. When installing new parts, make certain that these parts are functioning properly before firing the gun. When inspecting a gun, make certain it is unloaded; but *always* handle it as if it were loaded. Make sure that you are competent, confident and understand the principles of a job before attempting it. If in doubt, seek advice from a professional.

Proofing loads for modern arms. Most gunsmiths who proof and test various rifles usually use a couple of grains of powder over maximum. To proof yourself, a rest may be made by using an old tire with the gun butt set inside and the forearm resting and secured over the tire on the opposite side. A string is then tied to the trigger and the muzzle pointed in a safe direction so the bullet will strike a backstop. Stand back a safe distance and preferably behind an object such as a building or tree. Let off a round by pulling the string, and if the rifle safely handles five overloads, I would reach the conclusion that the firearm is reasonably safe to fire standard loads.

Black Powder Safety

In most cases, it is best to retire the old-timers to museums, gun cabinets or wall hangers, but some black powder enthusiasts insist on shooting the old weapons anyway. With the large array of reproduction arms available that are well built and tested, I really can't see any purpose in doing so, but perhaps it's like my fondness for pre-'64 modern arms. I know I can buy a good, safe new firearm in, say, .270 Winchester, but I'd still

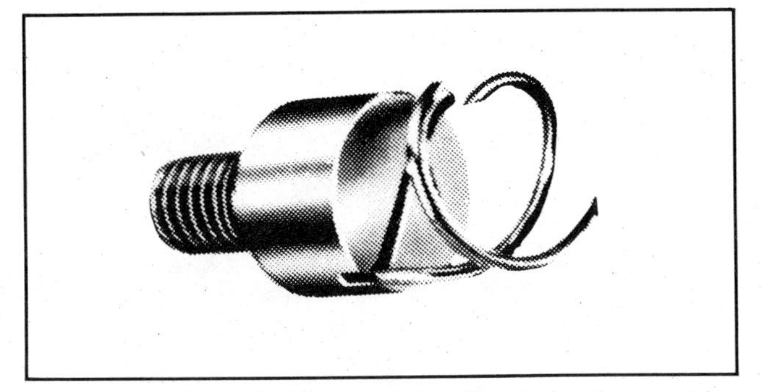

To remove obstacles in muzzleloading barrels, you can use a "worm" or a wood screw soldered onto the end of a cleaning rod. Insert the rod into the muzzle, then twist to attach the worm or screw into the patch or whatever blockage is present. Do not use steel screws, though, since they could set off a charge.

rather shoot my pre-World War II Winchester Model 70 than the ones manufactured today. There's something classic about the earlier model that just isn't captured in the later versions. So, perhaps the black powder enthusiasts have similar reasons for wanting to restore and shoot the old muzzleloaders.

Assuming that you have obtained a muzzleloader from the last century, and you want to put it into shootable condition, the first thing you should consider is whether the gun is loaded or not! The original owner of the weapon may have loaded it with shot and ball to keep it ready for game or to scare off intruders. Upon his death, the gun—probably still loaded—was inherited by his son or daughter, to be stashed away in the attic for decades. The gun may have eventually been auctioned off to a dealer and you, in turn, purchased it from him. More than likely the gun was never checked to see whether it was loaded. Then, another owner of the gun —thinking it was not loaded—may have loaded it again; another owner again, and so on. You never know what surprises you'll encounter with old guns.

To check a muzzleloading shotgun or rifle, run the ramrod all the way down the bore, and mark the rod where it's flush with the muzzle. Withdraw the rod and place it alongside the barrel, with the mark again lined up with the muzzle. If the rod extends all the way to the breech, chances are the gun is okay. If not, there's a good chance the gun has one or more charges of shot and ball in it. Of course, a wasp may have built a nest in it, or other debris may have gotten crammed into the bore, but, by all means, investigate further at this point.

In trying to "disarm" a loaded muzzleloader, it's a good idea to deaden the powder with water before beginning. If the nipple will unscrew and come out, you may be able to squirt in some water from this angle. You may even be able to get some in through the nipple hole. Once the charge has been water soaked, let it stand for about an hour before working on the arm further. It should now be relatively safe to work on, but always be extra cautious and keep your head, hands and other parts of your anatomy away from the muzzle.

To remove obstacles in a muzzleloading barrel, most people use a "worm" or a wood screw soldered to the end of a cleaning rod. The worm or screw, attached to the rod, is inserted into the muzzle until contact is made with the obstacle. The rod is then twisted clockwise to screw the worm or screw into the lead ball, patch or whatever. It is a good idea not to use steel screws in this operation, because steel can spark and set off the charge of black powder that may still be in the bore. And during this operation, keep your head well back and away from the muzzle. Once the screw makes contact, twist the rod with a pair of pliers so you can also keep your hands out of the way. The muzzle, of course, should be pointed in a safe direction.

A surer way to check for charges in black powder arms is to remove the breech plug. This will also allow you to examine the bore readily for its condition. If the bore is rusted and pitted to a point where accuracy will be poor, there is really no sense in shooting the gun anyway. However, removing the breech plug from many of these old muzzleloaders is easier said than done! Some were soldered or welded in place, while others have been welded naturally by plain old red rust for the past hundred years or so.

To remove the breech plug, first make relatively sure that no powder and/or shot charge is in the barrel. Then remove the barrel from the wood stock. Do this very carefully because the stocks will splinter easily. A special wrench is required, such as the B-Square Breech Plug Wrench. The special, cutout design of this wrench transfers all clamp force directly to the plug's wrenching surface, and, if this wrench won't remove it, nothing will. B-Square also offers vise jaws especially designed for octagonal barrels.

Before tightly securing the barrel in a vise, apply plenty of penetrating oil such as WD-40 or Liquidwrench. Squirt some down the barrel, around the plug/breech junction and through the nipple hole. Allow the oil to work for at least 30 minutes. Use the special vise jaws and wrench and tap the wrench handle with a hammer; don't pound on it, merely tap it lightly. If the plug doesn't break free, repeat the penetrating oil-soaking procedure. If the plug is still frozen, you can try the oil-soak process once more, but give up on this method if it doesn't work by the third try; the plug or wrench can be damaged by too many blows with the hammer.

The next step should be tried only if you are absolutely certain there is no powder in the breech area. If you're positive there is none, heat the breech plug with a torch until it's too hot to touch; not red hot—just too hot to touch. Let the plug cool by itself; that is, don't apply oil or water. Now heat the breech end of the barrel until it, too, is about the temperature of a hot clothes iron and, before it cools, try the special wrench again. If this doesn't do it, heat the breech end of the barrel again and apply pressure and tapping to the wrench, gripping the breech plug. Should the plug still refuse to release, I'd give up the idea and retire the gun to the wall for decoration.

(Applying heat to the breech plug this way and to the temperature of a clothes iron is not a particularly dangerous procedure with black powder arms. Using heat on a modern cartridge gun is much more risky, as I mentioned before, although caution should be exercised in both cases.)

If you do get the plug free, clean it and the internal threads thoroughly; then clean the entire bore of the barrel. How does it look? If the barrel is somewhat pitted, you may be able to restore some accuracy by lapping, or you may want to have the barrel bore enlarged and re-rifled to a larger caliber.

When everything is clean, screw the plug back into the bore, preferably with hand force only. The plug should stop about ⅛ inch short of the travel necessary to prevent gas from escaping when the gun is fired. A wrench is then necessary for final tightening. However, if the plug screws pass the alignment point with only

A safe way to check for charges in muzzleloaders is to remove the breech plug completely. B-Square's breech plug wrench and vise jaws can be especially helpful in performing this black powder safety function.

hand pressure, your rifle is unsafe without further modification. A lead or brass washer may be cut to a thickness that permits the breech plug to align perfectly with only a light tapping of the wrench.

During the time the breech plug is out is a good time to determine the exact size of the bore if you don't already know it. You can measure across lands and grooves with an inside caliper, or run a lead ball down the barrel (a lead ball slightly larger than the grooves) and measure across the raised lands on the ball with a micrometer; this will provide you with the groove diameter and the proper ball size to use. However, you normally use a ball .01 of an inch smaller than groove diameter to allow room for the patch. Therefore, if the groove diameter is .50 caliber, you'd use a .490-inch round ball.

If everything else operates as you think it should, the next step is to "proof" your muzzleloader, which means firing a shot charge that generates from 20 to 30 percent more breech pressure than the maximum load you intend to use in the arm. Such loads should always be fired by using a rest to support the firearm; tie a string or other means to the trigger, get back and behind some barrier and let go. If the gun remains intact after several firings, the gun should be relatively safe for reduced loads.

Muzzleloaders do blow up occasionally, as do modern firearms. In the older guns, blow-ups usually occur due to metal crystallization, loss of temper in locking lugs and other critical areas through careless application of heat, cracked welds or tiny fissures resulting from excessive loads. There may also be imperfections such as seams in new metal or minute cracks resulting from machining and grinding. One method of detecting these flaws is called "Magnafluxing," which is really magnetic particle inspection. In general, it is based on the attraction of magnetic particles to a "leak field" created in the smallest crack or fissure when the metal is magnetized.

The larger manufacturers use certain scientific systems and implements to test the surface hardness of steels. Of these, the Rockwell instrument is the best known. In general, the Rockwell test is based on the principle of forcing a point or small ball of a given size and hardness with a given amount of pressure against the metal to be tested. The depth of the impression, when related to the read-out scale, indicates the hardness. But this method measures surface hardness only. The best, and least expensive, way is to test the guns with proof loads.

In summary, don't shoot an old gun until it has been disassembled, carefully examined and found safe. To be safe, the breech plug must be tight, the drum and nipple tight and clean. The barrel must be clean and have no obstructions in it. The muzzle may have to be trued to be accurate and also the bore will probably have to be re-rifled or lapped to be of use.

12. Firearm Security: Protecting Your Collection

It's no secret that holding on to our guns is becoming more and more of a problem. It seems that whatever the pro-gun control groups leave will eventually be cleaned out by thieves. Dead bolts, security alarm systems, metal doors, and the like, help to keep out or alert us to intruders, but if they want to break into your home or shop, somehow they succeed—often without getting caught.

Measures to Take First

Immediately after acquiring a firearm—collector item or not—record the make, model, serial number and other outstanding identifying features. These data, plus photos of the guns, should be kept in a secure place, such as a safe deposit box, along with the sales receipts. Also keep a second copy of this information in another place . . . just in case!

Adequate insurance is something that few gun owners have, except for rare and expensive collections. The theft of firearms kept in the home should fall under, and be covered by, your conventional home-owner's policy. However, many underwriters are eliminating firearms from their policies since the theft of firearms has increased tremendously over the past 10 years. If this is the case, among the better policies are those available through the National Rifle Association. Write them at 1600 Rhode Island Ave., N.W., Washington, D.C. 20036 for information.

Should any of your guns be stolen, immediately notify your local law enforcement agency, giving them the serial numbers and descriptions so they can be entered into the national computer. Although it may take years, many guns will be recovered because the owners recorded this information. Not too long ago, Val Forgett Jr. of Navy Arms in New Jersey had two finely engraved pistols that had been stolen from him over 10 years ago returned by the New Jersey State Police. A priceless item that is stolen can be heartbreaking, but think of the joy if it should be returned.

Serial numbers can be altered, and some firearms manufactured before 1968 have no serial numbers at all. In such instances, it would be extremely difficult to identify positively one of your stolen guns—unless you added some personalized identification.

Collector items, as a rule, should not be altered or marked upon as either will lower the value. However, what would be wrong with inscribing your name on a small piece of sheet brass and inserting it in, say, the recessed bolt screw hole in the buttstock? The butt plate would keep the brass sheet in place and probably go unnoticed until identification of the arm was needed.

Engraving your name on certain portions of your firearms is one sure way to identify any questionable weapon. For example, a handgun may be engraved on the frame under the grips. When the grips are replaced, the markings will not show. Your name stamped on the buttstock, under the butt plate is also a good place, or you can merely scribe your name into the butt plate itself. The inside of a floor plate is another good location. In other words, you want to "brand" your guns so the markings will be there when you need them, but not be readily detected. Then, should you have to prove that a firearm is yours, state where the markings should be; if a lawman disassembles the arm and finds your name where you indicated, there should be no question about rightful ownership.

What is the best way to mark your guns? You can use metal stamps which will also work on wood, vibrating tools, engraving tools, rotary tools with dental burrs, and the like. If you have only a few guns to mark, the cheapest way is to take them to your local jeweler and have him do the engraving. However, if you have several arms, it might pay to purchase one of the vibrating tools, especially if you can use the tool for other projects around the house or shop.

One of the handiest gadgets for marking all kinds of metal is a device called "Etch-O-Matic," which marks all tools and metals in seconds. It puts anything you can type, write, draw, etc., on the stencils provided as deep as .003 of an inch in only seconds. It marks any thickness, even thin metal foil, without cracks or stress and any flat or round surface as small as 1/16 inch diameter. The device works on the electrochemical etching principle and uses standard 120-volt household current. The kit contains marker, ground plate, two-ounce electrolyte, 10 stencils, deep-etching adapter clip and instructions. Etch-O-Matic is available from many sources, but mine came from Jensen Tools Inc., 1230 South Priest Drive, Tempe, Arizona 85281. Besides this etching tool, they have hundreds of other tools and it would pay any gun owner to write for their free catalog.

"Securing" Your Collection

The best, and often the least expensive, way to keep guns out of the hands of intruders is to hide them so they can't be found. A burglar usually doesn't have all night to look for guns once he has broken into your home. Most go to the obvious places such as closets, chests, etc., and, if nothing is found, they leave hurriedly—especially if the premises are protected by a security system.

There are so many good ways to hide your guns cleverly that it would be impractical to list all of them here. Besides, we don't want to put too many ideas into the heads of thieves who buy books like this just for that purpose. However, let's look at one particular way that was used to hide a small gun collection.

The underside of a "door" on a trapdoor butt plate being marked with the Etch-O-Matic metal marking kit. Once the stencil is cut and placed in the holder, all that is necessary is to press the etcher onto the metal for a period of about 10 seconds.

A local contractor and gun collector was renovating a large commercial building in which the main electrical distribution panel had to be replaced. I'm not talking about the little two-pole, 30-ampere switch boxes that are used for electric water heaters or clothes dryers. This was a large 800- or 1200-ampere, three-phase switch box. The old switch box was removed and taken home. The contractor removed the interior components of the switch; that is, the fuse holders, bus bars, connectors, etc. The handle, however, was left intact, since this protruded to the outside of the box. Therefore, when the cabinet door was closed, it looked like an authentic, workable fusible switch box. Some carpentry work was done on the interior to provide a rack for about eight guns, a regular padlock keeps the door from readily being opened, and a bright orange sign on the front of the switch reads, DANGER—HIGH VOLTAGE.

If you'd like to try a similar project, make sure the cabinet is placed in a utility room or other location where the electrical panel would normally be. Of course, you won't have any electrical wiring running to the box, but to set the stage right, you should simulate a true-to-life situation—having a piece of electrical conduit (pipe), with locknuts, bushings and the works running from the cabinet to, say, the ceiling of the room, and terminate it right there. This gives the impression that the cabinet is actually fed by electrical conductors. A smaller fuse box connected to the side of the cabinet, or perhaps a bank of push buttons will make the scene even more realistic. An OSHA sign reading DANGER—HIGH VOLTAGE should be installed on the front of the panel. The cabinet may be locked with a padlock—the way most electrical switches are.

Now you don't want to buy a new 1200-amp safety switch from an electrical supplier; the cost of such a switch prohibits doing so. Look for buildings that are being renovated around your area. Such projects usually require the complete rewiring of the building, which means that all new switch gear, panel boards, and the like will be replaced. Architects and consulting engineers seldom allow used equipment to be installed in any building, so the existing electrical equipment will usually be junked. Find one of these projects, and chances are the contractor or foreman will give you a large safety switch suitable for a gun cabinet. He'll also be able to advise you how to make the housing look real in your home or place of business. If not, look at the electrical equipment room in the building where you work. One arrangement is shown in the accompanying drawing.

For a few handguns only, the smaller 100- or 200-amp switch boxes will suffice. The following dimensions of one manufacturer's switch-box housings will give you an idea of what size you will need for your own application.

Gun Safes. Many gun owners are turning to gun safes, not only for added protection, but also to help protect their children from their own basic curiosity and fascination with firearms. Add to this the fact that gun safes and vaults are fully tax deductible, if used to protect firearms you later expect to sell at a profit, and will often lower insurance rates considerably; so any gun owner has a good reason to purchase one. Here is an alphabetical listing of some of the makers of gun safes and vaults, and the type of security equipment they produce. See Appendix III for a more complete listing, with addresses.

A&A Sheet Metal Products, Inc. Two models of all-steel gun cabinets are available from this company. Each is constructed of 18-gauge welded steel, with piano hinges that secure double-swinging doors.

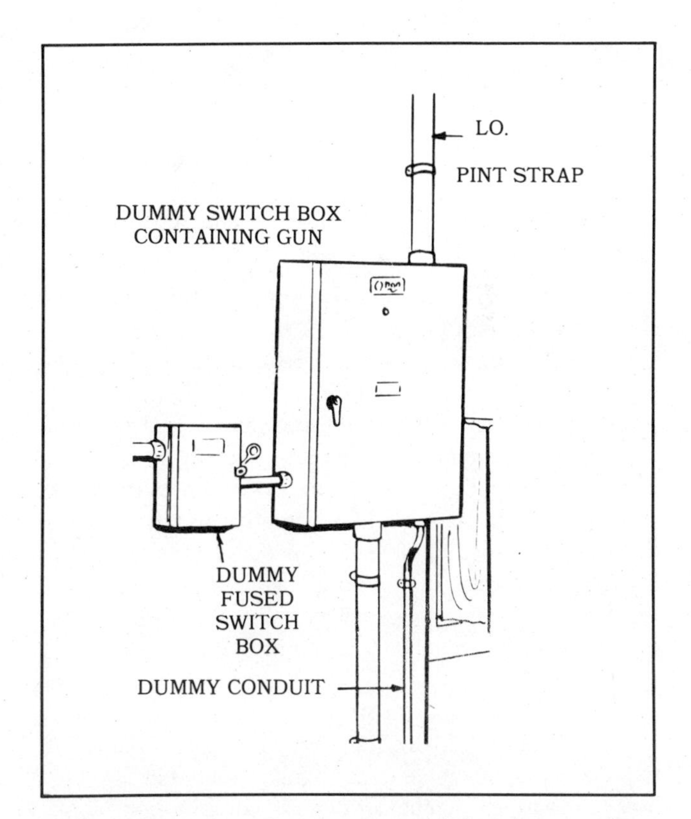

Typical layout for a dummy electrical fuse box used to house guns.

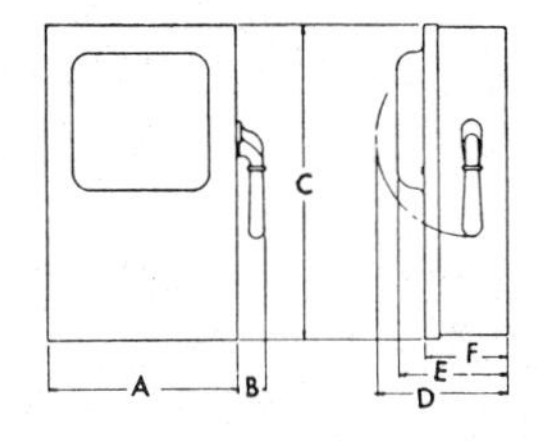

Safety Switches—Enclosure Dimensions

Type TH Safety Switch Cat. No.	See Fig. 1						Type TH Safety Switch Cat. No.	Fig. 1					
	A	B	C	D	E	F		A	B	C	D	E	F
TC36261	9 7/8	1 11/16	11 1/16	6 15/16	5 1/4	3 7/8	TC72321SN	7 3/8	1 11/16	10 11/16	6 15/16	5 1/4	3 7/8
TC36262	11 3/8	1 3/4	13 5/16	7 11/16	5 5/8	3 7/8	TC72322	11 3/8	1 3/4	18 1/16	7 11/16	5 5/8	3 7/8
TC36263	14 3/8	2	24 1/16	9 7/16	7 1/8	5 1/8	TC72322SN	9 1/8	1 3/4	15 5/16	7 11/16	5 5/8	3 7/8
TC36264	10 7/8	2	21 1/16	9 13/16	7 15/16	5 7/16	TC72323	14 3/8	2	24 1/16	9 7/16	7 1/8	5 1/8
TC36265	21	2 1/2	30 3/16	14 3/8	10 3/8	7 7/8	TC72323SN	14 3/8	2	24 1/16	9 7/16	7 1/8	5 1/8
TC36266	23	2 1/2	32 11/16	14 11/16	11 1/4	8 3/4	TC72324	15 1/2	2	30 11/16	9 13/16	8	5 1/2
TC36361	9 7/8	1 11/16	11 11/16	6 15/16	5 1/4	3 7/8	TC72324SN	11	2	28 7/16	9 13/16	8	5 1/2
TC36362	11 3/8	1 3/4	13 5/16	7 11/16	5 5/8	3 7/8	TC72325SN	17	2 1/2	37 3/16	14 3/8	10 3/8	7 7/8
TC36363	14 3/8	2	19 1/16	9 7/16	7 1/8	5 1/8	TC72326SN	23 1/8	2 1/2	44 7/8	14 11/16	11 5/16	8 13/16
TC36364	15 3/8	2	21 1/16	9 13/16	7 15/16	5 7/16	TC72361	9 7/8	1 11/16	14 9/16	6 15/16	5 1/4	3 7/8
TC36365	21	2 1/2	30 3/16	14 3/8	10 3/8	7 7/8	TC72362	11 3/8	1 3/4	18 1/16	7 11/16	5 5/8	3 7/8
TC36366	23	2 1/2	32 11/16	14 11/16	11 1/4	8 3/4	TC72363	14 1/2	2	26 3/16	9 1/2	7 3/16	5 3/16
TC36367	31 3/4	2 9/16	43 11/16	18 3/8	–	10 9/16	TC72364	15 1/2	2	30 11/16	9 13/16	8	5 1/2
TC36368	37 1/8	2 9/16	44 3/8	18 3/4	–	11 9/16	TC72365	21	2 1/2	40 3/16	14 3/8	10 3/8	7 7/8
TC36461	12 3/8	1 11/16	14 15/16	6 15/16	5 1/4	3 7/8	TC72366	23 1/8	2 1/2	44 7/8	14 11/16	11 5/16	8 13/16
TC36462	14 3/8	1 3/4	13 5/16	7 11/16	5 5/8	3 7/8	TC72267	41 1/2	2 1/2	53 1/8	18 3/8	–	10 3/4
TC36463	17 1/2	2	26 5/16	9 1/2	7 3/16	5 3/16	TC72268	47 1/8	2 1/2	60 9/16	18 3/4	–	11 3/4
TC36464	19 1/2	2	21 3/16	9 13/16	7 15/16	5 7/16	TC72367	41 1/2	2 1/2	53 1/8	18 3/8	–	10 3/4
TC72221	7 3/8	1 11/16	10 11/16	6 15/16	5 1/4	3 7/8	TC72368	47 1/8	2 1/2	60 9/16	18 3/4	–	11 3/4
TC72222	9 1/8	1 3/4	15 5/16	7 11/16	5 5/8	3 7/8	TC72421SN	9 7/8	1 11/16	11 1/16	6 15/16	5 1/4	3 7/8
TC72223	14 3/8	2	24 1/16	9 7/16	7 1/8	5 1/8	TC72422SN	11 3/8	1 3/4	18 1/16	7 11/16	5 5/8	3 7/8
TC72224	11	2	28 7/16	9 13/16	8	5 1/2	TC72423SN	14 3/8	2	24 1/16	9 7/16	7 1/8	5 1/8
TC72261	9 7/8	1 11/16	14 9/16	6 15/16	5 1/4	3 7/8	TC72424SN	15 1/2	2	30 11/16	9 13/16	8	5 1/2
TC72262	11 3/8	1 3/4	18 1/16	7 11/16	5 5/8	3 7/8	TC72425SN	21	2 1/2	40 3/16	14 3/8	10 3/8	7 7/8
TC72263	14 1/2	2	26 3/16	9 1/2	7 3/16	5 3/16	TC72426SN	23 1/8	2 1/2	44 7/8	14 11/16	11 5/16	8 13/16
TC72264	15 1/2	2	30 11/16	9 13/16	8	5 1/2	TC72461	12 3/8	1 11/16	14 15/16	6 15/16	5 1/4	3 7/8
TC72265	21	2 1/2	40 3/16	14 3/8	10 3/8	7 7/8	TC72462	14 3/8	1 3/4	18 1/16	7 11/16	5 5/8	3 7/8
TC72266	23 1/8	2 1/2	44 7/8	14 11/16	11 5/16	8 13/16	TC72463	17 1/2	2	26 5/16	9 1/2	7 3/16	5 3/16
TC72321	9 7/8	1 11/16	11 1/16	6 15/16	5 1/4	3 7/8	TC72464	19 1/2	2	30 11/16	9 13/16	8	5 1/2

Dimensions of fusible switch boxes manufactured by General Electric.

Shelves are fabric-lined and a seven-pin tumbler security door lock is used.

Cemco Security Systems. Several models of security safes are produced by this firm for all types of firearms. All are constructed of extra-heavy, quarter-inch plate steel and feature a one-piece seamless interior. The reinforced doors are made of 3/8-inch plate steel, providing a safe of bank-like size and weight. Besides the bank-type locking device, a special designed relocking trigger protects the safes against drilling and punching. Cemco offers a five-year warranty on all its vaults; prices range between $850 to about $1,500.

Center Manufacturing Co. This firm produces insulated gun vaults for protection against both fire and theft. Five large 3/4-inch plated bolts lock all four sides of the heavily constructed doors against forced entry. The bolt operating mechanism and combination lock, similar to those used by banks, are rigidly assembled and protected by a drill-resistant steel plate. The handle operating the five large bolts has a shear pin to protect against any type of forced entry.

Special insulation is solid cast and fully encased between the heavy steel inner and outer sheets of the vault's body and door, offering heat resistance in case of fire. Tongue-and-groove door mouldings fit the body and door jamb to retard the penetration of heat during fires. A relocking device is built into each safe so that if the lock is forced, the locking mechanism becomes inoperative.

Metro Enterprises, Inc. Carpeted security vaults backed with a five-year limited warranty are manufactured by Metro Enterprises. All vault doors are secured by a three-point sliding bar and a Medeco lock. Hardened 1/4-inch internal steel hinges prevent prying or sawing the door.

Nesci Enterprises, Inc. A wide variety of safes is manufactured by this firm for all types of firearms. All safes are made from heavy 14-gauge sheet steel and each door has extra-heavy hinges. Padlocks are positioned so they cannot be reached by a burglar's cutting tool. Several soft sheet plastic or sponge rubber separators are provided to protect the finish on firearms. The company has a five-year guarantee against forcible entry. The approximate retail price is $800 at this writing.

Pro-Steel Security Safes. A division of Provo Steel & Supply Co., this company manufactures a wide variety of safes for both long arms and handguns. These safes feature sophisticated, bank-type locking devices positioned on the inside of all models, requiring that an intruder must penetrate the safe wall before getting to the locking system. Further security is provided by the drill-resistant, hardened-steel plate, so locks cannot be drilled or cut with a torch. Prices range from about $700 to over $2,000.

San Angelo Co., Inc. This is another firm that manufactures security vaults for all types of firearms, each lined with heavy carpet-like fabric and long-pile velour covering on the shelves to serve as cushioning for the firearms. The locking system of each safe comprises two hardened-steel sliding pins with Medeco high-security inner cylinders.

Stowline, Inc. A variety of firearm security products is offered by this firm. Components include heavy-gauge steel plates, piano-type hinges, strong welded reinforcements, a key-locking, three-point deadbolt system and acrylic pile lining. Retail prices range between $300 and $350.

Tread Corporation. The popular "Treadlok" security chests are offered in both upright and horizontal models to house all types of firearms, from handguns to long-barreled muzzleloaders. Tread Corporation also makes chests to fit in the space behind the seat of a pickup truck, along with storage chests for other types of vehicles.

The chests are constructed of 12-gauge, continuously welded steel and remain locked and secure even if the door latch and hinges are removed. Each Treadlok security chest is guaranteed against forcible entry for a period of three years from date of purchase. The average retail price is around $450.

Westfield Sheet Metal Works, Inc. This firm recently introduced a new, fire-retardant security safe designed for all types of firearms. It's constructed of heavy-plate double-wall steel and employs a six-point sliding bar keyed door lock. The weight is 500 pounds and can be bolted to concrete or wood for added security. As with most safes, it is carpeted inside which provides cushioned support for its contents.

Gun Cabinets. Wood and glass gun cabinets do not offer the amount of protection that security vaults do, but they do provide a degree of protection from improper handling. How many times have you had your neighbors over for cocktails and upon seeing your firearms displayed on an open rack, immediately take one down and start pointing it at various objects in the room? Locked gun cabinets prevent this, and also deter children from handling the firearms.

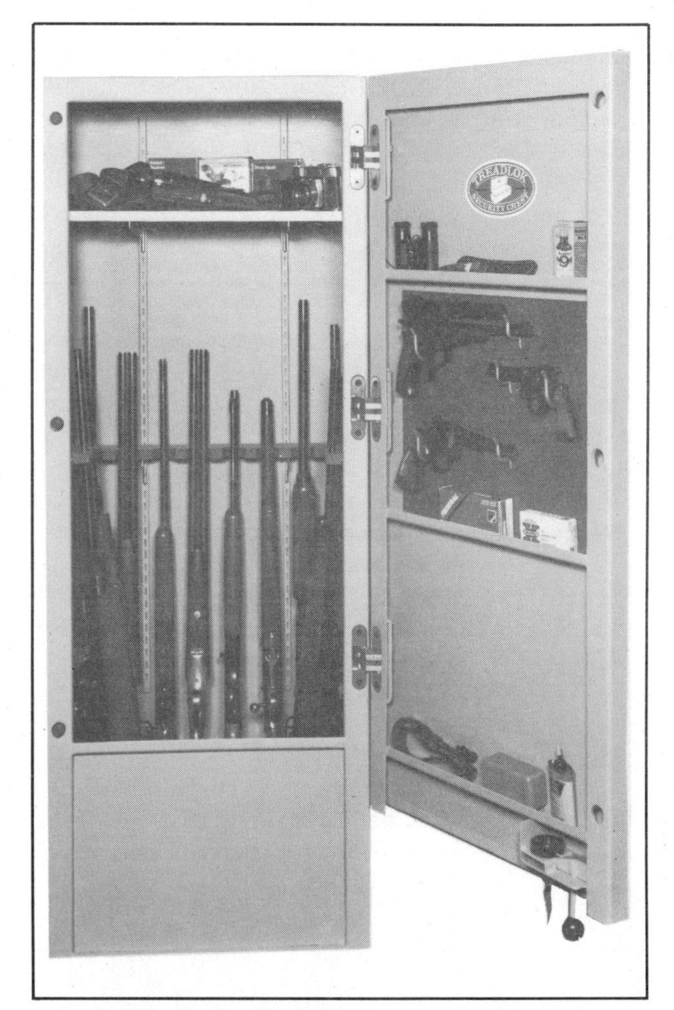

Treadlok Model 1204 upright security chest which houses long guns, handguns and accessories. Chest is constructed of 12-gauge continuously welded steel.

Gun cabinets are also attractive for displaying firearms. If you are interested, write to the manufacturers listed in Appendix III to find out about the various products they have to offer.

Safe deposit boxes. Certain rare guns that cannot be replaced at any price require the utmost protection against deterioration, fire and theft. Probably the safest place to store such guns would be in a safe deposit box at a bank or similar facility. Bank vaults are seldom robbed and are relatively resistant to almost any type of fire. The only problem is caring for the guns while in the vault. However, if the guns are given a thorough cleaning prior to depositing them, and then a protective coating of oil or gun grease is applied, they should not be subject to rust for at least six months—depending upon the area. Most owners who utilize bank deposit boxes for gun storage usually visit the bank about once a month to inspect the guns. If any show signs of needing care, the owner checks them out, takes them home, cleans them, then returns them to the bank.

In recent months there have been rumors about firearm depositories being planned; that is, high-security installations designed especially for housing guns. Atmospheric conditions are perfectly maintained; fireproof structure and security guards provide the highest protection for guns. Trained personnel also inspect all weapons periodically and clean them when needed. Such services, however, are nothing new. Many of the gun clubs in Europe have had similar arrangements for years—with their own in-house gunsmiths to handle repairs and custom work.

Security/Fire Alarm Systems

In general, an alarm system is for the protection of life and property, as well as anything of value—including guns. The typical fire-alarm system consists of sensors placed at strategic locations throughout a building and connected, usually by electric wires, to a power source. When any of these sensors detects either heat or smoke that is above the building's norm, the sensors send a signal to the central control panel. Electronic devices in this panel, in turn, send a signal to an alarm device—which may be a horn, bell, siren—or may even dial the fire department to inform firefighters of the fire.

Security or burglar alarms work in a similar manner in that they also have sensors that detect an illegal entry into a building or lot. These sensors are in the form of contacts that break when a window or door is opened—devices capable of detecting motion, sounds or vibrations. When a sensor detects an intruder, in most cases, it sends a signal to the central control panel and again an alarm is sounded to warn of illegal entry.

All alarm systems have three functions in common: detection, control and annunciation (or alarm) signaling. Many systems incorporate switches or relays that operate when entry, movement, pressure, infrared-beam interruption and other intrusions occur. The control senses the operation of the detector with a relay and produces an output that may operate a bell, siren or silent alarm, such as telephone dialers, to law enforcement agencies. The controls frequently contain ON/OFF

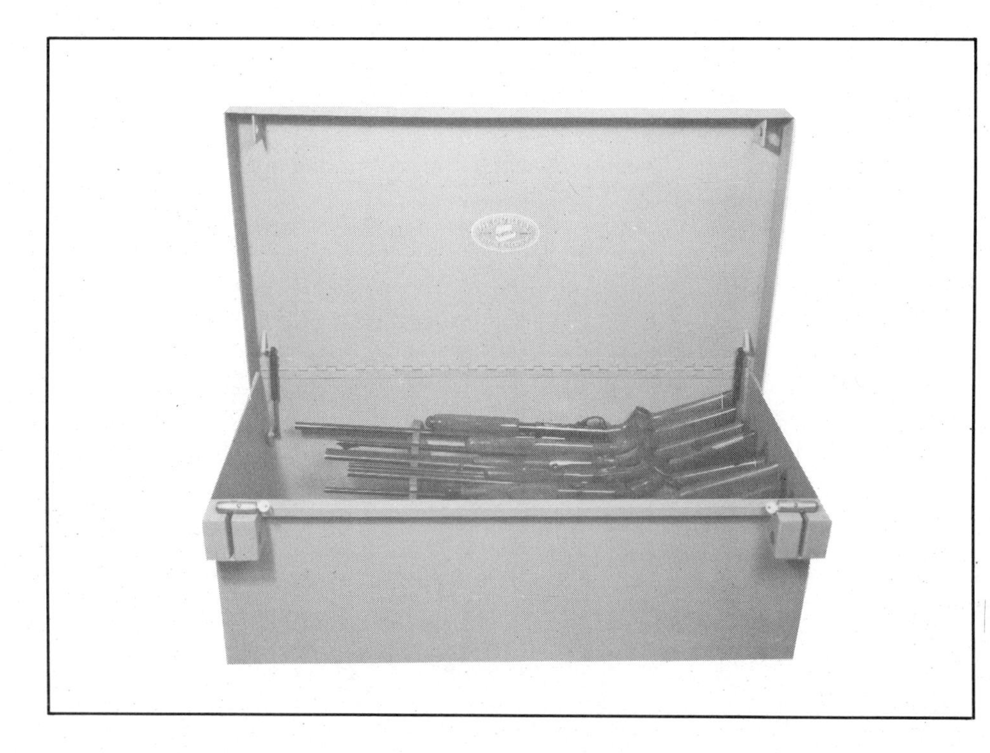

As all Treadlok models, this Model 101R horizontal security chest is guaranteed against forcible entry for three years after purchase.

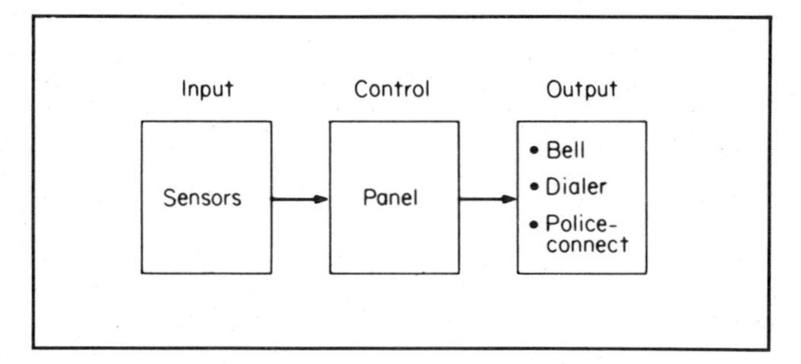

Basic subdivisions of an alarm system.

switches, test meters, time delays, power supplies, standby batteries and terminals for connecting the system together. The control output usually provides power on alarm to operate signaling devices or switch contacts for silent alarms. See the accompanying diagram.

An example of a basic closed-circuit alarm system is also shown. The detection, or input, subdivision in this drawing shows exit/entry door or window contacts. However, the detectors could just as well be smoke or heat detectors, switch mats, ultrasonic detectors, etc. The control subdivision for this system consists of switches, relays, a power supply, a reset button and related wiring. The power supply shown is a 6-V nickel-cadmium battery that is kept charged by a plug-in transformer unit. Terminals are provided on the battery housing to accept 12-V AC charging power from the plug-in transformer, which provides 4- to 6-V power for the detection (protective) circuit and power to operate the alarm or output subdivision.

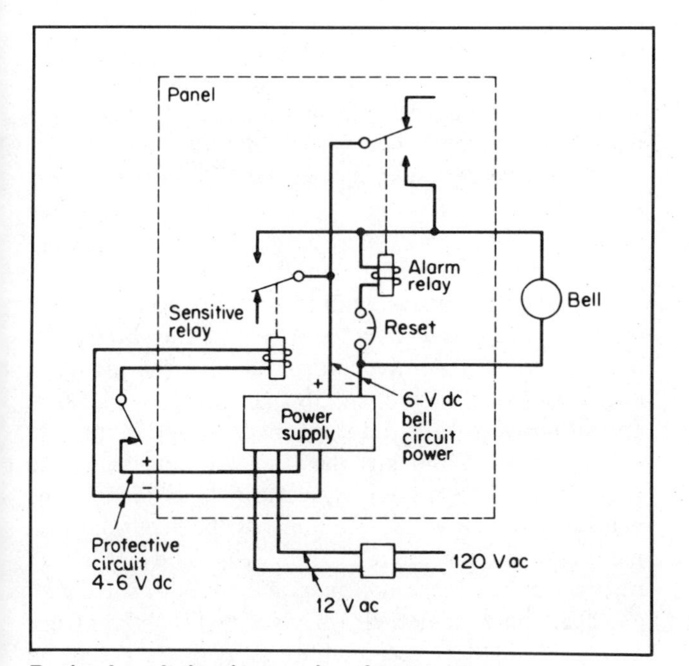

Basic closed-circuit security alarm system.

The third diagram (next page) shows another closed-circuit system. The protective circuit consists of a DC energy source, any number of normally closed intrusion-detection contacts (wired in series), a sensitive relay (R_1) and interconnecting wiring. In operation, the normally closed intrusion contacts are connected to the coil of the sensitive relay. This keeps the relay energized, holding its usually closed contacts open against spring pressure —the all-clear condition of the protective circuit. The opening of any intrusion contact breaks the circuit, which de-energizes the sensitive relay and allows spring force to close the relay contacts. This action initiates the alarm.

The key-operated switch shown is provided for opening the protective circuit for test purposes. A meter (M) is activated when the switch is set to CIRCUIT TEST. The meter gives a current reading only if all intrusion contacts are closed. All three sections of the switch (S_1, S_2, S_3) make contact simultaneously as the key is turned.

Opening of intrusion contacts is not the only event that causes the alarm to activate. Any break in protective-circuit wiring or loss of output from the energy source has the same effect. The circuit is broken, which de-energizes the sensitive relay and allows spring force to close the relay contacts, thus sounding the alarm. Any cross or short circuit between the positive and negative wires of the protective circuit also keeps current from reaching the relay coil and causes dropout, which again sounds the alarm.

Other components of the alarm circuit include a second energy source, an alarm bell and a drop relay (R_2). When the key switch is at ON, dropout of the sensitive relay R_1 and closing of its contacts completes a circuit to energize the coil of drop relay R_2. Closing of the drop relay's normally open contacts rings the bell and latches in the drop-relay coil so that R_2 stays energized even if the protective circuit returns to normal and opens the sensitive relay's contacts. As a result, the bell continues to ring until the key switch is turned away from ON to break the latching connection to the R_2 coil.

Drop relays often have additional contacts to control other circuits or devices. The extra contacts shown are for turning on lights, triggering an automatic telephone dialer, etc. But the two main functions of the

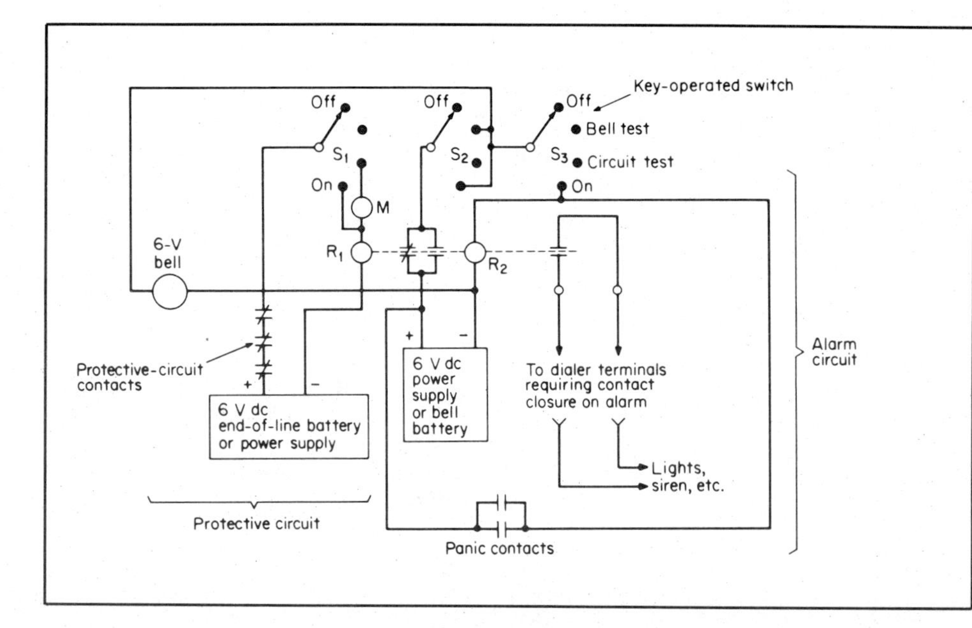

Closed-circuit security alarm system, consisting of a DC energy source, any number of normally closed intrusion-detection contacts, a sensitive relay (R_1) and interconnecting wiring.

drop relay are actuation of the alarm and latching the coil to keep the circuit in the alarm condition.

Almost all burglar systems use a closed-loop protective circuit, so only a brief description of an open-circuit system will be given here. In general, the system consists of an annunciator connected to a special design contact on each door and window and a relay so connected that when any window or door is opened, it will cause current to pass through the relay. The relay, in turn, will operate to close a circuit on a bell, horn or other type of annunciator, which will continue to sound until it is shut off, thereby alerting the occupants or law enforcement agencies.

Wire sizes for the majority of low-voltage systems range from No. 22 to No. 18 AWG. However, where larger-than-normal currents are required or when the distance between the outlets is long, it may be necessary to use wire sizes larger than specified to prevent excessive voltage drop.

Most closed systems use two-wire No. 22 or No. 24 AWG conductors and are color-coded to identify them. A No. 18 pair normally is adequate for connecting bells or sirens to controls if the run is 40 feet (12 meters) or less. Many, however, prefer to use No. 16 or even No. 14 cable.

The wiring of any alarm system is installed like any other type of low-voltage system; that is, locating the outlets, furnishing a power supply and, finally, interconnecting the components with the proper size and type of wire.

A summary of the various components for a typical security/fire-alarm system is depicted in the following illustration.

The installation of a security system to protect your firearms as well as other valuables is not beyond the capabilities of most gun owners. However, a sketch of the building should be prepared or the original blueprints should be obtained. The sketch should be drawn to scale and should show the location of all windows, doors, chases, closets, etc. A simple riser diagram showing the various components, such as smoke and heat sensors, control panel and alarm signals, should also appear on the sketch. When this is completed, the installer can begin the design of the security/fire-alarm system. Many suppliers will help you lay the system out—often at no charge.

The installation of a protective security/fire-alarm circuit should always start at the protective-circuit energy source, as if it were an end-of-line battery—a battery remote from the control panel—even though it may actually be a power supply installed in the panel. A pair of wires is run from this power source to the first contact location, but just the positive wire is cut and connected to the two contact terminals as shown. The neutral or common wire is not cut, but continues on parallel with the positive or "hot" wire. The pair is then run to the next contact—door, window, sensor, etc.—and again only the hot wire is connected to the contacts. This procedure is repeated until all contacts are wired in series, and then the pair of wires is run from the last

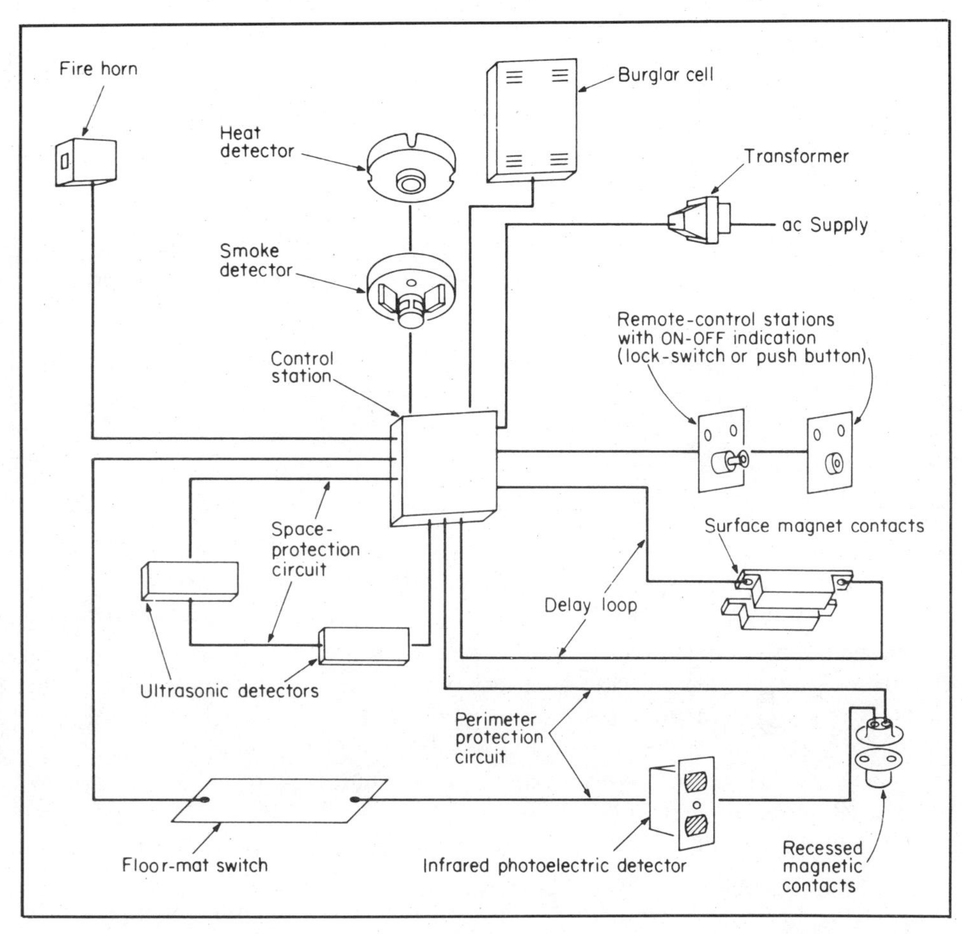

Various components for a typical security/fire-alarm system, among them an infrared photoelectric detector, ultrasonic detectors, smoke detector and heat detector.

contact device in the system to the protective-circuit terminals in the panel. Although the markings will vary from manufacturer to manufacturer, the terminals for the starting connections will read something like LOOP POWER OUT, while the terminating terminals will read IN or a similar term.

A simple circuit of the wiring connections described above is shown in the illustration at right. Obviously, the system would operate with just a single-wire, positive-leg circuit run from contact to contact, with the negative power-supply terminal connected directly to the negative protective-circuit terminal within the cabinet. However, manufacturers discourage this practice, since trouble-shooting a single-wire circuit can be extremely time-consuming, and the single wire is more vulnerable to defeat by an intruder with no trouble symptoms occurring to warn the user of the loss of protection.

An exit/entry delay relay is sometimes used on security systems so that authorized personnel may exit and enter (using their door keys) without activating the alarm. However, a shunt switch is most often preferred. The purpose of the shunt lock is to enable an authorized

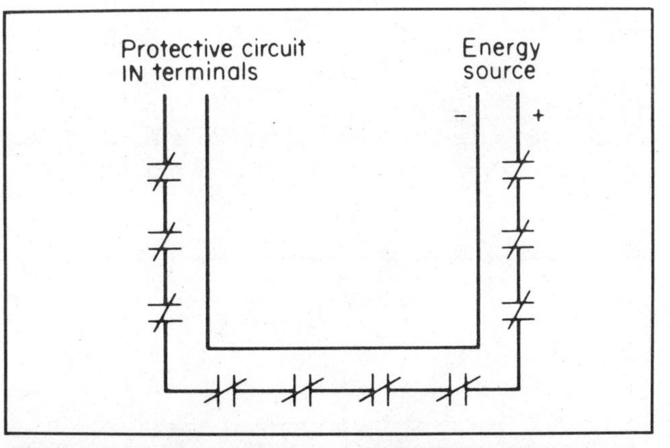

The negative conductor is run with the positive conductor to all contacts, even though the system would operate with just a single, positive-leg wire run from contact to contact.

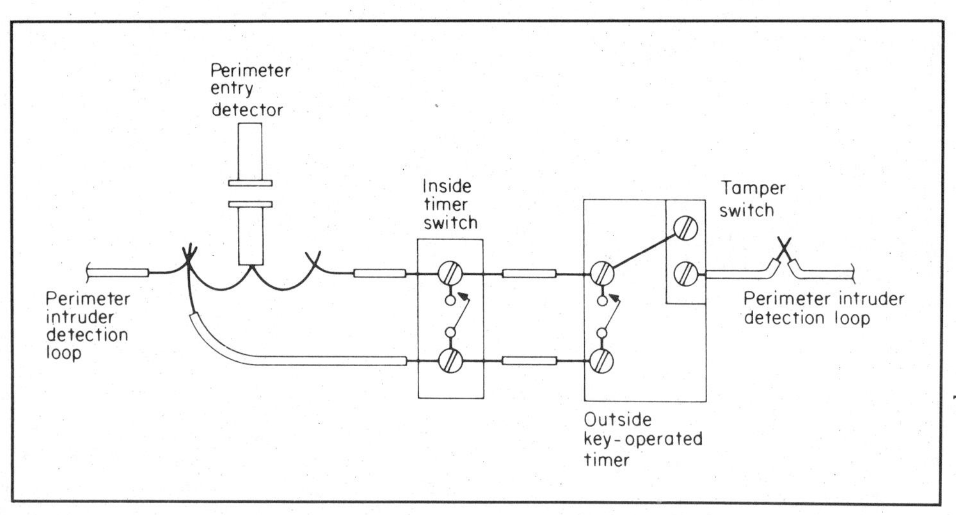

Typical shunt switch circuit.

person with a key to shunt out the contacts on the door used for entry/exit, allowing him or her to enter or leave the premises without causing an alarm when the alarm system is turned on. The shunt lock does extend outside the protected premises, however, and it is a potential weak link in the system. Following the two procedures suggested below makes defeat of the shunt lock much more difficult:

1. Install the shunt lock at the door that is most brightly illuminated and most readily visible to passersby.

2. Wire the shunt lock switch to the magnetic contact terminals. This arrangement traps the lock, so any attempt to pull it out to gain access to its terminals will break the positive side of the protective circuit and cause an alarm to sound.

Contacts used to signal the opening of doors, windows, gates, drawers, etc., are usually mounted on the frame of the object, while the magnet unit is mounted on the moving part itself. The two units should be positioned so the magnet is close to and parallel with the switch when the door or window, etc., is closed. This keeps the shunt lock actuated, but opening the door or window moves the magnet away and releases the switch mechanism.

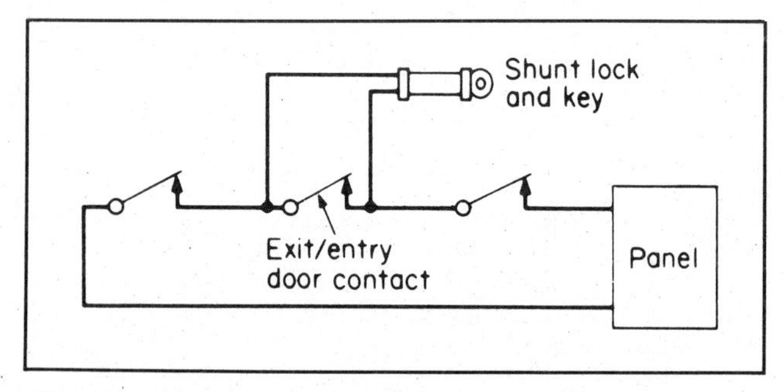

Wire the shunt lock switch to the magnetic contacts as shown. This traps the lock so any attempt to pull it out to gain access to its terminals will break the positive side of the protective circuit, thus sounding an alarm.

As long as the faces of the switch and magnet are parallel and in close proximity when the door or window is closed, they may be oriented side-to-side, top-to-top or top-to-side. Mounting spacers may be used under the units, if necessary, to improve their alignment and proximity.

Terminal covers are available for most makes of door contacts to give the installation a more finished look and also to protect the terminal connections against tampering.

Selecting equipment. Dozens of manufacturers offer security/fire-alarm systems with a wide selection of accessories to fill practically every need. The selection of a particular system for a given application will usually depend upon the following factors:

1. Type of building to be secured;
2. Allotted budget;
3. Availability of equipment;
4. Availability of service.

The accompanying diagram illustrates various components of a residential security/fire-alarm system as distributed by NuTone Housing Products. The surface magnetic detector is the most versatile entry detector for residential alarm systems and should be considered first as a method of protecting any movable door or window. These detectors can be mounted on wood, metal, and even glass, if necessary. They can be mounted with screws, double-sided tape or epoxy. Obviously, the tape and epoxy are useful on glass, aluminum or any other surface where screws cannot be used. However, when using tape or epoxy, make certain that the surface is clean, dry, smooth and at least 65°F. (18°C.) when applied.

Where the appearance of surface-mounted systems may be objectionable, recess-mounted magnetic protectors may be used. These detectors are more difficult to install, requiring greater care on the installer's part, but few problems develop if the following precautions are adhered to:

1. Be careful not to damage or destroy any weatherproofing seal around windows, doors or other openings.

2. If a recess-mounted entry detector is installed in the window sill, you must prevent water seepage to the switch by applying a sealant under the switch flange and around the switch body.

3. When drilling holes to accept each half of the detector, be sure the holes line up and there is no more than ¼-inch (0.6-cm.) space between the two sections of the detector.

4. Be certain there is enough space between the window and its frame (or door and its frame) when each is closed; that is, there must be enough space (usually equaling 1/16 inch or 0.16 cm.) for the protrusion of both sections when they meet.

5. If the window frame is not thick enough to accept the magnetic section of the detector, the detector can be mounted in the side frame.

In most cases where it is difficult to protect a window or door by mounting any of the direct-type detectors, the area directly inside the door or window can be

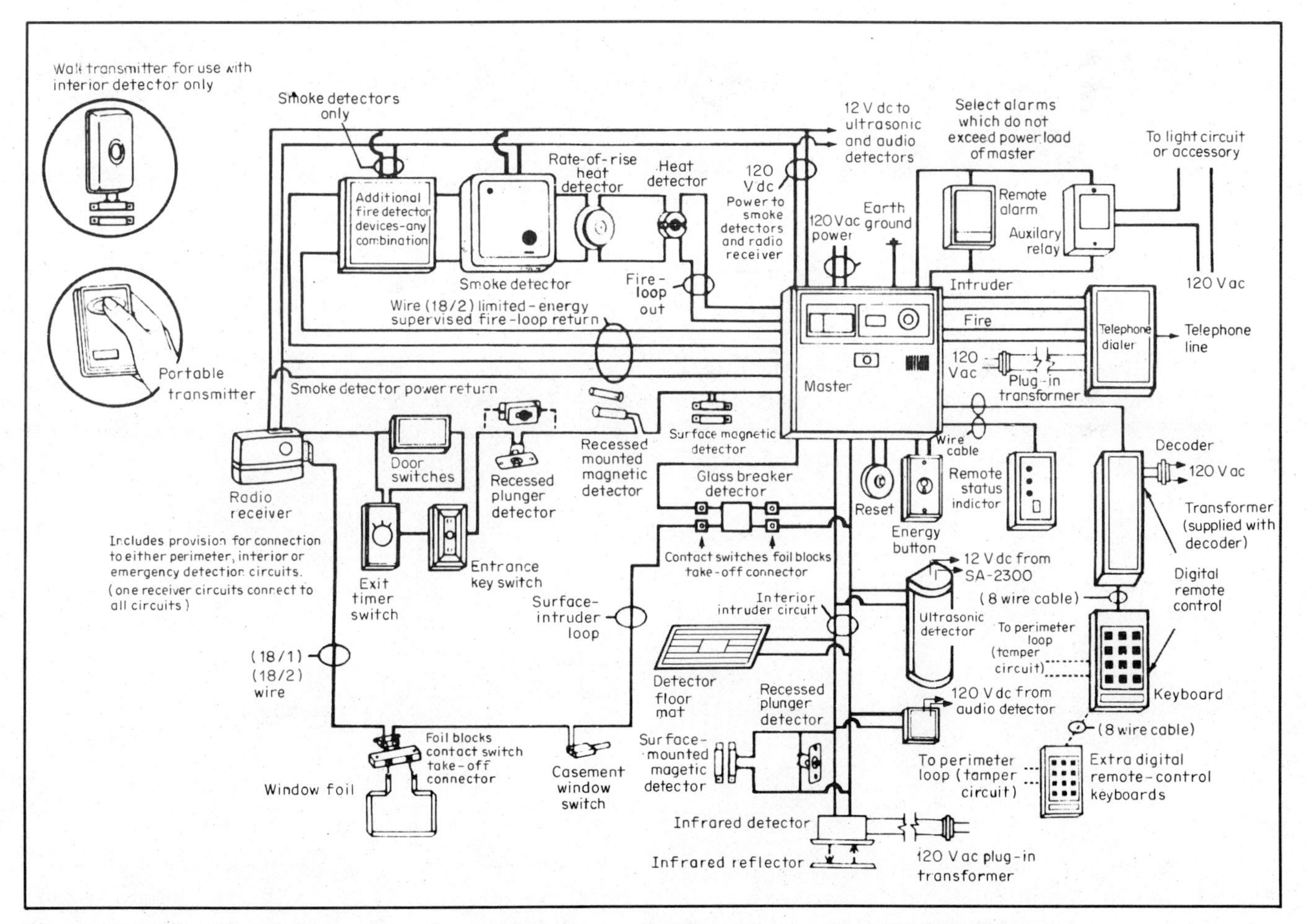

Diagram of the various components of a residential security/fire-alarm system distributed by NuTone Housing Products.

Vibration detectors are an excellent means of protecting the premises and usually require the least amount of labor to install.

protected with interior "space" detectors, such as a floor-mat detector or an ultrasonic motion detector.

Floor-mat detectors are easily concealed under rugs at doors, windows, tops or bottoms of stairways or any other area on which an intruder is likely to step. A light pressure on the mat triggers the alarm.

There are also rolls of super-thin floor matting that can be cut to any desired length. These rolls can be used on stair treads and in areas near sliding glass doors or other large glass areas, entrance foyers, etc. In households with unrestricted pets, these mats are almost useless, since the pets roam around the home and are certain to step on one of the mats and trigger the alarm.

Other space detectors include ultrasonic motion detectors, audio detectors and infrared detectors. Care must be used with any of these units because the protected area is limited both in width and depth, depending upon the particular unit.

The ultrasonic motion detector can be used in large glass-walled rooms that might otherwise be difficult to

Infrared light detectors sense persons crossing their paths. Note that this device resembles a conventional duplex electrical receptacle.

Surface-mounted door contact used to protect a back entryway in a gunshop. When "armed," any break in the system, such as when the door is opened, will trigger the alarm.

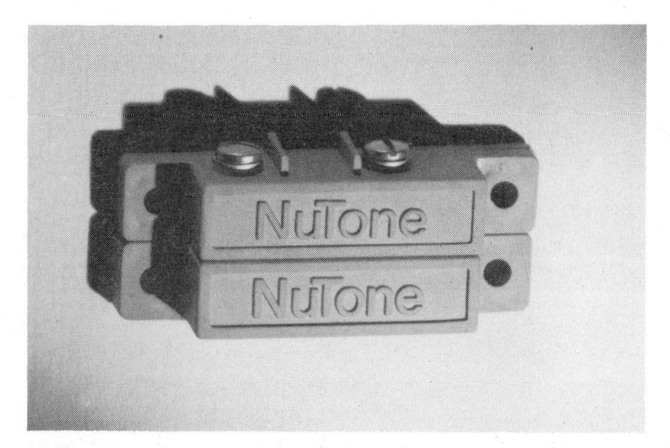

NuTone surface-mounted door or window contact.

protect and in hallways or entries or in virtually any area an intruder would have to pass through in moving about a home. They are especially useful as added protection (when conventional detectors are also used) to monitor a "valuables" room or area.

Most ultrasonic motion detectors are designed for mounting on either the wall or ceiling. They emit inaudible high-frequency sound waves in an elliptical pattern that ranges from 12 feet (4 m.) to 35 feet (11 m.) by 5 feet (2 m.) to 20 feet (6 m.) for most residential models. When an intruder moves within the secured area, movement interrupts the established pattern of sound waves and sounds the alarm. Some designs of motion detectors can be rotated up to 180 degrees for maximum coverage of the area being monitored.

Another type of motion detector is the audio detector. This type senses certain sharp sounds known to be present in forced entry, such as wood splintering or glass breaking. When these sounds are received through the unit's miniature microphone, the detector triggers the control unit to sound an alarm.

Audio detectors are best utilized in areas that are seldom used, such as an attic, garage or closed-off wing. They can be used in other areas, but when such areas are subject to frequent daytime activity, it is recommended that they be activated only at night when the family retires or they are away from home.

Infrared detectors are another type of motion detector. A combination transmitter-receiver is used to project an invisible pulsating beam at a special bounce-back reflector on an opposite wall. Any interruption of the beam activates the system's alarm. Infrared detectors can be wired either to the perimeter or interior circuit, but for faster response, it is recommended that they be connected to the interior circuit. Infrared detectors are designed for indoor areas such as entries, hallways, rooms, etc. Most cover a span from 3 feet (1 m.) to 75 feet (23 m.), so they may be used in practically any indoor area or room.

13.
Caring for Used Guns

A well-built firearm will last a lifetime—several lifetimes—if it is reasonably cared for. Besides longer life, increased accuracy and smoother operation will also result when gun owners spend a little time keeping their firearms in first-class condition. A firearm that has not been badly neglected needs only a few minutes of cleaning at regular intervals to keep it in good working order. However, once a firearm has been neglected, it becomes increasingly difficult to clean satisfactorily.

The necessary implements for keeping any sporting arm in good condition are few and inexpensive. All that is required is one of the basic cleaning kits available at any sporting goods store. These kits contain a cleaning rod, rod tips, powder solvent, gun oil and grease, wire brush and cleaning patches. There are, of course, other items, such as a gun cleaning rack, that will make the job easier, but the contents of the gun cleaning kit will usually suffice if the firearm to be cleaned has not been seriously neglected.

Basic Cleaning

Using the cleaning kit, soak a gun patch in powder solvent (bore cleaner) and push the patch through the slotted tip attached to the end of the cleaning rod. Insert the tip into the barrel—preferably from the breech end—and run the patch the full length of the barrel, and return. Repeat this operation as many times as is necessary to saturate the powder residue thoroughly—usually 15 or 20 times. Then use a dry patch to dry the bore. During this operation, change patches often until the last one comes out perfectly clean. Finish the bore cleaning by lightly oiling a clean patch and running it up and back through the bore.

Badly neglected bores will require the use of a wire bronze or brass bristle brush. Soak a clean patch with bore cleaner; run it through the bore as discussed previously to partially loosen the sticky powder fouling. Again, working from the breech end, if possible, dip the bristle brush into the powder solvent (bore cleaner) and run the brush up and down the bore with the cleaning rod. The brush should be pushed completely out of the barrel on each down stroke, because reversing the direction of the brush inside the bore will ruin the brush.

After running the brass brush up and down the bore a half dozen times or more, repeat the first operation; that is, install the patch-holding tip on your cleaning rod, insert a patch with powder solvent and swab the bore out again. Then use a clean patch, with no solvent, to wipe out the excess solvent. This may require as many as six clean patches. Run the first patch down, up, down and out at the muzzle end, but run the remaining patches through the bore only once—discarding each at the muzzle end. The final patch should show perfectly clean and dry. If not, the preceding operations

The minimum requirement needed to keep most sporting arms in good operating condition is a basic cleaning kit, such as the one available from Hoppe's.

must be repeated for a proper cleaning job.

The final step is oiling with light gun oil. This will protect the gun for a period of approximately one month, depending on atmospheric conditions and how the gun is stored. If the gun is to be stored for a period longer than a month, use gun grease instead of light oil.

The outside of the firearm should also be cleaned and lightly rubbed with gun oil. Leather slings should be coated with a leather preservative and gun stocks should also be treated, as discussed later in this chapter.

When cared for properly, guns will rarely be ruined by rust, fouling or corrosion from routine handling and shooting.

Gun Cleaning Racks. For very little expense you can build a suitable gun-cleaning rack out of scraps found in your basement or shop. Rifles are easily held in place for cleaning by constructing a simple jig as shown in the accompanying illustrations. Two chocks, cut from either a 2 × 6-inch or 2 × 8-inch wooden board are merely nailed or screwed to a baseboard the same width as the chocks. Shotguns as well as rifles can be clamped in a standard bench vise, using pads on the vise jaws to protect the finish. You can also make a simple wood vise with a 2 × 4-inch piece of pine wood by drilling a hole to fit the barrel through the narrow sides

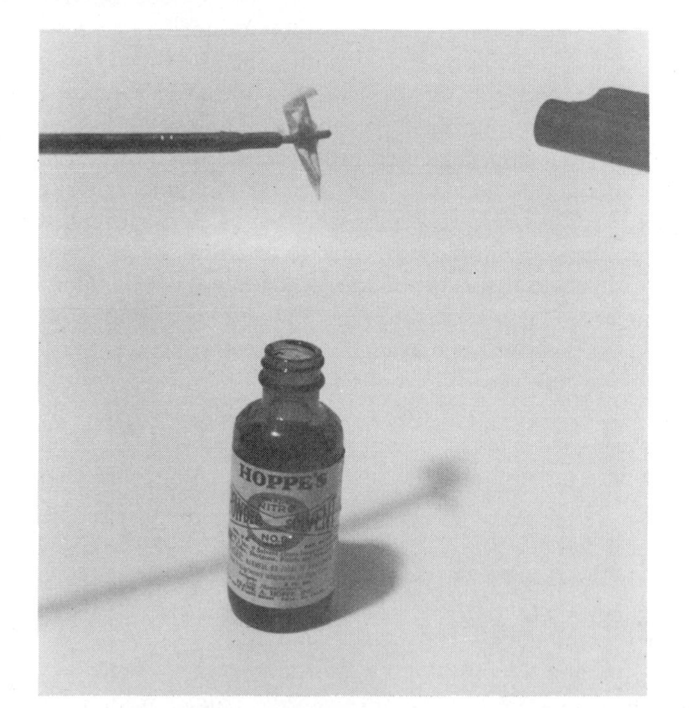

One of the first basic cleaning steps is to clean the bore: soak a cloth patch in bore cleaner and push it through the bore on a slotted tip attached to the end of a cleaning rod. Push it back and forth about 15 to 20 times, then use a dry patch to dry the bore.

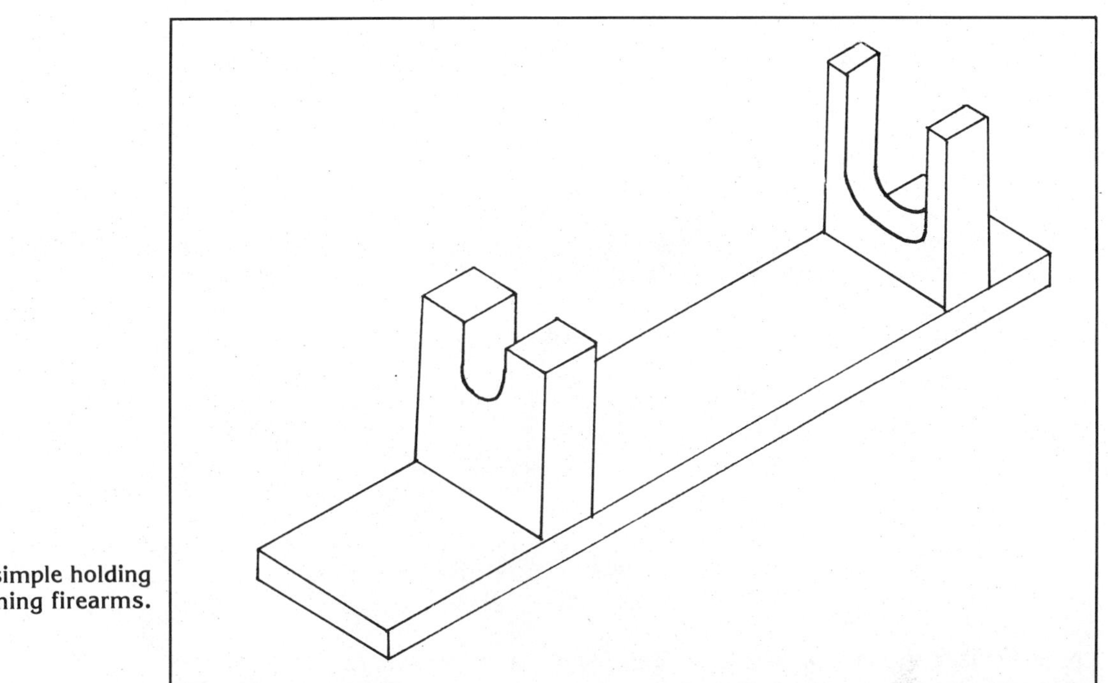

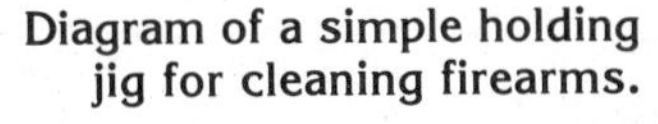
Diagram of a simple holding jig for cleaning firearms.

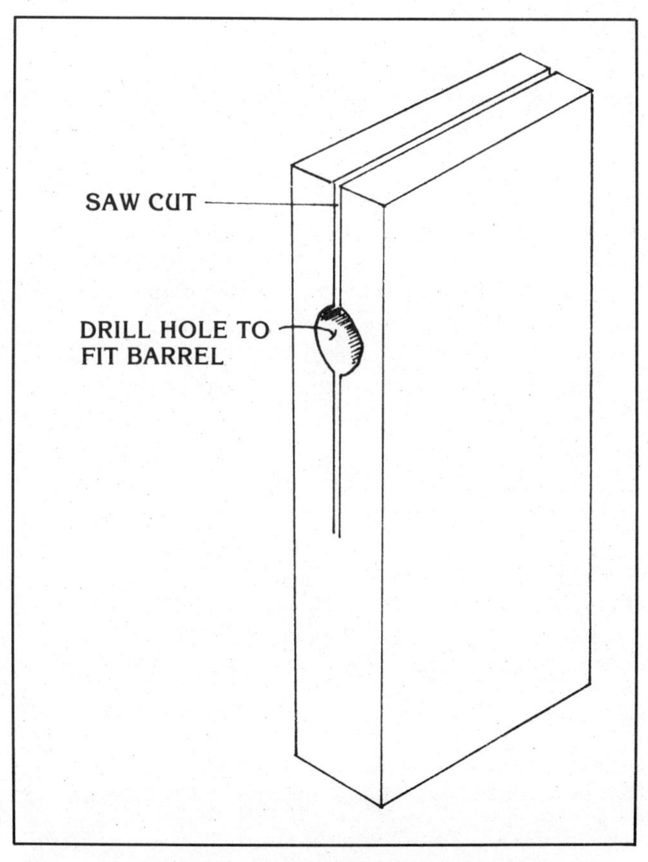

You can construct a simple vise by using a scrap piece of 2 x 4 lumber and drilling a hole to fit the barrel.

of the wood member, and then slitting it as shown. A conventional "C" clamp is used to apply pressure to the top of the vise to secure the firearm in place.

If you don't care to go to the trouble of building your own, the Decker Shooting Vise is reasonably priced and greatly simplifies the operation of gun cleaning. Properly used, the Naugahyde covering at all locations touching the gun will completely eliminate all scratching and marring. The base can be secured to a workbench or the kitchen table with C-clamps, or it can be permanently mounted with screws or bolts. This vise is also excellent for holding firearms while mounting sights, bore sighting and zeroing rifles.

Metal Fouling

Besides powder fouling, the shooter must sometimes give consideration to metal fouling—especially on some of the used guns you will undoubtedly purchase that have been seriously neglected. Metal fouling is caused by the deposit of metal left by the bullet in the bore. When the fouling is caused by jacketed bullets, the term *metal fouling* is used; when caused by lead bullets, it's called *leading*.

Regardless of the cause, metal fouling can cause poor accuracy until the problem is corrected. Examine the bore with a bore light. Any fouling will be visible by showing long streaks, flaky deposits or perhaps

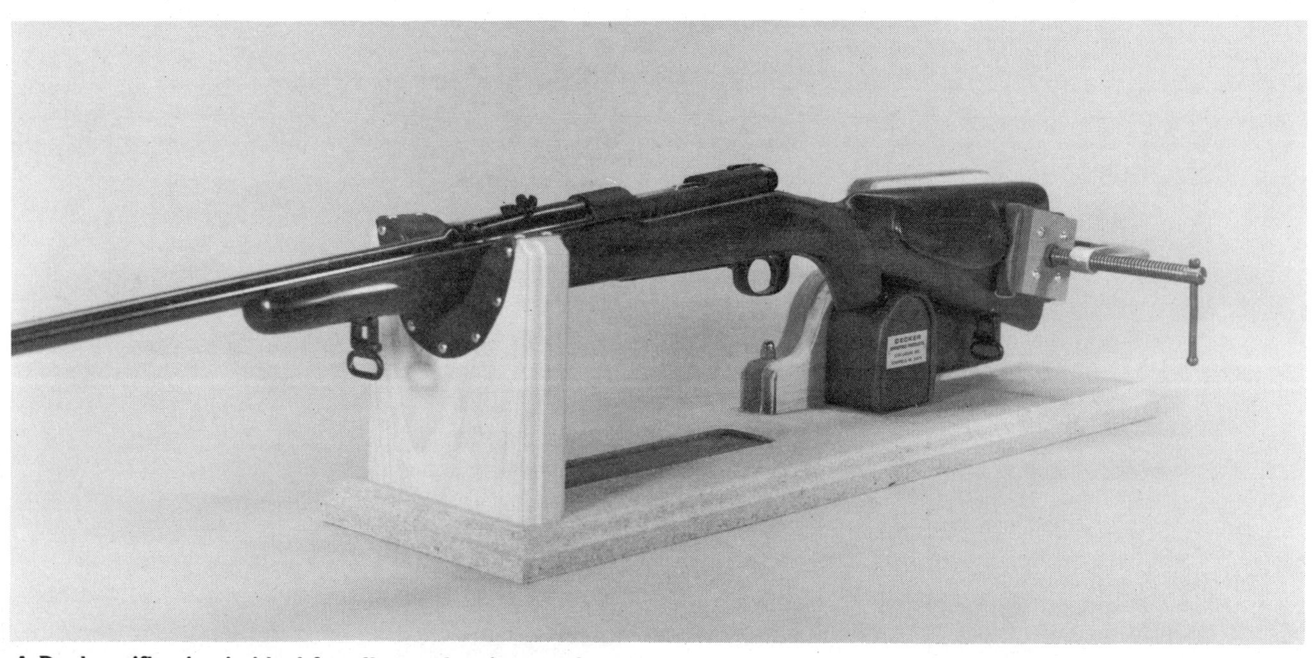

A Decker rifle vise is ideal for all gun cleaning needs.

lumps of metal particles sticking to the lands and the grooves of the barrel.

For light fouling, purchase a quantity of J-B Non-Imbedding Bore Cleaning Compound. Besides removing lead, metal and powder fouling from all types of firearms, it is guaranteed by the manufacturer to improve the accuracy of any firearm it is used on. It will not injure the finest bore and will also help guard against rust.

To get rid of heavy fouling, make a solution of the following: 1 ounce ammonium persulfate; 200 grams ammonium carbonate; 4 ounces water; and 6 ounces strong ammonia. You should be able to purchase the ammonium compounds and the ammonia at any pharmacy. To prepare the solution, stir the first two powders together and in a glass jar dissolve them in the water; add the ammonia and mix. Store in a dark glass bottle.

Before using this de-fouling solution, be aware that it should only come in contact with the *inside* of the barrel. Any of the solution that is accidentally spilled on the stock and metal finish will surely ruin them.

First, plug the chamber end of the barrel with a cork or plastic stopper, making sure the cork is perfectly tight so none of the liquid will leak out the breech end. Brace the barrel in a vertical position in a bench vise with padded jaws so the chamber end is at the lower end. Now, insert a plastic funnel into the muzzle end of the barrel. Be absolutely certain that this funnel fits well into the bore; remember, you don't want any of the solution to spill onto the outside surface of the firearm. With everything in place, carefully pour the solution into the barrel, being very careful not to let the solution run over.

At first, the solution will appear colorless, but it will soon take on a blue appearance as it begins to dissolve the metallic deposits. Allow it to set for about 15 minutes before pouring it out. Again, be very careful not to let any of the solution remain on the outside finish. Have a clean cloth handy and, as soon as the last of the solution has left the barrel, immediately wipe off the muzzle; better yet, flush it with water for a few minutes. Then perform the basic cleaning procedure of the firearm as previously discussed. Also repeat the basic cleaning steps perhaps twice a week for the next two weeks.

Leading can be removed with a wire brush, the metal-fouling method just outlined or mercuric ointment on a flannel patch. Some shooters pour a few ounces of mercury into the barrel after plugging one end. Then while holding a finger over the opposite end, the barrel is tilted up and down a few times. Common vinegar will sometimes do the job, too. Exercise caution if you use mercury because it is poisonous.

When you find that a rough bore does not "cure" itself, lapping should be done to correct the problem. Heat the muzzle to a moderate temperature, then pour molten lead into the barrel. The lead should fill about three inches of the barrel.

Lapping

A perfectly smooth bore will pick up very little lead or metal fouling, so if you keep your guns in good shape, you'll seldom need to perform the above mentioned tasks. On the other hand, a badly pitted bore will always foul to some extent, causing poor accuracy.

In the case of lead bullets, a rough bore will sometimes "cure" itself after several firings as lead fills up the pits. However, if the problem persists, the barrel should be lapped. This job is usually best left to a qualified gunsmith, but many hobbyists have been known to perform the operation at home successfully. Here's how it's done.

A steel rod, slightly smaller than the bore diameter, is used in the barrel. One end is notched both lengthwise and crosswise. The other end of the rod is set in a cross-handle with a ball bearing so the rod can turn freely and follow the twist of the rifling when it is pushed through the barrel.

First, clean the barrel of all foreign matter, then apply a film of light gun oil to the bore. (Of course, the barrel should be removed from the stock during the entire lapping operation.) Push a cotton string wrapped tightly around the front of the rod, the tip of which is fluxed, through the barrel from the breech end until the tip is within an inch of the muzzle. Using a propane torch, heat the muzzle of the barrel to a medium temperature, about the same as heating bullet moulds prior to casting bullets. If great care is taken, you can perform this operation without seriously discoloring the bluing on the firearm. In the meantime, melt lead in a pot at about 650 to 700 degrees F. Then, with the rod in place, the first few inches of the muzzle heated, pour the molten lead into the barrel, which should fill about three inches of the barrel—the distance from the cotton string to the rod tip. When cool, push the lead a short distance out of the muzzle so it can be trimmed.

The lap is then coated with oil and carefully pushed a couple of inches out of the muzzle, but never entirely out. Should the lap be pushed completely out accidentally, you'll have to start over again—melting the old lap down and repouring a new one. This couple of inches of exposed lead is also oiled and then a compound, such as valve lapping compound, Clover lapping compound, etc., is applied to the lap. You'll notice that the lap has

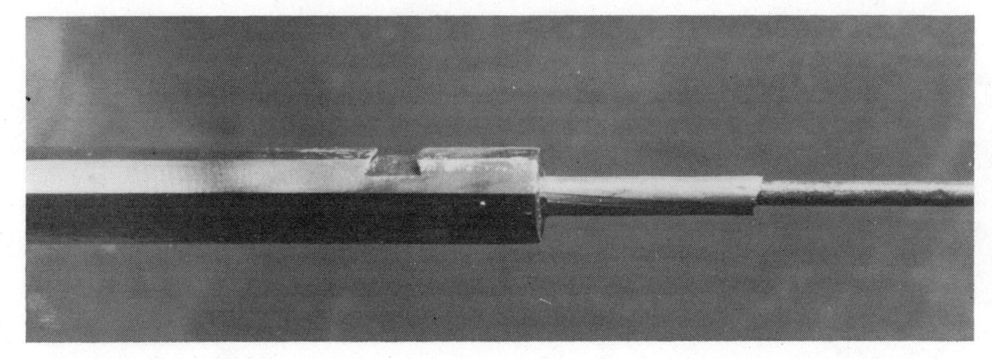

When cool, the lead is pushed a short distance out of the muzzle so it can be trimmed. Then apply oil and lapping compound, pushing and pulling the lap through the bore until the barrel has a uniform feel.

taken the shape of the bore, showing rifling and all. These rifling grooves in the lap will follow the twist of the rifling down the bore as the lap is being pushed back and forth.

Depending on the extent of pitting, work the lap carefully through the bore from 10 to 50 times, recoating it with more lapping compound every 10 cycles. The lap should be pushed and pulled with steady tension until the barrel has the same feel the entire length. The rod must be free to turn with the rifling of the barrel or serious damage will result to the bore. Once a smoothness is obtained throughout the complete length of the barrel, remove the lap and clean the barrel with bore cleaner; then slug the bore by lightly driving a lead bullet through the bore and measuring it with a micrometer. This will give you the exact size of the lands and grooves and the precise bore diameter.

Polishing Shotgun Bores

Shotgun barrels and chambers may be easily lapped or polished by the hobbyist since they are smooth bored. However, care must be taken not to remove the choke. Light pits, for example, may be removed by inserting one end of a cleaning rod in an electric hand drill and attaching a wire brush to the opposite end. Wrap fine steel wool around the brush, insert the assembly into the bore and switch on the drill motor. As the steel wool revolves, slowly push it back and forth in the bore until the desired polish is obtained. Just don't polish about the first four inches of the muzzle too heavily to insure that the choke will not be removed.

Deep pits in shotgun barrels usually cannot be removed. First of all, the thin tubes will not stand too much metal being removed. Even if it were possible, the final result would be a wavy barrel (or else an enlarged barrel), probably causing shot patterns to go wild.

Removing Rust

There is little doubt that ferric oxide, or plain old red rust, gives gun owners perennial problems—on new as well as older guns. Usually, proper cleaning of firearms will solve the rust problem. The frequency of the cleaning will vary with the use of the guns and the weather to which they are subjected. In most cases, a thorough cleaning after each day's hunt or firing will suffice, except when a gun is used or stored near salt water or in humid areas. In these cases, it may be necessary to clean the gun every few days and wipe it off with an oil-soaked cloth every day. I still remember those days in boot training at Parris Island, S.C. Our barracks were located right on a canal and the salty air from Beaufort Bay swept over the entire island. Light rust would sometimes appear on the Parkerized finish of our M1's in only a day or two if they were not properly cleaned. Therefore, as I recall, we were required to clean our weapons daily.

You can usually remove light rust from a firearm by first spraying the rusted area with WD-40, then rubbing the affected area with a rough bath towel. Little, if any, bluing will be removed by this method, provided the bluing was satisfactory to begin with. It might take a lot of elbow grease, but if you keep at it, the rust will eventually come off.

When purchasing used guns, you may find that some will be so heavily rusted that the best solution may be to have them completely refinished. However, some collectibles should not be refinished or their value will be lowered tremendously. Instead of refinishing the gun, try using No. 0000 steel wool dampened with WD-40 or G66 Gun Cleaner. A relatively new product called "707" is another excellent product for removing rust, as is Naval Jelly. With the steel wool dampened with any of these solutions, rub the rusted area lightly until all rust is removed.

For badly rusted areas, you have one of two choices. Either oil the gun frequently and leave it like it is or remove all the rust and have the gun refinished. Of course, all of the original finish must be removed in this latter method and, in some cases, it may be best to leave the gun just the way it is.

Gunstock Maintenance

During normal use, the wood on firearms will be subjected to scratches from briars, barbed wire fences and other sharp objects. It will also suffer chips, dents and perspiration stains. Again, on some guns it is desirable to preserve the original finish to the greatest extent, so you don't want to refinish the whole stock unless it is absolutely necessary.

For rejuvenating gunstocks, I've found a product called Patina Rub, available from Brookstone, Peterborough, New Hampshire 03458 to be about the best on the market, especially for the older, pre-lacquer finishes. To use it, remove all metal from the stock with the possible exception of the butt plate and dip a felt pad (included with the kit) in the solution. Rub the stock with moderate pressure in straight strokes with the

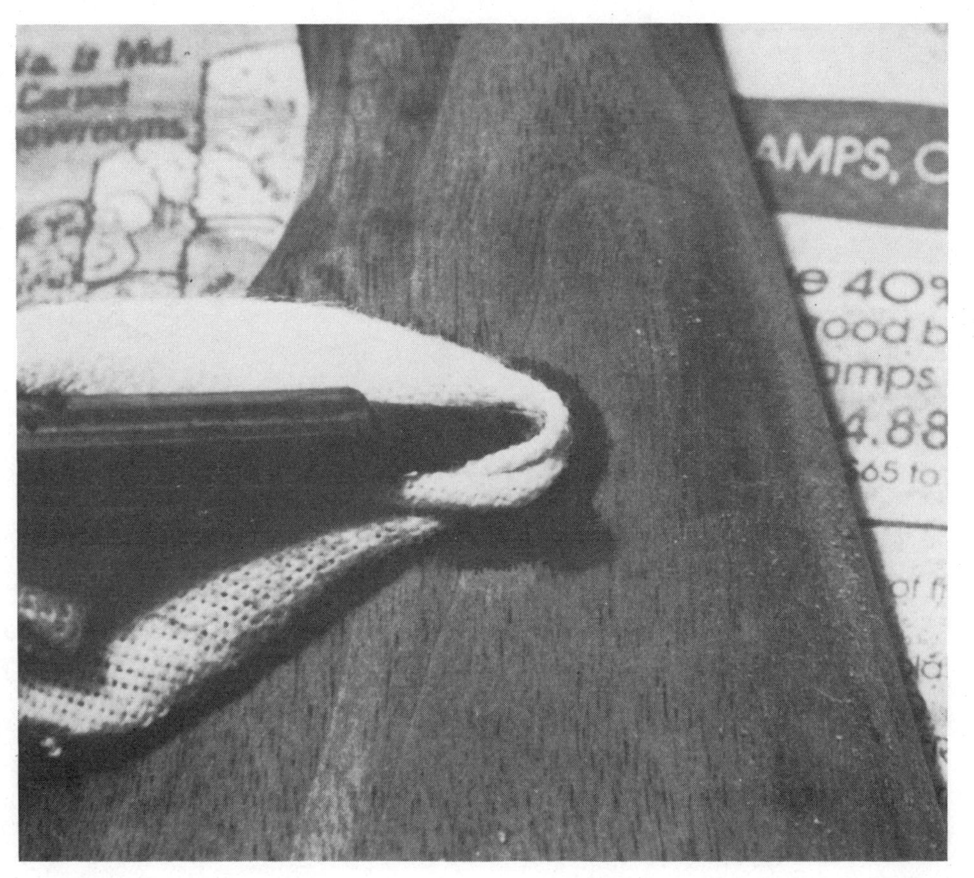

Minor dents in gunstocks can be raised with a damp cloth and a soldering iron. Just be careful not to apply too much heat.

grain of the wood. Check your work frequently to avoid cutting through the existing stock finish. I've restored several stocks in this manner, yet I'm able to keep the original finish. All but the worst scratches will be hidden, all dirt and perspiration stains will be removed and the stock will look practically new if the job is done correctly.

Minor dents in gunstocks can be raised without completely refinishing the wood. Merely wet an old washcloth, place it over the dent and apply a hot soldering iron on the wet rag at the exact location of the dent. You don't want to leave the iron on very long, because the heat may burn the wood or cause the finish to bubble; leave it on just long enough to cause the steam to swell the wood fibers and raise them to the surface. Repeat the operation as often as is necessary until the dent is raised.

Chips or gouges in a gunstock require the advice of a professional if a good match is desired. In general, the damaged area is sawed or routed square, with flat sides, so another piece of wood can be spliced in. The area is then sanded flush with the existing surface and finished to match the present finish. Sometimes it is necessary to stain the repaired area to match.

Professional Gun Cleaning Methods

Many times I have purchased used guns that looked as though the internal receiver parts had never been cleaned . . . and they probably weren't. Cakes of crud, grease and powder covered all internal parts, making the action sluggish and often not functional at all. In cases like these, the gun should be completely disassembled and given a thorough cleaning. Such cleaning is also recommended once or twice a year for any firearm that is used frequently. It will help to eliminate malfunctions that continually occur in the action of semiautomatics and other repeating rifles, shotguns and pistols due to a buildup of sediment.

Just how far you have to go with the disassembly will depend on what type of method you use for cleaning. An ultrasonic cleaning tank, for example, is capable of cleaning the most remote areas of a gun action

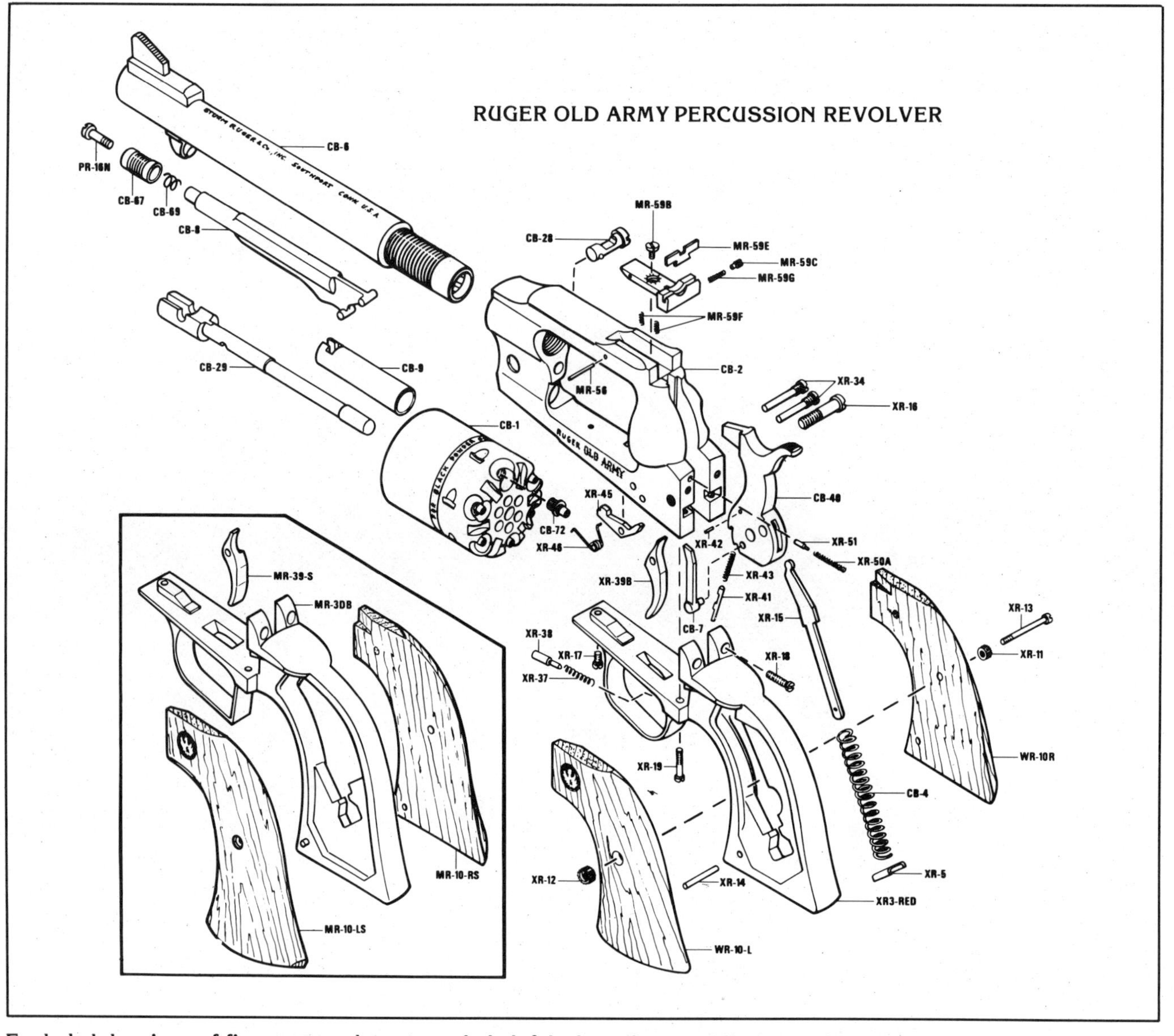

Exploded drawings of firearms can be extremely helpful when disassembling arms for cleaning. Most important, they will enable you to get the gun back together without having parts left over.

with the minimum of disassembly—just enough so the parts will fit in the tank. However, we are talking about a $200 to $500 investment—too much for the average gun owner to spend, since the tank will be used only once or twice a year. A gun shop owner, on the other hand, can profit from such an investment.

Ultrasonic radio waves make the tank vibrate, creating billions of tiny bubbles whose creation and bursting adds an intense scrubbing action to the solvent. This scrubbing action gets to every little hole and crevice—places that would otherwise be impossible to get to without completely disassembling the parts.

A somewhat less expensive method would be to purchase a gallon of Brownell's d'SOLVE Gunsmith Cleaning Solution and also one of the plastic bluing tanks such as those sold by Birchwood Casey. A plastic tank filled with the d'SOLVE diluted with water will clean even the most dirty parts. Just allow the parts to soak in the solution while you're doing other work around the shop or home. After they are clean, lift them from the tank, dry them and spray a light coat of WD-40 on all surfaces.

If you have compressed air available, use it to blow loose grime from the gun immediately upon lifting it from the tank. This air may also be used to dry the parts prior to oiling.

Cleaning Black Powder Firearms

Black powder is a mixture of charcoal, sulfur and saltpeter which are ground together, pressed into hard cakes and subsequently broken into small pieces to pass through sieves of the proper mesh to obtain the desired granulation. The grains are then coated with graphite to retard the absorption of moisture, which gives the powder the shiny black appearance from which it gets its name.

Black powder will create powder fouling in all types of firearms much faster than smokeless powder. Therefore, those who own or shoot these types of weapons must take extra care in cleaning them. If possible, cleaning should commence after each shot by running a water-dampened patch down the bore, letting it remain for perhaps 10 seconds to dissolve the powder residue. Then use a dry patch to absorb any moisture in the bore or powder chamber.

The finest accuracy can only be obtained by cleaning a rifle or pistol after each shot. Furthermore, this practice eliminates any sparks that may be present immediately after the shot. If there were a spark left in the bore and you immediately poured the next charge of black powder into the barrel, well, you can imagine the results!

Even if you clean after each shot, muzzleloading arms will eventually build up an accumulation of hard fouling in the cylinder passage. This causes misfires and will eventually close the passage so the percussion cap cannot ignite the powder. To prevent this from happening, the cylinder should be removed after a hundred or so shots. Clean out the fouling by immersing the cylinder in cold water. Water is the most effective solvent for black powder residue. Of course the cylinder should be dried before screwing it back in the barrel.

Some shooters like to disassemble their weapons after a hundred shots or so and clean all metal parts with soapy water. These are then rinsed in clean water and dipped into a tank of boiling water for about 15 minutes. Many parts will dry immediately upon being lifted from the tank due to the heat absorbed by the metal. Dry other parts in question; then liberally coat the bore with a good gun grease. Also, give the same attention to other metal parts, such as the hammer, lock, plate and nipple.

Iron and steel barrels of muzzleloading firearms will rust very quickly in warm, humid temperatures unless they are adequately protected. Those that have seen neglect will surely need some fancy cleaning to put them in good shooting condition and, even then, they may be unsafe to fire. All such questionable arms should be proofed as discussed in Chapter 11.

14. Restoring Firearms

Restoring used guns can be a touchy subject—especially among collectors. Many valuable firearms have been completely ruined by hobbyists who were not aware of the guns' value and tried to "fix 'em up" a bit. A good rule of thumb for restoring antique firearms is to try to halt deterioration, preserve their current appearance and, if possible, not rework any parts. Restoring modern firearms can also be a no-no. For example, any firearm manufactured before 1964 which possesses 80 percent or more of its original finish should remain in that condition and be "restored" only to the extent of retarding further deterioration, especially if the gun has, or will have, collector's appeal in the future.

On the other end of the ladder, there are models that are definitely in the collectible class, but have been seriously neglected through the years. Perhaps the wood has been cracked or gouged; certain parts have rusted badly; and pits have formed in the metal. Such a gun will normally have little collector's value, unless it is really a rarity. If the gun can be restored to a good appearance and working order, restoration is certainly legitimate and should be encouraged.

The main objective in restoring an old firearm is to maintain the gun's original identity. If, for example, the metal finish is to be restored, it should follow the original finishing process, if this is known, or at least one of the processes of the period in which it was originally produced. The same is true for the wood. Any missing parts should be replaced with original parts, if available; if not, try to obtain reproduction parts that are as authentic as possible. There are several people who deal in obsolete gun parts, and almost any part you will need is available or can be made (see Appendix III). Of course, expect to pay a pretty penny for custom-made replacement parts.

Determining Whether and/or How Much to Restore

The first step should be a careful and minute inspection of the entire gun with a magnifying lens, making notes during the process. Look for hairline cracks in the metal and wood parts; note rust and pits—both inside and out—without disassembling the firearm at this time; check the action for proper functioning, using dummy ammo during this test.

Having become familiar with the gun's exact condition, give it a thorough cleaning from muzzle to butt, using methods described in Chapter 13. Try to remove all foreign matter, but none of the original finish. At this point, it may be wise to remove the stock from the firearm since different cleaning methods usually will be required for each. During this cleaning and after, more defects will probably turn up; include these in your notes.

To determine the extent of restoration necessary on a gun you are sure will profit from it, first do a careful inspection. A magnifying lens will show up the tiniest scratches and rust pits. Then make notes to aid in estimating the cost of the restorative work, including any unusual problems and their solutions, if possible.

If the gun functions okay and cleans up rather well, it is usually best to leave it as is, and not try to restore it further. On the other hand, if the gun is not functional in its present condition, and if it is not a real rarity, some restoration may be called for. For example, a few months ago, a 12-gauge Parker Trojan shotgun was purchased by one of the dealers in my area. Although a coveted Parker, the buttstock was broken completely in half, the forearm badly cracked and the right barrel had bulged and cracked about two inches from the muzzle. The gun was nearly worthless in its present condition and was certainly a candidate for reconditioning.

The project began by first disassembling the firearm, and while one gunsmith worked on the new buttstock, another shortened the barrels to 26 inches, polished out the light pits inside and out and then hand polished the barrel for bluing. The slow rust process was used, giving it that satin blue-black look. New chokes, improved cylinder and modified, were cut into the shortened barrels and a new bead sight was installed.

Once the buttstock was finished and checkered to match the existing checkering, it looked so good that it was decided to shape a new forearm rather than repair the old one. The end result was an attractive Parker shotgun, looking almost like it came out of the box. Of course, the gun offered little attraction to a true Parker shotgun collector since it had been refinished, but it was a fine shotgun for hunting. In fact, this restoration turned an otherwise almost worthless shotgun into one that brought over $600 from a customer who wanted it strictly for hunting.

So, before any restoring is done to a firearm, you should first clean it thoroughly without removing any of the original finish. Look at the model and type of gun you have and decide if it's best to leave the gun alone at its present collector value, or restore it to a more attractive condition, keeping in mind that restoring often requires replacing or repairing worn parts.

A gun owner contemplating having a gun restored should keep several other things in mind. If it is a functional "working" gun—one that will be used extensively for hunting—as long as it functions safely and is not in too bad condition, the owner would probably be better off stopping any deterioration and leaving it as it is. However, the owner may want to hunt with the arm in question, but still have a nice-looking weapon. Unless it is a very rare firearm, restoration may be warranted. But, first, the owner should ask if the gun is really worth restoring—bearing in mind that it will probably lose some collector value (unless it's a piece of junk to begin with) if it is restored.

Many badly abused firearms have come into my

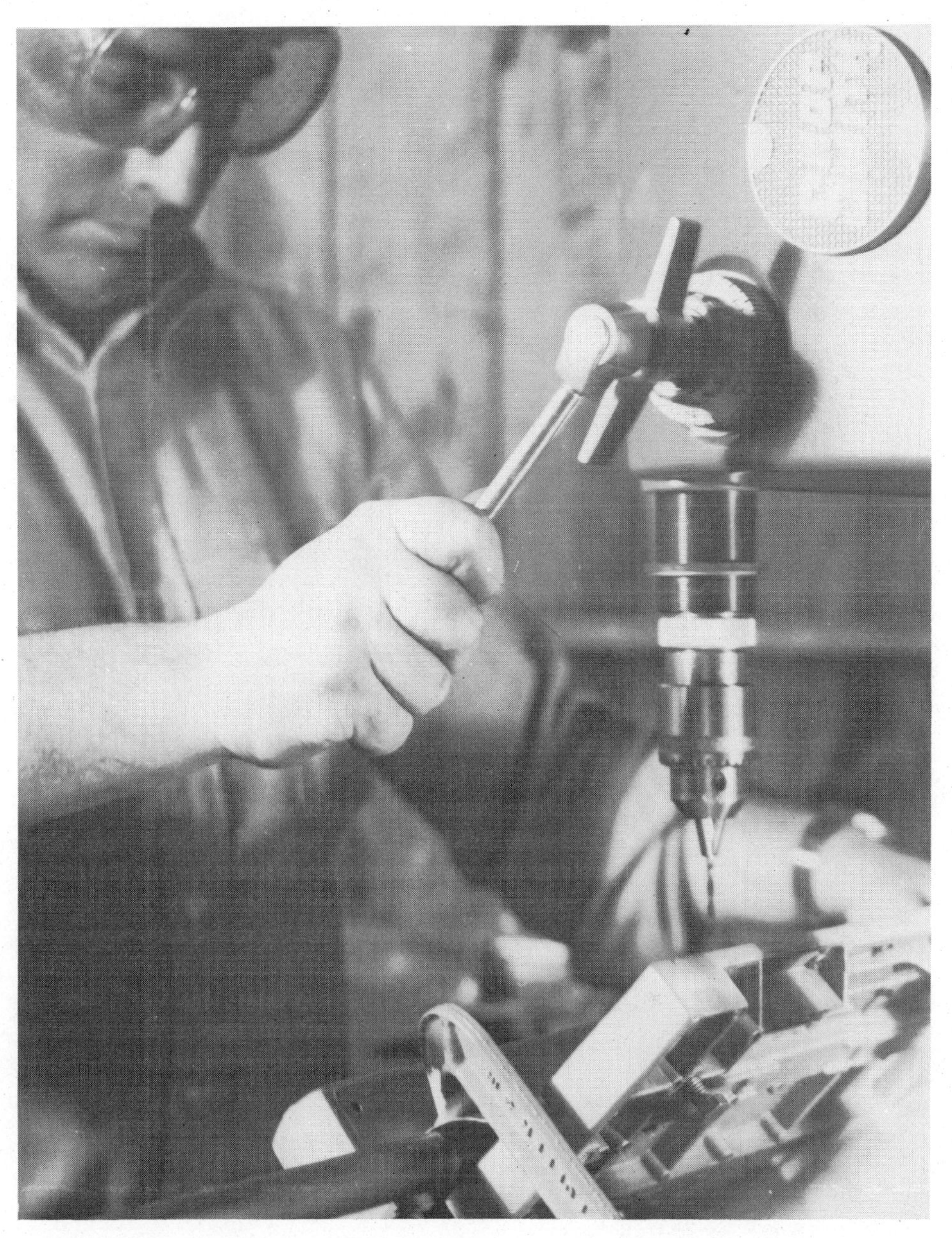

A damaged shotgun barrel has been cut off and rechoked and is now being drilled for a new front sight. If such restoration can make an otherwise useless gun function properly again, such work is highly recommended.

shop that had sentimental value to the owner. "This was my great-grandpa's duck gun and I want to hang it over the fireplace in my home," said one customer. "Can you fix it up so it looks halfway decent?" Unless it's a real rarity, I usually comply, although the work may consist of only a thorough cleaning and halting any further deterioration. I've seen many old double-barreled shotguns with Damascus barrels come in that were badly rusted and pitted, the wood dented and cracked or broken beyond repair. Most of these are worth about $75 on today's market, as most of them are cheap mail-order guns that were sold around the turn of the century. After explaining that the cost of the work is going to be more than double what the gun is worth, and if the owner still wants it done, I can restore the shotgun to like-new condition. In most cases, the customer does not object much to the high cost, since the gun does have sentimental value to him. In this case, the restoration is legitimate even though the gun will be a wall hanger and never be fired.

This pre-'64 Winchester Model 94 rifle had holes in the receiver filled in, then the entire rifle was reblued. Note the screw where normally there is an access hole to enable removal of the finger lever pin. Since this hole had previously been enlarged and threaded, it was decided to use a plug screw here instead of leaving it out.

Another example is the Marlin Model 27 pump rifle in .25-20. This particular customer used the gun frequently on his farm for hunting and plinking, and killed numerous deer and groundhogs with it for over 40 years. Now it wouldn't shoot worth a darn, and he wanted it rebarreled, primarily because he liked the firearm and wanted to continue using it. The wood looked like it had been previously refinished, but the original bluing was in excellent condition. The present worth of the gun is about $175, but had he had it rebarreled, the value would have dropped to around $100. Yet, since it was a "working" gun, he wanted it to be accurate. There were several alternatives: reboring to .32-20; relining; or lapping the bore. The third choice would be the least expensive, and also lower the firearm's value the least.

The barrel was lapped, and the shooter also changed to jacketed bullets. He was again able to group the shots within a 1½-inch circle at 50 yards with iron sights and was well pleased with my recommendations. The gun may have been slightly more accurate with a new barrel, but it would have lost its identity as well as some of its collector value. Perhaps this owner didn't care about the collector value, since he used it to hunt with, but what about his grandchildren or others who might eventually inherit the gun?

To cite one more example, a Winchester Model 94 (late pre-'64) rifle was recently brought into my shop for evaluation. Although the outside finish showed some wear, the bore was perfect and the action functioned beautifully. The chief problem was that a previous owner had drilled and tapped the right side of the receiver for scope mounts (apparently he was left-handed). In other words, there were three additional screw holes back from, and in line with, the finger lever pin hole. This drilling and tapping ruined the arm as a collector gun. Since the owner wanted it solely as a hunting arm, I recommended that he leave it alone, because it was quite functional as it was.

However, he didn't like the appearance of the holes in the side of the receiver and wanted them filled in. In this case, the work turned out to be a customizing job rather than a restoration. Threaded studs were tightly and closely turned in to fill the screw holes and then the entire receiver was polished and reblued. The outline of where the holes had been are noticeable to the trained eye, but for all practical purposes—as a hunting gun—the appearance had been enhanced. We also checkered the stock and forearm styled after a Winchester pattern popular around the turn of the century.

Therefore, a firearm may be restored because it has been badly abused and the owner wishes to put it back into service; it has sentimental value; or it is less-than-adequate for a gun collection. In all cases, however, the gun should be in less-than-good condition before a restoration is attempted. Although there are exceptions, use this as a rule of thumb.

The extent of a restoration can range from the replacement of a small defective part, through lapping the bore, to a complete overhaul of the gun—removing all pits, rejuvenating engraving, rebluing and replacing or refinishing the stock and forend. It depends entirely on the value of the firearm and what the customer wants. Just keep in mind that in nearly all instances, a collectible firearm will lose some value (unless it's already a wreck) when it is restored. That's the reason why most restored guns are "working" guns, rather than those that should remain in a bank vault due to their high value.

Let a Professional Do the Job

Many gun enthusiasts have such a love for the better, older firearms that they are now turning to restoring badly abused models or those that are no longer complete, rather than sticking strictly to firearms in mint or excellent condition. This practice also enables a collector to obtain a larger quantity of firearms due to the greatly reduced cost in the less-than-adequate items.

Restoration of a valuable firearm requires repair or replacement of broken or badly worn parts, careful duplication of original polishing and bluing methods, duplication of original wood and checkering and, oftentimes, the replication of a part of the engraving. Color case-hardening of receivers and other gun parts is also often necessary. Firms specializing in such gun restoration are rare indeed—the total number could probably be counted on both hands.

Every qualified gunsmith will occasionally do some type of firearm restoration, but the average gunsmith is unlikely to have the knowledge, expertise and the tools required to restore the classic, high-quality obsolete arms in the manner in which they should be. To be able to restore the finer firearms necessitates much study, years of experience and a lot of natural talent. J.J. Jenkins, for example, has long been a specialist in this kind of work, concentrating on fine shotguns, rifles and the rarer variations of Lugers and other collectible automatic pistols. He is located at 375 Pine Avenue, No. 25, Goleta, California 93017. Prices are quoted on each individual job.

John Kaufield of Small Arms Engineering, 7698 Garden Prairie Road, Garden Prairie, Illinois 61038, is another artisan who specializes in restoring badly abused firearms into factory-new condition. Care is taken to use the same techniques of refinishing as were used when the gun was originally built—providing a finish as close as possible to the original. Cut-off barrels can be restored to their original length; deep pits in the metal can be filled by welding; and original markings are restamped or engraved.

Lester Womac, P.O. Box 17210, Tucson, Arizona 85710, also does repair and restoration work; his specialty is renewing commercial Mauser sporting rifles, using original factory techniques.

Although David Trevallion's specialty is gunstocks, he also does complete metal and wood restoration of antique and modern arms. He would be a good choice for having any of the finer English shotguns and double-barreled rifles restored, since he learned his trade as an apprentice with one of England's top gunmakers. Quotes on prices are on an individual job basis and may be obtained by writing to him at 6524 N. Carrollton Avenue, Indianapolis, Indiana 46220.

Vic's Gun Refinishing, 6 Pineview Drive, Dover Point, Dover, New Hampshire 03820, offers complete refinishing services, with original-type polishing and hot or rust bluing as appropriate. He also does color case-hardening and other gunsmithing operations. A detailed price list is available.

The Paul Jaeger gunsmithing firm of Jenkintown, Pennsylvania 19046, has long been noted for its fine custom rifles, but they are also highly capable of restoring valuable firearms, time permitting.

Reinhart Fajen and E.C. Bishop & Son, both of

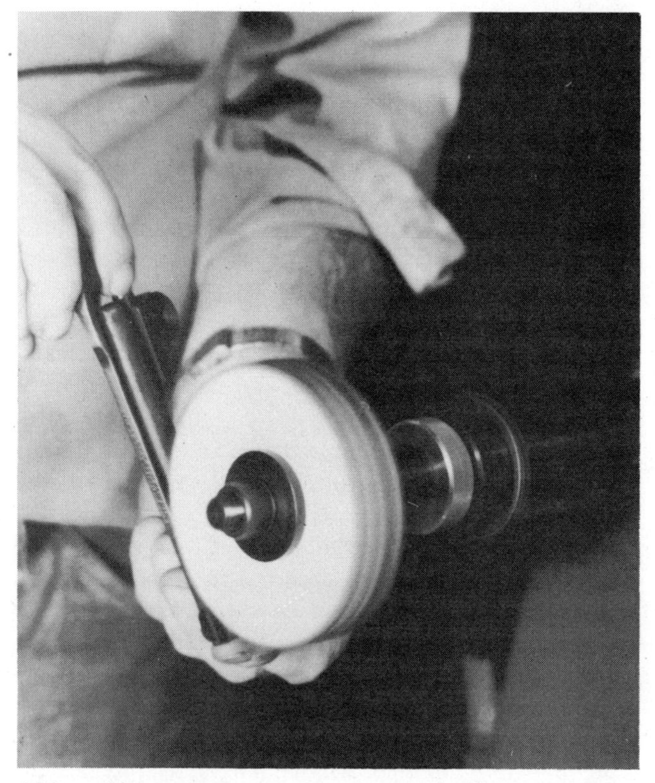

Although a restorer may use a power buffer to remove pits in the metal, usually the final polishing must be accomplished by hand.

Warsaw, Missouri, turn out excellent reproductions of stocks for obsolete arms. I also understand that E.C. Bishop does some metal restoration as well.

Traister Arms Company, Route 1, Box 300, Bentonville, Virginia 22610, specializes in restoring badly abused pre-'64 Winchesters only. They will also halt deterioration of any Winchester in good or better than good condition, but will not refinish, nor recommend refinishing, those Winchesters in good condition.

Restoration Techniques

In general, modern gunsmithing methods cannot be used satisfactorily on old guns with the desired results. Power metal polishing, for example, cuts too much metal and closes the pores so the coveted satin blue-black finish cannot be obtained. A restorer may use a power buffer to remove some pits in the metal, but the final polishing must be done by hand.

The hot caustic bluing method is another forbidden practice. The glossy black appearance of this finish, which, incidentally, is used on most modern firearms, just doesn't look authentic on the older guns. Besides that, this method attacks soft soldering—the type used to secure barrel ribs and join tubes on double-barreled shotguns. The slow rust or possibly the hot water method are the only two acceptable methods for restoring the majority of these high-quality guns. This brings us to another problem.

If a poll were taken, I'd be willing to bet my prewar Winchester Model 70 against a J.C. Higgins .22 rimfire single shot that less than a third of the 7,000 odd full- and part-time gunsmiths in this country bother with any bluing method other than the hot caustic method. Rust bluing is just too time-consuming, and the average customer is not willing to pay the price. I'm not saying they don't know how to rust blue, I'm just saying that they don't want to go to all the trouble.

Another technique that adds to the value and authenticity of many older firearms is color case-hardening, a technique of hardening metals that also results in mottled blues, browns, grays and blacks. Few gunshops offer this service, mainly because most formulas call for the addition of lethal cyanide to the hardening compound and one tiny speck in an open cut, mouth or corner of the eye can mean "curtains." Actually, good color case-hardening can be obtained without the use of cyanide, but the process takes longer and, like slow rust bluing or other older gunsmithing techniques, this method has taken a back seat.

There are other details that must be adhered to if an authentic finish is to be obtained. English flat-checkering may be one of them—a technique that almost always must be done by hand. The bright mirror blue finishes found on early Smith & Wesson handguns are difficult to duplicate. These handguns were blued by a method known as the carbonia process, in which the gun parts to be blued were suspended on rods inside a large metal container partially filled with a special powdered chemical. The metal container was rotated and heated to 700 degrees F. As the powder fell on the heated metal surfaces, it produced a deep, lustrous mirror blue that is often considered to be the finest in the firearms industry. However, the system is a complicated one that requires considerable expense to set up and is more dangerous to use than most other methods. A few experts have been able to come close to this finish by using a technique known as fume bluing. Another master can, or so I am told, duplicate the S&W mirror blue in a skillet on a stove, but such methods must be learned by "feel" and long experience.

Some gunsmiths have been fortunate enough to ob-

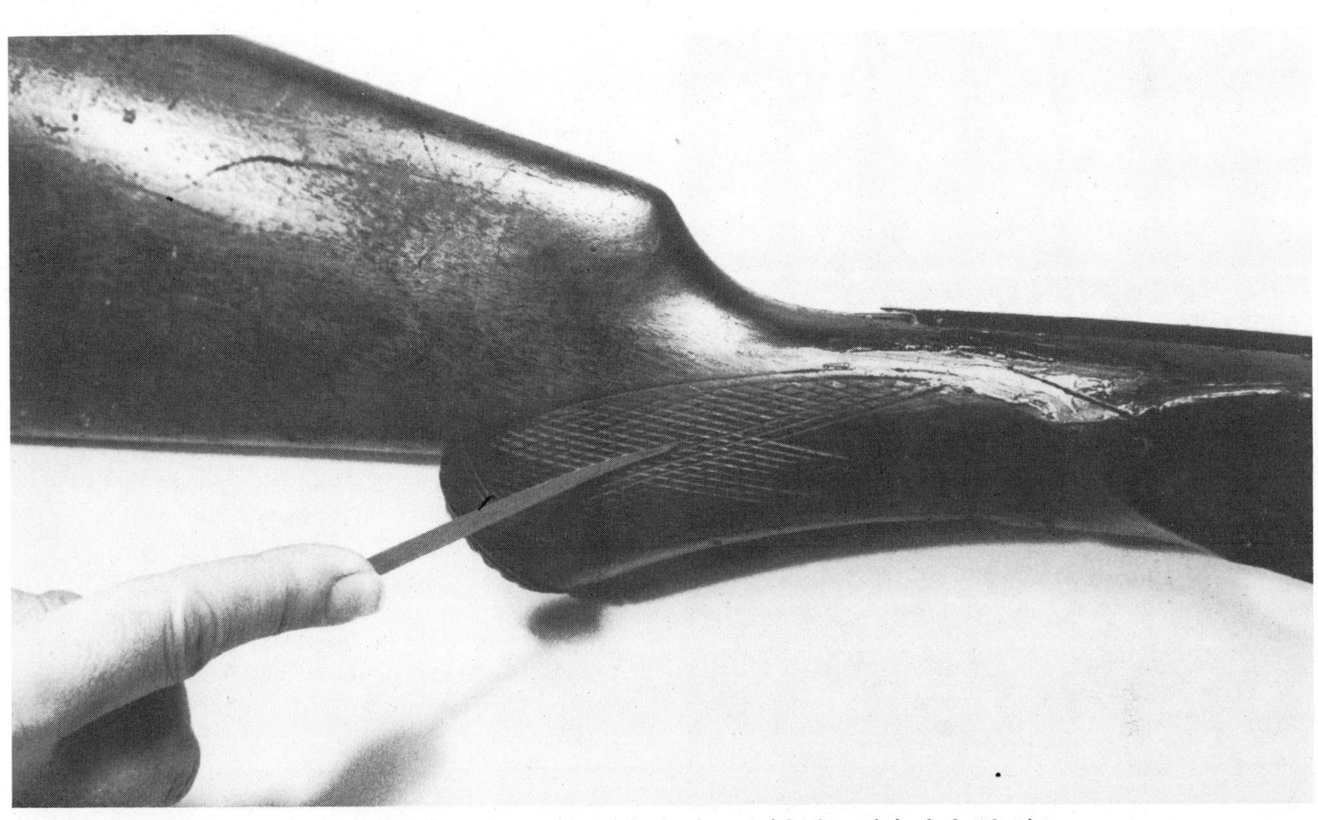

This particular shotgun stock looks almost hopeless (shown here with the original checkering being recut), but an expert can apply his knowledge and have it looking almost brand new.

tain the original bluing formula used on some of the older firearms, have had their pharmacist mix them exactly as specified, but still have been unable to obtain the desired results. The exact techniques seem to have been lost, requiring that the restorer be a chemist, gun historian, as well as be willing to take the time to experiment with several methods until the right one is developed. Such a person must be dedicated to his profession and have a higher level of expertise than the average gunsmith. When a person reaches this level, seldom will he take on general gunsmithing jobs. For a gun to be worthy of restoring by methods that took years to develop, it must be one of high quality or historical value, or both.

One of the most difficult items to restore on a firearm is the engraving. A majority of the finer metal engravers had their own style and technique, and you can well imagine the difficulty a good modern-day engraver experiences duplicating the work of a master. It's like trying to duplicate a Picasso painting. Fortunately, most gun engravings do not have to be completely re-etched. Rather, it's a matter of perhaps deepening lines that are already there, which does not require the artistic ability involved with an original engraving. For example, the trigger guards on some of the finer double-barreled shotguns have a simple border engraving on them. These same trigger guards are subject to rust and pits and, in many cases, removing the pits means removing the engraving also. So the average gunsmith will either remove the engraving entirely during the polishing process prior to bluing or leave the pits in, resulting in a less-than-adequate restoration. An expert restorer, on the other hand, will first make an exact pattern of the original border engraving and also take close-up photos before any polishing begins. The pits are then removed, taking off as little metal as possible. The restorer or his engraver re-cuts the engraved border following the original pattern prior to bluing, maintaining the original appearance of the firearm.

By this time, it should be evident that any firearm restorer worth his salt must be a highly dedicated indi-

In some cases, it may be best to customize an entire rifle. Here, Ben Toxvard of Shenandoah Guns prepares to unscrew a barrel from the receiver for a rechambering job.

vidual, have an above-average expertise in firearm history, know the techniques of the period, and how to apply them to his work. He, of course, must have an appreciation of high craftsmanship. To quote J.J. Jenkins, "You have to have an appreciation for what the original designer was thinking as he developed the firearm in question. And also an appreciation for what he was trying to accomplish, always bearing in mind the state of the gunmaker's art during the period the gun was made."

Customizing

Occasionally, it may be best to customize an old rifle, rather than try to have it restored. Let's take a pre-'64 Winchester Model 70 with a shot-out barrel, a broken stock and a badly scratched receiver. An original barrel and a stock for this model—when available—will run over $200 minimum. Add the labor involved in replacing them and also possibly having them refinished and you're talking about $300 to $400. Then you won't have an original Model 70.

You can buy a good Model 70 at this writing for around $550, so why bother to have it restored? You'd probably be better off trading it in or selling the action to a gunsmith to be made into a custom rifle, then buying a good used Model 70 from a dealer. On the other hand, you may have always dreamed of having a custom-built rifle of your own, and it's hard to find a better bolt-action than that of the Winchester pre-'64 Model 70, at least in my opinion. A competent gunsmith can take your beat-up rifle and turn it into a thing of joy with practically any design of stock you want or whatever your pocketbook will afford. In other words, it may sometimes be best to customize rather than restore. Again, it depends upon the rarity of the gun in question, your personal desires and several other factors.

One word of caution, be sure to check out your restorer thoroughly before entrusting him with a priceless firearm. Advertisements are not always what they appear to be. Also, if there is any doubt in your mind as to whether you should have a particular gun restored or not, let it sit for awhile. You can always have the work done later; but once it's done, it's done! Like reversing "Band-Aid" surgery, it may be possible sometimes, but more than likely, it may not.

When a person turns to the problem of restoring a gun, his first thoughts should concern the functioning of the arm. The firearm should first be repaired to function safely and properly because the finish is sometimes altered during the repair, requiring additional work to restore the finish.

The wood of a particular firearm should be the next consideration. A careful examination will reveal if the stock should be replaced entirely or if it's feasible to repair and refinish the existing one. If the latter route is taken, any existing checkering should be cleaned out first, the area masked off and then the remaining surfaces sanded.

Gun Metal Finishes Through the Years

Metal refinishing seems to be the most critical task involved in restoring valuable firearms. First of all, engravings, sharp corners and lettering can be obliterated in seconds with a power buffing wheel if care is

Many custom rifles are built on wildcat cartridges, which means they must be specially chambered.

not taken. Second, deep pits in metal are difficult to remove without altering the original shape or removing some of the original markings. Finally, the methods used to color the metal vary from era to era and to get an authentic finish, these methods should be known. The following gives a brief description of the bluing methods used on firearms for the past 100 years. Details of these methods may be obtained in the book *Professional Care and Refinishing Gun Metal*, published by TAB Books, Blue Ridge Summit, Pennsylvania 17214.

Slow rust bluing. Around the early part of the 19th century, a modified browning process came into use that resulted in a blue-black finish. This modified finish became known as "bluing" in the United States. The British, however, prefer to call any gun finish, regardless of the color, "browning."

The earliest bluing solutions consisted of a mixture of nitric and hydrochloric acids with steel shavings or iron nails dissolved in them. The process used in applying the solution to the gun metal is generally known as the "slow rust process."

In general, the slow rust process consists of polishing the metal parts to be blued to the desired luster and then degreasing the parts by boiling them in a solution of lime and water or lye and water. Without touching the metal parts with the bare hands or otherwise letting them become contaminated, the metal is swabbed with the bluing solution in long, even strokes until all parts are covered. The metal is then allowed to stand and rust from six to 24 hours. The rust that forms is carded off with steel wool or a wire brush to reveal a light gray or bluish color underneath.

The surface, still free of oil, is again swabbed with the solution and allowed to rust another day. When this second coat of rust is carded off, the metal beneath reveals an even darker shade of blue. The process is repeated until the desired color is obtained—anywhere from one to two weeks on the average. Then the parts are boiled in water for about 15 minutes to stop further rusting, and then oiled. The result is a beautiful, long-wearing gun finish that is still admired by lovers of high-quality firearms. The time required for this process, however, makes it impractical for the average gunsmith unless it is used on a high-quality double-barreled shotgun, which would make the extra hours and costs worthwhile.

Hot water bluing. The time required to obtain a perfect finish on a firearm by the slow rust process forced gunsmiths and manufacturers to seek a faster and easier process. The process developed has been

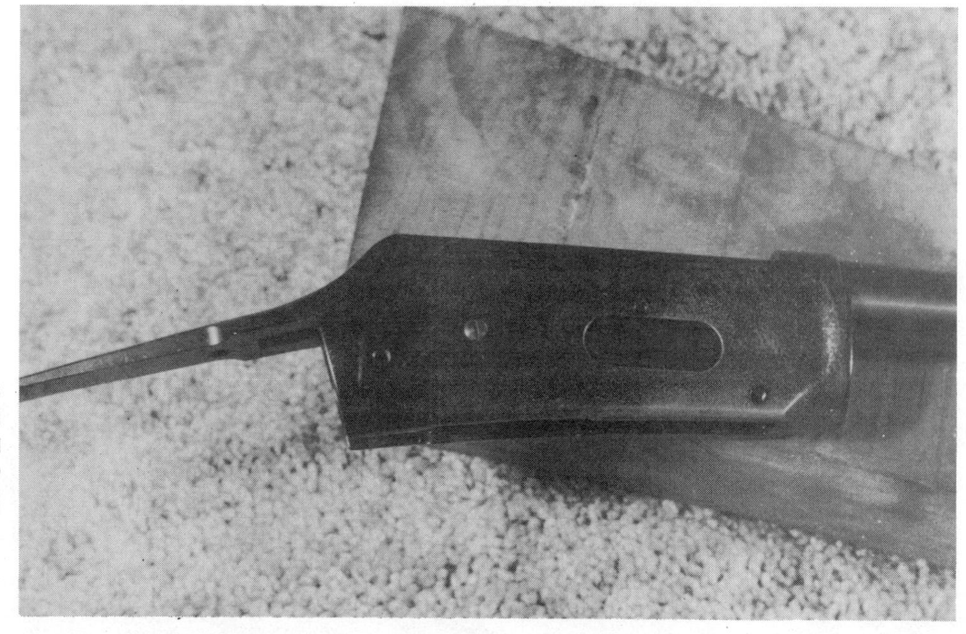

A post-'64 Winchester Model 94 rifle had this badly pitted, rusted receiver. Correct polishing and bluing restored it to "new" condition, making the gun once again an attractive hunting weapon.

called many names, such as "20-minute blue," " express blue," and the like, but "hot water bluing" is the generally accepted term.

Hot water bluing is based on the fact that steel, when heated, rusts more rapidly than when it is cold, due to the rapid absorption of the oxygen which forms ferric oxide or red rust. So, new formulas were developed which reacted favorably on metal that was polished, degreased, then heated in boiling water prior to applying the bluing solution. Once boiled for five to ten minutes, the metal parts are lifted from the boiling water, after which they dry almost immediately due to the heat of the steel.

The bluing solution, often also heated, is then applied to the hot metal in long, even strokes. Rust forms at once on the metal. But before carding, the parts are again dunked into the boiling water for about five more minutes. The first carding usually produces a light gray color on the metal parts and each successive coat deepens the color until it is a dark, velvet blue-black color. Depending upon the metal, it may take anywhere from four to a dozen or more coats to obtain the desired finish.

Hot caustic bluing. Around the turn of the century, the black oxide process of bluing was patented. Although it did not gain popularity in the firearms industry until sometime later, it is now used in practically every gunshop and by every firearm manufacturer in the U.S. Once the parts are polished and cleaned in the conventional way, this bluing process is essentially a 15-minute to 30-minute, simple boiling process in a strong, alkaline solution. The method works exceptionally well on a wide variety of steel and is much more economical for mass production than any other process known. Another advantage of this method is that the number of guns that can be blued at one time is limited only by the size of the tanks and the heating facilities.

Bluing salts were introduced to the public in the mid-1930's and most of them came in "dry" form. The bluing solution was made by mixing them with water. Early suppliers of the black oxide bluing salts included A.F. Stoeger Co., who produced Stoeger's Black Diamond Lightning Bluer; E.G. Houghton & Co., producing Hough-To-Black; and Bob Brownell of Brownells Inc., who produced "How-To-Blue," now manufactured under the name of "Oxynate 7," which is still available to the trade.

Carbonia bluing. In the early 20th century, Colt, Smith & Wesson and some other firearms manufacturers produced a bluing method known as the carbonia process. This process required that the parts to be blued be suspended on rods inside a large metal container. The container was partly filled with a special chemical in powdered form, and heated to 700 degrees F. while it was being rotated. As the powder fell onto the hot metal surfaces, it resulted in a beautiful brilliant blue, considered by some as the finest in the firearms industry. However, the process is complicated and requires considerable expense to set up; in addition, it is more dangerous to use than most other methods. So, like the big dance bands and a nickel cup of coffee, the carbonia bluing process has been left behind in another era.

Parkerizing. To obtain a more durable finish than bluing, the military used a process—beginning with its Springfield 1903 service rifles—called Parkerizing. The process consisted of boiling the parts to be finished in a solution of "Parko Powder," composed of specially prepared powdered iron and phosphoric acid. During the process, small surface particles on the parts are dissolved and replaced by insoluble phosphates which are rust-resistant. The resulting finish is a gray, non-reflecting surface, which, while less attractive than bluing, is far more practical from a military standpoint.

Plating. Nickel plating has been one of the favorite finishes for use on handguns and certain small parts of long guns since before the turn of the century. Traditionally, the finish was applied by a process called "electroplating," which uses an electric current to deposit the nickel onto the steel surface. The steel part to be plated is suspended in a solution containing a high concentration of nickel along with a bar or sheet of pure nickel. The negative wire from a battery or other source of direct current is connected to the steel part (making it the cathode) and the positive wire is connected to the nickel bar (making it the anode). By carefully controlling the current, the nickel in the solution is deposited onto the steel part. At the same time, an equal amount of nickel is removed from the nickel bar to replenish that which is taken out of the solution.

Case-hardening. Case-hardening is the process by which soft metal parts of iron or steel can be hardened to make them more durable and wear-resistant. When these parts are properly case-hardened, the surface resists wear even better than tempered tool steel, while the soft, tough metal inside provides strength.

Color case-hardening, which adds patterns of color as well as strength, is accomplished by heating the metal, usually in a cast-iron vessel containing carbonaceous materials, to a cherry red (not above 1400° F.), then plunging it into cold water and alternating the hot and cold treatment until the desired hardness is achieved. Years ago, pulverized bones, hoofs and the horns of animals were often used, as was soot. Today, bone meal is frequently the additive. The addition of these substances changes the structural formation of the metal and binds the fibers into a fine-grained mass.

If you are interested in trying simple case-hardening on some of your gun parts (without the coloring aspects), several commercial chemical products are available that will enable you to do so safely with a minimum amount of effort. The two most popular compounds are Brownell's Hard 'N' Tuff and the Kasenit Surface Hardening Compound. The only other element you'll need is a propane torch; instructions for use are included on the containers of each compound.

The entire gun trading scene is continually changing, necessitating the need to keep constantly abreast of current circumstances and prices. Those guns that are commonplace today may be collectors' items tomorrow. The truly successful gun trader must maintain unceasing watch so that he or she can stay up-to-date with ever-vacillating prices and the arms that are most in demand. The person who buys and sells used guns has an obligation, if only to himself, to acquire the proper knowledge of gun dealing so that neither the buyer nor the seller gets hurt—financially or physically. HOW TO BUY AND SELL USED GUNS has been designed for that purpose and I hope that you, the reader, will enjoy and profit more in your gun trading by using it.

Appendix I
Firearms Curios and Relics

The curios and relics listed below have currently been determined by the Bureau of Alcohol, Tobacco and Firearms (ATF) to have special value as collectors' items. Since one of the requirements for a firearm to be classified in this category is that the gun (not including replicas) must have been manufactured at least 50 years ago, this list will increase each year. One good source for determining the age of firearms is Paul Wahl's GUN TRADER'S GUIDE.

Other qualifications for classification as a curio or relic are: the weapon must be certified by the curator of a municipal, state or federal museum exhibiting firearms to be of museum interest; and a substantial part of the weapon's monetary value must be derived from the fact that it is novel, rare or bizarre, or was associated with some historical figure, period or event.

Collectors who wish to obtain a curio or relic determination from the ATF on a specific firearm not appearing in this listing may submit a letter to the Chief of the Firearms Technology Branch, Bureau of Alcohol, Tobacco and Firearms, Washington, DC 20226. The letter should include a complete physical description of the firearm, reasons why the weapon in question is believed to merit classification as a relic or curio and any supporting data concerning the history of the firearm.

A

Armand Gevage .32 ACP-caliber semiautomatic pistol, as manufactured in Belgium prior to World War II.

Astra M 300 pistols, calibers 7.65mm and 9mm Kurz, marked with German Waffenamt acceptance stamp, 1939-1945.

Astra M 400 pistol, German Army Contract, caliber 9mm Bergmann-Bayard, serial number range 97351-98850.

Astra Model 400 semiautomatic pistol, second German Army Contract, caliber 9mm Bergmann-Bayard, serial number range 92851-97350.

Astra M 600 pistol, caliber 9mm Parabellum, marked with German Waffenamt acceptance stamp, 1939-1945.

Astra M 800 Condor Model pistol, caliber 9mm Parabellum.

B

Baker Gun and Forging Company, all firearms manufactured from 1899 to 1919.

Bannerman Model 1937, Springfield rifle, caliber 30-06.

Bayard Model 1923 semiautomatic pistols, calibers 7.65mm and .380, Belgian manufacture.

Beretta Model 1915 pistols, calibers 6.35mm, 7.65mm and 9mm Glisenti.

Beretta Model 1915/1919 (1922) pistol (concealed hammer), caliber 7.65mm.

Beretta Model 1919 pistol (without grip safety), caliber 6.35mm.

Beretta Model 1923 pistol, caliber 9mm Glisenti.

Beretta Model 1931 pistol, bearing Italian Navy

Crest consisting of the letters "RM" and an anchor on the grip medallion, caliber 7.65mm.

Beretta Model 1932 pistol, having smooth wooden grips with "PB" medallion, caliber 9mm.

Beretta Model 1934 pistol, caliber 9mm, post-war variations bearing Italian Air Force eagle markings.

Beretta Model 1934 pistol, caliber 9mm, produced in 1945 or earlier, serial numbers within the following ranges—500000 to 999999, F00001 to F120000, G0001 to G80000, 00001AA to 10000AA, or 00001BB to 10000BB. This classification does not include any post-war variations dated subsequent to 1945 or bearing post-war Italian proof marks.

Beretta Model 1934 pistol, lightweight model, marked "Tipo Alleggerita" or "All" having transverse ribbed barrel, caliber 9mm.

Beretta Model 1935 pistol, Rumanian Contract, marked "P. Beretta—Cal. 9 Scurt—Mo. 1934—Brevet." on the slide, caliber 9mm.

Beretta Model 1935 pistol, Finnish Home Guard Contract, marked "SKY" on the slide, caliber 7.65mm.

Beretta Model 1935 pistol, caliber 7.65mm, produced during 1945 and earlier and having serial numbers below 620799.

Beretta M1951 pistol, Egyptian Contract, caliber 9mm Parabellum.

Beretta M1951 pistol, Israeli Contract, caliber 9mm Parabellum.

Bergmann-Bayard M1908 pistol, caliber 9mm Bergmann-Bayard.

Bernardelli Model 1956, experimental pistol, caliber 9mm Parabellum.

Bern Arsenal Experimental Gas-Locked pistol, caliber 9mm Parabellum.

Bern Arsenal Experimental 16-shot pistol, caliber 9mm Parabellum.

FN Browning, Model 1902 (usually known as the Model 1903), semiautomatic pistol, caliber 9mm Browning Long.

Browning Centennial Model High-Power Pistol, caliber 9mm Parabellum.

Browning Centennial Model 92 lever-action rifle, caliber .44 Magnum.

Browning Superposed Centennial, consisting of a 20-gauge superposed shotgun supplied with extra set of .30-06 caliber superposed barrels.

Browning Hi-Power pistol, caliber 9mm with German Waffenamt inspector's marks.

Browning M1935 Hi-Power pistol, Canadian, Congolese, Indian and Nationalist Chinese Contracts, caliber 9mm Parabellum.

Browning "Baby" Model pistol, Russian Contract, caliber 6.35mm.

Browning M1910 and M1922 pistols, Contract pieces; M1910 Dutch Navy, M1922 Dutch or French Navy, and M1922 Yugoslavian Army calibers 7.65mm and 9mm Kurz.

Browning M1922 pistol, caliber 7.65mm, bearing Germany Navy acceptance stamps.

Browning M1922 pistol, caliber 9mm, bearing German Waffenamt acceptance stamp, 1939–1945.

Browning Model 1922 pistol, caliber 7.65mm, bearing German NSDAP or RFV markings.

Browning Model 1922 pistols, calibers 7.65mm and 9mm Kurz, marked with the Greek letters Epsilon Sigma denoting issue to the Greek Army.

Browning Model 1922 pistols, calibers 7.65mm and 9mm Kurz, marked "T.C. Subay," denoting issue to the Army of the Turkish Republic.

Browning Model 1922 pistols, calibers 7.65mm and 9mm Kurz, marked "C.P.I.M.," denoting issue to the Belgian Political Police.

Browning Model 1922 pistols, calibers 7.65mm and 9mm Kurz, marked "S.P." and/or bearing the crest of the Kingdom Thailand.

Budischowsky, Model TP70, semiautomatic pistol, caliber .25 ACP, with custom serial number DB1.

C

Campo-Giro Model 1913 and 1913/16 pistol, caliber 9mm Largo.

Chinese Communist Types 51 and 54 Tokarev pistols, caliber 7.62mm.

Chinese, Peoples Republic of China, copy of Japanese Type Sigiura Shiki semiautomatic pistol, caliber 7.65mm.

Chylewski semiautomatic pistol manufactured by S.I.G. Switzerland, caliber 6.35mm (.25 ACP).

Clement pistol, Belgian manufacture, caliber 5mm Clement.

Colt Ace Service Model semiautomatic pistol, caliber .22, manufactured by Colt from 1935 to 1945, serial number range from SM1 to SM13803, including those marked "UNITED STATES PROPERTY" on right side of frame.

Colt Ace semiautomatic pistol, caliber .22, manufactured by Colt from 1931 to 1947, serial number range from 1 to 10935, including those marked "UNITED STATES PROPERTY" on right side of frame.

Colt Aircrewman revolver produced between 1951 and 1959, caliber .38 Special, marked "Property of U.S. Air Force" on back strap, having Air Force issue numbers of 1 through 1189 and in the serial number range 1902LW through 90470IW.

Colt Army Model double-action revolver, any caliber, manufactured between 1899 and 1907.

Colt, First Model, Match Target Woodsman, caliber .22, semiautomatic pistol, manufactured from 1938 to 1944, serial numbers MT1 to MT15000.

Colt, J frame, Officer's Model Match, .38 Special revolver manufactured from 1970 to 1972, identified by a J serial-number prefix.

Colt Lightning Model double-action revolver, any caliber manufactured between 1899 and 1909.

Colt Model 1900 semiautomatic pistol, caliber .38, in original configuration.

Colt Model 1902 semiautomatic pistol, sporting model, caliber .38, in original configuration.

Colt Model 1902 semiautomatic pistol, military model, caliber .38, in original configuration.

Colt Model 1903 Pocket (exposed hammer), semiautomatic pistol, caliber .38 ACP.

Colt Model 1903 Pocket (hammerless), semiautomatic pistol, caliber .32.

Colt Model 1908, caliber .25 ACP, hammerless semiautomatic pistol having a grip safety, originally manufactured in Connecticut by Colt prior to 1956.

Colt Model 1908 Pocket (hammerless) semiautomatic pistol, caliber .380.

Colt Model 1911, "Commercial Model" semiautomatic pistol, caliber .45 ACP, serial numbers C1 through C130000.

Colt Model 1911 pistol, English Contract, caliber .455

Colt Model 1911-A1, "Commercial Model," caliber .45, bearing Egyptian inscription meaning police on upper forward right-hand side of trigger guard and having serial numbers within the range of C186000 to C188000.

Colt Model 1911-A1 pistol, caliber .45, manufactured by Union Switch and Signal Company, prototype model, bearing serial number US & S Exp. 1 to US & S Exp. 100.

Colt Fourth Model Deringer, caliber .22 Short Rimfire, cased as set of two pistols in leather book titled, "Colt Deringer, Limited Edition, by Colt," on spine of book and "A Limited Edition by Colt," on cover.

Colt Government Model pistol, caliber .45 ACP, BB Series.

Colt MK IV Series 70 semiautomatic pistols, all calibers, which were incorrectly marked at the factory with both Colt Government Model markings and Colt Commander markings.

Colt, Ned Buntline Commemorative, .45 caliber revolver.

Colt New Service revolvers, all calibers, all variations, manufactured between 1898 and 1944.

Colt Officers Model (1904-1930), .38 caliber revolver.

Colt Officers Model (1930-1949), .22 caliber revolver.

Colt Officers Model Match (1953-1969), .22 and .38 caliber revolvers.

Colt Officers Model Special (1949-1952), .22 and .38 caliber revolvers.

Colt Officers Model Target (1930-1949), .32 and .38 caliber revolvers.

Colt, Single Action Army (Bisley, Standard and target variations), all original, manufactured from 1899 to 1946, serial number range from 182000 to 357869.

Colt, Abercrombie and Fitch, "Trailblazer," .45 New Frontier.

Colt, Alabama Sesquicentennial, .22 caliber.

Colt, Alamo, .22 and .45 calibers.

Colt, Abilene, (Kansas Cowtown Series), .22 caliber.

Colt, Appomattox Court House Centennial, .22 and .45 calibers.

Colt, Arizona Ranger Model Commemorative, .22 caliber revolver.

Colt, Arizona Territorial Centennial, .22 and .45 calibers.

Colt, Arkansas Territory Sesquicentennial, .22 caliber.

Colt, Battle of Gettysburg Centennial, .22 caliber.

Colt, Belleau Wood, (World War I Series), .45 pistol.

Colt, California Bicentennial, .22 caliber.

Colt, California Gold Rush, .22 and .45 calibers.

Colt, Camp Perry, single-shot target pistol, .22 Long Rifle or .38 Special calibers.

Colt, Carolina Charter Tercentenary, .22 and .22/.45 calibers.

Colt, Chamizal Treaty, .22 and .45 calibers.

Colt, Chateau Thierry, (World War I Series), .45 pistol.

Colt, Cherry's Sporting Goods 35th Anniversary, .22/.45 caliber.

Colt, Chisholm Trail, (Kansas Trail Series), .22 caliber.

Colt, Civil War Centennial Single Shot, .22 caliber.

Colt, Coffeyville, (Kansas Cowtown Series), .22 caliber.

Colt, Colorado Gold Rush, .22 caliber.

Colt, Colonel Samuel Colt, Sesquicentennial, .45 caliber.

Colt, Colt's 125th Anniversary, .45 caliber.

Colt, Columbus (Ohio) Sesquicentennial, .22 caliber.

Colt, H. Cook, "1 of 100," .22/.45 caliber.

Colt, Dakota Territory, .22 caliber.

Colt, Des Moines, Reconstruction of Old Fort, .22 and .45 calibers.

Colt, Dodge City, (Kansas Cowtown Series), .22 caliber.

Colt, Wyatt Earp, Buntline Special, (Lawman Series), .45 caliber.

Colt, Wyatt Earp, (Lawman Series), .22 and .45 calibers.

Colt, European Theater, (World War II Series), .45 pistol.

Colt, Florida Territory Sesquicentennial, .22 caliber.

Colt, General Nathan Bedford Forrest, .22 caliber.

Colt, Fort Findlay (Ohio) Sesquicentennial, .22 caliber.

Colt, Fort Hays, (Kansas Fort Series), .22 caliber.

Colt, Fort Larned, (Kansas Fort Series), .22 caliber.

Colt, Fort McPherson (Nebraska) Centennial Deringer, .22 caliber.

Colt, Fort Scott, (Kansas Fort Series), .22 caliber.

Colt, Fort Stephenson (Ohio) Sesquicentennial, .22 caliber.

Colt, Forty-Niner Miner, .22 caliber.

Colt, Pat Garrett, (Lawman Series), .22 and .45 calibers.

Colt, Geneseo (Illinois) 125th Anniversary, Deringer, .22 caliber.

Colt, Golden Spike Centennial, .22 caliber.

Colt, Wild Bill Hickock, (Lawman Series), .22 and .45 calibers.

Colt, General Hood, Tennessee Campaign Centennial, .22 caliber.

Colt, Idaho Territorial Centennial, .22 caliber.

Colt, Indiana Sesquicentennial, .22 caliber.

Colt, Kansas Centennial, .22 caliber.

Colt, Maine Sesquicentennial, .22 and .45 calibers.

Colt, Bat Masterson, (Lawman Series), .22 and .45 calibers.

Colt, General George Meade, Pennsylvania Campaign, .22 and .45 calibers.

Colt, Meuse Argonne, (World War I Series), .45 pistol.

Colt, Montana Territory Centennial, .22 and .45 calibers.

Colt, Missouri Sesquicentennial, .22 caliber.

Colt, General John Hunt Morgan, Indiana Raid, .22 caliber.

Colt, Joaquin Murieta, "1 of 100," .22/.45 caliber.

Colt, Nebraska Centennial, .22 caliber.

Colt, Nevada Centennial, .22 and .45 calibers.

Colt, Nevada Centennial, "Battle Born," .22 and .45 calibers.

Colt, New Jersey Tercentenary, .22 and .45 calibers.

Colt, New Mexico Golden Anniversary, .22 caliber.

Colt, NRA Centennial, single-action revolver, .357 Magnum and .45 calibers.

Colt, NRA Centennial, Gold Cup National Match pistol, .45 caliber.

Colt, Oklahoma Territory Diamond Jubilee, .22 caliber.

Colt, Oregon Trail, (Kansas Trail Series), .22 caliber.

Colt, Pacific Theater, (World War II Series), .45 pistol.

Colt, Pawnee Trail, (Kansas Trail Series), .22 caliber.

Colt, Peacemaker Commemorative, .22 and .45 calibers.

Colt, Pony Express, Russell, Majors and Waddell, Presentation Model, .45 caliber.

Colt, Pony Express Centennial, .22 caliber.

Colt, Rock Island Arsenal Centennial Single Shot, .22 caliber.

Colt, St. Augustine Quadricentennial, .22 caliber.

Colt, St. Louis Bicentennial, .22 and .45 calibers.

Colt, Santa Fe Trail, (Kansas Trail Series), .22 caliber.

Colt, Second (2nd) Marne, (World War I Series), .45 pistol.

Colt, Shawnee Trail, (Kansas Trail Series), .22 caliber.

Colt, Sheriff's Model, .45 caliber.

Colt Single Action Army revolver, caliber .45, serial number 85163A, engraved and inlaid with bust of President Abraham Lincoln.

Colt, Texas Ranger, .45 caliber.

Colt, "The Right to Keep and Bear Arms" Commemorative, .22 caliber Peacemaker Buntline, single-action revolver, 7½-inch barrel inscribed with "The Right to Keep and Bear Arms," serial number range G0001RB through G3000RB.

Colt, United States Bicentennial Commemorative, Python revolver, .357 caliber.

Colt, United States Bicentennial Commemorative, single-action Army revolver, .45 caliber.

Colt, West Virginia Centennial, .22 and .45 calibers.

Colt, Wichita, (Kansas Cowtown Series), .22 caliber.

Colt, Woodsman, caliber .22, semiautomatic target pistol, manufactured from 1915 to 1943, serial numbers 1 to 157000.

Colt, Wyoming Diamond Jubilee, .22 caliber.

Colt, 1873 Peacemaker Centennial 1973, single-action revolver, .40/44 or .45 calibers.

Czechoslovakian CZ50 pistol, caliber 7.65mm.

Czechoslovakian CZ52 pistol, caliber 7.62mm.

Czechoslovakian CZ27 pistol, caliber 7.65mm, with flanged barrel for silencer and bearing German Waffenamt acceptance stamp, 1939-1945.

Czechoslovakian CZ38 pistol, caliber 9mm Kurz, with or without German Waffenamt acceptance stamp.

Czechoslovakian Model 24 pistol, caliber 9mm Kurz, marked with German Navy acceptance stamps, Navy proof marks or issuance marks.

Czechoslovakian Model 27 pistol, caliber 7.65mm, marked with German Navy acceptance stamps, Navy proof marks or issuance marks.

Czechoslovakian Model 1927 pistol, caliber 7.65mm, bearing German Waffenamt acceptance markings.

Czechoslovakian Model 1952 and 1952/57, calibers 7.62 × 45mm and 7.62 × 39mm, semiautomatic rifles (Puska Vzor 52, 7.62 × 45mm, and Puska Vzor 52/57, 7.62 × 39mm).

D

Danish M1910/1921 Bayard pistol, caliber 9mm Bergmann-Bayard.

Davis Warner Infallible, semiautomatic pistol, caliber .32.

Dreyse Military Model 1910 pistol, caliber 9mm.

E

Egyptian Hakim (Ljungman) 7.92mm semiautomatic rifle as manufactured in Egypt.

Esser-Barratt, English manufacture, slide-action rifle, caliber .303.

F

French S.A.C.M. Model 1935A pistol, caliber 7.65 Long, marked with German Navy acceptance stamps, Navy proof marks or issuance marks.

French M1935 pistol, caliber 7.65 French Long, bearing German Waffenamt acceptance stamp for period 1939-45.

French Model 1949 semiautomatic rifle, caliber 7.5mm, (Fusil Mle. 1949 [MAS] 7.5mm).

G

German P38 pistol, caliber 9mm Parabellum, manufactured prior to 1947.

Gustloff semiautomatic pistol, caliber 7.65mm, manufactured by Gustloff Werke, Suhl, Germany.

H

Hammond or Grant Hammond pistols, all models, variations or prototypes, made by Grant Hammond Corporation, New Haven, Connecticut.

Hammond/High Standard semiautomatic pistols, caliber .45.

Harrington & Richardson Abilene Anniversary revolver, caliber .22.

Harrington & Richardson Centennial Officer's Model Springfield rifle, .45-70 Govt.

Harrington & Richardson Centennial Standard Model Springfield rifle, .45-70 Govt.

Harrington & Richardson self-loading semiautomatic pistol, caliber .32.

Hartford Arms and Equipment Company single-shot target pistol, caliber .22 LR.

Hartford Arms and Equipment Company repeating pistol, caliber .22 LR.

Hartford Arms and Equipment Company Model 1928 pistol, caliber .22 LR.

High Standard experimental electric free pistol, caliber .22 Long Rifle.

High Standard Model P38 semiautomatic pistol, caliber .38 Special.

High Standard experimental Model T-3 semiautomatic pistol, caliber 9mm Luger.

High Standard Model C/S smoothbore .22-caliber shot semiautomatic pistols, bearing serial numbers 59279, 59473, 59478 or 59460.

High Standard experimental ISU rapid-fire semiautomatic pistol, caliber .22 Short.

High Standard Model A pistol, caliber .22 LR.

High Standard Model B pistol, caliber .22 LR.

High Standard Model C pistol, caliber .22 Short.

High Standard Model D pistol, caliber .22 LR.

High Standard Model E pistol, caliber .22 LR.

High Standard Model H-A pistol, caliber .22 LR.

High Standard Model H-B pistol, First Model, caliber .22 LR.

High Standard Model H-B pistol, Second Model, caliber .22 LR.

High Standard Model H-D pistol, caliber .22 LR.

High Standard Model H-E pistol, caliber .22 LR.

High Standard Model USA-HD pistol, caliber .22 LR.

High Standard Model HD-Military pistol, caliber .22 LR.

High Standard Model G-380 pistol, caliber .380.

High Standard Model G-B pistol, caliber .22 LR.

High Standard Model G-D pistol, caliber .22 LR.

High Standard Model G-E pistol, caliber .22 LR.

High Standard Model G-O (First Model Olympic) pistol, caliber .22 Short.

High Standard Supermatic Trophy, Model 107, .22 pistol Olympic Commemorative Model.

Hungarian Frommer Model 1937 pistol, caliber 7.65mm, marked with German Navy acceptance stamps, Navy proof marks or issuance marks.

Hungarian Model 1937 pistol, caliber 7.65mm, bearing German Waffenamt acceptance markings.

I

Italian Brixia M1906, pistol, caliber 9mm Glisenti.

Italian Glisenti M1910, pistol, caliber 9mm Glisenti.

Ithaca double-barreled shotguns, manufactured before 1950 in Ithaca, New York, by the Ithaca Gun Company. All gauges and all models, having barrels of at least 18 inches in length and overall lengths of at least 26 inches.

Ithaca Gun Company single-barreled break-open trap guns, all gauges and all models manufactured in Ithaca, New York, before 1950.

Ithaca, Model 49, St. Louis Bicentennial, .22 rifle.

J

Japanese Type I Hamada (1941), pistol, caliber 7.65mm.

Japanese Type II Hamada, pistol, caliber 7.65mm.

Japanese Type 14 (1925), pistol, caliber 8mm Nambu.

Japanese Type 94 (Model 1934), pistol, caliber 8mm Nambu (8 × 21mm cartridge), manufactured in Japan 1934-1945.

Japanese "Grandpa" Nambu, Model 1904, pistol, caliber 8mm Nambu.

Japanese "Baby" Nambu, pistol, caliber 7mm Nambu.

Japanese Type Sigiura Shiki semiautomatic pistols, calibers 7.65mm and 6.35mm.

Jieffeco pistol, Belgian manufacture, caliber 7.65mm.

Jieffeco semiautomatic pistol, caliber .25 ACP, marked "Davis Warner Arms Corp., N.Y."

K

Kimball pistols, all models, all calibers.

Kolibri pistols, calibers 2.7mm and 3mm Kolibri.

L

L.C. Smith shotguns manufactured by Hunter Arms Company and Marlin Firearms Company from 1899 to 1971.

Lahti L-35 pistol, Finnish manufacture, caliber 9mm Parabellum.

Luger, pistol, all models and variations manufactured prior to 1946.

Luger, Mauser commercial manufacture, semiautomatic pistol, caliber 9mm, 70 Jahre, Parabellum-Pistole, Keiserreich Russland, commemorative.

Luger, Mauser commercial manufacture, semiautomatic pistol, caliber 7.65mm, 75 Jahre, Parabellum-Pistole, 1900-1975, commemorative.

Luger, Mauser commercial manufacture, semiautomatic pistol, caliber 7.65mm, 75 Jahre, Parabellum-Pistole, Königreich Bulgarien, commemorative.

M

MAB Model D pistol, caliber 7.65mm, bearing German Navy acceptance stamp.

MAB Model D pistol, caliber 7.65mm, bearing German Waffenamt acceptance stamp for period 1939-1945.

MAB Model R pistol, caliber 9mm Parabellum.

Makarov pistol, Russian and East German, caliber 9mm Makarov.

Mannlicher pistols, M1900, M1901, M1903 and M1905, caliber 7.63mm Mannlicher.

Marlin 90th Anniversary, Model 39A, .22 rifle.

Marlin 90th Anniversary, Model 39A, .22 carbine.

Original military bolt-action and semiautomatic rifles, manufactured between 1899 and 1946.

Mauser, semiautomatic pistols, any caliber, manufactured prior to 1946.

Menz Liliput, German manufacture, caliber 4.25mm.

Menz PBIII, caliber 7.65mm, manufactured by August Menz, Suhl, Germany.

Menz PBIIIA, caliber 7.65mm, manufactured by August Menz, Suhl, Germany.

Menz, PBIV, caliber 7.65mm, manufactured by August Menz, Suhl, Germany.

Menz, PBIVa, caliber 7.65mm, manufactured by August Menz, Suhl, Germany.

Menz Special, caliber 7.65mm, manufactured by August Menz, Suhl, Germany.

Mexican Obregon, pistol, caliber .45 ACP.

Mugica Model 120, pistol, caliber 9mm Parabellum.

N

North Korean Type 1964, pistol, caliber 7.62mm Tokarev.

Norwegian M1914, pistol, caliber .45 ACP.

P

PAF "Junior" semiautomatic pistol, caliber .25, manufactured by Pretoria Arms Factory Ltd., South Africa.

PAF pistol, marked "BRF," caliber .25, manufactured by Pretoria Arms Factory Ltd., South Africa.

Phoenix (U.S.A.) pistol, caliber .25 ACP.

Polish FB "VIS," M1935 (Radom), pistol, caliber 9mm Parabellum, original Republic of Poland model with an eagle crest and Polish inscription on left side of slide. Dated 1936, 1937, 1938 and 1939 and having small-sized serial numbers in the range 1 through 50000 without letter or number prefix or suffix.

Polish VB "VIS" Model 1935 (Radom) pistol, caliber 9mm Parabellum, bearing German military acceptance markings.

R

Reising semiautomatic pistol, .22 caliber.

Remington Canadian Territorial Centennial, Model 742, rifle.

Remington Model 51 semiautomatic pistol, calibers .32 ACP and .380 ACP.

Remington 150th Anniversary Model 1100SA semiautomatic shotgun, caliber 12 gauge.

Remington 150th Anniversary Model 870SA slide-action shotgun, caliber 12 gauge.

Remington 150th Anniversary Model 742ADL slide-action rifle, caliber .30/06.

Remington 150th Anniversary Model 760ADL slide-action rifle, caliber .30/06.

Remington 150th Anniversary Model 552A semiautomatic rifle, caliber .22 LR.

Remington 150th Anniversary Model 572A slide-action rifle, caliber .22 LR.

Remington 150th Anniversary Model Nylon 66 semiautomatic rifle, caliber .22 LR.

Remington Montana Territorial Centennial, Model 600, rifle.

Roth Steyr 1907, semiautomatic pistol, caliber 8mm.

Ruger Canadian Centennial, Matched No. 1 Rifle Sets, Special Deluxe.

Ruger Canadian Centennial, Matched No. 2 Rifle Sets.

Ruger Canadian Centennial, Matched No. 3 Rifle Sets.

Ruger Canadian Centennial, Model 10/22, carbine.

Ruger Blackhawk revolvers, flattop, calibers .44 Magnum and .357 Magnum, all barrel lengths, made from 1955 through 1962.

Ruger Single-Six, flattop, .22-caliber revolvers with flat side loading gate, all barrel lengths, made from 1953 through 1956.

S

Sauer 38(h), pistol, caliber 7.65mm, marked with Third Reich police acceptance stamps of Eagle C, F, K or L.

Sauer 38H pistol, caliber 7.65mm, bearing German Waffenamt acceptance markings.

Savage Arms semiautomatic pistols, caliber .45 ACP, all models.

Savage Prototype pistols, calibers .25, .32 and .38, made between 1907 and 1927.

Savage Model 1907 pistols, calibers .32 and .380.

Savage Model 1907 pistol, caliber .45, military contract.

Savage Model 1911 pistol, caliber .45, Prototype.

Savage Model 1915 pistols, calibers .32 and .380.

Savage Model 1917 pistols, calibers. 32 and .380.

Smith & Wesson Model 66 revolver, U.S. Border Patrol 50th Anniversary Commemorative, caliber .357 Magnum, stainless steel.

Smith & Wesson Model .22/32 Hand Ejector (Bekeart Model), caliber .22 LR, serial numbers 138220 to 534636 (no letter).

Smith & Wesson K-22 Hand Ejector, caliber .22 LR, serial numbers 632132 to 696952 (no letter).

Smith & Wesson K-32 Hand Ejector (K-32 Masterpiece), caliber .32 S&W Long, serial numbers 653388 to 682207 (no letter).

Smith & Wesson .38 Hand Ejector Military and Police, caliber .38, serial numbers 1 to 241703 (no letter).

Smith & Wesson .357 Magnum Hand Ejector, caliber .357 Magnum, serial numbers 45768 to 60000 (no letter).

Smith & Wesson .44 Hand Ejector, all calibers, serial numbers 1 to 62488 (no letter).

Smith & Wesson .455 Mark II Hand Ejector, caliber .455.

Smith & Wesson Mercox Dart Gun, caliber .22 rimfire, blank.

Smith & Wesson .22/32 Kit Gun, caliber .22 LR, serial numbers 525670 to 534636 (no letter).

Smith & Wesson .32 Double Action Top Break, caliber .32 S&W, serial numbers 209302 and higher.

Smith & Wesson .32 Safety Hammerless Top Break (New Departure), caliber .32 S&W, serial numbers 91401 and higher.

Smith & Wesson .38 Double Action Top Break, caliber .38 S&W, serial numbers 382023 and higher.

Smith & Wesson .38 Double Action Top Break Perfected Model, caliber .38 S&W.

Smith & Wesson, .38 Safety Hammerless Top Break (New Departure), caliber .38 S&W, serial numbers 119901 and higher.

Smith & Wesson pistol, caliber .35, all variations.

Smith & Wesson 2nd Model, single-shot pistols, calibers .22 rimfire, .32 S&W and .38 S&W.

Smith & Wesson 3rd Model, single-shot pistols, caliber .22 rimfire, .32 S&W and .38 S&W.

Smith & Wesson 1st Model, Ladysmith revolver, caliber .22 rimfire long.

Smith & Wesson 2nd Model, Ladysmith revolver, caliber .22 rimfire long.

Smith & Wesson 3rd Model, Ladysmith revolver, caliber .22 rimfire long.

Smith & Wesson Model 39-1 (52-A), pistol, caliber 9mm Parabellum.

Smith & Wesson Model 39, steel-frame pistol, caliber 9mm Parabellum.

Smith & Wesson pistol, caliber .32 ACP.

Smith & Wesson Model Straight Line, single-shot pistol, caliber .22 rimfire Long Rifle.

Smith & Wesson Model 16 (K-32 Masterpiece), caliber .32 S&W Long, "K" serial number series.

Smith & Wesson .38/44 Outdoorsman & Heavy Duty, caliber .38, serial numbers 36500 to 62023 (no letter).

Smith & Wesson Model 19 revolver, 150th Anniversary Texas Ranger Commemorative.

Smith & Wesson Model 10 Victory Model, identified by the letter "V" prefix to the serial number, in the original .38 Special chambering, with U.S. Navy acceptance marks.

Smith & Wesson U.S. Army Model of 1917, caliber .45, serial numbers 1 to 163476.

Standard Arms Co. rifle/shotgun combination, U.S., Model "Camp," caliber .50, slide-action.

Standard Arms Co. Rifle Model G, slide-action or gas-operated, caliber unknown.

Standard Arms Co. Rifle Model M, slide-action, calibers .25-.35, .30 Rem. and .35 Rem.

Star Model B semiautomatic pistol, caliber 9mm Parabellum, having German military acceptance marks, serial number range 21597 through 249687.

Steyr-Hahn M1912, pistol, caliber 9mm Steyr.

Steyr-Hahn M1912, pistol, caliber 9mm Parabellum marked with Third Reich police acceptance stamps of Eagle C, F, K or L.

Sosso pistol, caliber 9mm, manufactured by Guilio Sosso, Turin, Italy, or Fabrica Nationale D'Armi, Brescia, Italy.

T

Tauler Model military and police pistol.

Tokagypt 58, pistol, caliber 9mm Parabellum.

U

Unique Kriegsmodell pistol, French manufacture, caliber 7.65mm, bearing German Waffenamt acceptance stamp for period 1939-1945.

U.S. Model 1911 semiautomatic pistol, military series, caliber .45, serial number range from 1 to 629500, all original variations regardless of manufacture, including: The North American Arms Company, Model 1911; the Springfield Armory, Model 1911 with NRA markings; the Remington Arms-UMC, Model 1911; and any Model 1911 cutaways.

U.S. pistol, Model 1911-A1, caliber .45, manufactured by the Singer Manufacturing Company in 1942, serial number range from S800001 to S800500.

U.S. Model 1911-A1 semiautomatic pistol, caliber .45, manufactured by Remington Rand, bearing serial number prefix of ERRS.

U.S. Model 1911-A1 semiautomatic pistol, caliber .45, produced as original factory cutaways.

U.S. Rifle, caliber .30 MC-1952, equipped with telescopic sight mount MC, telescopic sight MC1, marked U.S.M.C. or kollmorgan.

W

Walther pistols, all models, all calibers, manufactured at Zella-Mehlis prior to 1946.

Webley Model 1909, pistol, caliber 9mm Browning Long.

Webley and Scott Model 1910 and 1913 high-velocity pistols, caliber .38 ACP.

Webley and Scott M1913, Navy or Commercial, self-loading pistol, caliber .455.

Webley-Fosbury semiautomatic revolvers, all models, all calibers.

Winchester 1980 Alberta Diamond Jubilee Commemorative carbines, Model 94, caliber .38/55.

Winchester Alaskan Purchase Centennial, Model 1894, carbine.

Winchester Antlered Game Commemorative, Model 94, carbine, caliber .30-30.

Winchester Apache Commemorative carbine, commemorative edition of Model 1894 Winchester, with serial number prefix AC.

Winchester Bicentennial 76, Model 94, carbine.

Winchester Buffalo Bill, Model 1894, carbine.

Winchester Buffalo Bill, Model 1894, rifle.

Winchester Canadian 1967, Centennial Model 1894, carbine.

Winchester Canadian 1967, Centennial Model 1894, rifle.

Winchester Centennial Model 1866, carbine.

Winchester Centennial Model 1866, rifle.

Winchester Comanche Commemorative carbine, commemorative edition of Model 1894 Winchester with serial number prefix CC.

Winchester Cowboy Commemorative, Model 94, carbine.

Winchester Golden Spike, Model 1894, carbine.

Winchester Illinois Sesquicentennial, Model 1894, carbine.

Winchester Klondike Gold Rush Commemorative, Model 94, carbine.

Winchester Legendary Lawman Commemorative, Model 94, carbine, caliber .30-30.

Winchester Legendary Frontiersman, Model 94, rifle, caliber .38-55.

Winchester "Limited Edition II," Model 94, rifle, caliber .30-30.

Winchester Little Big Horn Centennial, Model 94, carbine.

Winchester Lone Star Commemorative, Model 94, carbine.

Winchester Lone Star Commemorative, Model 94, rifle, .30-30.

Winchester "Ducks Unlimited" Commemorative shotgun, Model 12, bearing serial numbers DU-001 through DU-800.

Winchester "Matched Set of 1000," cased pair consisting of Winchester Model 94 rifle, caliber .30-30, and Winchester Model 9422 rifle, caliber .22.

Winchester Model 52, rifle, bearing serial numbers 1 to 6500.

Winchester Model 53, original, manufactured from 1924 to 1947 with 16-inch or longer barrel and 26-inch or longer overall length.

Winchester Model 54, rifle, speed-lock variation, caliber .270.

Winchester Model 65, original, manufactured from 1933 to 1947 with 16-inch or longer barrel and 26-inch or longer overall length.

Winchester Model 70 Ultra Match Target Special Grade rifle, caliber .308.

Winchester rifles, Model 70, calibers .308, .270 Winchester and .30-06, 19-inch barrel, Mannlicher-type stock, made from 1968 to 1971.

Winchester Model 71, original, manufactured from 1936 to 1958, with 16-inch or longer barrel and 26-inch or longer overall length.

Winchester Limited Edition, Model 94 carbine, caliber .30-30, serial numbers 77L1 through 77L1500.

Winchester Model 1873, original, manufactured from 1899 to 1925, with 16-inch or longer barrel and 26-inch or longer overall length.

Winchester Model 1885, single-shot rifle, original, manufactured from 1899 to 1920, with 16-inch or longer barrel and 26-inch or longer overall length.

Winchester Model 1886, original, manufactured from 1899 to 1945, with 16-inch or longer barrel and 26-inch or longer overall length.

Winchester Model 1892, original, manufactured from 1899 to 1947, with 16-inch or longer barrel and 26-inch or longer overall length.

Winchester Model 1894 rifles and carbines manufactured prior to January 2, 1964, and having serial numbers below 2700000, provided barrel length is at least 16 inches and overall length, at least 26 inches.

Winchester Model 1895, original, manufactured from 1899 to 1938, with 16-inch or longer barrel and 26-inch or longer overall length.

Winchester Nebraska Centennial, Model 1894, carbine.

Winchester NRA Centennial rifle, Model 94, caliber .30-30.

Winchester Model NRA Centennial, Model 94, carbine.

Winchester Mounted Police, Model 94, carbine.

Winchester Northwest Territories Centennial Rifle.

Winchester Royal Canadian Mounted Police Centennial, Model 94, carbine.

Winchester 150th Anniversary Texas Ranger Commemorative, Model 1894, carbine.

Winchester Theodore Roosevelt, Model 1894, carbine.

Winchester Theodore Roosevelt, Model 1894, rifle.

Winchester Wells Fargo and Company Commemorative, Model 94, carbines.

Winchester Wyoming Diamond Jubilee, Model 94, carbine.

Winchester Yellow Boy Indian, Model 94, carbine.

Appendix II
Gun Shows and Organizations That Sponsor Them

Alabama

Huntsville Gun & Knife Show
c/o Harry G. Martin
Park Plaza 1122-J
Huntsville 35801
(205) 539-3839

Arizona

Ft. Smith Dealers and Collectors Association
P.O. Box 941
Ft. Smith 72901

Mesa Gun Show Collectorama
201 N. Center Street
Mesa 85004
(602) 838-9631

California

Las Vegas Western Americana Arms and Knife Show
c/o The Show Factory
42452 Tioga Drive
Box M33-8
Big Bear Lake 92315
(714) 866-8709

Quincy Elks Lodge Gun Show
c/o Rod Day
Box 1846
Quincy 95971
(916) 283-3291

Santa Barbara Historical Arms Association, Inc.
P.O. Box 6291
Santa Barbara 93111
(805) 968-6386

Turlock Gun Show
c/o Merenda Enterprises
137 Dakota Avenue
Modesto 95351
(209) 522-1550

Florida

Exhibitors Unlimited
P.O. Box X
Venice 33595
(813) 485-7997

Jacksonville Gun Show
9900 Normandy Boulevard
Jacksonville 32201
(904) 781-4557

Idaho

Pendleton Gun & Antique Show
c/o Lewis Clark Trader
Box 219
Lewiston 83501
(208) 743-8811

Illinois

Fox Valley Arms Fellowship Gun Show
c/o Fred Doederlein
110 Railroad
East Dundee 60118
(312) 426-3455

Illinois Gun Show
c/o Frontier Gun Shop
2277 N. Grand Avenue E.
Springfield 62702
(217) 528-5490

Iowa

Sioux City Gun Show
c/o Pete's Guns
920 Morningside Avenue
Sioux City 51106
(712) 276-0676

Kansas

Hutchinson Gun Show
c/o McClellan Enterprises
Box 2413
Hutchinson 67501

Louisiana

Baton Rouge Gun & Knife Shows, Inc.
c/o Alex Chauffe Jr.
P.O. Box 265
Maringouin 70757
(504) 625-2126

Maryland

Baltimore Antique Arms Association
c/o Stanley I. Kellert
E30 2600 Insulator Drive
Baltimore 21230
(301) 342-8200

Michigan

Ypsilanti Gun & Knife Show
Huron Valley Gun Collectors, Inc.
(313) 663-8249

Minnesota

Anoka Gun Show
c/o Minnesota Weapons Collectors Association
P.O. Box 662
Hopkins 55343
(612) 721-5423

Missouri

Eureka Gun Show
Guns Unlimited
c/o Rick Avila
709 Boca Chica
Fenton 63026
(314) 326-0625

Montana

Bozeman Trail Gun Show
Box 814
Bozeman 59715
(406) 586-5703

Nebraska

Nebraska Rifle Club Gun Show
c/o Alliance Rifle Club
304 Potash
Alliance 69301
(308) 762-5437

New Hampshire

Portsmouth Gun Show
c/o J.R. LaRue
260 Miller Avenue
Portsmouth 03801

New Mexico

S.E.N.M. Gun Shows
105 N. Third
Carlsbad 88220
(505) 887-2810

Silver City Gun Show
Box 2481
Demming 88030
(505) 538-3172

New York

Adirondack Gun-Knife Show
11 Pearl Street
Glen Falls 12801
(518) 668-5044

North Carolina

Boone Gun Show
c/o Clayton Cooke
P.O. Box 63
Boone 28607

Carolina Gun Collectors' Association
c/o Jerry M. Ledford
Route 10, Box 144
Hickory 28601
(704) 327-0055

Oklahoma

Muskogee Gun & Knife Show
c/o John Forrest
102 North T Street
Muskogee 74401
(918) 682-8133

Oklahoma City Gun Shows
P.O. Box 14718
Oklahoma City 73113
(405) 348-6858

Pennsylvania

Lancaster Gun Show
c/o R. Buckwalter
1701 Bridge Road
Lancaster 17602

Lehigh Valley Military Collectors Association
c/o Jay Solomon
P.O. Box 72
Whitehall 18052

South Carolina

Aiken Gun & Knife
Box 1431
Aiken 29801
(803) 649-9852

South Dakota

South Dakota Gun Show
c/o Ed Benson
P.O. Box 236
Sioux Falls 57101
(605) 332-4554

Tennessee

Memphis Gun Show
P.O. Box 11137
Memphis 38111

Texas

The Texas Gun & Knife Association, Inc.
c/o Don or Deressa Hill
P.O. Box 15044
Austin 78761
(512) 926-2372

The Texas Weapon Collectors Association
c/o Mile Morris
Star Route Box 17-D
Devine 78016
(512) 663-5124

Washington County Gun Collectors Association
222 East Alamo
Brenham 77833
(713) 836-0098

Utah

Salt Lake City Gun Show
c/o Lynn Templeton
332 Mountain Road
Laysville 84037
(801) 544-9125

Virginia

The Exchange Club's Gun Show
c/o B. Russell Atwood
P.O. Box 305
Harrisonburg 22801
(703) 433-2546

Wisconsin

Green County Conservation League Gun Show
c/o Jeffrey E. Wells
Route 3, Box 205
Monroe 53566
(608) 966-3430

Appendix III
Firearms Trade Sources

Cleaning and Touch-up Supplies and Equipment

A 'n A Company
Box 571
King of Prussia, Pennsylvania 19406

Armite Labs
1845 Randolph Street
Los Angeles, California 90001

Armology Company of Fort Worth
204 East Daggett Street
Fort Worth, Texas 76104

B-Square
Box 11281
Fort Worth, Texas 76109

Birchwood Casey
7900 Fuller Road
Eden Prairie, Minnesota 55344

Bisonite Company, Inc.
P.O. Box 84
Kenmore Station
Buffalo, New York 14217

Blue Ridge Machine and Tool Company
165 Midland Trail
Hurricane, West Virginia 25526

Brookstone Company
125 Vose Farm Road
Peterborough, New Hampshire 03458

Brownells, Inc.
Route 2, Box 1
Montezuma, Iowa 50171

Browning Arms
Route 4, Box 624-B
Arnold, Missouri 63010

J.M. Bucheimer Company
P.O. Box 280
Airport Road
Frederick, Maryland 21701

Burnishine Products Company
8140 North Ridgeway
Skokie, Illinois 60076

Caddie Products Corporation
Division of Jet-Aer
Paterson, New Jersey 07524

Blue and Gray Products, Inc.
R.D. #6 Box 348
Wellsboro, Pennsylvania 16901

Jim Brobst
299 Poplar Street
Hamburg, Pennsylvania 19526

Chem-Pak, Inc.
Winchester, Virginia 22601

Chopie Manufacturing, Inc.
531 Copelend
La Crosse, Wisconsin 54601

Clenzoil Company
Box 1226 Station C
Canton, Ohio 44708

Clover Manufacturing Company
139 Woodward Avenue
Norwalk, Connecticut 06856

Decker Shooting Products
1729 Laguna Avenue
Schofield, Wisconsin 54476

Dixie Gun Works
Gunpowder Lane, P.O. Box 130
Union City, Tennessee 38261

Dri-Slide, Inc.
Industrial Park 1210 Locust Street
Fremont, Michigan 49412

Forty-Five Ranch Enterprises
119 South Main Street
Miami, Oklahoma 74354

Gun-All Products
Box 244
Dowagiac, Michigan 49047

H & R, Inc.
GB Products Department
Industrial Rowe
Gardner, Massachusetts 01440

Frank C. Hoppe Division
Penguin Industries, Inc.
Airport Industrial Mall
Coatesville, Pennsylvania 19320

J & G Rifle Ranch
Box S 80
Turner, Montana 59542

Jensen Tools Inc.
1230 South Priest Drive
Tempe, Arizona 85821

Jet-Aer Corporation
100 Sixth Avenue
Paterson, New Jersey 07524

Kellog's Professional Products, Inc.
P.O. Box 1201
Sandusky, Ohio 44870

K.W. Kleindorst
R.D. #1 Box 113B
Hop Bottom, Pennsylvania 18824

LPS Chemical Products
Holt Lloyd Corporation
4647 Hugh Howell Road
Tucker, Georgia 30084

LEM Gun Spec.
Box 31
College Park, Georgia 30337

Liquid Wrench
Box 10628
Charlotte, North Carolina 28201

Lynx Line Gun Products Division
Protective Coatings, Inc.
20626 Fenkell Avenue
Detroit, Michigan 48223

Marble Arms Company
420 Industrial Park
Gladstone, Michigan 49837

Micro Sight Company
242 Harbor Boulevard
Belmont, California 94002

Mirror-Lube
P.O. Box 693
San Juan Capistrano, California 92675

New Method Manufacturing Company
Box 175
Bradford, Pennsylvania 16701

Northern Instruments, Inc.
6680 North Highway 49
Lino Lake, Minnesota 55014

Numrich Arms Company
West Hurley, New York 12491

Old World Oil Products
3827 Queen Avenue North
Minneapolis, Minnesota 55412

Original Mink Oil, Inc.
P.O. Box 20191
10652 Northeast Holman
Portland, Oregon 97220

Outers Laboratories
Route 2
Onalaska, Wisconsin 54650

Radiator Spec. Company
1400 Independence Boulevard
Charlotte, North Carolina 28201

Reardon Products
103 West Market Street
Morrison, Illinois 61270

Rice Gun Coatings
1521 - 43rd Street
West Palm Beach, Florida 33407

Rig Products Company
Division of Mittan, Inc.
21320 Deering Court
Canoga Park, California 91304

Rusteprute Labs
Sparta, Wisconsin 54656

San/Bar Corporation
Break-Free Division
9999 Muirlandson Boulevard
Irvine, California 92714

Saunders Sporting Goods
338 Somerset
North Plainfield, New Jersey 07060

Schultea's Gun String
67 Burress
Houston, Texas 77022

Schwab Industries, Inc.
330 Alta Avenue
Santa Monica, California 90402

Service Armament
689 Bergen Boulevard
Ridgefield, New Jersey 07657

Shenandoah Guns
Ben Toxvard
P.O. Box 89
Berryville, Virginia 22611

Silicote Corporation
Box 359
Oshkosh, Wisconsin 54901

Silver Dollar Guns
P.O. Box 475, 10 Frances Street
Franklin, New Hampshire 03235

Sportsmen's Labs, Inc.
Box 732
Anoka, Minnesota 55303

Taylor & Robbins
Box 164
Rixford, Pennsylvania 16745

Testing Systems, Inc.
220 Pegasus Avenue
Northvale, New Jersey 07647

Texas Platers Supply Company
2453 West Five Mile Parkway
Dallas, Texas 75233

Totally Dependable Products, Inc.
P.O. Box 277
Zieglerville, Pennsylvania 19492

C.S. Van Gorden
120 Tenth Avenue
Eau Claire, Wisconsin 54701

WD-40 Company
1061 Cudahy Place
San Diego, California 92110

West Coast Secoa
3915 U.S. Highway 98S
Lakeland, Florida 33801

Williams Gun Sight Company
7389 Lapeer Road
Davison, Michigan 48423

Winslow Arms, Inc.
P.O. Box 783
Camden, South Carolina 29020

Wisconsin Platers Supply Company
2453 West Five Mile Parkway
Dallas, Texas 75233

Woodstream Corporation
P.O. Box 327
Litilz, Pennsylvania 17543

Zip Aerosol Products
31320 Deering Court
Canoga Park, California 91304

Firearm Restoration

E.C. Bishop & Son, Inc.
Box 7
Warsaw, Missouri 65355

Reinhart Fajen, Inc.
Box 338
Warsaw, Missouri 65355

Paul Jaeger Inc.
211 Leedom Street
Jenkintown, Pennsylvania 19046

J.J. Jenkins
375 Pine Avenue
North 25
Goleta, California 93017

Small Arms Engineering
7698 Garden Prairie Road
Garden Prairie, Illinois 61038

Traister Arms Company
Route 1, Box 300
Bentonville, Virginia 22610

Trevallion Gunstocks
6524 North Carrollton Avenue
Indianapolis, Indiana 46220

Vic's Gun Refinishing
6 Pineview Drive
Dover Point
Dover, New Hampshire 03820

Lester Womack
P.O. Box 17210
Tucson, Arizona 85710

Gun Cabinets

Brenik, Inc.
925 West Chicago Avenue
Chicago, Illinois 60622

Collector's Armoury, Inc.
P.O. Box 1061
Alexandria, Virginia 22313

Ebonite Corporation
1400 N.W. 57th Court
Miami Lakes, Florida 33014

Fort Harrison Products Corporation
1229 Eighth Avenue
Terre Haute, Indiana 47804

Harbor House
12508 Center Street
South Gate, California 90280

IPCO, Inc.
331 Lake Hazeltine Drive
Chaska, Minnesota 55318

Morton Booth Company
P.O. Box 123
Joplin, Missouri 64802

Possibilities Unlimited
9409 Sacramento Avenue South
Evergreen Park, Illinois 60642

Traditions
221 South Jessica
Sioux Falls, South Dakota 57103

Western Woodcraft
2651 Gravel Street
Fort Worth, Texas 76118

Gun Parts

Alaskan Rifles
Box 30
Juneau, Alaska 99801

American Import Company
1167 Mission Street
San Francisco, California 94103

American International
103 Social Hall Avenue
Salt Lake City, Utah 84111

Antique Gun Parts, Inc.
1118 South Braddock Avenue
Pittsburgh, Pennsylvania 15218

Armoury Inc.
Route 202
New Preston, Connecticut 06777

Artistic Arms, Inc.
Box 23
Hoagland, Indiana 46745

Badger Shooter's Supply
Box 397
Owen, Wisconsin 54460

Century Arms, Inc.
3-5 Federal Street
St. Albans, Vermont 05478

Cornwall Bridge Gun Shop
P.O. Box 67
Cornwall Bridge, Connecticut 06754

Walter Craig, Inc.
Box 927-A
Selma, Alabama 36701

Philip R. Crouthamel
513 East Baltimore
E. Lansdowne, Pennsylvania 19050

David E. Cumberland
3509 Carlson Boulevard
El Cerrito, California 94530

Darr Tool Company
P.O. Box 117
Bliss, New York 14024

Dixie Gun Works, Inc.
Gunpowder Lane, P.O. Box 130
Union City, Tennessee 38261

Charles E. Duffy
Williams Lane
West Hurley, New York 12491

Eastern Firearms Company
790 S. Arroyo Parkway
Pasadena, California 91105

Federal Ordnance Inc.
9634 Alpaca Street
So. El Monte, California 91733

Fenwick's Gun Annex
P.O. Box 38
Weisberg Road
Whitehall, Maryland 21161

Jack First
The Gunshop, Inc.
44633 Sierra Highway
Lancaster, California 93534

Greg's Winchester Parts
P.O. Box 8125
W. Palm Beach, Florida 33407

Hunter's Haven
Zero Prince Street
Alexandria, Virginia 22314

Hunter's Lodge
200 South Union
Alexandria, Virginia 22313

Kindig's Log Cabin Sport Shop
R.D. 1 P.O. Box 275
Lodi, Ohio 44254

Lever Arms Service Ltd.
771 Dunsmuir Street
Vancouver, B.C., Canada V6C 1M9

Edward E. Lucas
32 Garfield Avenue
East Brunswick, New York 08816

Lyman Products Corporation
Route 147
Middlefield, Connecticut 06455

Markwell Arms Company
2413 West Devon
Chicago, Illinois 60645

Mars Equipment Corporation
3318 West Devon
Chicago, Illinois 60645

National Gun Traders
225 Southwest 22nd
Miami, Florida 33135

Numrich Arms Company
West Hurley, New York 12491

The Outrider, Inc.
3288 LaVenture Drive
Chamblee, Georgia 30341

Pacific International Merch. Corporation
2215 "J" Street
Sacramento, California 95816

Plainfield Ordnance Company
Box 447
Dunellen, New Jersey 08812

Potomac Arms Corporation
Box 35
Alexandria, Virginia 22313

Replica Models, Inc.
610 Franklin Street
Alexandria, Virginia 22314

Martin B. Retting, Inc.
11029 Washington
Culver City, California 90230

Riflemen's Headquarters
Route 3 R.D. 550-E
Kendallville, Indiana 46755

Ruvel & Company
3037 North Clark
Chicago, Illinois 60614

S & S Firearms
88-21 Aubrey Avenue
Glendale, New York 11227

Sarco, Inc.
323 Union Street
Sterling, New Jersey 07980

Service Armament Company
689 Bergen Boulevard
Ridgefield, New Jersey 07657

Sherwood Distributors, Inc.
18714 Parthenia Street
Northridge, California 91324

Simms
2801 J Street
Sacramento, California 95816

Clifford L. Smires
R.D. Box 39
Columbus, New Jersey 08022

C.H. Stoppler
1426 Walton Avenue
New York, New York 10452

N.F. Strebe Gunworks
4926 Marlboro Pike S.E.
Washington, D.C. 20027

Triple-K Manufacturing Company
568 - 6th Avenue
San Diego, California 92101

C.H. Weisz
Box 311-D
Arlington, Virginia 22210

W.H. Wescombe
P.O. Box 488
Glencoe, California 95232

Gun Safes, All-Steel

A&A Sheet Metal Products, Inc.
P.O. Box 547
La Porte, Indiana 46350

Cemco Security Systems
P.O. Box 1113
Yuba City, California 95911

Center Manufacturing Company
540 Goodrich Road
Bellevue, Ohio 44811

Dara-Nes Division
P.O. Box 119
East Hampton, Connecticut 06424

Kingsberry Manufacturing Corporation
Crystal City, Texas 78839

Metro Enterprises, Inc.
317 Kirby Street, Suite 210
Garland, Texas 75242

Nesci Enterprises, Inc.
P.O. Box 119
East Hampton, Connecticut 06424

R.A. Pearson
P.O. Box 33, R.D. 4
Centerville, Pennsylvania 16404

Pro-Steel Security Safes
P.O. Box 977
Provo, Utah 84603

Ready Metal Manufacturing Company
4500 West 47th Street
Chicago, Illinois 60632

San Angelo Co., Inc.
P.O. Box 984
San Angelo, Texas 76901

Stowline, Inc.
811 South First Street
Kent, Washington 98031

Tread Corporation
P.O. Box 13207
Roanoke, Virginia 24032

Westfield Sheet Metal Works, Inc.
Monroe Avenue & Eighth Street
Kenilworth, New Jersey 07033

Gunstocks

Adams Custom Gun Stocks
13461 Quito Road
Saratoga, California 95070

Don Allen
Route 4
Northfield, Minnesota 55057

Jim Baiar
490 Halfmoon Road
Columbia Falls, Montana 59912

Joe J. Balickie, Custom Stocks
Route 2, Box 56-G
Apex, North Carolina 27502

Donald Bartlett
16111 S.E. 229th Place
Kent, Washington 98031

Al Biesen
West 2039 Sinto Avenue
Spokane, Washington, 99201

Stephen L. Billeb
Box 219
Phillipsburg, Montana 59858

E.C. Bishop & Son
Box 7
Warsaw, Missouri 65355

John M. Boltin
P.O. Box 1122
No. Myrtle Beach, South Carolina 29582

Border Gun Shop, Garry Simmons
2760 Tucson Hiway
Nogales, Arizona 85621

Garnet D. Brawley
8931 Stanwin Avenue
Arleta, California 91331

Brown Precision Company
P.O. Box 270W.
Los Molinos, California 96055

Lenard M. Brownell
Box 25
Wyarno, Wyoming 82845

E.J. Bryant
3154 Glen Street
Eureka, California 95501

Jack Burres
10333 San Fernando Road
Pacoima, California 91331

Calico Hardwoods, Inc.
1648 Airport Boulevard
Windsor, California 95492

Dick Campbell
365 West Oxford Avenue
Englewood, Colorado 80110

Winston Churchill
Route 1 Box 29B
Proctorsville, Vermont 05153

Crane Creek Gun Stock Company
25 Shepard Terrace
Madison, Wisconsin 53705

Reggie Cubriel
15502 Purple Sage
San Antonio, Texas 78255

Jack Dever
8520 Northwest 90
Oklahoma City, Oklahoma 73132

Charles De Veto
1087 Irene Road
Lyndhurst, Ohio 44124

David R. Dunlop
Route 1 Box 199
Rolla, North Dakota 58367

Jere Eggleston
P.O. Box 50238
Columbia, South Carolina 29250

Bob Emmons
238 Robson Road
Grafton, Ohio 44044

Reinhart Fajen, Inc.
Box 338
Warsaw, Missouri 65355

N.B. Fashingbauer
P.O. Box 366
Lac Du Flambeau, Wisconsin 54538

Ted Fellowes
Beaver Lodge, 9245 16th Avenue S.W.
Seattle, Washington 98106

Phil Fischer
2625 N.E. Multnomah
Portland, Oregon 97232

Clyde E. Fischer
Route 1, Box 170-M
Victoria, Texas 77901

Jerry Fisher
1244 - 4th Avenue
Kalispell, Montana 59901

Flaig's Lodge
Millvale, Pennsylvania 15209

Donald E. Folks
205 West Lincoln Street
Pontiac, Illinois 61764

Dale Goens
Box 224
Cedar Crest, New Mexico 87008

Gary Goudy
263 Hedge Road
Menlo Park, California 94025

Gould's Myrtlewood
1692 North Dogwood
Coquille, Oregon 97423

Charles E. Grace
10144 Elk Lake Road
Williamsburg, Michigan 49690

Rolf R. Gruning
315 Busby Drive
San Antonio, Texas 78209

The Gunshop
R.D. Wallace
320 Overland Road
Prescott, Arizona 86301

Half Moon Rifle Shop
490 Halfmoon Road
Columbia Falls, Montana 59912

Harris Gun Stocks, Inc.
12 Lake Street
Richfield Springs, New York 13439

Hal Hartley
147 Blairsfork Road
Lenoir, North Carolina 28645

Richard Hodgson
5589 Arapahoe, Unit 104
Boulder, Colorado 80301

Hollis Gun Shop
917 Rex Street
Carlsbad, New Mexico 88220

Jackson's
Box 416
Selman City, Texas 75689

Paul Jaeger, Inc.
211 Leedom Street
Jenkintown, Pennsylvania 19046

Johnson Wood Products
R.R. 1
Strawberry Point, Iowa 52076

Monte Kennedy
P.O. Box 214
Kalispell, Montana 59901

Don Klein
Box 277
Camp Douglas, Wisconsin 54618

LeFever Arms Co., Inc.
R.D. 1
Lee Center-Strokes Road
Lee Center, New York 13363

Lenz Firearms Company
1480 Elkay Drive
Eugene, Oregon 97404

Stanley Kenvin
5 Lakeville Lane
Plainview, New York 11803

Philip D. Letiecq
AQ Wagon Box Road
Story, Wyoming 82842

Al Lind
7821 76th Avenue S.W.
Tacoma, Washington 98498

Bill McGuire
1600 North Eastmont Avenue
East Wenatchee, Washington 98801

Gale McMillan
28638 N. 42nd Street, Box 7870
Cave Creek Stage
Phoenix, Arizona 85020

Maurer Arms
2366 Frederick Drive
Cuyahoga Falls, Ohio 44221

John E. Maxson
Box 332
Dumas, Texas 79029

Leonard Mews
Spring, Box 242
Hortonville, Wisconsin 54944

Robt. U. Milhoan & Son
Route 3
Elizabeth, West Virginia 26143

C.D. Miller Guns
Purl Street
St. Onge, South Dakota 57779

Milliron Custom Guns & Stocks
1249 N.E. 166th Avenue
Portland, Oregon 97230

Nelsen's Gun Shop
501 South Wilson
Olympia, Washington 98501

Bruce Nettestad
R.R. 1 Box 140
Pelican Rapids, Minnesota 56572

Oakley & Merkley
Box 2446
Sacramento, California 95811

Jim Norman
Custom Gunstocks
11230 Calenda Road
San Diego, California 92127

Maurice Ottmar
Box 657, 113 East Fir
Coulee City, Washington 99115

Pachmayr Gun Works
1220 South Grand Avenue
Los Angeles, California 90015

Paulsen Gunstocks
Rt. 71 Box 11
Chinook, Montana 59523

Peterson Machine Carving
Box 1065
Sun Valley, California 91352

R. Neal Rice
5152 Newton
Denver, Colorado 80221

Richards Micro-Fit Stocks
P.O. Box 1066
Sun Valley, California 91352

Carl Roth Jr.
4728 Pineridge Avenue
Cheyenne, Wyoming 82001

Matt Row
Lock, Stock 'N Barrel
8972 East Huntington Drive
San Gabriel, California 91775

Royal Arms, Inc.
10064 Bert Acosta Court
Santee, California 92071

Sanders Custom Gun Service
2358 Tyler Lane
Louisville, Kentucky 40205

Saratoga Arms Company
Walter Shultz
1752 North Pleasantview Road
Pottstown, Pennsylvania 19464

Roy Schaefer
965 West Hilliard Lane
Eugene, Oregon 97404

Shaw's
The Finest in Guns
9447 West Lilac Road
Escondido, California 92025

Hank Shows, The Best
1202 North State
Ukaih, California 95482

Sile Distributor
7 Center Market Place
New York, New York 10013

Six Enterprises
6564 Hidden Creek Drive
San Jose, California 95120

Ed Sowers
8331 DeCelis Place
Sepulveda, California 91343

Fred D. Speiser
2229 Dearborn
Missoula, Montana 59801

Sport Service Center
2364 North Neva
Chicago, Illinois 60635

Sportsman's Haven
Brent L. Umberger
R.R. 4
Cambridge, Ohio 43725

Sportsmen's Equipment Company
915 West Washington
San Diego, California 92103

Keith Stegall
Box 696
Gunnison, Colorado 81230

Stinehour Rifles
Box 84
Cragsmoor, New York 12420

Surf N' Sea, Inc.
62-595 Kam Highway
Box 268
Haleiwa, Hawaii 96712

Swanson Custom Firearms
1051 Broadway
Denver, Colorado 80203

Talmage Enterprises
43197 East Whittier
Hemet, California 92343

John Vest
6715 Shasta Way
Klamath Falls, Oregon 97601

Weatherby's
2781 Firestone
South Gate, California 90280

Cecil Weems
Box 657
Mineral Wells, Texas 76067

Frank R. Wells
4025 North Sabino Canyon Road
Tucson, Arizona 85715

Western Gunstocks Manufacturing Co.
550 Valencia School Road
Aptos, California 95003

Duane Wiebe
P.O. Box 497
Lotus, California 95651

Bob Williams
P.O. Box 143
Boonsboro, Maryland 21713

Williamson-Page Gunsmith Service
117 West Pipeline
Hurst, Texas 76053

Robert M. Winter
Box 484
Menno, South Dakota 57045

Mike Yee
4700 - 46th Avenue S.W.
Seattle, Washington 98116

Russell R. Zeeryp
1601 Foard Drive
Lynn Ross Manor
Morristown, Tennessee 37814

Metalsmiths

The following people are metalsmiths who can perform certain restorative work on gun parts, such as duplicating a broken trigger guard and the like. Some 'smiths will require the broken part in order to duplicate it; others are able to design missing parts from "scratch." It is recommended that readers contact them directly to obtain information on the type of metalsmithing they do, and the prices for such services.

Ted Blackburn
85 East 700 South
Springfield, Utah 84663

Tom Burgess
180 McMannamy Draw
Kalispell, Montana 59901

Dave Cook
Dave's Gun Shop
720 Hancock Avenue
Hancock, Michigan 49930

Homer Culver
1219 North Stuart
Arlington, Virginia 22201

John H. Eaton
8516 James Street
Upper Marlboro, Maryland 20870

Phil Fischer
2625 N.E. Multnomah
Portland, Oregon 97232

Geo. M. Fullmer
2499 Mavis Street
Oakland, California 94601

Harkrader's Custom Gun Shop
825 Radford Street
Christiansburg, Virginia 24073

Huntington's
P.O. Box 991
Oroville, California 95965

Paul Jaeger, Inc.
211 Leedom Street
Jenkintown, Pennsylvania 19046

Ken Jantz
Route 1
Sulphur, Oklahoma 73086

Terry K. Kopp
Highway 13
Lexington, Missouri 64067

R.H. Lampert
Route 1 Box 61
Guthrie, Minnesota 56451

Mark Lee
2323 Emerson Avenue, N.
Minneapolis, Minnesota 55411

Bruce Nettestad
R.R. 1 Box 140
Pelican Rapids, Minnesota 56572

Paul's Precision Gunworks
420 Eldon
Corpus Christi, Texas 78412

Dave Talley
Route 10, Box 249-B
Easley, South Carolina 29640

John Vest
6715 Shasta Way
Klamath Falls, Oregon 97601

Herman Waldron
Box 475
Pomeroy, Washington 99347

Edward S. Welty
R.D. 2, Box 25
Cheswick, Pennsylvania 15024

Dick Willis
141 Shady Creek Road
Rochester, New York 14623

Appendix IV
Recommended References

For those of you who trade in used guns, the following references are highly recommended. While some of the books may be out of print and unavailable through traditional sources, they can most often be found in public libraries or used book stores. You may also want to contact the dealers listed below who specialize in out-of-print books, reprints and rare and antique gun catalogs. Write for their price lists and/or current offerings. In addition, look for rare gun catalogs advertised in periodicals such as *Shotgun News* and *The American Rifleman.*

Dealers

Dixie Gun Works, Inc.
Gunpowder Lane, P.O. Box 130
Union City, Tennessee 38261
(antique arms catalog)

Fairfield Book Company, Inc.
P.O. Box 289
Brookfield Center, Connecticut 06805
(books)

Ray Riling Arms Books Company
6844 Gorsten Street
P.O. Box 18925
Philadelphia, Pennsylvania 19119
(books, catalogs, reprints)

Rutgers Book Center
127 Raritan Avenue
Highland Park, New Jersey 08904
(books)

Periodicals that contain current used gun prices:

American Rifleman, The
National Rifle Association of America
1600 Rhode Island Avenue, NW
Washington, D.C. 20036

Gun Week
Hawkeye Publishing, Inc.
P.O. Box 411, Station C
Buffalo, New York 14209

Investing in Guns
Matlock Advertising
4468 Zarahemla Drive
Salt Lake City, Utah 84117

Shotgun News
Snell Publishing Company, Inc.
Box 669
Hastings, Nebraska 68901

Books

American Gun Makers. Satterlee, L.D., and Gluckman, Arcadi. Buffalo: Otto Ulbrich Co., 1945.

American Handgun Patents 1802-1924. Macewicz, Joseph. Ontario: Museum Restoration Service, 1978. A must for the serious handgun collector.

American Sporting Arms of the 18th & 19th Century. Houze, Herbert G. Chicago: Chicago Historical Society, 1975. Catalog of the Chicago Historical Society collection of antique sporting and martial firearms.

Antique European and American Firearms at the Hermitage Museum. Tarassuk, Leonid. Arma

Press, 1973. Selected from the museum's 2,500 firearms dating from the 15th to 19th centuries; includes the Colt rifle and pistols presented by Samuel Colt to Czars Nicholas I and Alexander II.

Antique Firearms. Wilkinson, Frederick. San Rafael, CA: Presidio Press, 1978. Traces the history of firearms from their introduction in 14th-century Europe through the appearance of the modern repeating rifle.

Bannerman Catalogue of Military Goods—1927. Francis Bannerman Sons. Northfield, IL: DBI Books, 1980. Replica edition. Virtually a museum in print; thousands of items catalogued; soft cover.

Book of Colt Firearms, The. Sutherland, Robert Q., and Wilson, R.L. Kansas City, MO: Robert Q. Sutherland, 1971.

Book of the Garand. Hatcher, Julian S. Washington: Infantry Journal Press, 1948.

Book of Pistols and Revolvers, The, 6th Edition. Smith, W.H.B., and Bellah, Kent. Harrisburg, PA: Stackpole Books, 1965.

Book of Rifles, The. Smith, W.H.B. Harrisburg: Stackpole Books, 1963. Encyclopedic reference about shoulder arms; includes rifles of all types, arranged by country of origin.

Book of the Springfield, The. Crossman, Edward C., and Dunlap, Roy F. Georgetown, SC: Small-Arms Technical Publishing Co., 1951.

Brassey's Infantry Weapons of the World. Owen, J.I.H., editor. Second edition. Elmsford, N.Y.: Pergamon Press, 1979.

Brassey's Warsaw Pact Infantry and its Weapons. Owen, J.I.H., Editor. London: Brassey's Publishers, Ltd., 1976.

Breech-Loader in the Service, The. Fuller, Claude E. Reprint. New Milford, CT: N. Flayderman & Co., 1965.

John M. Browning, American Gunmaker. Browning, John, and Gentry, Curt. Garden City, NY: Doubleday & Co., 1964.

Buxton's Guide, Foreign Firearms. Greenwich, CT: John S. Herold Inc., 1963.

Carbine Handbook. Wahl, Paul. New York: Arco Publishing Co., 1964.

Collector's Guide to American Cartridge Handguns. Sell, DeWitt E. Harrisburg, PA: Stackpole Books, 1963.

Collector's Handbook of U.S. Cartridge Revolvers 1856-1899, The. Fors, W. Barlow. Chicago: Adams Press, 1973. Over 600 brand-name listings for revolvers; historical sketches of over 80 makers.

Colt Automatic Pistols. Bady, Donald B. Alhambra, CA: Borden Pub. Co., 1974. Revised and enlarged version of 1956 edition. Complete information on Colt autos.

Colt Commemorative Firearms, 2nd Edition. Wilson, R.L. Geneseo, IL: Robert E.P. Cherry, 1973.

Colt Firearms Catalog, 1934. Topsfield, MA: Americana Archives, 1976 (reprint). Excellent survey of the Colt company and its products, updated with new SAA production chart and commemorative list.

Colt Firearms, 1836-1960. Serven, James E. Santa Ana, CA: Serven Books, 1960.

Colt Heritage, The. Wilson, R.L. New York: Simon & Schuster, 1979. "The official history of Colt firearms from 1836 to the present," with luscious color photos and the most complete and current information regarding serial numbers.

Colt's 100th Anniversary Firearms Manual: A Century of Achievement. Hartford: Colt's Patent Fire Arms Mfg. Co., 1937.

Colt Peacemaker Dictionary & Encyclopedia Illustrated. Cochran, Keith A. Rapid City, SD: Colt Collectors Press, 1976. Over 1,300 entries pertaining to everything there is to know about the Colt Peacemaker.

Complete Illustrated Encyclopedia of the World's Firearms, The. Hogg, Ian V. New York: A & W Publishers, 1978. An A-Z directory of military and civilian firearms from 1830 to the present.

Dixie Gun Works Antique Arms Catalog. Union City, Tennessee: Pioneer Press. Updated frequently.

Encyclopedia of Modern Firearms. Compiled and published by Bob Brownell, Montezuma, IA, 1959. Massive accumulation of basic information for nearly all modern arms.

Firearms Encyclopedia. Nonte, George C., Jr. New

York: Harper & Row, 1973. A to Z coverage of gun and shooting terms, plus complete appendix of useful information.

Firearms Identification. Mathews, J. Howard. C.C. Thomas, 1973. Carefully researched, authoritative work published in three volumes: Vol. 1. *The Laboratory Examination of Small Arms, Rifling Characteristics in Hand Guns and Notes on Automatic Pistols*; Vol. 2. *Original Photographs and Other Illustrations of Handguns*; Vol. 3. *Data on Rifling Characteristics of Handguns and Rifles* (plus photos and other illustrations of handguns).

Firearms Investigation, Identification and Evidence. Hatcher, Jury and Weller. Harrisburg, PA: Stackpole Books, 1977. Reprint of 1957 classic on forensic ballistics; indispensable for those interested in firearms identification and criminology.

Firearms Past and Present. Lugs, Jaroslav. English edition. London: Grenville Publishing Co., 1975.

Firearms Price Guide, The. Byron, David. New York: Crown Publishers, 1980.

Flayderman's Guide to Antique American Firearms, Second Edition. Flayderman, Norm. Northfield, IL: DBI Books, 1980. All values in this new edition have been completely updated and a number of guns not covered in the first edition added.

French Military Weapons, 1717-1938. Hicks, James E. Reprint. New Milford, CT: N. Flayderman & Co., 1964.

German Military Handguns, 1879-1918. Walter, John. London: Arms and Armour Press, 1980. Also Story Creek, Ontario: Fortress Publications, 1980. Fully illustrated study of the principal German handguns of the Second Reich, with comprehensive information on the two commission-designed revolvers of 1879 and 1883, the Parabellums of 1904, 1908 and 1913 and the Mauser C96 taken into emergency service in 1915.

German Weapons, Uniforms, Insignia, 1841-1918. Hicks, Major J.E. Revised Edition. La Canada, CA: James E. Hicks & Son, 1958.

Gun Collector's Fact Book, The. Steinwedel, Louis W. New York: Arco Publ. Co., 1975. Illustrated introduction to gun collecting—where and how to buy antique guns, points that affect their value, hints on restoration.

Gun Collector's Handbook of Values: 1980-1981. Chapel, Charles E. New York: Coward, McCann & Geoghegan, Inc., 1979. Price guide for collectors.

Gun Digest Book of Exploded Firearms Drawings. Murtz, H.A., ed. Second edition. Northfield, IL: DBI Books, 1977.

Gun Digest Book of Modern Gun Values, 3rd Edition. Lewis, Jack. Northfield, IL: DBI Books, 1981. Invaluable guide for buying, selling, trading and identifying guns; handguns, rifles and shotguns covered in separate sections; feature articles relate to collecting and values.

Gun Trader's Guide. Wahl, Paul. So. Hackensack, NJ: Stoeger Publishing Co. 10th edition, 1982. Considered by many to be the best reference/pricing guide currently available; over 4,000 listings and over 400 pages.

Gunmarks. Byron, David. New York: Crown Publishers, Inc., 1980. Trade names, codemarks and proofs from 1870 to present.

Handbook on the Primary Identification of Revolvers & Semi-Automatic Pistols, A. Millard, John T. Springfield, IL: C.C. Thomas, 1974. Practical outline of the basic phases of primary firearm identification with emphasis on revolvers and semiautomatics.

History of the Colt Revolver, A. Haven, Charles T., and Belden, Frank A. New York: Outlet Books, 1978. Information and pictures about the most cherished American revolver.

History of Smith & Wesson. Jinks, Roy G. North Hollywood, CA: Beinfeld Publishing Inc., 1977.

History of Winchester Firearms 1866-1980, The. Watrous, George R. Updated and revised by Duncan Barnes. New York: Winchester Press, 1980. Standard, comprehensive reference including specifications on all Winchester firearms; background on design, manufacture and use; serial numbers listed.

Hopkins & Allen Gun Guide and Catalog (circa 1913). Lake Wales, FL: Wagle Publ., 1972. Facsimile of the original catalog; shows the firm's rifles, shotguns and pistols; includes prices.

Illustrated Encyclopedia of Modern Small Arms

of the World. Myatt, Frederick. New York: Outlet Book Co., 1978. Comprehensive directory of the most important small arms developed and used in the 20th century.

International Armament. Johnson, George B., and Lockhaven, Hans Bert. Cologne: International Small Arms Publishers, 1965.

Introduction to Modern Gunsmithing. MacFarland, Harold E. New York: Barnes and Noble, 1975.

Jane's Infantry Weapons. Edited by Hobart, F., and Archer, Denis H.R. New York: Franklin Watts Inc., 1975, 1976, 1977.

Japanese Hand Guns. Leithe, F.E. Alhambra, CA: Borden Publ. Co., 1968. Covers models produced since the late 19th century; brief text gives history, descriptions, markings.

Know Your .45 Auto Pistols—Models 1911 & A1. Hoffschmidt, Edward J. Alhambra, CA: Borden Pub. Co., 1976. Concise history with a wide variety of types and copies; illustrated. (Included in *Know Your Gun.*)

Know Your Walther P.38 Pistols. Hoffschmidt, Edward J. Alhambra, CA: Borden Pub. Co., 1976. Covers the Walther models, Armee, M.P., H.P., P-38; history and variations. (Included in *Know Your Gun.*)

Know Your Walther P.P. and P.P.K. Pistols. Hoffschmidt, Edward J. Borden Pub. Co., 1976. Concise history with a guide to varieties and types. (Included in *Know Your Gun.*)

Krag Rifles. Brophy, William S. No. Hollywood, CA: Beinfeld Pub., Inc., 1978. Comprehensive work detailing the evolution and various models of both military and civilian Krags.

Krieghoff Parabellum, The. Gibson, Randall. Midland, TX: Randall Gibson, 1980. In-depth study of the Luger pistols manufactured by Heinrich Krieghoff; 11 pages of color and hundreds of b/w photos, the majority first-time published.

Lee-Enfield Rifle, The. Reynolds, E.G.B. New York: Arco Publishing Co., 1962.

Luger, 1875-1975. Walter, John. London: Arms and Armour Press, 1977. Full coverage of the world's most famous pistol.

Luger Pistol, The. Datig, Fred A. Beverly Hills: FADCO Publishing Co., 1955.

Luger Tips. Reese, Michael, II. Union City, TN: Pioneer Press, 1976.

Lyle Official Arms and Armour Review 1980, The. Anderson, Margaret. Selkirkshire, Scotland: Lyle Publications, 1979. Compiled prices (in pounds sterling and U.S. dollars) of edged weapons, firearms and militaria from the auctions of Wallis & Wallis.

Manhattan Firearms. Nutter, Waldo E. Harrisburg, PA: Stackpole Books, 1958. Excellent specialized reference and complete history of the Manhattan Firearms Mfg. Co. and its products.

Marlin and Ballard Firearms and History. West, Bill. Azusa, CA: Bill West, 1968.

Mauser Bolt Rifles, 3rd Edition. Olson, Ludwig. Montezuma, IA: F. Brownell & Son, Publishers, 1976.

Mauser, Walther and Mannlicher Firearms. Smith, W.H.B. Harrisburg: Stackpole Books, 1971.

Military Small Arms of the 20th Century. Hogg, Ian V., and Weeks, John. London: Arms and Armour Press, 1977. New and enlarged edition covering small-caliber firearms from 1900 to 1977.

M1 Carbine, Design Development and Production. Ruth, Larry. Cornville, AZ: Desert Publications. Complete history of one of the world's most famous and largest produced firearms.

Modern Guns, Identification and Values, 2nd Revised Edition. Quertermous, Russel, and Quertermous, Steven. Paducah, KY: Collector Books, 1980. Descriptive, illustrated reference with realistic gun values.

Modern Small Arms. Myatt, Frederick. Los Angeles: Crescent Pubns., Inc., 1978. Illustrated encyclopedia of famous military firearms from 1873 to present.

Notes on United States Ordnance. Volume I. Small Arms, 1776 to 1946. Hicks, James E. Harrisburg, PA: Stackpole Books, 1971.

NRA Firearms Assembly Guidebook to Handguns. Washington, D.C.: National Rifle Association, 1973.

NRA Gun Collectors Guide, The. Washington, D.C.: National Rifle Association, 1972. Wealth of information on collecting and collector arms.

Official Price Guide to Antique and Modern Firearms, The. House of Collectibles, 1980. Over 20,000 current collectors' values for over 600 manufacturers of American- and foreign-made firearms; special sections on collector cartridges and commemorative guns.

Official Price Guide to Military Collectibles, The. Rankin, Robert H. House of Collectibles, 1981. 10,000 prices and listings of the largest accumulation of military objects—15th century to date; special Luger section with prices and photographs; armor, edged weapons, firearms, flags, helmets, medals, posters, uniforms, etc.

John Olson's Book of the Shotgun. Olson, John. Chicago: Philip O'Hara, Inc., 1975. Covers all phases, from design and manufacture to field use and performance.

Outdoor Life Gun Data Book. Rice, F. Philip. New York: Harper & Row, 1975. Packed with formulas, data and tips essential to the modern hunter, target shooter, gun collector and all gun enthusiasts.

Parker, America's Finest Shotgun. Johnson, Peter H. 2nd Edition. Harrisburg: Stackpole Books, 1963.

Parker Gun, The. Baer, Larry L. Two volumes. North Hollywood: Beinfeld Publishing, Inc., 1974, 1976.

Parker Guns Catalog 1930. Santa Fe, NM: Empire Press, 1979. Facsimile reprint showing all models, including the Parker single-barreled trap gun.

Peacemaker and Its Rivals, The. Parsons, John E. New York: William Morrow & Co., 1950.

Pistol Guide. Nonte, George C., Jr. So. Hackensack, NJ: Stoeger Publishing Co., 1980. Unique and detailed examination of a very specialized type of gun—the autoloading pistol.

Pistols, Rifles, and Machine Guns. Allen, W.G.B. London: English Universities Press, 1953.

Pistols of the World. Hogg, Ian V., and Weeks, John. London: Arms and Armour, 1978. A comprehensive illustrated encyclopedia of the world's pistols and revolvers from 1870 to the present day.

Plans and Specifications of the L.C. Smith Shotgun. Brophy, William S., Lt. Col. Montezuma, IA: F. Brownell & Son, Publishers, Inc.

Practical Book of Guns, The. Warner, Ken. New York: Winchester Press, 1978. Delves into the important things about firearms and their uses.

Professional Care and Refinishing Gun Metal. Traister, John. Blue Ridge Summit, PA: TAB Books, 1981.

Rare and Valuable Antique Arms, The. Serven, James E. Union City, TN: Pioneer Press, 1976. Guidelines for the collector.

Remington Arms in American History. Hatch, Alden. New York: Rinehart & Co., 1956.

Remington Arms and History. Azusa, CA: Bill West, 1971.

Remington Handguns. Karr, Charles Lee, Jr., and Karr, Carroll Robbins. Harrisburg, PA: Military Service Publishing Co., 1947.

Remington Tips. Larson, E. Dixon. Union City, TN: Pioneer Press, 1975. Pointers for collectors of Remington handguns.

Revolver Guide. Nonte, George C., Jr. So. Hackensack, NJ: Stoeger Publ. Co., 1980. Guide to selecting, shooting, collecting and care of revolvers of all types.

Rifle in America, The. Sharpe, Philip B. 2nd Edition. New York: Funk & Wagnalls Co., 1947.

Ruger Automatic Pistols and Single Action Revolvers With Check List. Lueders, Hugo A. Houston, 1978. Useful tool for the Ruger collector in identifying major variations.

Savage Arms Co. 1900 Catalog. Reprint. Marlow, NH: Sand Pond Gun Shop, 1978. Shows all grades of engraving for the Model 99 Savage, sporting and military rifles, cartridges, etc.

Savage Automatic Pistols. Carr, James R. St. Charles, IL: Published by the author, 1967. Guide to Savage pistols, models 1907-1922; features; production data; illustrated.

Savage and Stevens Arms and History. Azusa, CA: Bill West, 1971.

Sharps Firearms. Sellers, Frank. No. Hollywood, CA: Beinfeld Publ., Inc., 1977. First complete review of Sharps Firearms Co., with detailed examination of each product.

Shotgun Book, The. O'Connor, Jack. New York: Alfred A. Knopf, 1978. Indispensable for every shotgunner, containing authoritative information on every phase of the shotgun.

Shotguns by Keith. Keith, Elmer. Harrisburg, PA: Stackpole & Heck Inc., 1950.

Single-Shot Rifles. Grant, James J. New York: William Morrow & Co., 1947.

Small Arms. Wilkinson, Frederick. New York: Hawthorne Books, Inc., 1966. History of small firearms; techniques of the gunsmith; equipment used by combatants, sportsmen and hunters.

Small Arms Makers: A Directory of Fabricators of Firearms, Edged Weapons, Crossbows, and Polearms. Gardner, Robert E. New York: Crown Publishers, 1963.

Small Arms of the World. Ezell, Edward Clinton. 11th revised edition. Harrisburg, PA: Stackpole Books, 1977.

L.C. Smith Shotguns. Brophy, William S. North Hollywood: Beinfeld Publishing Inc., 1977.

Smith & Wesson Handguns. McHenry, Roy C., and Roper, Walter F. Huntington, WV: Standard Publications Inc., 1945.

Smith and Wesson 1857-1945. Neal, Robert J. and Jenks, Roy J. NY: A.S. Barnes and Co., 1975. Especially for knowledgeable enthusiasts and collectors; examines the series of handguns produced by this prestigious company.

Special Forces Foreign Weapons Handbook. Moyer, Frank A. Boulder, CO: Panther Publications, 1970.

Sporting Arms of the World. Bearse, Ray. New York: Outdoor Life/Harper & Row, 1976.

Standard Directory of Proof Marks, The. Steindler, R.A. Paramus, NJ: The John Olson Co., 1976. Comprehensive directory of proof marks of the world.

Stevens Pistols and Pocket Rifles. Cope, K.L. Ottawa: Museum Restoration Service, 1971. All are shown, identified, detailed, etc.

Textbook of Automatic Pistols. Wilson, R.K. Plantersville, SC: Small-Arms Technical Publishing Co., 1943.

Textbook of Small Arms 1929. British War Office. London: H.M. Stationery Office, 1929.

200 Years of American Firearms. Serven, James. Follett, 1975. Covers the evolution of firearms in America from those carried by Spanish explorers to the M-16 rifle.

Waffen-Lexikon. Mahrholdt, Richard. Munich: F.C. Mayer Verlag, 1952.

Walther Models PP and PPK, 1929-1945. Rankin, James L. Coral Gables, FL: J.L. Rankin, 1977. Complete coverage of the subject as to finish, proof marks, etc.

Walther Volume II, Engraved, Presentation and Standard Models. Rankin, James L. Coral Gables, FL: J.L. Rankin, 1977. Features embellished versions and standard models.

Whitney Firearms, The. Fuller, Claud. Huntington, WV: Standard Publications, 1946. Authoritative history of all Whitney arms and their makers.

Williams Blue Book of Gun Dealing 1977-78. Davison, MI: Williams Gun Sight Co., 1977. Enlarged edition of the modern guide to gun values.

William M. Locke Collection, The. Berryman, Robert B., et al. East Point, GA: The Antique Armory, Inc., 1973. Magnificent book, illustrated with hundreds of photographs of guns from one of the finest collections of American firearms.

Winchester Book, The. Madis, George. Dallas: George Madis, 1961.

Winchester for Over a Century. Azusa, CA: Bill West, 1966.

Winchester, The Gun that Won the West. Williamson, Harold F. Washington: Combat Forces Press, 1952.

Winchester Sales Manual 1938. Facsimile reprint of manual given to the sales personnel to familiarize them with the company's history and products.

World of Lugers: Proof Marks, Vol. 1. Costanzo, Sam. Mayfield Heights, OH: Sam Costanzo, 1977. Complete listing of different variations of proof marks on the Luger; limited, signed edition.

World of Lugers: Volume I, Serial Numbers of Lugers Issued to German Agents in the U.S. 1913-16. Costanzo, Sam. Wickliffe, OH: Sam Costanzo, 1975. Lugers issued by Hans Tauscher to German espionage agents in the U.S. and Canada; includes government correspondence used as evidence in the Tauscher trial.